Experimental Methodology

Larry B. Christensen
Texas A & M University

Experimental Methodology
second edition

Allyn and Bacon, Inc.
Boston   London   Sydney   Toronto

to my dear wife

who provides continuous support
for my time-consuming projects

Library of Congress Cataloging in Publication Data

Christensen, Larry B   1941–
    Experimental methodology.

    Bibliography: p.
    Includes index.
    1. Psychology, Experimental.   2. Psychology—
Experiments.   3. Experimental design.   I. Title.
BF181.C48 1980   150'.7'24   79–24363
ISBN 0-205-06960-6

Printed in the United States of America.

Series Editor: Bill Barke
Production Editor: Margaret Pinette

Contents

Preface   xi

1 What Is Science?   1

Stereotypes of Science   2
Definition of Science   3
Method Versus Technique   4
Characteristics of the Scientific Approach   6
Methods of Acquiring Knowledge   10
Objectives of Science   13
Role of the Scientist in Science   17
Basic Assumption Underlying Science   19
Summary   20

Contents

2 The Experimental Approach 22

Causation   23
Descriptive Research Approaches   27
Experimental Research Approach   34
Steps in Conducting the Psychological Experiment   44
Reality and the Research Steps   46
Summary   48

3 Problem Definition and Hypothesis Formation 51

Sources of Problems   53
Review of the Literature   56
Formulation of the Research Problem   59
Formulating Hypotheses   61
Summary   63

4 Decisions Preceding Research Design 65

The Independent Variable   66
The Dependent Variable   82
Summary   89

5 Control in Experimentation 91

Extraneous Variables to be Controlled   94
Subject-Experimenter Effects to be Controlled   100
Sequencing Effect to be Controlled   114
Additional Extraneous Variables to be Held Constant   114
Summary   115

Contents

6 Techniques for Achieving Constancy 118

Randomization   119
Matching   123
Counterbalancing   132
Control of Subject Bias   141
Control of Experimenter Effects   146
Likelihood of Achieving Control   152
Summary   153

7 General Research Design 156

Faulty Research Design   160
Requirements of Good Research Designs   165
Pretesting Subjects   168
Appropriate Research Designs   170
Application of the Research Designs   177
Choice of a Research Design   190
Summary   195

8 Quasi-Experimental Designs 197

Before-After Quasi-Research Designs   199
Time-Series Design   217
Cross-Lagged Panel Design   224
Summary   230

9 Single-Subject Research Techniques 233

Single-Subject Designs   235
A-B-A Design   237

Contents

Interaction Design   243
Multiple-Baseline Design   248
Multiple Schedule Design   252
Changing-Criterion Design   255
Methodological Considerations in the Use of Single-Subject
    Designs   258
Rival Hypotheses   265
Multisubject or Single-Subject Designs   266
Summary   268

10 Evaluation Research   272

Types of Evaluation Research Activities   274
Phases of Comprehensive Evaluation   279
Issues in Conducting Summative or Impact Evaluation   285
Summary   291

11 Data Collection and Hypotheses Testing   293

Subjects   294
Instructions   302
Debriefing or Postexperimental Interview   303
Procedure   306
Data Collection   307
Hypothesis Testing   308
Potential Errors in the Statistical Decision-Making Process   311
Summary   312

Contents

12 Generalization   315

Population Validity   316
Ecological Validity   322
Summary   327

13 Ethics   329

Ethical Principles to Follow in Conducting Human
    Research   322
Possible Consequences of Adopting the Code of Ethics   341
Ethics of Animal Research   348
Summary   350

14 The Research Report   351

The APA Format   352
Preparation of the Research Report   378
Writing Style   384

Bibliography   385

Index   409

Preface

When I first attempted to revise this experimental methodology text, my first thought was that maybe I should wait because the area of experimental methodology does not change that rapidly. However, during the intervening years since the first edition was published I kept a file on recent articles and books relating to experimental methodology. I was completely amazed at the speed with which my file grew. The revised edition incorporated over 100 new citations and an even larger number were reviewed but not included. This indicates that subtle revisions and refinements are continuously being made even in an area that seems to be very stable. Naturally, the greatest amount of work has taken place in the newer areas of single-subject research and quasi-experimental design.

xii   In this second edition of the book I have maintained the emphasis of the first edition, focusing attention on methodology rather than on statistical concepts, tests, or content areas. Therefore, some parts of the second edition of the book have remained virtually unchanged. Other parts show little resemblance to the material in the first edition. The major change is the incorporation of separate chapters on quasi-experimental designs and single-subject designs. These two topic areas have undergone the most change and development, and the new edition reflects the advancements that have taken place in these areas. Another major change is a separate chapter on evaluation research. During the past decade there has been a tremendous growth and demand for investigators to evaluate social programs adequately. However, the methodology and intricacies of this type of research are not those of the typical laboratory study. Consequently, this methodology has been, and still is being, developed. The chapter on evaluation research reflects the current thinking on the appropriate way to conduct an evaluation research study. Other changes in the current edition reflect more minor, but still significant, alterations in basic experimental methodology.

Again I am greatly indebted to many people for the assistance they have given me in completing this edition of the book. I want to thank the reviewers for their thorough comments on the book, especially Bill Fremouw of West Virginia University and Joe Sgro of Virginia Polytechnic Institute. Once again, I could not incorporate all the suggestions which were made; however, I did seriously consider each suggestion, and hope I have not offended those whose suggestions I have not followed. I also want to thank the authors and publishers who granted permission to quote material and reproduce figures.

What Is Science?

The book which you are beginning to read is one that will attempt to give you some understanding of the process by which psychologists uncover facts about the behavior of organisms. By the time you finish your program of courses, you will have taken a number of courses in psychology, particularly if that is your major area of study. In these courses you will have learned much of what is currently known about behavior, but these courses also reveal that our knowledge in that area is quite incomplete. While we understand much of the behavior of humans and infrahumans, we still have an inadequate understanding of, for example, alcoholism or childhood autism. Much research and experimentation must still be conducted on human behavior; how-

2   ever, the ability to do so does not come easily. It is not an ability that is acquired from taking content courses in psychology, which in my experience teach little in terms of insight into how the facts, theories, and data were acquired. You know that they were acquired from research, but the actual research procedure still seems to elude you.

Since learning course content is not sufficient in providing knowledge of the ways psychologists conduct research, it is necessary to provide this knowledge more directly by taking a course that is oriented toward teaching the research process. Some students may object to such a course on the grounds that it is not important to their education. Although students who intend to seek an advanced degree in psychology must learn the research process, those of you who do not have such expectations may consider it to be an unnecessary requirement. However, even for students who have no intention of engaging in the research process, knowledge of it can frequently be quite helpful. As we go about our daily lives we are continuously bombarded with claims ranging from the most effective aspirin to the relationship between saccharine and cancer. If you understand the research process you will be in a better position to evaluate such claims.

The purpose of this book is to help you gain an understanding of what science is and how psychologists proceed in their scientific endeavors. You will learn the language and approach of science in order to understand the scientist's approach to the solution of problems. Ultimately you will use science to solve problems in which you are interested.

Stereotypes of Science

When people talk about science and its achievements, many connotations and misconceptions are generated by the uninformed. If asked to define science, people identify it with a variety of inappropriate phenomena, ranging from a specific subject matter such as chemistry to some tremendous technological achievement. For whatever reason, it seems that the scientific process has been encompassed in a shroud of secrecy. The lack of correct information has led to the development of a variety of stereotypes of science.

Kerlinger (1964) presents three popular stereotypes that have contributed to the pervasive misunderstanding surrounding scientific activity. The first stereotype can be called the "white coat-stethoscope-laboratory" view of the scientist. This stereotype depicts an individual working in a laboratory in which he or she is conducting experiments to generate facts that ultimately will improve mankind. Television commercials frequently use this stereotype to lend credibility to their statements about products. An individual wearing a white laboratory coat and giving the appearance of a scientist states that product X—a toothpaste—has been shown to be superior to product Y—another toothpaste. The viewer gives such a statement credibility because this "scientist" supposedly has conducted the experiments that substantiate such a claim.

The second stereotype is the scientist as the brilliant person in the ivory tower. Scientists are seen as rather impractical individuals who are concerned with complex theory generation rather than the solution of practical problems confronting mankind. They are perceived as persons who are off in their own little world doing their own thing. If their products happen to be of value, they are praised; however, it is not mandatory that a scientist's product be of any use. Frequently, the scientist working in an academic setting is perceived as conforming to this stereotype.

The third stereotype equates scientific endeavors with technological advances. People marvel at the ability to send an astronaut to the moon, to construct a 60-story building, or to design a structure such as the Golden Gate bridge. They comment on the tremendous advancement in science that has allowed us to accomplish such feats. In this role the scientist is perceived as a highly skilled engineer striving to improve society.

These stereotypes represent false notions of what science is. They must first be eradicated to make room for an accurate conception of science.

Definition of Science

So far we have looked at what science is *not* rather than what it is. Science has at various times been equated with "a body of knowledge":

> But that means about as much as saying that you find all the works of Shakespeare in the dictionary, because all the words are there. One of the things which blocked scientific progress for nearly two thousand years was the idea that the Greeks had had the last word for it, that the knowledge existed. And such knowledge, untested by experiment, could be adapted or interpreted to suit the beliefs of the time, or to conform to doctrine. A "body of knowledge" unchallenged and unreplenished goes sick and may become itself superstition—like astrology which started off as that exercise of observation and reason which we call astronomy, the charting of the stars in their courses. No, science is not just knowledge; it is

4   knowledge working for its living, correcting itself, and adding to itself.[1]

If science is not a body of knowledge, then what is it? Most philosophers of science define science as a process or a *method*—a method for generating a body of knowledge. Science, therefore, represents a *logic of inquiry,* or a specific method to be followed in solving problems and thus acquiring a body of knowledge. Knowledge is not distinct from science—rather, it is the product of science. All knowledge, however, is not scientific knowledge. Knowledge acquired through the scientific method is the only type that is *scientific knowledge.*

At this point there seem to be three questions that need to be answered. What is unique about the scientific approach to acquiring knowledge? What are other methods of acquiring knowledge as opposed to the scientific method? What is the purpose of gaining knowledge using the scientific method? However, before each of these questions are answered, a distinction needs to be made between scientific method and technique.

Method Versus Technique

The scientific method represents the fundamental logic of inquiry, and technique refers to the specific manner in which one implements the scientific method. The distinction seems to be important because some individuals confuse *methodology* with *technique.* In their confusion they have asserted that psychology uses a different scientific method. Such an assertion means that psychologists use a logic of inquiry that is somewhat different from that of other sciences. "To hold such a view . . . is to deny that all of science is characterized by a common logic of justification in its acceptance or rejection of hypotheses or theories" (Rudner, 1966, p. 5).

To state that psychology uses a different scientific method is inaccurate, but it would be accurate to state that psychology uses different techniques in applying the basic scientific method. The techniques used in applying the scientific method vary in as many ways as there are different types of problems and disciplines. Specifically, technique varies with the nature of the subject matter, the nature of the specific problem, and the stage of inquiry.

1. From Calder, R. *Science makes sense.* London: George Allen and Unwin Ltd., 1955, p. 37.

Variation in technique as a function of subject matter can be illustrated by contrasting the various fields of inquiry as well as by contrasting the techniques used in the various areas of psychology. Consider, for example, the different observational techniques used by the astronomer, the biologist, and the psychologist doing research on small groups. The astronomer uses a telescope and, more recently, interplanetary probes in his or her investigations, whereas the biologist uses the microscope and the small-group researcher may use a one-way mirror to unobtrusively observe subjects' interactions. The scientists in these various fields are all using the same scientific method, the key aspect being controlled inquiry, but the techniques they must use in implementing this method differ. When looking at the variety of techniques used, it is not at all obvious that the techniques used in different fields vary more than the techniques used in the different areas of psychology. The physiological psychologist might use stimulation electrodes in investigating cortical processes, whereas the learning psychologist uses reinforcement techniques.

Variation in technique as a function of the nature of the specific problem can be illustrated by two studies, one conducted by Bandura, Ross, and Ross (1961) and one conducted by King (1957). Both of these studies used the scientific method in investigating the general area of aggression. The difference in the two studies was that different problems related to aggression were being investigated. Bandura et al. were concerned with the influence of an aggressive or nonaggressive model on subsequent aggressive acts of children. To conduct this experiment the children had to observe either aggressive or nonaggressive models, and the experimenter then noted the model's differential effect on the children's subsequent display of aggression.

King was also concerned with aggression but his study was concerned with a slightly different problem. He was interested in identifying some of the variables that produce adult aggression. King gave each of 10 groups of rats different social experiences. Within each social experience group he paired the rats, placed each pair in a fighting box, and then observed the length of time required for fighting to begin. This technique or procedure for implementing the scientific method differs from that used by Bandura et al. (1961) in spite of the fact that both studies were investigating aggression. Bandura et al. used a modeling technique to investigate aggression, whereas King used a social exposure technique. Different techniques had to be used since their problems were different. However, both studies still used the scientific method in investigating aggression. They both identified problems and inquired scientifically into these problems by making a controlled inquiry and by operationally defining their terms. For example, Ban-

6 dura controlled for the subjects' level of aggressiveness by matching those in the experimental and control groups on the basis of ratings of their aggressive behavior at nursery school while engaged in social interaction. King controlled for handling effects by avoiding it for all rats prior to the aggression test. Operational definition was adhered to in both studies when defining terms such as aggression. Bandura et al. defined aggression as a physical response (sitting on the Bobo doll) or a verbal response ("kick him") whereas King defined aggression as fighting response latency. All scientific studies use the same logic of inquiry, but they may use widely discrepant techniques in implementing it, ranging from different control techniques, through different observational techniques, to different research techniques.

The stage of inquiry, or the point in the research process at which one has arrived, also dictates the technique used. If one is at the data collection stage, then data collection techniques such as questionnaires, verbal responses, pressing a bar, or any of numerous other techniques could be used. The technique used is determined by the demands of the study. Likewise, if one is at the data analysis stage, the appropriate statistical technique has to be selected from the numerous ones available.

The wide differences that exist among different fields and even among different areas within a field are, therefore, primarily a function of different techniques used in applying the same scientific method.

Characteristics of the Scientific Approach

Science has been defined as a specific method or logic of inquiry. This definition suggests that the method of science is somehow unique and different from other methods of inquiry or that it has specific rules or characteristics that have to be followed. Indeed the scientific method does have specific characteristics. These characteristics, while necessary to distinguish science, are not limited to the realm of science. Each of the characteristics could also exist outside of science; however, science could not exist without these characteristics. The three most important characteristics of science are control, operational definition, and replication.

Control

Control is perhaps the single most important element in the scientific methodology. Control is so very important because it enables scientists to identify the causes of their observations. Experiments are

conducted in an attempt to answer certain questions. They represent 7
attempts to identify why something happens, what causes some event,
or under what conditions an event occurs. In order to provide unambiguous answers to such questions, control is necessary. Marx and
Hillix (1973, p. 8) present an example of how control is necessary in
answering a practical question.

> A farmer with both hounds and chickens might find that at least
> one of his four dogs is sucking eggs. If it were impractical to keep
> his dogs locked away from the chicken house permanently, he
> would want to find the culprit so that it could be sold to a friend
> who had no chickens, or to an enemy who does. The experiment
> could be run in just two nights by locking up one pair of hounds
> the first night and observing whether eggs were broken, if so, one
> additional dog would be locked up the second night, and the
> results observed. If none were broken, the two dogs originally
> released would be locked up with one of the others, and the results
> observed. Whatever the outcome, the guilty dog would be isolated.
> A careful farmer would, of course, check negative results by giving
> the guilty party a positive opportunity to demonstrate his pre-
> sumed skill, and he would check positive results by making sure
> that only one dog was an egg sucker.[2]

In this example the farmer, in the final analysis, controlled for the
simultaneous influence of all dogs by releasing only one dog at a time
to isolate the egg sucker. To answer questions in psychology, we also
have to eliminate the simultaneous influence of many variables to
isolate the cause of an effect. Controlled inquiry is an absolutely
essential process in science because without it the cause of an effect
could not be isolated. The observed effect could be due to any one or a
combination of the uncontrolled variables. A historical example will
serve to illustrate the necessity of control in arriving at causative
relationships.

In the thirties, Norman Maier presented a paper at a meeting of the
American Association for the Advancement of Science. In this paper
(Maier, 1938) he presented a technique for producing abnormal
symptoms in rats by presenting them with a discrimination problem
that had no solution. Shortly thereafter, other investigators examined
the procedure used by Maier and became interested in one of its
components. Maier had found that the rats, when confronted with the
insoluble problem, normally refused to jump off the testing platform.
To induce jumping behavior, a blast of hot air was directed at an
animal. Shortly thereafter, Morgan and Morgan (1939) duplicated

8   Maier's results by simply exposing rats to the high pitched tones of the hot air blast that Maier had used to make his rats leave the jumping stand. The significant point made in the Morgan and Morgan study was that conflict or the elaborate discrimination training was not necessary to generate the abnormal symptoms. This led to a controversy regarding the role of frustration in fixation that lasted for a number of years (Maier, 1949).

The important point for our purposes is that the potential effect of the *auditory* stimulus was not controlled. Therefore, one could not conclude from Maier's 1938 study that the insoluble discrimination problem produced the abnormal behavior since the noise could also have been the culprit. Exercise of control over such variables is essential in science.

Operational Definition

The principle of operational definition was originally set forth by Bridgman (1927) and was incorporated into psychology shortly thereafter. Operationism means that terms must be defined by the steps or operations used to measure them. Such a procedure is necessary to eliminate confusion in meaning and communication. Consider the statement, "Hunger causes one to perceive food-related objects selectively." One might ask, "What is meant by hunger?" Stating that hunger refers to being starved or some other such term only adds to the confusion. However, stating that hunger refers to 8 or 10 hours of food deprivation communicates a clear idea. Now others realize what hunger means and, if they so desire, they could also generate the same degree of hunger. Stating an operational definition forces one to identify the empirical referents for terms. In this manner ambiguity is minimized. This does not mean, as Stevens (1939) has pointed out, that operationism is a panacea. It is merely a statement of one of the requirements of science that must eventually be used if science is to provide communicable knowledge.

One of the early criticisms of operationism was that the demands of operationism were too strict. If everything had to be defined operationally, one could never begin the investigation of a problem. It would have been virtually impossible to formulate a problem concerning the functional relationships between events. Instead of stating a relationship between hunger and selective perception, one would have had to talk about the relationship between number of hours of food deprivation and inaccurate description of ambiguous stimuli presented tachistoscopically.

Operationism, however, does not preclude verbal concepts and higher level abstraction. Problems and questions are originally formulated in nonoperational terms such as hunger, anxiety, and frustration.

Once the problem is formulated, then the terms must be operationally defined. Verbal concepts are, therefore, admissible and useful in the pursuit of science.

Another criticism leveled at operationism was that each operational definition completely specified the meaning of the term. Any change in the set of operations would specify a new concept which would lead to a multiplicity of concepts. Such a notion suggests that there is no overlap between the operations, that (for example) there is no relationship between three different operational measures (responses to a questionnaire, GSR readings, and amount of urination and defecation by rats in an open-field situation) of a concept such as anxiety or that they are not concerned with the same thing. Stevens addresses this issue and notes that this "process of generalization proceeds on the basis of the notion of classes" (Stevens, 1939, p. 233). Verbal concepts such as anxiety merely represent the name or symbol that has been given to that class of events. Each of the many operational definitions that can be given to a verbal concept merely represents a member of that class. Each operational definition is only a partial representation of the verbal concept and consequently the various operational definitions of a verbal concept are concerned with the same thing.

More recently Deese (1972) has criticized operationism as being a hocus-pocus procedure. In conducting research we must translate abstract concepts such as hunger or intelligence into events or procedures that can be unambiguously understood by others. This is where the problem arises according to Deese. For example, consider the concept of intelligence. If we were to use the concept of intelligence in a study we would want to define it operationally. One way to define it is to identify intelligence as a score on a specific intelligence test. Doing this has satisfied the criteria of operationism. However, Deese states that although we have operationally defined intelligence in terms of a score on a specific intelligence test, we still may not know whether we have really measured intelligence or how or why intelligence tests measure intelligence. Although it is appropriate for Deese to question our knowledge and ability to measure intelligence, this does not seem to be related to operationism. Operationism merely refers to defining terms by the operations used to obtain them. In the case of intelligence this was done. It is quite another matter apart from operationism as to whether the operational definition is in fact an accurate or valid operational definition.

Replication

A third requirement of science is that the observations made must be replicable. To be replicable the data obtained in an experiment must be

10 reliable, that is, the same results must be found if the study is repeated. That science has such a requirement is quite obvious since it is attempting, in a scientific manner, to obtain knowledge about the world. If observations are not repeatable, then our descriptions and explanations are likewise unreliable and therefore useless.

Reproducibility of observations can be investigated by making intergroup, intersubject, or intrasubject observations. Intergroup observations would consist of attempting to duplicate the results on another group of subjects; intersubject observations involve assessing the reliability of observations on other individual subjects; and intrasubject observations consist of attempting to duplicate the results with the same subject on different occasions.

Methods of Acquiring Knowledge

Science has been defined as a specific method for generating knowledge. Is knowledge acquired in this way better or more appropriate than that acquired in other ways? How do other approaches differ from the scientific approach? To answer these two questions it is necessary to look at the various approaches to acquiring knowledge. Helmstadter (1970) presents five unscientific approaches to acquiring knowledge. Each successive approach represents a more acceptable means of acquiring knowledge.

Tenacity

The first approach can be labeled "tenacity," defined in the dictionary as "the quality or state of holding fast." This approach to acquiring knowledge seems to boil down to the acquisition and persistence of superstitions, because superstitions represent beliefs that are reacted to as if they were fact. A gambler, for example, may easily acquire such a superstition by observing that he has won a number of times when he has worn a certain hat. He makes the association between winning and wearing the hat and comes to the conclusion that he must wear the hat in order to win. In the future, winning while wearing the hat will only strengthen this association. The gambler has generated the belief that the hat promotes winning and therefore he must wear the hat when gambling. The acquisition of such superstitious behavior has been described by Skinner (1948).

Intuition

Intuition is the second approach to acquiring knowledge. The dictionary defines intuition as "the act or process of coming to direct knowl-

edge or certainty *without reasoning or inferring."* Psychics such as
Edgar Cayce *seem* to have derived their knowledge from intuition. The
predictions and descriptions of psychics are not based on any known
reasoning or inferring process; therefore such knowledge must be intuitive knowledge. This does not mean that knowledge acquired from
psychics is undesirable or inappropriate, only that it is not scientific
knowledge.

Authority

Authority, as a method of acquiring knowledge, represents an acceptance of information or facts stated by another because that person is a
highly respected source. An example exists within the various religions. A religion typically has a sacred text, tribunal, or person, or
some combination of these that represents finality. These represent
the facts, which are considered indisputable. This example is not
meant to be critical of religions, but is used only to demonstrate that
the authority approach to gaining knowledge differs from the scientific
approach. Another example comes from the political-social arena. On
July 4, 1936, the Central Committee of the Communist Party of the
Soviet Union issued a "Decree against Pedology" (Woodworth and
Sheehan, 1964) which, among other things, outlawed the use of standardized tests in schools. Since no one had the right to question such a
decree, it had to be accepted as fact.

The authority approach should not be confused with our increasing dependence upon experts for information. Experts do transmit
scientific knowledge, and they usually base their opinions on scientific
knowledge. The distinction between the authority approach and an
appeal to an expert is that the authority approach dictates that we
accept whatever is decreed, whereas the appeal to an expert does not
dictate such indiscriminate acceptance. We are free to accept or reject
whatever the expert says.

Rationalism

A fourth way of gaining knowledge is the rationalistic approach. This
approach uses reasoning to arrive at knowledge and assumes that valid
knowledge is acquired if the correct reasoning process is used. Consider the following classical syllogism:

> All men are mortal.
> Socrates is a man.
> Therefore, Socrates is mortal.

Few individuals would argue with the conclusion, even though it does
depend upon the validity of the first two statements. While the first
two statements may be correct and therefore would lead to a valid

12 conclusion, such is not the case with all syllogisms. Consider the following example provided by Helmstadter (1970, p. 11).

> Two weeks ago, Team A beat Team C in football.
> Last week, Team C beat Team B in football.
> Therefore, next week Team A will beat Team B in football.

Is the conclusion valid? The major or minor premises have frequently happened, yet the conclusion may or may not be true, depending on the performance of the two teams. Performance is highly variable, and therefore the conclusion could turn out to be true as well as false. It is not uncommon for an upset to occur in any sport, which illustrates the variability of performance. However, the premises do not take such variability into account and one may thus arrive at a faulty conclusion. It is such assumptions that reveal the limitations of the rationalistic approach to gaining knowledge.

Does this mean that science does not use the reasoning process? Obviously, the answer to this question is No! Reasoning is essential to the scientific process; however, reasoning is not synonomous with the scientific process. Reasoning is used, for example, to arrive at hypotheses. These hypotheses are then tested, using the scientific method, to determine their validity.

Empiricism

The empirical approach constitutes the fifth and final unscientific approach to gaining knowledge. This approach says, "If I have experienced something, then it is valid and true." Therefore, any facts that concur with experience are accepted and those that do not are rejected. What is wrong with this approach? Frequently you hear people say, "I won't believe it until I see it." Such a statement illustrates the empirical approach and indicates that we tend to believe the information acquired through our senses.

While this approach is very appealing and has much to recommend it, several dangers exist when using only this approach. Our perceptions are affected by a number of variables that lead us to form inaccurate perceptions. Research has demonstrated that variables such as past experiences and our motivations at the time of the perceiving can drastically alter what we see. Research has also revealed that our memory for events does not remain constant. Not only do we tend to forget things, but at times an actual distortion may take place. Also we tend to experience only a small number of the total possible number of situations that could occur. The situations we experience may represent a biased sample that could lead to an inaccurate conclusion. If, for example, you had had contact with 10, and only 10, females, all of whom were extremely tall, you would probably conclude that all women were extremely tall. However, these 10 women represented a biased sample of all women, which led to the inaccurate conclusion. Factors such as these limit the veridicality of the empirical approach.

Again, I am not saying that empiricism is not included in the scientific approach, because it is. Empiricism is a vital element in science. However, the scientific approach requires more than just empiricism.

Scientific Approach

We have just taken a look at five nonscientific approaches to acquiring knowledge. Empiricism, the last approach, is the most acceptable one to the scientist. The last method for gaining knowledge is the scientific approach, which uses the scientific method. This approach differs from the others in terms of the aforementioned characteristics of control, operational definition, and replication. It is much more demanding in its requirements and, therefore, knowledge thus acquired is much more exact. Calder (1955, p. 42) presents a good description of the scientific approach.

> The scientific man in the prosecution of his art of discovery has to practise three things: He must *observe* and choose his facts; he must form a *hypothesis* which links them together and provides a plausible explanation of them; he must carry out numerous and repeated *experiments* to prove, or disprove, his hypothesis.[3]

Calder's description reveals that the scientific approach requires time and patience in progressing through the steps required. He indicates three basic steps are involved: observing, forming a hypothesis, and testing the hypothesis. Other writers list many more steps. For our purposes we will list five steps: (1) identifying the problem and hypothesis formation; (2) designing the experiment; (3) conducting the experiment; (4) hypothesis testing; and (5) communicating the results. These steps will be elaborated on in Chapter 2.

Objectives of Science

Ultimately, the objective of science is to understand the world in which we live. This objective pervades all scientific disciplines in the sense that each attempts to understand its subject matter. However, to

---

3. From Calder, R. *Science makes sense.* London: George Allen and Unwin Ltd., 1955, p. 42.

14 say that the objective of science is understanding is rather nebulous. Ordinary people as well as scientists demand understanding. Is there a difference in the level of understanding referred to by the scientist and the ordinary person? The answer obviously is yes. Understanding on the part of the nonscientist most typically consists of being able to provide, however crude it may be, some explanation for the occurrence of a phenomenon. Most people, for example, do not totally understand the operation of the internal combustion engine. Some individuals are satisfied with only knowing that it requires turning a key in the ignition switch and simultaneously depressing the accelerator. Other individuals are not satisfied until they acquire additional information. For the ordinary person, understanding—or knowing the reasons—ceases when curiosity rests.

Science is not satisfied with such a superficial criterion for understanding a phenomenon. Science demands a detailed examination of a phenomenon. Only when a phenomenon is accurately described and explained, and therefore predictable and in most cases capable of being controlled, will science say that it has understanding. Consequently, scientific understanding requires the four specific objectives of (1) description, (2) explanation, (3) prediction, and (4) control.

Description

The first objective of science is to describe accurately the phenomenon of interest. Basically, the process of description requires one to portray an accurate picture of the phenomenon, to identify the variables that exist, and then to determine the degree to which they exist. For example, the initial data collected on children consisted of baby biographies or a description of the behavior of young children. Usually any new area begins with the descriptive process because it identifies the variables that exist. Only after we have some knowledge of which variables do and do not exist can we begin to explain why they exist. For example, we would not be able to explain the existence of separation anxiety—the crying behavior and visual searching behavior engaged in by infants when the mother departs—if we had not first identified this behavior. Scientific knowledge typically begins with description.

Explanation

The second objective is to explain the phenomenon, and this requires knowledge of why the phenomenon exists or what causes it. Therefore, we must be able to identify the antecedent conditions which result in the occurrence of the phenomenon. Assume the behavior connoting separation anxiety existed when an infant was handled by few adults other than its parents and did not exist when handled and left with many adults other than parents. We would conclude that one of the antecedent conditions of this behavior was frequency of handling by adults other than parents. Note that frequency was only *one* of the antecedents. Scientists are cautious and conservative individuals. They recognize that most phenomena are multidetermined and that new evidence may necessitate replacing an old explanation with a better one. As the research process proceeds, we acquire more and more knowledge as to the causes of a phenomenon. With this increasing knowledge comes the ability to predict and possibly control the phenomenon.

Prediction

Prediction represents the third objective of science and refers to the ability to anticipate the occurrence of an event prior to its actual occurrence. We can, for example, predict very accurately when an eclipse will occur. Making an accurate prediction such as this requires knowledge of the antecedent conditions that produce such a phenomenon. It requires knowledge of the movement of the moon and earth and knowledge of the fact that the earth, moon, and sun have to be in a particular position before an eclipse can occur. In short, prediction requires knowledge of antecedent conditions. If we knew the combination of variables that resulted in academic success, we could then very accurately predict who would and would not succeed academically. To the extent that we cannot accurately predict a phenomenon, we have a gap in our understanding of it.

Control

The fourth objective of science is control. Control as an objective of science refers to the manipulation of the conditions that determine a phenomenon. Note that the emphasis is on the *conditions that determine a phenomenon*. Control, in this sense, refers to having knowledge of the causes or the antecedent conditions of a phenomenon. When the antecedent conditions are known, they can be manipulated so as to produce the desired phenomenon. Psychologists, therefore, do not directly control behavior. Rather they investigate and try to control the variables that result in a behavior.

Frequently, it has been stated that the psychologist is interested in the control of behavior. Books such as *Walden Two* (Skinner, 1948) and *Beyond Freedom and Dignity* (Skinner, 1971) have promoted such statements because readers of these books note that Skinner is explaining or laying out a scheme for making people behave in a certain way. Thus they conclude that psychologists destroy or have eliminated people's free will and have the ability to control their behavior. The

16   point that most nonscientists miss is that Skinner's concern is with identifying the antecedent variables that generate the behavior of concern. Skinner believes that behavior is determined and that the psychological task is to isolate the antecedent conditions.

Psychologists are interested in behavior, but their main interest lies in the conditions that produce behavior. Once these conditions are understood, the behavior can be controlled by allowing or not allowing the conditions to exist. Consider the frustration-aggression hypothesis: "Frustration leads to aggression." Assume this hypothesis is completely correct. Aggression is produced by the condition of frustration. Knowing this, the behavior of aggression can be controlled by allowing or not allowing a person to be frustrated. As can be seen, control refers to the manipulation of conditions that produce a phenomenon such as aggression and not to the phenomenon itself.

At this point it seems appropriate to provide some additional insight into the concept of control. So far, control has been discussed in two slightly different ways. When discussing the characteristics of the scientific approach, control was referred to in terms of holding constant or eliminating the influence of extraneous variables in an experiment. In the present discussion, control refers to the antecedent conditions determining a behavior. Boring (1954) noted that the word "control" has three meanings attached to it. First, control refers to a check or verification in terms of a comparison. Second, control refers to a restraint—keeping conditions constant or eliminating the influence of extraneous conditions from the experiment. Third, control refers to a guidance or directing in the sense of producing an exact change or a specific behavior. The second and third meanings identified by Boring are those used in this book so far. Since all these meaningy will be used at various times, it would be to the student's advantage to memorize them.

The Objectives Illustrated

An experimental example will illustrate the objectives of science and reveal their interdependence. Haughton and Ayllon (1965) attempted to demonstrate the control that some environmental events can have on behavior. To demonstrate this relationship, Haughton and Ayllon systematically observed, using a time-sampling technique, the behavior of a female psychiatric patient for over a year. This observation period provided a baseline or a description of her behavior as it typically occurred. The baseline data revealed that her waking time was divided between lying in bed (60%); sitting and walking (20%); and eating, grooming, and elimination (20%). Throughout all of these behaviors, she maintained a high rate of smoking behavior. This data conformed to the ward reports that, for the past 13 years, she had **17** refused to do anything except smoke.

To demonstrate the relationship between environmental events and behavior, the arbitrary response of holding a broom while in an upright position was selected. To develop this behavior, one staff person would give her the broom while she was in an upright position and, while she held it, another would give her a cigarette. In this manner the patient was reinforced for broom holding. The cigarette was selected as a reinforcer since this was the only real behavior she would engage in. Within a few days the patient had developed a stereotyped behavior of pacing while holding the broom.

This study can illustrate the four objectives of science. Description of the patient's behavior was the first step. To accomplish the purpose of the study, it was necessary to describe the phenomenon accurately. In this case the phenomenon was the behavior of the patient. Next the broom-holding behavior was shaped through reinforcement. Since it was shaped through reinforcement we understand the behavior; we know the antecedent conditions which caused it. Since we know the antecedent conditions, we could have predicted the behavior and controlled it as was done in this study. Therefore, we can see that description assists explanation; once we have explanation we have the ability to predict and, in most cases, control behavior.

The Haughton and Ayllon study has been cited as an example of the goals of science. All four goals were represented in this study. However, one should not assume that all four goals are represented in every study. Haughton and Ayllon were conducting a study of only one person in a restricted environment where total behavior could be observed and all stimuli were under the control of the investigators. Most studies are conducted on more than one subject and in relatively nonrestricted environments where the subjects are potentially influenced by numerous stimuli. Therefore, a study typically focuses on only one of the goals of science rather than on all four of them.

Role of the Scientist in Science

One very significant component in the scientific approach is the scientist. This is the individual who employs the scientific approach and ultimately makes science possible. Is the scientist just any person or does he or she possess special characteristics? As might be expected, certain characteristics are necessary. A scientist is any individual who rigorously employs the scientific method in the pursuit of knowledge. However, nature's secrets are revealed reluctantly even when the sci-

18 entific method is used. The scientist must actively search and probe nature to uncover orderly relationships. As a result, the scientist must, among other things, be curious, patient, objective, and tolerant of change.

Curiosity

The scientist's goal is the pursuit of knowledge. The scientist attempts to uncover the laws of nature or attempts to answer the questions: What? When? Why? How? Under what conditions? With what restriction? These questions not only represent the starting point of scientific investigation but continue throughout the investigation. To ask these questions the scientist must be inquisitive, must exhibit curiosity, and must never think the ultimate solution is reached in any area. If questions such as these ever cease, then the scientific process also ceases.

The scientist must maintain an open mind, never becoming rigid in orientation or experimentation. Such rigidity could cause him or her to become blinded and incapable of capitalizing on, or even seeing, unusual events. This relates to Skinner's "fifth unformalized principle of scientific practice . . . serendipity—the art of finding one thing while looking for another" (1972, p. 112). Without being inquisitive and open to new and different phenomena, scientists would never make the accidental discoveries that periodically occur.

Patience

The reluctance of nature to reveal secrets is seen in the slow progress made in scientific inquiry. When individuals read or hear of significant discoveries in some field of scientific inquiry, they marvel at such ability and think of the excitement and pleasure that must have surrounded the discovery. Indeed, such excitement and pleasure does exist. However, most individuals do not realize the many months or years of tedious, painstaking work that went into achieving this advancement in knowledge. Many failures are frequently encountered before success is achieved. As a result the scientist must be extremely patient and must be satisfied with rewards that are few, with long periods of time frequently existing between them. Note the many years of effort that have gone into cancer research. While many advances have been made, a cure is still not available.

Objectivity

One of the prerequisites of scientific inquiry is that the scientist be objective, or free of bias. The scientific method requires objective

observation—observation free of the investigator's own wishes and
attitudes. This requirement is probably one that can only be approximated since the scientist is only human. No matter how severe the attempt to eliminate this, the scientist still has certain desires—desires that influence the research being conducted. Rosenthal (1966), for example, has repeatedly demonstrated that experimenter expectancies may influence the results of experiments.

Change

Scientific investigation necessitates change. The scientist is always devising new methods and new techniques for investigating phenomena. This process typically results in change. When a particular approach to a problem fails, a new approach must be devised which also necessitates change. Consequently, change is a necessary ingredient. When change no longer exists, the scientific process ceases, because then we continue to rely upon and accept old facts and methods of doing things. We are no longer asking questions and are basically saying that we have solved all problems. Change does not necessitate abandoning all past facts and methods, it merely means the scientist must be critical of the past and constantly alert to facts or techniques that represent an improvement over the past.

Basic Assumption Underlying Science

In order for the scientist to have confidence in the fact that scientific inquiry can achieve a solution to questions and problems, he or she must accept one basic axiom. This axiom or assumption of science is related to the nature of the object, events, or things with which the scientist works. It is an axiom concerning the uniformity of nature. The scientist, implicitly or explicitly, must believe that there is uniformity in nature because otherwise there can be no science. Skinner (1953, p. 13), for example, has stated that science is "a search for order, for uniformities, for lawful relations among the events in nature." If there were no uniformity in nature there could be no understanding, explanation, or knowledge about nature. Without uniformity we could not develop theories, laws, or facts. Implicit in the assumption of uniformity is the notion of determinism. In our efforts to uncover the uniform laws of behavior we attempt to identify the variables which are linked together. We construct experiments which attempt to identify the effects produced by given events and in this way attempt to determine the events which produce a given behavior or set of behaviors.

20   Summary

Many individuals seem to have inadequate definitions of science which have been promoted by several false stereotypes. Science is a method for generating a body of knowledge, or a logic of inquiry. As such, science must be distinguished from technique, which represents the specific manner in which one implements the scientific method. The various fields which use the scientific method for generating data make use of a wide variety of techniques. It is these techniques that differ across various fields and across areas within a given field of study. However, the logic of inquiry or the method of inquiry used is identical.

The scientific method as a logic of inquiry has certain rules or characteristics that must be followed. *Control* is the most important characteristic because it enables the scientist to identify causation. Without control, it would be impossible to identify the cause of a given effect. A second characteristic of the scientific method is *operational definition*, which refers to the fact that terms must be defined by the steps or operations used to measure them. Defining terms operationally is necessary to eliminate confusion in meaning and communication. The third characteristic of the scientific method is *replication*. The scientific observations that are made must be replicable. If these characteristics are not satisfied, the results of an investigation are useless because they are not reliable.

The scientific method, as a means for generating knowledge, is the best and most rigorous approach but not the only approach. In fact there are five unscientific approaches. *Tenacity*, or the state of holding fast, seems to represent knowledge acquired through superstitions. *Intuition* refers to knowledge acquired in the absence of any reasoning or inferring. *Authority* represents knowledge acquired from a highly respected source of information. *Rationalism* represents knowledge acquired through correct reasoning. *Empiricism* represents knowledge acquired from experience.

Science, as a method for acquiring knowledge, has certain objectives that it strives to achieve in attempting to reach the ultimate goal of understanding the world in which we live. The first objective is *description*, which refers to the process of portraying an accurate picture of the phenomenon under study. The second objective is *explanation*, or determining why a phenomenon exists or what causes the phenomenon. The third objective is *prediction*, or the anticipation of an event prior to its occurrence. The fourth and last objective is *control*, in the sense of being able to manipulate the antecedent conditions that determine the occurrence of a given phenomenon.

In attempting to gain a body of knowledge through use of the **21** scientific method, the scientist must implement this methodology. Any individual who rigorously employs the scientific method is a scientist, but nature is reluctant to reveal its secrets. Therefore the scientist must be curious enough to ask questions needing solution and patient enough to gain the answers. The scientist must also be objective so as not to bias the data, and must accept change to allow him or her to incorporate new techniques and/or facts. While the scientist must have these characteristics, he or she must accept one basic axiom in order even to begin a scientific study. This axiom is that the scientist must believe that there is uniformity in nature.

Key Concepts

One way to test your mastery of the material that was presented in this chapter is to see if you know the meaning of the following terms. These terms were selected because they represent the key concepts. If you can define, identify, or otherwise explain each of the following terms without referring back to the material in the chapter, you can be assured that you have mastered the basics of the material that was presented. Just in case you cannot recall the meaning of a given term, the page on which it can be found appears in parentheses beside it.

science (p. 4)
technique (pp. 4–5)
control (pp. 6–7, 15–16)
operational definition (pp. 8–9)
replication (pp. 9–10)
description (p. 14)
explanation (pp. 14–15)
prediction (p. 15)
determinism (p. 19)

2

The Experimental
Approach

The experimental approach is defined as the technique that attempts to ferret out cause-and-effect relationships. "How does it accomplish such a task?" "How does this approach differ from other approaches that are used to attain scientific knowledge?" Answers to both of these questions can be obtained from a discussion of the experimental research approach and the descriptive research approaches. Such a discussion should give a clear idea of how the experimental method identifies causation and how it differs from the descriptive method. Before these research approaches are discussed, the reader should have an accurate definition of causation. Causation is one of those terms that people frequently use but probably don't really understand. People are continually asking questions such as "What causes cancer?" "What causes a person to murder someone else?" "What causes a man to beat his wife?" What do they really mean? Common sense suggests that causality refers to a condition in which one event—the cause—generates another event—the effect. As you shall see, causality is much more complex.

Causation

The concept of causality has generated much discussion from both philosophers and scientists. John Stuart Mill (1874), a British philosopher, tackled the problem of causality and set forth a number of canons that could be used for experimentally identifying causality. These canons seem to be quite important since they form the basis of many of the approaches currently used.

The first canon is the *Method of Agreement*. The method of agreement identifies causality by observing the common elements that exist in several instances of an event. This canon can be illustrated by the frequently cited case of the man who wanted to find out scientifically why he got drunk. To attempt to isolate the cause of getting drunk, he drank rye and water on the first night and became drunk. On the second night, he drank scotch and water and became drunk once again. On the third night, he got drunk on bourbon and water. He therefore decided that the water was the cause of his getting drunk because it was the common element each time. This method, as you can see, is inadequate in unequivocally identifying causation because many significant variables, such as the alcohol in the rye, scotch, and bourbon, may be overlooked.

The second canon is the *Method of Difference*. This method attempts to identify causality by observing the different effects produced in two situations that are alike in all respects except one. The method of difference represents the approach taken in many psychological experiments. In an experiment designed to test the effect of a drug on reaction time, the drug will be given to one group of subjects and a placebo will be given to another group of matched subjects. If the reaction time of the drug group differs significantly from the placebo group, the difference is usually attributed to the drug (the causal agent). This method provides the basis for a great deal of work in psychology which is aimed at identifying causality.

24   The third canon set forth by Mill is the *Joint Methods of Agree-ment and Difference.* This method is exactly what the name implies. The method of agreement is first used to observe common elements. The common elements observed are then formulated as hypotheses to be tested by the method of difference. In the case of the man who wanted to find out why he got drunk, the common element of water should have been formulated as a hypothesis to be tested by the method of difference. Using the method of difference, one group of subjects would drink water and another matched group would be given another liquid such as straight bourbon. Naturally the group drinking only water would not get drunk, indicating that the wrong variable had been identified even though it was a common element.

The fourth canon is the *Method of Concomitant Variation.* This method states that a variable is either a cause or an effect, or is connected through some factor of causation if variation in the variable results in a parallel variation in another variable. Plutchik (1974) inter-prets this canon to be an extension of the method of difference in that, rather than just using two equated groups in an experiment, three or more are used, with each one receiving a different amount of the variable under study. In the previously cited drug example, rather than using just a placebo group and a drug group, one placebo and several drug groups could be used, with each drug group receiving a different amount of the drug. Reaction times would then be observed to deter-mine if variation in the drug results in a parallel variation in reaction time. If this parallel variation is found, then the drug is interpreted as being the cause of the variation in reaction time. Others interpret this canon as also including correlation studies. When including correla-tional studies under this canon, one is on extremely shaky ground in attempting to infer causative relationships, since most correlational studies represent descriptions of degree of relationship. Identification of of causation requires direct manipulation of the variables of interest. However, recent work is making strides in enabling causation to be inferred from correlational studies.

When looking at the works of people like Mill, one gets the idea that we have a fairly adequate grasp of what causation is and how to obtain evidence of it. This belief is further confirmed when we see that the way in which experiments are conducted to obtain evidence of causation tends to follow the canons set forth by Mill. However, such philosophizing and experimentation have not completely clarified the meaning of the word *cause.* Morison (1960, pp. 193–194), in his discus-sion of the history of attempts to find the cause of malaria, illustrates the ambiguity of this word:

Whatever the reason, medical men have found it congenial to assume that they could find something called *The Cause* of a particular disease. If one looks at the history of any particular disease, one finds that the notion of its cause has varied with the state of the art. In general, the procedure has been to select as *The Cause* that element in the situation which one could do the most about. In many cases it turned out that, if one could take away this element or reduce its influence, the disease simply disappeared or was reduced in severity. This was certainly desirable, and it seemed sensible enough to say that one had got at the cause of the condition. Thus in ancient and medieval times malaria as its name implied was thought to be due to the bad air of the lowlands. As a result, towns were built on the tops of hills, as one notices in much of Italy today. The disease did not disappear, but its incidence and severity were reduced to a level consistent with productive community life.

At this stage it seemed reasonable enough to regard bad air as the cause of malaria, but soon the introduction of quinine to Europe from South America suggested another approach. Apparently quinine acted on some situation within the patient to relieve and often to cure him completely. Toward the end of the last century the malaria parasite was discovered in the blood of patients suffering from the disease. The effectiveness of quinine was explained by its ability to eliminate this parasite from the blood. The parasite now became *The Cause,* and those who could afford the cost of quinine and were reasonably regular in their habits were enabled to escape the most serious ravages of the disease. It did not disappear as a public health problem, however; and further study was given to the chain of causality. These studies were shortly rewarded by the discovery that the parasite was transmitted by certain species of mosquitoes. For practical purposes *The Cause* of epidemic malaria became the Mosquito, and attention was directed to control of its activities.

Entertainingly enough, however, malaria has disappeared from large parts of the world without anyone doing much about it at all. The fens of Boston and other northern cities still produce mosquitoes capable of transmitting the parasite, and people carrying the organism still come to these areas from time to time; but it has been many decades since the last case of the disease occurred locally. Observations such as this point to the probability that epidemic malaria is the result of a nicely balanced set of social and economic, as well as biological, factors, each one of which has to be present at the appropriate level. We are still completely unable to describe these sufficient conditions with any degree of accuracy, but we know what to do in an epidemic area because we have focused attention on three or four of the most necessary ones.

Can we state precisely what is meant by the word *causation?* To be classified as a causative agent, the effect must not occur unless the *cause* is present. In the example just presented of the attempt to identify the cause of malaria, Morison concluded that we cannot describe the sufficient conditions that cause malaria but we do know some of the most important necessary conditions. This suggests that finding the cause of an effect requires discovering both the *necessary* and *sufficient* conditions for the occurrence of an event. A *necessary* condition refers to a condition that must be present in order for the effect to occur. To become an alcoholic you must consume alcohol. A *sufficient* condition refers to a condition that will always produce the effect. Destroying the auditory nerve always results in a loss of hearing.

A condition must be both necessary and sufficient to qualify as a cause because under such a situation the effect would never occur unless the condition were present and whenever the condition was present the effect would occur. If a condition were only *sufficient* then the effect could occur in other ways. There are several ways one can lose one's hearing in addition to destruction of the auditory nerve. In like manner, a necessary condition does not mean that the effect will necessarily occur. All people who consume alcohol do not become alcoholics; however, one must have consumed alcohol to become an alcoholic.

To state that we have found the cause for an event means that both the *necessary* and *sufficient* conditions have been found. It means that a complete explanation of the occurrence of the event has been isolated and *no change* in the explanation, unlike that noted with the malaria example, *will ever occur.*

Where does this leave the psychologist? The behavior of organisms in which the psychologist is interested is extremely complex and multidetermined. It would be rather presumptuous for anyone in the field to assume that all necessary and sufficient conditions for the occurrence of behavior could be identified. As scientists, we are continuously concerned with discovering necessary and sufficient conditions, but it is unlikely that we will discover all of these conditions. It seems more appropriate to take a probabilistic approach. Through experimentation, more and more of the necessary and sufficient conditions for the occurrence of a behavior will be identified. With this increase in knowledge of behavior, we increase the probability of correctly identifying the causes of behavior.

The position which has just been elaborated regarding causation is the traditional view and one which is typically accepted and advocated by researchers. However, there is another more complex and perhaps more appropriate view of causation. This orientation views causation (Deese, 1972) as a large network of cause and effect relations. Any given cause and effect relation which is isolated in a study is only one cause and effect relation which is embedded in a matrix of other cause and effect relations. Consider the case of Morison's discussion of malaria. In this discussion Morison illustrates the covariation between a number of events and malaria which could be considered a specific cause and effect relationship. The bad air of the lowlands was found to covary with the incidence of malaria. Later it was found that the presence of a parasite covaried with the appearance of malaria, and even later it was found that a certain species of mosquitoes caused malaria because they carried the malaria parasite. Note that a number of specific cause and effect relationships, in terms of covariation of events, were identified in the history of trying to identify the cause of malaria. However, it is also apparent none of these specific relationships that were identified could be labeled as *the* cause of malaria, since many of the so-called causative events, such as the mosquitoes, still exist and yet the presumed effect of malaria no longer occurs. Such a state of affairs suggests, as Morison pointed out, that a nicely balanced system of interrelated conditions must exist for a given effect to occur. For malaria to occur, it is necessary for the mosquitoes and parasites to exist in a system of other specific social and economic conditions. Any one condition by itself is not sufficient to produce the effect. This view of causation advocates study of the relationship between the levels or amounts of the variables operating within a system, rather than focusing on the covariation between one variable, which can be labeled the cause, and another, which can be labeled the effect. Such a viewpoint sees any given study as representing only a small part of the overall system, and the relationship found in a given study exists only if certain relationships exist among the remainder of the elements of the system.

Descriptive Research Approaches

The primary characteristic of the descriptive method is that it represents an attempt to provide an accurate description or picture of a particular situation or phenomenon. This approach does not try to ferret out the so-called cause-and-effect relationships. Instead, it attempts to identify variables that exist in a given situation and, at times, to describe the relationship that exists between these variables. Therefore, the descriptive approach is widely used and of great importance. We see the results of the descriptive approach whenever the Gallup polls on presidential popularity or other issues are reported, or the results of other surveys are reported. Helmstadter (1970, p. 65) has even gone so far as to state that the "descriptive approaches are the most widely used . . . research methods."

The descriptive method is of such great value because of its role in seeking solutions to questions. When initially investigating a new area, the descriptive method is necessary to identify the factors that

28 exist and to identify relationships that exist among the factors. Such knowledge is used to formulate hypotheses that are subjected to experimental investigation. Also, the descriptive method is frequently used to describe the status of a situation once a solution, suggested by experimental analyses, has been put into effect. Here the descriptive method can provide input regarding the effectiveness of the proposed solution and also provide hypotheses as to how a more effective solution could be reached. As you can see, the descriptive method has its place in the process of attaining knowledge through the scientific method. It is useful in both the initial and final stages of investigation into a given area.

Naturalistic Observation

Naturalistic observation is a technique that enables the investigator to collect data on naturally occurring behavior. Ebbesen and Haney (1973), for example, were interested in determining the relationship between the proportion of drivers who turned in front of an oncoming car and the risk of a collision with that car. The investigators naturally hypothesized that an inverse relationship would exist. To obtain data to test the hypothesis, an unobtrusive observer was situated in a parking lot next to the T-shaped intersection that was selected for study. Results of the study supported the hypothesis. However, it was also observed that males took significantly greater risks than females, and that risk taking increased if drivers had to wait in a line of cars before being allowed to turn, particularly if they had no passengers with them.

A study such as this illustrates the characteristics of naturalistic observation. Perhaps a unique characteristic is the unobtrusiveness of the observer. Rather than taking an active part in the experiment, the observer must remain completely aloof in order to record natural behavior. If subjects had known they were being observed, their behavior would probably not have been the same. A second and related characteristic is the lack of artificiality of the situation. The subjects are not behaving in an environment removed from real life. They are left in their natural environment so as to eliminate any artificial influence that may be caused by bringing the organism out of its natural habitat.

For certain types of studies it is necessary that these characteristics exist. If a research project were directed at answering the question of what baboons do during the day, naturalistic observation would be the technique to use. Such research would also generate hypotheses that could be tested with field or laboratory experimentation. If we observe that baboons fight when conditions *a*, *b*, *c*, and *d* exist, and we wanted to know *why* they fight, we could conduct an experiment to determine this. Condition *a* would be presented without *b*, *c*, or *d*, and we would observe whether fighting occurs. Then condition *b* would be presented without *a*, *c*, or *d*, and so forth, until all conditions and combinations had been presented. We have now moved from observation to experimentation. Another situation in which naturalistic observation is necessary is when one is conducting a study that is not amenable to experimentation. It is not experimentally feasible, for example, to study suicide or other similar topics.

While there are many positive components of naturalistic observation, it also has a number of constraints. Naturalistic observation is great for obtaining an accurate description, but causes of behavior are almost impossible to isolate. Any given behavior could be produced by a number of agents operating independently or in combination and observation does not provide any means of ferreting these out. In no way could the Ebbesen and Haney study have isolated why males take more risks than females. Also the observational approach is very time consuming. Observers in the Ebbesen and Haney study spent about a month observing drivers at selected time intervals between 10:00 A.M. and 5:00 P.M. to collect data for just one portion of the study. These are just some of the difficulties encountered in such a study.

Field Studies

A second descriptive research approach is the field study approach. Field studies are similar to naturalistic observation in that both are conducted in the real world. Consequently, both approaches avoid the criticism of artificiality of the environments in which the data are collected. However, the field studies differ from naturalistic observation in several important ways. First, the investigator intervenes in the data collection. A prerequisite for a study to be classified as naturalistic observation is that the investigator remains unobtrusive. In field studies the investigator actively interacts with subjects in the collection of data. Second, the observations of interest to the investigator are typically focused on a more specific aspect of behavior than are those in a naturalistic observation study. Third, field studies use a variety of diverse approaches whereas naturalistic observation uses one general procedure. The approaches that fall under the classification of field studies are the survey, correlational studies, longitudinal and/or cross-sectional studies, and the field experiment. The field experiment will not be included in the present discussion since it represents an experimental approach and will be discussed under that topic. Each of the others will be briefly discussed.

THE SURVEY.   Webster's dictionary defines a survey as a "critical inspection, often official, to provide exact information; often, a study of an area with respect to a certain condition, or its prevalence; as, a *survey* of the schools." The survey represents a probe to describe a given state of affairs that exists at a given time. Therefore, direct contact has to be made with the individuals whose characteristics, behaviors, or attitudes are relevant to the investigation.

Probably the most widely known surveys are those conducted by the Gallup organization. Gallup polls are frequently conducted to survey the voting public's opinions on such issues as the popularity of the president or a given policy, or to determine the percentage of individuals who will be expected to vote for a given candidate at election time. Surveys are initially conducted to supply answers to the questions of "how many" and "how much." But such frequency data are only a preliminary phase of the research in many survey studies. Frequently studies want to answer the questions of "who," and "why." Who votes for the Republican candidate and who votes for the Democratic candidate? Why do people buy a particular make of car or brand of a product? Such information aids in our understanding of why a particular phenomenon took place, and increases our ability to predict what will happen.

While the survey technique is applicable to a wide range of problems, a number of disadvantages are associated with it. The three most obvious disadvantages are sampling error, time constraints, and constraints in the length of the survey.

Sampling error arises from the fact that most surveys are not administered to the total population of individuals. Population refers to all of the events, things, or individuals to be represented. Rather, a sample (any number less than the population) of individuals is selected for inclusion in the study, and the results obtained from this sample are considered to be the same as those that would have been obtained if the survey had been administered to the total population. The Gallup polls, for example, do not survey all voting members in the United States. They select perhaps 1500 to survey and base their predictions on these 1500 individuals' responses. Since the survey is based on a sample, it is subject to sampling error. Investigators have devised sampling techniques which have minimized, but not eliminated, the magnitude of sampling bias which exists. Employment of these sampling procedures does increase the time required to conduct a survey, but the benefits accrued far outweigh the time disadvantage. Without the use of appropriate sampling procedures, the information attained would be virtually worthless. Aside from this, surveys do typically require a considerable investment of time and manpower (the second disadvantage) not only in data collection but in terms of constructing the survey, coding the data once it is obtained, and then analyzing the data after it is coded.

The third constraint of length of the survey questionnaire is also very important. In any survey there are numerous significant questions that can be asked. But every data-gathering instrument has an optimal length for the population to which it is being administered. After a certain point the respondent's interest and cooperation diminish. The survey researcher must, therefore, insure that the questionnaire is not too long, even though some important questions may have to be sacrificed.

CORRELATIONAL STUDIES. A correlational study, in its simplest form, consists of measuring two variables and then determining the degree of relationship that exists between them. Consequently, a correlational study can be incorporated into any of the descriptive research approaches. A relatively old but commonly cited study in introductory and developmental texts is the study by Conrad and Jones (1940). They were interested in the relationship between the IQ scores of parents and their offspring. To accomplish the goals of this study, Conrad and Jones measured the IQs of the parents and correlated them with their children's IQ. In this way a descriptive index was obtained that accurately and quantitatively portrayed the relationship between these two variables. As you can see, correlational studies do not make any attempt to manipulate the variables of concern but measure them in their natural state.

The correlational approach enables us to accomplish the goals of prediction. If a reliable relationship is found between two variables, then we have not only described the relationship between these two variables but also gained the ability to predict one variable from a knowledge of the other variable. Sears et al. (1953), for example, found that a positive relationship existed between severity of weaning and later psychological adjustment. Knowledge of this relationship enables one to predict a child's psychological adjustment when given knowledge only of the severity with which the child had been weaned.

The weakness of the correlational approach is apparent in the Sears et al. study. Given knowledge of the relationship that they found, some individuals are prone to say that severity of weaning was the agent causing the later psychological maladjustment. Such an inference is not justified. Causation is frequently inferred from correlational studies but these studies provide no such evidence. If evidence of causation is found between the two correlated variables, it will typically be found by the experimental approach. The later psychological maladjustment found by Sears et al. was probably due to generally inappropriate parent-child relationships, which, among other things, were manifested in severe weaning.

32   Let us look at a hypothetical example to drive this point home. Assume we find a correlation between the number of inches of rainfall in the Dallas-Fort Worth area each month and the number of babies born each month. Could we then say that the monthly rainfall in the Dallas-Fort Worth area caused a certain number of babies to be born or vice versa? Certainly not! It does, however, reveal the fallacy of assuming causation from correlation. There are some rather complex correlational procedures that do give evidence of causation. However, the two-variable cases just presented do not.

The fallacy of assuming causation is not inherent in the correlational study, only in the user of the results of such a study. If the purpose of an investigation is to describe the degree of relationship which exists between variables, this approach is the appropriate one to use.

LONGITUDINAL AND CROSS-SECTIONAL STUDIES.   Longitudinal and cross-sectional studies are of the developmental type of studies since they investigate developmental changes that take place over time. However, the approaches that these two basic techniques use are somewhat different. The longitudinal approach involves selecting a single group of subjects and measuring them repeatedly at selected time intervals to note changes that occur over time in the selected characteristics. Brown, Cayden, and Bellugi-Klima (1969), for example, were interested in language development of children. They systematically recorded the verbalizations and language productions of three children for almost two years. On the other hand, a cross-sectional study identifies representative samples of individuals at specific age groups and notes the changes in the selected characteristics of subjects in these different age groups. Liebert et al. (1969), for example, took this approach in their developmental study of language development. They identified three relatively large groups of children at three different age levels, and observed and recorded the differences among these three groups of subjects.

The longitudinal and cross-sectional descriptive approaches to developmental research have frequently been used in the past, and much discussion has been generated about the relative advantages and disadvantages of each technique. One significant point regarding these two techniques is the fact that they have not always generated similar results. Schaie (1965) presents a general model for studying developmental problems that subsumes the two traditional approaches as special cases and explains why the two traditional approaches are frequently not in agreement. A discussion of Schaie's model is beyond the scope of this book. However, the student interested in developmental research would be advised to read and adhere to his suggestions.

Ex Post Facto Studies

Ex post facto inquiries are actually of the field type of studies because they meet the criterion of field studies. They are given separate status here for two reasons. First, although they are field studies, many of them closely resemble an experiment. Second, some studies have combined the ex post facto and the experimental approaches into a single study. Therefore, a discussion of ex post facto studies seems to represent a good transition into experimental studies.

Ex post facto studies are studies in which the variable or variables of interest to the investigator are not subject to direct manipulation but have to be chosen after the fact. The investigator begins with two or more groups of subjects that are already different on a variable, and then records their behavior to determine if they respond differently in a common situation. These and other characteristics of the ex post facto research are revealed in Dunn and Lupfer's 1974 study which assessed black versus white boys' performance in two categories of sports activities. They hypothesized that black children would prefer reactive sports activities (boxing, batting in baseball, or defense in football) and white children would prefer self-paced sports activities (golf, pitching in baseball, or quarterbacking in football). To test their hypothesis they devised a game that included both types of activities and had each boy play each position. All subjects were measured on both performance and preference for each sports activity. Results revealed that blacks excelled on the reactive sports activity whereas whites excelled on the self-paced activity, but there was no difference in the preference for either activity.

The Dunn and Lupfer study has the appearance of a field experiment by virtue of the fact that the racial variable was manipulated, which allowed the investigators to compare performance of the black and white boys. However, the manipulation of the racial variable represents the ex post facto nature of the study. The experimenters did not have manipulative control of this racial variable. The subjects' *initial* difference (being black or white) determined the group they were in, which means that the subjects *assigned themselves* to the groups on the basis of the characteristics they possessed. As you can see, the variables of interest to the investigator in an ex post facto study cannot be directly manipulated because the variables of interest represent organismic variables such as age and sex. It would have been impossible to have randomly assigned subjects to be either black or white. Consequently, the investigator does not have manipulative control over the variables of interest. It is this self-selection process that represents the ex post facto nature of the research as well as the weakness of this research. Subjects that comprise different groups because of some self-selected characteristic, as black versus white,

34   may also differentially possess traits or characteristics extraneous to the research problem. It may be these characteristics and not the one of interest that produces the observed difference between the groups. Dunn and Lupfer were aware of this weakness and, instead of just concluding that racial affiliation was the causative factor of the observed differences, they discussed the possible contribution of other variables, including number and position of siblings and racial balance of the school attended, to the observed difference. As can be seen, ex post facto studies resemble correlational studies by virtue of the fact that the obtained relationships may have been produced by variables other than those investigated in the study.

Even though ex post facto research has built-in limitations, it seems to be a valuable and necessary type of research. If such research were not conducted, a great deal of the knowledge that has been acquired in psychology, sociology, and education would not exist, since many important and significant variables do not lend themselves to experimental inquiry. Research on variables such as sex, type of mental disorder, participation versus nonparticipation in a riot, intelligence, and parental upbringing do not lend themselves to experimental manipulation. Such investigation requires the controlled inquiry of ex post facto studies.

Experimental Research Approach

The research approach that is most frequently used to identify causation is the experimental approach. Through experimentation cause-and-effect relationships can be isolated because this approach allows one to observe, under controlled conditions, the effects of systematically varying one or more variables. Because of its ability to identify causation, the experimental approach has come to represent the prototype of the scientific method for solving problems. The status of this approach can be seen by the fact that, for example, some books have been titled "*Experimental* Child Psychology," or "*Experimental* Social Psychology," or "*Experimental* Psychology" to denote the specific approach that has been used in acquiring knowledge in that area of psychology. The assumption seems to be that the knowledge acquired in this fashion is somehow better than that acquired by the descriptive method. This assumption seems to be promoted by the fact that evidence of causation can be attained from this approach. We will take a look at the advantages and disadvantages of this approach, from which students can draw their own conclusions.

The Psychological Experiment

Zimney (1961) presents probably one of the better definitions of the psychological experiment. An analysis of this definition, with one minor alteration, should provide a definition of an experiment, an appreciation of the many facets of experimentation, and a general understanding of how experimentation enables causative relationships to be identified. Zimney (1961, p. 18) defines an experiment as "objective observation of phenomena which are made to occur in a strictly controlled situation in which one *or more* factors are varied and the others are kept constant" (italics mine). This definition seems to be one of the better ones because of the components that it includes. Each of these components will be examined separately.

OBJECTIVE.   Objectivity or impartiality and freedom from bias on the part of the investigator were previously discussed as characteristics that the scientist must exhibit. In order to be able to identify causation from the results of the experiment, the experimenter must avoid doing anything that may influence the outcome of the experiment. Rosenthal (1966) has demonstrated that the experimenter is probably capable of greater biasing effects than one would expect. In spite of this, and recognizing that complete objectivity is probably impossible to attain, freedom from bias is the goal for which the investigator must strive.

OBSERVATION.   Science requires that we make empirical observations in order to arrive at answers to questions that are posed. Observations are necessary because they provide the data base used to attain the answers. To provide correct answers, the observations and the recording of these observations must be accurate. Experimenters, even though they are scientists and make a concerted effort to avoid any mistakes, are only human and therefore are subject to errors in recording and observation. For example, work in impression formation has revealed the biased nature of impressions of others. These biases are so pervasive that Gage and Cronback (1955, p. 420) have stated that social impressions are "dominated far more by what the Judge brings to it than by what he takes in during it."

Once scientists realize that they are capable of making mistakes, they can proceed to guard against them. Zimney (1961) presents three rules that investigators should follow to minimize recording and observation errors. The first rule is to accept the possibility that mistakes can occur. This rule is actually stating that we accept the fact that we are not perfect, that our perceptions and therefore our responses are influenced by our motives, desires, and other biasing factors. Once we accept this fact we can then proceed to attempt to identify where the

36 mistakes are likely to occur (the second rule). To identify potential mistakes we must carefully analyze and test each segment of the entire experiment in an attempt to anticipate the potential sources and causes of the errors. Once the situation has been analyzed, then the third rule can be implemented. The third rule states that the experimenter should take the necessary steps to avoid the errors. Many times this involves constructing a more elaborate scenario or redesigning or just appropriately designing equipment, procedures, etc. In any event, every effort should be expended in constructing the experiment so that accurate observations are recorded.

PHENOMENON. Webster's dictionary defines phenomenon as "an observable fact or event." In psychological experimentation, phenomenon refers to any publicly observable behavior such as actions, appearances, verbal statements, responses to questionnaires, and physiological recordings. Focusing on such observable behaviors is a must for psychology to meet the previously discussed characteristics of science. Only by focusing on such phenomena can we meet the characteristics of operational definition and replication of our experiments.

Defining phenomenon as publicly observable behavior would seem to have excluded the internal or private processes and states of the individual. In the introductory course and other courses in psychology, processes such as memory, perception, personality, emotions, and intelligence are discussed. Is it possible to retain these processes if we only study *publicly* observable behavior? Certainly these processes have to be retained since they also play a part in determining an individual's responses. Without getting into intervening variables and hypothetical constructs and the controversy over these (Marx, 1963, pp. 24–31), the student should realize that such processes are studied diligently by many psychologists. In studying these processes researchers investigate publicly observable behavior and infer from these observations the existence of internal processes. It is the behavioral manifestation of the inferred processes that is observed. Intelligence, for example, is inferred from responses to an intelligence test, or aggression is inferred from verbal or physical attacks on another person.

You should also realize that all psychologists do not accept this position. Notably, B. F. Skinner considers the inferring of internal states as inappropriate and not the subject matter of psychology. Psychology should only study environmental phenomena and forget anything that cannot be observed or has to be inferred. Such psychologists state that we should investigate only those environmental sequences, such as stimuli-response reinforcement, that determine behavior, and they have had a great deal of success with this approach. Pribram (1971, p. 253) makes two cogent points regarding this issue. First, the behaving organism is required to define each of the environmental variables. Only the organism can tell you what is reinforcing. Likewise, the response of the organism defines the stimulus and the stimulus defines the response. Second, it is the *internal* processes of the organism that enable the sequencing of events to take place. In order to determine what makes the sequencing occur we must return to the organism and the things taking place inside of that organism.

PHENOMENA THAT ARE MADE TO OCCUR.　In the discussion of control as a goal of science, we saw that the psychologist does not have a direct controlling influence on behavior. The psychologist arranges the antecedent conditions that result in the behavior of interest. In an experiment, the experimenter precisely manipulates one or more variables and objectively observes the phenomena *that are made to occur* by this manipulation. This part of the definition of experimentation refers to the fact that the experimenter is manipulating the conditions that cause a certain effect. In this way experimenters ferret out the cause-effect relationships from experimentation by noting the effect or lack of effect produced by their manipulations.

IN A STRICTLY CONTROLLED SITUATION.　This part of the definition refers to the need for eliminating the influence of variables other than those manipulated by the experimenter (Boring's second meaning of the word control). As you have seen, control is one of the most pressing problems facing the experimenter and one to which considerable attention is devoted, since without control, causation could not be identified. Because of the magnitude of this issue, it will be given extended coverage in later chapters.

IN WHICH ONE OR MORE FACTORS ARE VARIED AND THE OTHERS ARE KEPT CONSTANT.　The ideas expressed in this phase of the definition are epitomized by the *rule of one variable,* which states that all conditions in an experiment must be kept constant except one, this one is to be varied along a defined range, and the result of this variation is to be measured on the response variable.

　　Two major ideas are expressed in the rule of one variable, constancy and variation. The idea of constancy refers to controlling or eliminating the influence of all variables except the one or ones of interest. This requirement is necessary to determine the cause of the variation on the response variable. If this constancy component of the rule is violated, cause for the variation cannot be determined and the experiment is ruined. A learning experiment can easily illustrate

38   the constancy portion of the rule. Assume you were interested in the effect of the length of a list of words on speed of learning. How does increasing the length influence the speed with which you learn that list of words? The length of the list of words could be systematically varied and related to the number of trials required to learn the list. In such an experiment, a number of factors that could influence learning speed need to be controlled, including the factors of difficulty level of the words, ability level of the subjects, familiarity with the words, and motivation level of the subjects. Only if these factors are held constant, and therefore do not exert an influence, can you say that the difference in speed of learning is a function of the change in the length of the list of the words.

The idea of variation means that one or more variables must be deliberately and precisely varied by some given amount to determine their effect on behavior. In the learning experiment, the length of the list of words must be changed by an exact predetermined amount. The question that frequently arises is how, and how much, is the variable to be varied? The answer to this question will be discussed at a later point in the book.

Advantages of the Experimental Approach

The first and foremost advantage of the experimental approach is the control that can be exercised. Control, as was stated in Chapter 1, is the most important characteristic of the scientific method and the experimental approach enables one to effect the greatest degree of control. In an experiment you are seeking an answer to a specific question. In order to obtain an unambiguous answer to the question, it is necessary to institute control over irrelevant variables by either eliminating their influence or holding their influence constant. Such control can be achieved by bringing the experiment into the laboratory and thereby eliminating many extraneous influences such as noise, the presence of others, or other potentially distracting stimuli. Control is also achieved by use of techniques such as random assignment and matching. Since a whole chapter will be devoted to control techniques, they will not be discussed further at this point. Suffice it to say that the primary advantage of experimentation is the rigor afforded by the ability to utilize excellent control techniques.

A second advantage of the experimental approach is the ability to manipulate precisely one or more variables of the experimenter's choosing. If one were interested in studying the effects of crowding on any of a variety of behaviors, crowding could be manipulated in a very precise and systematic manner by varying the number of people in a constant amount of space. If interest also existed in the effects of sex of the subject and degree of crowding on some subsequent behavior, male and female subjects could be included in both the crowded and non-crowded conditions. In this way the experimenter has precisely manipulated two variables, sex of subject and degree of crowding. The experimental approach enables one to control precisely the manipulation of variables by specifying the exact conditions of the experiment. In this manner the results can be interpreted unambiguously since the subjects should be responding primarily to the variables introduced by the experimenter.

A third advantage of the experimental approach is a completely pragmatic one. Use of the experimental approach has produced results that have lasted over time, that have suggested new studies, and, perhaps of most importance, that have suggested solutions to practical problems. This approach has proved to be extremely useful, which makes it important.

Disadvantages of the Experimental Approach

The most frequently cited, and probably the most severe, criticism leveled against the experimental approach is that laboratory findings are obtained in an artificial and sterile atmosphere that precludes any generalization to a real life situation. Bannister (1966, p. 24) epitomizes this approach by stating, "In order to behave like scientists we must construct situations in which subjects are totally controlled, manipulated and measured. We must cut our subjects down to size. We must construct situations in which they can behave as little like human beings as possible and we do this in order to allow ourselves to make statements about the nature of their humanity."

Is such a severe criticism of experimentation justified? It seems to me as though the case is overstated. Underwood (1959) takes a totally different point of view in that he does not see the artificiality problem as a problem at all. He states:

> One may view the laboratory as a fast, efficient, convenient way of identifying variables or factors which are likely to be important in real-life situations. Thus, if four or five factors are discovered to influence human learning markedly, and to influence it under a wide range of conditions, it would be reasonable to suspect that these factors would also be important in the classroom. But, one would *not* automatically conclude such; rather, one would make field tests in the classroom situation to deny or confirm the inference concerning the general importance of these variables.[1]

1. Benton J. Underwood, "Verbal Learning in the Educative Processes," *Harvard Educational Review*, 29, Spring 1959, 107–117. Copyright © by President and Fellows of Harvard College.

40 The artificiality issue seems to represent a problem only when an individual makes a generalization from an experimental finding without first determining if the generalization can be made. Competent psychologists rarely blunder in this fashion since they realize that laboratory experiments are contrived situations.

Additional difficulties of the experimental approach include such factors as difficulty in designing the experiment and the fact that the experiment may be extremely time-consuming. It is not an unusual situation when the experimenter must go to extreme lengths to set the stage for the subject, to motivate the subject, and occasionally to deceive the subject. Then, when the experiment is actually conducted, it is not uncommon for the experimenter and maybe one or two assistants to spend quite some time with each subject.

More recently a new twist has been added to the list of criticisms levied at the experimental approach. This new twist states that the experimental approach as a method of scientific inquiry into the study of human behavior is inadequate. Gadlin and Ingle (1975) advocate that there are a number of anomalies inherent in the experimental approach that make it an inappropriate paradigm for use in the study of human behavior. For example, they state that the experimental approach promotes the view that humans are manipulable mechanistic objects because twentieth-century psychology mirrors the mechanistic method and assumptions of nineteenth-century physics. As a result of these anomalies Gadlin and Ingle recommend the search for an alternative methodology that is not fraught with such inadequacies. However, when such criticisms are given close inspection, they do not hold up. Kruglanski (1976) took a close look at each of the criticisms Gadlin and Ingle levied at the experimental approach, and revealed the inadequacies of each. For example, the mechanistic manipulable assumption exists only to the extent that the experimenter arranges a set of conditions that may direct the individual's behavior in a given manner. This, however, in no way "suggests that the subject is an empty machine devoid of feelings, thoughts, or a will of his own" (Kruglanski, 1976, p. 656). In the final analysis, it again appears that we must resort to use of the experimental approach for the answers to our research questions. This does not mean that it is the only approach, and that adherence to it will enable us to accomplish great strides in understanding human behavior. However, at the present time it seems to be one of the better approaches available to us.

Illustrative Example

To drive home the advantages and disadvantages of the experimental approach, we will take a detailed look at a laboratory experiment conducted by Aronson and Mills (1959). They set out to test the hypothesis that individuals who go through severe initiation procedures in order to be admitted to a group are more attracted to that group than are individuals who go through less severe initiation procedures.

To test this hypothesis, 63 female volunteer subjects were obtained to participate in a study ostensibly investigating the "dynamics of the group discussion process." The subjects were randomly assigned to either a severe initiation condition, a mild initiation condition, or a control condition. Following participation in one of these three conditions the subject joined a group discussion by listening to a tape recording which ostensibly represented an ongoing discussion of the psychology of sex. Each subject then evaluated the discussion group.

The advantages of control of extraneous variables and precise manipulation of the variable of interest can easily be demonstrated. This study required control of a number of extraneous variables, which was possible because it represented a laboratory study. The subjects' initial motivation for joining a group was controlled by random assignment of the subjects to groups. Likewise the stimulus that all subjects received, the actual discussion, had to be identical; otherwise the evaluations of attractiveness may have been a function of the differences in the actual discussion, rather than the severity of initiation. Similarly, the discussion could not be extremely attractive because such a condition may override the effect of severity of initiation. These two variables were controlled by having subjects listen to a tape recording of individuals conducting a very uninteresting discussion of the secondary sex behavior in lower animals.

It was also necessary to manipulate precisely the severity of initiation variable. This was possible by having subjects in the severe initiation group read aloud 12 obscene words. In the mild condition, subjects read aloud five nonobscene but sex-related words, and in the control or no-initiation group no words had to be read. In this manner an exact amount of initiation was administered to each subject.

The disadvantages of the experimental approach can also be readily demonstrated. The difficulty of designing the study and the time-consuming nature of the study can be seen throughout. It was necessary to construct an elaborate scenario at several points to conduct the experiment successfully. First subjects had to be deceived regarding the true purpose of the experiment. They were told that the purpose was to study the dynamics of the group discussion process and that sex was chosen as the topic because of its interest. Second, it was necessary to disguise the fact that the subject was actually listening to a tape recording and not an actual group discussion. This was accomplished by telling subjects that one of the difficulties with using a topic such as sex was that many people tend to be rather shy when discussing it. Such shyness would be detrimental to the experiment. Since, as was explained to each subject, shyness is primarily a function of the presence of others, each person in the group would be placed in a separate room and would communicate through an intercom system. This enabled the use of a tape recording since headphones were used and others were not present. However, one other wrinkle had to be included. The subjects could not interact with the tape-recorded group discussion lest they discover that the group was nonexistent. To insure that subjects did not participate in the discussion (since it was a recording), they were told that all subjects had prepared for the discussion by reading a particular book. Since the subject had not read the book she would be at a disadvantage so it would be best if she remained silent the first day.

The third problem that had to be overcome was somehow to justify administering the variable of severity of initiation. This manipulation was justified by stating that some subjects were too embarrassed to discuss the sex topic and to screen new people they were given an embarrassment test. The stage was now set to administer the various conditions which manipulated severity of initiation.

After this elaborate scenario was developed, each subject had to be tested individually. The scenario and individual testing, I believe, adequately demonstrate the thought and difficulty encountered in designing many experiments, and the time-consuming nature of many experiments.

The disadvantage of departure from real life is also quite adequately demonstrated by the elaborate scenario that had to be created. Seldom if ever do we participate in group discussions without seeing the other members or verbally interacting with them. Also, the most severe initiation condition in the experiment was probably much milder than any actual initiation procedure that takes place outside the laboratory. Fraternities, for example, typically require some form of initiation that is much more severe than reading a list of obscene words.

Experimental Research Settings

The experimental approach is used in two different research settings—a laboratory setting and a field setting. Most of the experimental work has always been conducted in the laboratory. While the laboratory will probably continue to be the most frequent setting for experimentation, we are hearing pleas for more field experimentation. Field and laboratory experimentation both use the experimental approach but they have slightly different attributes. Therefore, a discussion of these two seems appropriate because of the differences that exist between them.

FIELD EXPERIMENTATION.   A field experiment is an experimental research study that is conducted in a real life setting. The experimenter actively manipulates variables and carefully controls the influence of as many extraneous variables as the situation will permit. Freedman and Fraser (1966), for example, wanted to find out if people who initially complied with a small request would be more likely to comply with a large request. The basic procedure used was initially to ask one group of housewives if they would answer a number of questions about what household products they used. Three days later the experimenter again contacted these same housewives and asked if they would allow a group of men to come into their home and spend approximately two hours classifying all their household products. Another group of housewives was contacted only once, during which the large request was made. Results revealed that the housewives who initially complied with the small request were significantly more likely to comply with the large request.

This study represents a field study because it is conducted in the housewives' natural setting of their home while they were engaging in daily activities. It also represents an experimental study because variable manipulation was present, small request followed by large request or just large request, and control was present by virtue of the fact that the subjects for each group were randomly selected from the telephone directory. Field experiments such as this one do not have to worry about the artificiality problem that exists with laboratory experiments, and field experiments are, therefore, excellent for studying many problems. The primary difficulty with such experiments is that control of extraneous variables cannot be accomplished as well as with laboratory experiments. In the Freedman and Fraser study, even though subjects were randomly selected from the telephone directory, only those subjects who were actually home could be included in the study. Consequently, a selection bias may exist. Even though it is more difficult to exercise control in field experiments, such experiments are necessary, and a number of individuals are saying that we need to get out of the laboratory and get more involved with field experimentation.

Tunnell (1977) has carried such a suggestion a step further. He states that we not only must engage in more field experimentation but also should do so in a manner which makes all variables operational in real world terms. Consider, for example, the study conducted by Ellsworth, Carlsmith, and Henson (1972). They had a confederate pedestrian stare at car drivers waiting at a red light to assess the

44   influence of staring on the speed with which the driver left the intersection. In this study Ellsworth et al. included the three dimensions of naturalness identified by Tunnell: natural behavior, natural setting, and natural treatment. The natural behavior investigated was speed of leaving the intersection when the light turned green. The natural setting was the individual remaining in his or her car as opposed to being brought into an artificial laboratory setting, and the natural treatment was the staring. In reality the treatment was imposed by a confederate but it mirrored a behavior that could have naturally occurred. These are the types of behaviors Tunnell says we must strive for when we conduct field experimentation, as opposed to studies that ask subjects for self-reports or for recalling their own behavior in some prior situation. Asking for such retrospective data only serves to introduce possible bias in the study.

LABORATORY EXPERIMENTATION.   The laboratory experiment is the same type of study as the field experiment except that where the field experiment is strong, the laboratory experiment is weak, and where the laboratory experiment is strong, the field experiment is weak. The laboratory experiment epitomizes the ability to control or eliminate the influence of extraneous variables. This is accomplished by bringing the problem into an environment apart from the subjects' normal routine. In this environment, outside influences, such as the presence of others and noise, can be eliminated. However, the price of this increase in control is the artificiality of the situation created. This issue was covered in detail when discussing the disadvantages of the experimental approach. While precise results can be obtained from the laboratory, applicability of these results to the real world must always be verified.

The laboratory experiment is a study conducted in the laboratory in which the investigator precisely manipulates one or more variables, and controls the influence of all or nearly all of the extraneous variables. Results from such studies probably yield stronger conclusions than from any other research technique. The Aronson and Mills severity of initiation study represents an example of a laboratory experiment.

Steps in Conducting the Psychological Experiment

All of the research approaches that have been discussed make use of the scientific methodology. In Chapter I we saw that use of the scientific method involves following a series of logical steps. A brief description of each of these steps as they relate to the experimental **45** approach will be presented here as a prelude to the remainder of the book. The rest of the book will constitute a detailed discussion of each of these steps. Discussion is delimited to the experimental approach since this is the primary focus of the book.

Identifying the Problem and Hypothesis Formation

The beginning point of any scientific inquiry involves identifying a problem. Identifying a problem which needs solution is actually a simple process. All one has to do is look at the events taking place and numerous problems that need solutions become readily apparent. Child abuse, cancer, alcoholism, and crime are just a few of the more apparent problems. However, it is not enough to just identify a problem and say you are going to investigate it. For a problem to be investigated it must be stated in a researchable way. The problem must be refined and frequently narrowed so that it is researchable. Once the problem has been stated in researchable terms, hypotheses are formulated which state the expected or predicted relationships between the variables. These hypotheses must in turn be stated in such a way that they are testable and capable of being refuted.

Designing the Experiment

This stage of the experiment is very crucial and demands a tremendous amount of preparation on the part of the experimenter to insure that the hypotheses stated are actually those tested. Proper controls over extraneous variables have to be established, and the experimental variable as well as the response variable has to be specified. These procedures are extremely important since this stage represents the outline or the scheme to be followed in conducting the experiment. This scheme or outline is one that is constructed to overcome the difficulties that would otherwise distort the results and to help insure that the data are properly analyzed and interpreted.

Conducting the Experiment

After the experiment has been designed the researcher must make a number of very important decisions regarding the actual conduct of the experiment. He must make decisions such as what subjects are to be used, what instructions are necessary, and what equipment or materials are necessary. These decisions must be made before any data are collected. Actually, this involves filling in the outline set forth in the design stage of the experiment. After these decisions have been

46 reached, the experimenter is ready to collect the data. He or she is to follow precisely the prescribed procedure and record responses made by the subjects. For some studies this involves little more than plugging in electronic equipment. Other studies are much more demanding since the experimenter must interact with the subjects and record the responses made by the subjects. In many experiments debriefing or post-interviews must be conducted with the subjects to determine their reaction to the experiment and/or to eliminate any undesirable influence which the experiment may have created.

Hypothesis Testing

At this point the data has been collected and the experimenter must now analyze and interpret the data to determine if the stated hypotheses have been supported. With the advent of the computer and statistical packages, the investigator is spared the task of making the necessary computations (some investigators prefer to use a desk calculator). Even though the computer is a marvelous piece of machinery, it still will do only what it is told to do. The investigator must decide on the appropriate statistical analysis. After the statistical analyses have been conducted, the investigator must interpret the results or specify exactly what they mean.

Writing the Research Report

After the data have been analyzed, the scientist wants to communicate the results to others. Communication most frequently takes place through the professional journals in a field. Consequently the scientist must write a research report that states how the research was conducted and what was found.

Reality and the Research Steps

The five steps of the research process just described represent the *logical* analysis of the scientific process. These steps also suggest that research flows in an orderly process from the first to the last step. Presenting a logical analysis such as this one has didactic value but is not an accurate representation of actual practice.

Selltiz et al. (1959, p. 9) identify two ways in which the actual research process differs from the model presented. First, the neat sequence of activities suggested is almost never followed. There tends to be a tremendous amount of overlap among the various activities outlined. Definition of the problem and statement of the hypotheses in part determine the design and conduct of the experiment. The design of the experiment in turn has a great deal to say about the method to be followed in collecting the data and the way the results are analyzed. The point is that there is a tremendous interaction between the various activities. One activity cannot be carried out without affecting another activity. Second, the research process involves many activities not included in published studies or the model presented. Frequently equipment breaks down, subjects do not show up at the designated time and place, experimenters have to be trained, cooperation has to be obtained not only from subjects (assuming human subjects are used) but also from administrative personnel. These are only a few of the additional activities which may be required as one conducts a study.

The veteran researcher moves back and forth through the research steps with ease to accomplish the goal of obtaining scientific knowledge. On the other hand, the student, who is a novice at research, performs better if the logical sequence of steps is followed. As a researcher gains more experience, rigid adherence to these steps declines. Skinner's 1956 talk, "A Case History in Scientific Method," depicts the informal nature of the scientific process that exists with the experienced researcher. This informality is depicted in his description of the "unformalized principles of scientific practice." These principles, derived from his own experience, are as follows:

1. When you run onto something interesting, drop everything else and study it.

2. Some ways of doing research are easier than others. (The now famous *Skinner Box* resulted from the fact that Skinner, in his early maze studies, saw no reason why he always had to retrieve the rat at the end of the runway or why the rat could not deliver his own reinforcement.)

3. Some people are lucky. (Skinner's construction of the cumulative recorder and observation of other aspects of the rate of responding was a result of not discarding an apparently useless appendage from the discarded apparatus from which he built his first food magazine.)

4. Apparatuses sometimes break down. (Jamming of the food magazine resulted in an extinction curve which he later investigated.)

5. Serendipity—the art of finding one thing while looking for another. (This principle led to his investigation of schedules of reinforcement.)

Skinner's principles reveal the informality of the scientific process and also reveal some of the previously discussed characteristics of

48 scientists. However, you should not get the impression that Skinner, because he has elaborated on the informality of the scientific process, is lax or fuzzy in his approach to experimentation. Quite the contrary. He advocates *more* careful control and thought about experimentation and *more* rigorous definition of terms and quantification of research findings.

Summary

One very frequently used but little understood concept is causation, and yet it is causative relationships that the experimental method attempts to identify. One of the many individuals who have attempted to tackle the problem was John Stuart Mill. He set forth four canons, the methods of agreement, difference, concomitant variation, and the joint methods of agreement and difference, which he said could be used in identifying causation. However, to be able to state that *the* cause of a given effect has been found, this condition must qualify as being both necessary and sufficient. Since behavior is multidetermined, it is highly unlikely that the variables causing behavior will ever be identified. All that can be hoped for is that the experimental approach will continue to identify more of the necessary and sufficient conditions.

The descriptive approach to gaining scientific knowledge differs from the experimental approaches in that it attempts to describe or paint a picture of a particular phenomenon. There are three basic research approaches used in attaining this objective. Naturalistic observation attempts to fulfill this objective by unobtrusively observing and recording naturally occurring behavior. Field studies attempt to accomplish the goal of description by collecting data through use of the survey, by conducting a correlational study, or by conducting a longitudinal or cross-sectional study. Ex post facto studies accomplish the goal of description by describing the relationship that exists between a given behavior and a variable on which groups of subjects naturally differ, such as on skin color. Although ex post facto studies resemble experimental studies, they are not, because the experimenter does not have control over the manipulated variable. However, it is not uncommon to find a study that includes both an ex post facto component and an experimental component.

The experimental approach is the research approach that attempts to identify cause-and-effect relationships. It attempts to accomplish this task by conducting an experiment. The psychological experiment accomplishes the goal of the experimental approach because it allows one to observe, under controlled conditions, the effects of systematically varying one or more variables. Use of the experimental approach has the primary advantage of providing for control of extraneous variables. However, it also gives one the advantage of being able to manipulate precisely one or more variables, of producing lasting results, of suggesting new studies, and of suggesting solutions to practical problems. Although the experimental approach has these excellent advantages, it also has the disadvantages or difficulties of having created an artificial environment and of frequently being difficult to design and time consuming.

The experimental approach is used in both a field and a laboratory setting. Using a field setting, the experimenter is conducting an experiment in a real life situation and therefore avoids the criticism of having created an artificial environment. However, one typically does not have as much control over extraneous variables. In a laboratory setting the experimenter brings the subjects into the laboratory where there is maximum control over extraneous variables. However, this typically means that an artificial environment has been created.

In conducting the psychological experiment there are five steps that must be carried out: (1) identify the problem and formulate the hypothesis, (2) design the experiment, (3) conduct the experiment, (4) test your hypothesis, and (5) write the research report. These five steps indicate an orderly sequence to research. However, this sequence is seldom followed for two reasons. First, there is tremendous overlap between the activities involved in each of the steps. A veteran researcher moves back and forth between the various steps rather than taking them in sequence. Second, the research process involves many activities not revealed by these steps, such as equipment breakdown.

Key Concepts

One way to test your mastery of the material that was presented in this chapter is to see if you know the meaning of the following terms. These terms were selected because they represent the key concepts. If you can define, identify, or otherwise explain each of the following terms without referring back to the material in the chapter, you can be assured that you have mastered the basics of the material that was presented. Just in case you cannot recall the meaning of a given term, the page on which it can be found appears in parentheses beside it.

causation (pp. 26–27)
necessary condition (p. 26)
sufficient condition (p. 26)
naturalistic observation (p. 28)
survey (pp. 29–30)
correlational study (p. 31)
longitudinal study (p. 32)
cross-sectional study (p. 32)
ex post facto study (p. 33)
psychological experiment (p. 35)
field experimentation (p. 43)
dimensions of naturalness (p. 44)
laboratory experimentation (p. 44)

3

Problem Definition and Hypothesis Formation

The purpose of research is to attempt to find a solution to problems through the use of scientific methodology. Research, therefore, begins with a problem that requires solution. Identification of a problem is frequently difficult for students. An inordinate amount of time is spent worrying about identifying a suitable problem. This worry is needless. Researchable problems are, in fact, numerous, and no one should have difficulty identifying a topic for research.

Why do individuals react in this manner when faced with the task of conducting research? Why do they have difficulty in identifying a

52 problem? Several reasons probably exist. The student may have a fear of failure, feeling a lack of ability to accomplish the task. Such a feeling seems to be stimulated by lack of knowledge and experience in the research process, and boils down to a fear of the unknown. The inadequacy feeling may also be promoted by a stereotype that a researcher has characteristics that the students do not possess and cannot develop. Such fears are probably common, perhaps even, at some time, among prominent researchers. These fears can be overcome by jumping in and conducting research studies with proper supervision. Another reason that students typically have difficulties in problem identification is that they think the study they conduct has to be *the* definitive piece of research in an area. They feel that the problem has to be of utmost importance, extremely interesting, and have no methodological flaws. A study should be methodologically sound. However no study, or at least none that I am aware of, is flawless. The beginning researcher has to learn that research is a progressive building process. After a study is conducted one can look back and see how the study could have been improved. Based upon the results of the study and the experience gained, a better study can be conducted. The second study should enable the researcher to eliminate some of the mistakes of the first study. Pilot studies, which will be discussed later, serve this purpose.

What about the importance or interest of the study? Underwood (1966, pp. 260–264) discusses the meaning given to the words "uninteresting" and "unimportant." A study would be labeled uninteresting if the outcome were obvious. A student might say that a study designed to measure the influence of being blindfolded on the ability to put various shaped blocks into holes designed for the blocks was uninteresting because the outcome was obvious. However, the facts do not always support the obvious predictions. If they did, scientific psychology would boil down to common sense. Some commonsense predictions are supported, but definitely not all of them. A study may also be labeled uninteresting if the phenomenon to be investigated seems to exist in isolation—that is, if the phenomenon does not seem to be related to known knowledge. However, the connection between current knowledge and the seemingly isolated phenomenon may not become apparent until additional knowledge is attained.

The label unimportant seems to be synonomous with the question, "What good is it?" If the value of the research is not readily apparent then it is considered unimportant. Underwood makes two cogent points regarding this issue. New knowledge, regardless of its practical utility, may reduce fear of the unknown and may provide aesthetic pleasure to many individuals. Also, the utility of new knowledge is not always immediately apparent. In any field there are exam-

ples of knowledge that did not seem useful when acquired, but later   **53**
was of tremendous practical value. One should be very hesitant to state
that a particular study or line of research is unimportant or has no
practical value.

Sources of Problems

Where do ideas or problems originate? Where should a student look for
a researchable problem? In all fields there are a number of common
sources of problems such as existing theories or past research. In
psychology we are even more fortunate. We have our own personal
experience and the events occurring in everyday life to draw upon. The
things we see, read about, or hear about can serve as ideas that can turn
into a research topic. However, the identification of these topics as
research topics requires an alert and curious scientist. Remember that
one of the characteristics of the scientist is to be a curious individual
always asking questions or making predictions about the events that
are encountered.

Researchable topics are numerous. A brief glance at the
psychological abstract index provides an indication of the many areas
within psychology that have problems in need of solution. The problems are there. However, it is the scientist who must identify them.

There are four sources from which problems typically originate—
theories, everyday life, practical issues, and past research.

Theories

A theory, defined as "a group of logically organized (deductively related) laws" (Marx, 1963, p. 9), is supposed to serve a number of distinct
functions. Marx states that theory is both a tool and a goal. The goal
function is evidenced from the proposition that laws are ordered and
integrated by theories. Theories summarize and integrate existing
knowledge. The tool function is evidenced from the proposition that
theories guide research. This is the proposition that is of interest to us.
A good theory goes beyond the goal function to suggest new relationships and make new predictions. Since theory has this tool function it
serves as a source of researchable ideas.

Leon Festinger's 1957 theory of cognitive dissonance is an example
of a theory that has stimulated an extraordinary amount of research in
the decade following its publication. From this theory, Festinger and
Carlsmith (1959), for example, made and validated the nonobvious
prediction that, after completing a boring task, subjects who were
given $1 to tell a stooge that the boring task was interesting and fun,

54   actually stated that they enjoyed the task more than subjects who were given $20 to do the same thing.

Everyday Life

As we proceed through the daily routine dictated by our current point in life, we come into contact with many phenomena that pose questions in need of solution. Parents want to know how to handle their children. Students want to know how to learn material faster. When we interact with others or see others react we can note many individual differences. When observing children on a playground individual differences are readily apparent. One child is very aggressive and another is much more reserved, holding back and waiting for others to encourage interaction. Differences in response also exist for one individual in different situations. In one situation a child may be very aggressive and in another situation very passive. One could ask, "Why do these differences exist not only among children but also within the same child? What produces these differences in response? Why are some people leaders and others followers, or why do we like some people and not others?" There are many such questions. The point is that numerous researchable problems can be identified from the interactions and personal experiences that everyone has.

Darley and Latané in the late 1960s began a series of investigations that epitomize the utility of life's experiences and the events taking place around us as a source of research problems. They were aware of the fact that bystanders frequently do not lend assistance in emergency situations. The frequently cited incident involving Kitty Genovese is a case in point. She was stabbed to death in New York City. Without having previous knowledge of the incident you may not think much of this until you are told that there were 38 witnesses to the longer than half-hour attack, and no one even called the police. Darley and Latané asked "Why?" They began a series of experimental studies to investigate the conditions that facilitate or inhibit bystander interventions in emergency situations.

Practical Issues

Many experimental problems arise from practical issues that require solution. Private industry is basically profit-oriented and has many practical problems, such as employee morale, absenteeism, turnover, and selection and placement, to name only a few that need solution. Such work currently is, has been, and will continue to be conducted. Clinical psychology is in need of a great deal of research to identify more efficient modes of dealing with mental disturbances. Units of the federal and state governments also support experimentation designed to solve practical problems. The government is spending large sums of money to find a cure for cancer. Large sums of money are also spent on trying to find better ways to conduct the educational process. Recently the federal government funded a number of projects that attempted to determine the influence of televised violence upon children. Liebert and Baron (1972) conducted a study, supported in part by a National Institute of Mental Health contract, designed to investigate the willingness of a child to hurt another child following exposure to televised violence. Results of this study indicated that children exposed to the aggressive program attacked their victims for longer periods of time and elicited greater degrees of aggressive play than those exposed to nonaggressive programs.

Past Research

Previously conducted experiments are an excellent source of research ideas. This may sound like a contradiction since research is designed to answer questions. One of the interesting features about research is that it tends to generate more questions than it asks. Each well-designed study does provide additional knowledge, but phenomena are multidetermined. In any experiment only a limited number of variables can be studied. Investigation of certain variables may lead to hypotheses as to the effects of other variables. The multidimensional nature of phenomena is also the frequent cause of disagreements between experimental results. An unidentified variable may be the source of conflict between various studies on a given problem, and experiments must be conducted to uncover this variable and thereby eliminate the apparent contradiction.

To illustrate what has just been said, consider the study conducted by Mellgren, Seybert, and Dyck (1978). They investigated the influence of presenting different orders of schedules of continuous reinforcement, nonreinforcement, and partial reinforcement on resistance to extinction. Prior research had revealed conflicting results when comparing resistance to extinction of subjects who had received continuous reward and then partial reward, versus those given only partial reward schedules. Some studies indicated that resistance to extinction decreased whereas others indicated that it increased, and still others revealed that the existence of an increase or a decrease in resistance to extinction depended upon the stage of extinction. Mellgren et al. attempted to resolve this inconsistency. Results of their study revealed that greatest resistance to extinction occurred when a large number of nonreinforced trials preceded a partial reinforcement schedule. Therefore, this study revealed which schedule produced the greatest resistance to extinction. Even though it did answer this question, it left other questions unanswered. The study, for example, did not provide an explanation as to why resistance to extinction was increased if a

56   large number of nonreinforced trials preceded partial reinforcement. This led to another study which attempted to answer this question. As you can see, each study leads to a subsequent study. This is why some people have spent their whole lives investigating a particular area. Research is an ongoing process.

Review of the Literature

From the sources just mentioned, a topic of research can be obtained. The next step in the research process is to become familiar with the information available on the topic. Practically all, if not all, psychological problems have had some prior work conducted on them.

At this point you might be asking yourself, "Why should I review the literature on my selected topic? Why not just proceed to the laboratory and find an answer to the problem?" There are several good reasons to do one's homework in the form of a literature review prior to conducting any experimentation. The general purpose of the library search is to gain an understanding of the current state of knowledge about the selected topic. Specifically, a review of the literature will tell you if the problem you have identified has already been researched. If it has, you should either revise the problem in light of the experimental results or look for another problem. If the topic you have identified has not been investigated, prior studies will indicate how you should proceed in attempting to reach an answer to the problem. A literature review should also point out methodological problems specific to the problem area. Are special control groups or special pieces of equipment needed to conduct the research? If they are, the literature can give clues as to where to attain the equipment or how to identify the particular groups of subjects needed. These are just a few of the more salient reasons for conducting a review of the literature.

Assuming you are convinced of the necessity of a literature review, you are now probably asking, "Where do I look? What sources should be investigated?" There are two primary sources that should be investigated when reviewing the literature, books dealing with the topic of interest and psychological journals. These are the two standard sources of information although additional sources are also available. Helmstadter (1970, Chapter 5) presents an extremely thorough review of the sources available for conducting the literature review.

Books

Books have been written about most, if not all, of the areas in psychology. These should be examined for material relating to the research topic. The pertinent material may consist of actual information or may point to where pertinent information may be obtained. One book that is frequently very profitable is the *Annual Review of Psychology.* Published yearly since 1950, this book presents an in-depth discussion by an expert of the principal work done during the preceding year on a variety of topics. One of the topics may relate to your topic and it would be worthwhile to check this source.

Psychological Journals

Most of the pertinent information about a research topic is usually found in the psychological journals. Frequently, if not always, a review that has started with books leads to the journals. Books are generally the outgrowth of work cited in journals so this progression from books back to journals is a natural one.

How should one proceed in reviewing the work cited in the journals? A survey of the number of psychological journals reveals that it would be an impossible task to go through each and every journal looking for relevant information. This is where *Psychological Abstracts* comes in. *Psychological Abstracts,* as the name implies, is a journal consisting of brief abstracts of published articles, books, and so forth from sources throughout the world but predominently the United States. Use of this source as a starting point can enable you to efficiently and economically identify sources of information related to your topic. To use *Psychological Abstracts* most efficiently, study the subject index to become acquainted with the various categories used. Then identify which of the many different categories available is related to your topic. Most topics relate to several categories and therefore it is necessary to survey the articles under each category to identify the references relating to your problem.

After you have identified the appropriate category, read each entry under each selected category and list the entries (represented by a number beside the entry). The next step is to find each selected entry and read the abstract to determine if the article is of value to your selected topic. Discard those judged irrelevant and record the reference of those judged relevant. Once you have finished this process you should have a workable reference list of articles pertaining to your study.

Information Retrieval Systems

Books and journals have been identified as the basic sources of information regarding a topic. However, the traditional practice of each individual investigator going to the library and manually performing a comprehensive literature search is becoming less and less practical.

58   The impracticality of this approach is due to the so-called information explosion. Helmstadter states that the number of published research articles doubles about every ten years. The validity of such a statement can be seen by just looking at the increase in size of *Psychological Abstracts.* The volumes have more than doubled in size in the past 10 years. Such an explosion of knowledge has drastically increased the amount of time and energy necessary to identify and record the results of relevant studies.

In an effort to overcome such problems, a number of attempts have been initiated to provide a comprehensive information storage and retrieval system. The one of importance for the psychologist is PASAR, *Psychological Abstracts* Search and Retrieval. PASAR, a nonprofit organization operated by the American Psychological Association, has a data base of over 250,000 records published in the *Psychological Abstracts* from 1967 to the present time. This data base is growing at the rate of about 2,400 records per month. For a fee ranging from about $40 to $60, PASAR will search these records and provide you with a list of relevant publications. A search of material earlier than 1967 still has to be conducted by the individual investigator. PASAR forms are located in the back of the *Psychological Abstract.* The investigator desiring use of this service can make a copy of this form, fill it in, and send it to the address given on the form.

There are additional information centers and exchanges in existence, such as ERIC (Educational Resources Information Center). However, these additional sources are more specific in purpose. Because of its more general orientation, PASAR seems to be the primary source for the student. Helmstadter (1970) describes each of these other sources, and it is recommended that the interested student investigate this material

Additional Information Sources

The regional and national psychological association meetings are an excellent source of *current* information. I emphasize *current* because of the publication lag that exists in journals and books. A research study that appears in these sources is anywhere from a few months to a few years old. Studies presented at professional meetings are typically much more recent. An additional advantage of securing information at professional meetings is that you can frequently interact with the investigator. You can exchange ideas with this individual and frequently come away with added enthusiasm and many more research ideas.

Frequently the beginning researcher also returns from meetings with renewed confidence in his or her developing research skills. The novice frequently feels that researchers at other institutions are more skilled or more adept at research. Attending professional meetings can illustrate that others use the same techniques and skills that he or she has acquired.

Information can also be acquired from direct communication with colleagues. It is not infrequent that one researcher calls or writes another to inquire about current studies or methodological techniques.

Formulation of the Research Problem

You should now be prepared to make a clear and exact statement of the specific problem to be investigated. The specific statement of the problem logically follows the review of the literature. The literature review has revealed not only what is currently known about the problem but also the ways in which the problem has been attacked in the past. Such information is a tremendous aid in formulating the problem and indicating how and by what methods the data should be collected. Unfortunately, the novice may attempt to jump from the selection of a research topic to the data collection stage. This does not preclude formulating the problem. Instead it means that the task of formulating the problem will remain unspecified and come after data collection, running the risk of not obtaining information on the problem of interest. An exact definition of the problem is very important since it guides the research process.

Definition of a Research Problem

What is a research problem? Kerlinger (1973, p. 17) defines a problem as "an interrogative sentence or statement that asks: 'What relation exists between two or more variables?' " For example, Milgram (1964) asked the question: "Can a group induce a person to deliver punishment of increasing severity to a protesting individual?" This statement conforms to the definition of a problem since it contains two variables—group pressure and severity of punishment delivered—and asks a question regarding the relation between these variables.

Are all problems that conform to the definition good research problems? Assume you posed the problem which asks: "How do we know that God influences our behavior?" This question meets the definition of a problem but obviously it cannot be tested. Kerlinger (1973) presents three criteria which good problems must meet. First, the variables in the problem should express a relation. This criterion, as you can see, was contained in the definition of a problem. The

60   second criterion is that the problem should be stated in question form. The statement of the problem should begin with "What is the effect of," "Under what conditions do," "Does the effect of," or some similar form. Frequently, only the purpose of a study is stated, which does not always communicate the problem to be investigated. The purpose of the Milgram study was to investigate the effect of group pressure on a person's behavior. Asking a question has the benefit of presenting the problem directly and in this way interpretation and distortion are minimized. The third criterion, and the one which most frequently distinguishes a researchable from a nonresearchable problem, states that "The problem statement should be such as to imply possibilities of empirical testing" (p. 18). Many interesting and important questions fail to meet this criterion and therefore are not amenable to scientific inquiry. Many philosophical and theological questions fall into this category. Milgram's problem meets all these criteria. A relation was expressed between the variables, the problem was stated in question form, and it was possible to empirically test the problem. Severity of punishment was measured by the amount of electricity supposedly delivered to the protesting individual and group pressure was applied by having two confederates suggest increasingly higher shock levels.

Specificity of the Question

A rule of thumb to follow in formulating a question is to be specific. Consider the difficulties facing the experimenter asking the following question: "What effect does the environment have on learning ability?" This question meets all the criteria of a problem and yet it is stated in such a vague way that the investigator could not pinpoint what was to be investigated. The concepts of environment and learning ability are vague. What environmental characteristics? Learning of what? The experimenter must specify what is meant by environment and by learning ability to be able to conduct the experiment. Contrast this question with the following question: "What effect does the amount of exposure to words have on the speed with which they are learned?" This question specifies exactly what the problem is.

The two examples of questions presented in the preceding paragraph demonstrate the advantages of formulating a specific problem. A specific statement helps insure that the experimenter understands the problem. If the problem is vaguely stated, the experimenter probably does not know exactly what he wants to study and therefore may design a study that does not provide a solution to the problem. Specificity of the problem also assists in the decisions that must be

made about such factors as subjects, apparatus, instruments, and mea-   **61**
sures. A vague problem statement assists very little in such decisions.
To drive this point home, go back and reread the questions given in the
preceding paragraph and ask yourself the following: "What subjects
should I use?" "What measures should I use?" "What apparatus or
instruments should I use?"

How specific should one be in formulating a question? Only a
general answer can be given. The primary purpose of formulating the
problem in question form is to insure that the investigator has a good
grasp of the variables to be investigated and to aid in designing and
carrying out the experiment. If the formulation of the question is
specific enough to serve these purposes, then additional specificity is
not needed. To the extent that these purposes are not met, additional
specificity and narrowing of the research problem is required. Therefore, the degree of specificity required is dependent on the purpose of
the problem statement.

Formulating Hypotheses

After the literature review has been completed and the problem has
been stated in question form, you should state your hypothesis.
Hypotheses represent predictions or tentative solutions to the problem. They represent predictions of the relation that exists between the
variables. Formulation of the hypothesis logically follows the statement of the problem for several reasons. The first and most obvious
reason is that one could not state a hypothesis without the existence of
a problem. This does not mean that the problem is always explicitly
stated. In fact, if you survey articles published in journals, you will find
that most of the authors do not present a statement of their specific
problem. However, you will find statements of their hypotheses. Just
because the problem is not explicitly stated does not mean that it does
not exist. It seems as though experienced researchers in a given field
have so much familiarity with that field that the problems, for them,
are so explicit and apparent that they are not stated. However, their
predicted solutions to these problems are not apparent and consequently these are stated.

The second reason that the formulation of the hypothesis comes at
this point is that the hypothesis to be tested is frequently a function of
the review of the literature. This is not the only source of hypotheses.
Hypotheses are also frequently formulated from theory. As stated earlier, theories guide research and one of the ways in which they do so is

62   by making predictions of possible relationships between variables. Hypotheses also, but less frequently, come from reasoning based on casual observation of events. There are even times in some situations in which it seems to be fruitless even to attempt to formulate hypotheses. When engaged in exploratory work in a relatively new area where the important variables and their relationships are not known, hypotheses serve little purpose.

More than one hypothesis can almost always be formulated as the probable solution to the problem. Here again the literature review can be an aid. A review of prior research can suggest the most probable relationships that may exist between the variables.

Regardless of the source of the hypothesis it *must* meet one criterion. A hypothesis must be stated so that it is capable of being either refuted or confirmed. In an experiment it is the hypothesis that is being tested and not the problem. One does not test a question such as the one Milgram posed; rather, one tests one or more of the hypotheses that could be derived from this question such as "group pressure increases the severity of punishment which subjects will administer." A hypothesis which fails to meet the criteria of testability, or is nontestable, removes the problem from the realm of science. Any conclusions reached regarding a nontestable hypothesis do not represent scientific knowledge.

At times individuals wonder why hypotheses should be set up in the first place. Why not just proceed to attempt to answer the question and forget about hypotheses? Hypotheses serve a valuable function. Remember that hypotheses are derived from knowledge obtained from the literature review of other experiments, theories, and so forth. Such prior knowledge served as the basis for the hypothesis. If the experiment confirms the hypothesis, then, in addition to providing an answer to the question asked, additional support is given to the literature that suggested the hypothesis. But what if the hypothesis is not confirmed by the experiment? Does this invalidate the prior literature? If the hypothesis is not confirmed, then either the hypothesis is false or some error exists in the conception of the hypothesis. If there is an error in conceptualization, it could exist in a number of categories. Some of the information obtained from prior experiments may be false or some relevant information may have been overlooked in the literature review. It is also possible that the experimenter misinterpreted some of the literature. These are a few of the more salient errors that could have taken place. In any event, failure to support a hypothesis may indicate that something is wrong and it is up to the experimenter to discover what it is. Once the experimenter uncovers what he or she thinks is wrong, a new hypothesis is made to be tested experimentally. The experimenter now has another study to be conducted. Such is the continuous ongoing process of science. Even if the hypothesis is false, knowledge has been advanced, for now we know an incorrect hypothesis and we must formulate another one to test in order to reach a solution to the problem.

Summary

In order to conduct research it is first necessary to identify a problem that is in need of a solution. Psychological problems arise from the rather traditional sources of theories, practical issues, and past research. Additionally, in psychology we have our own personal experience to draw upon for researchable problems since psychological research is concerned with behavior. Once a researchable problem has been identified one needs to review the literature relevant to this problem. A literature review will give you an understanding of the current state of knowledge about your selected topic. It will indicate ways of investigating the problem as well as point out methodological problems related to the topic. The literature review should probably begin with books written on the topic and progress from there to the actual research as reported in journals. In surveying the past research conducted on a topic, one can make use of one of the many information retrieval systems now in existence, one of which is operated by the American Psychological Association. In addition to these sources of information, one can also obtain related information by attending conventions or actually calling or writing other individuals conducting research on the given topic.

Once the literature review is completed the experimenter must make a clear and exact statement of the problem to be investigated. This means that the experimenter must formulate an interrogative sentence or statement asking about the relationship between two or more variables. This interrogative sentence or statement must express a relation and be capable of being tested empirically. The question must also be specific enough to assist in making the decisions regarding such factors as subjects, apparatus, and general design of the study.

Once the question is stated the experimenter needs to state hypotheses. These need to be stated because they represent the predicted relation that exists between the variables under study. Also, hypotheses frequently are a function of past research, and if they are confirmed, the results not only answer the question asked but provide additional support to the literature that suggested the hypotheses. In any event, there is one criterion that any hypothesis must meet. Regardless of the source or function served by the hypothesis, it must be stated so that it is capable of being either refuted or confirmed.

64   Key Concepts

One way to test your mastery of the material that was presented in this chapter is to see if you know the meaning of the following terms. These terms were selected because they represent the key concepts. If you can define, identify, or otherwise explain each of the following terms without referring back to the material in the chapter, you can be assured that you have mastered the basics of the material that was presented. Just in case you cannot recall the meaning of a given term, the page on which it can be found appears in parentheses beside it.

> uninteresting (p. 52)
> unimportant (p. 52)
> theory (p. 53)
> PASAR (p. 58)
> research problem (p. 59)
> specificity (pp. 60–61)
> hypothesis (pp. 61–62)

Decisions Preceding
Research Design

The term *design* refers to the outline, plan, or strategy conceived in an attempt to obtain an answer to a research question. Some individuals are tempted to perform this operation or design the experiment immediately after stating the hypothesis. Although this progression from hypothesis to design may seem logical, it is inappropriate at this stage of the research process since there are several decisions that should be made prior to the design stage. These play a significant role in the final outline or design conceived. Decisions have to be made regarding the independent variable (the antecedent conditions manip-

66   ulated by the experimenter), the dependent variable (the variable that measures the effects of the variation in the independent variable), and the variables to be controlled.

Consider the previously discussed Aronson and Mills study. Their basic design was randomly to assign subjects to three treatment groups—mild, severe, and no initiation treatment—and then statistically analyze the subjects' responses to the dependent variable to determine if the treatment conditions produced different results. In order to conceive their design, Aronson and Mills had to reach a decision regarding the independent variable, the dependent variable, and the extraneous variables that had to be controlled. First, in order to state that the design would have three treatment groups, the decision had to be made that only one independent variable would be used and that there would be three levels of variation of this independent variable. If this decision had not been made, there would be no basis for determining the number of treatment groups to be included in the design. Second, the design stated that one dependent variable would be used, different subjects were to be in each of the treatment groups, and each subject would be measured on the dependent variable only once. Another design could have stated that all subjects would participate in each of the three treatment conditions and would be measured on two dependent variables after participating in each condition. Therefore, decisions regarding the dependent variable can also affect the final design conceived. Third, Aronson and Mills randomly assigned subjects to groups. This random assignment was included because they knew they had to control for variables such as initial motivation for joining a group and random assignment would provide this control.

As you can see, there are a number of decisions that must be made before the final design can be conceived. If they are not, then the investigator must stop and do so while conceiving the design. Regardless of when it is done, the conclusion is the same. The design cannot be finalized until the decisions are made. It is best if these decisions are reached prior to attempting to develop the design. Therefore, an in-depth look at each of these decision points will be taken. In this chapter the independent and dependent variables will be discussed. The following two chapters will discuss extraneous variables.

The Independent Variable

The independent variable has been defined as the antecedent conditions which are manipulated by the experimenter. This is the variable that is of interest to the investigator because this is the variable which is hypothesized to be one of the causal variables producing the presumed effect. To obtain evidence of this hypothesized causal relationship, the investigator manipulates this variable *independent* of other variables. In the Aronson and Mills experiment, severity of initiation was independently manipulated and therefore it was the independent variable. King (1957), as discussed in Chapter 1, investigated the influence of early social experience upon later aggressive behavior. In this study early social experience was the independent variable because this was the variable independently manipulated by King. In an experiment that examines the influence of rate of presentation of words on speed of learning, the independent variable is speed of presentation. Variation in the rate of presentation from one to three seconds provides an independent manipulation which, with the control of other factors such as ability, enables one to identify the effect of rate of presentation upon learning speed.

These examples demonstrate the ease with which one can pick out the independent variable from a study. The examples also illustrate the requirements necessary for a variable to qualify as an independent variable. In all of the above examples the independent variable involved variation—variation in rate of presentation of words, early social experience, or severity of initiation. This variation was not a random form of variation but was under the direct control of the experimenter. In all cases the experimenter created the conditions that provided the type of variation desired. Here we have the two requirements necessary for a variable to qualify as an independent variable: variation and control of the variation. We shall look at each separately and also discuss other issues related to the independent variable. The issue of controlled variation will be discussed under the topic, "Establishing Variation in the Independent Variable."

Variation

For a variable to qualify as an independent variable, it must be manipulable. The variable must be presented in at least two forms even if this boils down to a presence versus absence type of variation. There are several ways in which the desired variation in the independent variable can be achieved. We will take a look at each of these.

PRESENCE VERSUS ABSENCE.   The presence versus absence technique for achieving variation is exactly what the name implies. One group of subjects receives the treatment condition, and the other group does not. The two groups are then compared to see if the group that received the treatment condition differed from the group that did not. A drug study can illustrate this type of variation. One group of

68   subjects is administered a drug and a second group is administered a placebo. The two groups of subjects are then compared on some measure such as reaction time to determine if the drug group had significantly different reaction times than did the placebo group. If they did, then the difference is attributed to the drug.

AMOUNT OF A VARIABLE.   A second basic technique for achieving variation in the independent variable is to administer different amounts of the variable to each of several groups. Erlebacher and Sekuler (1974), for example, varied the amount of time subjects were exposed to three different stimulus figures to investigate the influence of exposure duration upon perceived length. Subjects were exposed to the stimulus figures for periods of 30, 60, 120, 240, 480, 960, and 1920 msec and then were required to estimate whether the stimulus figure they had just seen was longer or shorter than a standard stimulus figure. The results revealed that the perceived length of the stimulus figure increased as the length of exposure increased. Note that in this experiment the presence-absence form of variation could not be used since subjects must be exposed to the stimulus figures for some period of time in order to have a basis for making their comparative judgments. Other studies may include a group that does not receive any amount of the independent variable. Such studies combine the technique of varying amount with the presence versus absence technique. A drug study represents an excellent candidate for combining these techniques as do many other types of studies. One group would receive a placebo, and three additional groups would receive three different amounts of drug being investigated. In such a study you could tell not only if the drug had an influence on the subjects' responses but also whether the different *amounts* of the drug influenced their responses.

One question that might come up with regard to establishing variation is "How many levels of variation should be induced?" An exact answer cannot be given other than that there must be at least two levels of variation and these two must differ from one another. The research problem, past research, and the experience of the investigator should provide some indication as to the number of levels of variation that need to be incorporated in a given experiment.

Also, the type of inference that is to be drawn from the results of the study will suggest the number of levels of variation that should be included. If, for example, the objective of a given drug study was to determine if a drug produced a given effect, you would probably use only two levels of variation. One group of subjects would receive a large dosage of the drug and another group would receive the placebo. However, if you were concerned with identifying the specific drug

dosage that produced a given effect, you would probably have many
levels of variation ranging in small increments from the placebo group
to the group of subjects receiving a massive drug dosage.

TYPE OF A VARIABLE.   A third means of generating variation in
the independent variable is to vary the type of variable under investigation. Assume you were interested in determining whether or not a
person's reactions toward others were affected by the label these others
were given. Such a study could be conducted by having a school
psychologist and a teacher discuss the teacher's pupils at the beginning
of a school year. In this discussion, the school psychologist could
appraise the teacher of the type of student he or she would be facing.
Some of the students would be labeled as trouble makers, some as the
average, run-of-the-mill students who may occasionally create a dis-
turbance, and a third group would be labeled ideal students, those who
never give any trouble. In actuality a matched group of students would
have been randomly assigned to the three groups. Some time after the
school term had begun, the teacher would be required to assess the
students in terms of problem behavior, for example, being asked to rate
each of the students in terms of the degree to which they were considered to be problem children; or the teacher could be asked to rank the
students in order from those who never gave any trouble to those who
were constantly a problem. If the assessments initially provided by the
school psychologist were confirmed by the teacher's ratings or rank
ordering, then support would be given to the hypothesis that giving a
child a certain *type* of label tends to generate that type of behavior. In
this hypothetical example, variation was generated in type of the
behavioral label given to each child.

Constructing the Independent Variable

In an experiment, we are attempting to determine if the independent
variable actually produces the hypothesized effect. In order to test the
hypothesis, we must translate the independent variable into concrete
experimental operations. We must specify exactly what we mean by
learning, guilt, reinforcement, and so on. If the independent variable
being investigated has specific empirical referents, no difficulty in
translation exists. If the independent variable is a drug, then the task is
merely one of obtaining and administering that drug. If rate of presentation of nonsense syllables is the independent variable, then one must
naturally use a specific time interval. Here the only problem lies in
deciding which time interval to use. In these cases the independent
variable required little if any translation because there were specific
empirical referents.

70   Other independent variables such as attitude, frustration, anxiety, learning, and self-esteem are not so specifically spelled out. Therefore, the scientist must find some way of translating the concepts into observable events. The scientist must specify exactly the specific behaviors or events that are used to generate the independent variable. This boils down to defining operationally the independent variable. However, the problem is one of specifying the operations to represent the independent variables. Anxiety may be defined as a score on a test or receiving electric shock. Frustration may be defined and thereby translated into empirical referents by putting children in a playroom which contained a number of highly attractive but inaccessible toys. Aronson and Mills translated severity of initiation into the concrete operations of reading obscene words. In any case, the abstract conceptual variable (memory, learning, reinforcement, fear, anxiety, or aggressiveness, for example) must be operationally defined.

For some types of research, operationally defining the conceptual variable, which does not have specific empirical referents, does not seem to be a major problem because standard agreed-upon techniques exist. A study of the effect of schedules of reinforcement upon strength of a response requires the construction of the different reinforcement patterns. The schedules of reinforcement identified by Skinner are standard and accepted in the field (the interested student is referred to Ferster and Skinner, 1957). These could immediately be incorporated in the study.

In other areas of research, such as in social psychology, difficulty is frequently encountered in constructing conditions that represent a realization of the independent variable specified in the problem. The reason for this is that relatively few standard techniques exist for manipulating the conceptual variable in such areas. Few of the manipulations of variables such as conformity, commitment, or aggression are identical. Aronson and Carlsmith (1968, p. 40) state that the reason for this lack of development of specific techniques is a function of the fact that the variables with which the social psychologist works must be adapted to the particular population with which he or she is working. A standard technique would not work with all populations. Therefore, the researchers must use ingenuity in accomplishing the task, capitalizing on previous work by borrowing ideas and innovations and incorporating them. However, there is one basic problem encountered when many researchers attempt to make the translation from such abstract concepts to concrete operational terms. Many researchers do not attempt to use prior ideas and innovations in an attempt to create a better translation of the abstract concept. Instead they "cling to settings and techniques that have been used before" (Ellsworth, 1977). Every translation has had its own quirks and characteristic

sources of error and, as Stevens (1939) has pointed out, each operational   **71**
definition or translation of an abstract concept represents merely a
partial representation of the abstract concept. Therefore, one should
not automatically assume that prior translations are the best or even
most appropriate translations. In fact, in any translation the investigator always has to compromise and sacrifice some methodological
advantages for others. Given this situation one should, when faced
with the problem of translating abstract concepts into operational
terms, first determine how the topic or phenomenon has been studied
in the past. Once you have determined how the concept has been
studied in the past you should then determine whether or not any of
these translations are appropriate for your study. In making this decision you should consider the overall research which has been conducted on the topic. It may be that most prior studies have focused
only on a narrow but typical translation of an abstract concept. If this is
the case then it would be more appropriate to identify another translation that would help approximate a more complete representation of
the abstract concept. For example, fear has typically been studied in
the laboratory. However, in this setting the range of fear that can be
generated is restricted because of the ethical restrictions of imposing
stimuli that may create extreme fear. Given this situation it may be
more appropriate to search for a naturalistic setting where extreme fear
was naturally created.

In other areas of research, the problem is not so much one of how
the conceptual variable will be translated into specific experimental
operations, but which of the many techniques available will be used.
Pluchik (1974) lists eight different techniques (including approach-
avoidance conflict and physiological measures) which Miller (1957)
identified for either producing or studying fear in animals. If you were
to study the conceptual variable of fear in animals, which one should
you use? What specific operations will be used to represent this conceptual variable of fear? To answer this question you have to determine
which of the available techniques most adequately represents the variable. This issue will be discussed at a later point in the chapter.

Why do several different techniques exist for constructing a single
variable such as learning, emotion, or fear? Variables such as fear are
concepts that refer to a general state or condition of the body. Therefore, there is probably no single index that is *the* way to produce such a
concept. There are probably some ways that are better than others, but
no one index can provide complete understanding of the concept. To
obtain a better understanding of the concept several indexes should be
investigated even though they may initially seem to give contradictory
results. As our knowledge of the concept increases, the initial results
that appear to be contradictory will probably be integrated.

72   Establishing Variation in the Independent Variable

Intimately tied in with the issue of constructing the independent variable is the need for establishing controlled variation in the independent variable. Not only must we specify the empirical referents for a variable such as fear, but also we must be able to generate some controlled variation of it. For some variables it is much more difficult to establish controlled variation than with other variables. In drug research it is typically easy to establish controlled variation. The drug under study is the independent variable, and controlled variation is achieved by administering various amounts to different groups of subjects. For other variables, the task is much more difficult. There seems to be a direct positive correlation between the ease of constructing the independent variable and the ease with which various degrees of controlled variation are attained. Contrast the ease with which variation can be established with drugs versus fear or anxiety.

We will now take a look at some concrete ways variation can be achieved and the difficulties each technique produces. There seem to be two basic ways in which variation can be achieved in psychological research. Variation can be generated through manipulation of the instructions to the subjects or it can be produced by some event that happens to the subject. Let us look first at each of these two ways of establishing variation and then at two other less appropriate ways of varying the independent variable.

MANIPULATION OF INSTRUCTIONS.   One possible technique for introducing variation is through manipulating instructions. One group of subjects receives one set of instructions and another group receives another set of instructions. Hall and Pierce (1974), for example, investigated the relationship between memory encoding instructions and both recognition and recall. In the first experiment, they randomly assigned subjects to three experimental conditions. The first group of subjects were in the association condition and were told to think of words that reminded them of the word presented to them. The second group of subjects, those in the repetition condition, were told to repeat each word that was presented over and over and to try not to think of anything else until the next word was presented. The third group of subjects participated in the neutral condition, and consequently they were not given any specific set of instructions. Rather, they were told to try to remember the word as best they could. Such a technique of manipulating variables has the advantage of being integrally related to the activity in which the subjects are to engage. Therefore, it is probably safe to say that such a technique will represent a successful manipulation.

Manipulation of variables through instruction is not without dangers. Two can readily be identified. First, one runs the risk of some subjects being inattentive when the instructions are given. These subjects will miss part or all of the instructions and therefore will not be operating according to the appropriate manipulation, introducing error into the results. The second danger is the possibility that subject-to-subject variation exists in the interpretation of the instructions. Some subjects may interpret the instructions to mean one thing while others interpret it in a different way. In this case, an unintentional variation is introduced that represents error or, actually, an uncontrolled variable. The danger of misinterpretation can be minimized if instructions are kept simple, given emphatically, and related to the activity to be engaged in. As a result of these two difficulties, probably no more than one variable should be manipulated through instructions. Manipulation of more than one variable will often result in too much complexity and length, rendering the manipulations ineffective by virtue of increasing inattentiveness, misinterpretation, and forgetting.

MANIPULATION OF EVENTS.   A second means of establishing variation in the independent variable is through manipulation of events. Drug research varies events such as drug dosages, and learning experiments may vary events such as meaningfulness of the material presented to subjects. Aronson and Mills, in their experiment, varied the severity of initiation administered to subjects. Most human experiments and almost all animal experiments use this method for achieving variation. Communication skills have been developed in chimpanzees (Fouts, 1973), enabling one to use instruction with these infrahumans. When a choice exists between using instructions or events to create the variation, the best choice is, in most cases, to use events. The reason for this choice is that events are more realistic or have more impact on the subject.

Consider the experiment conducted by Aronson and Linder (1965). They wanted to determine if liking for another is partially determined by the behavior exhibited by that other. To investigate this problem experimentally, they designed an experiment where a confederate and a subject interacted on seven different occasions. After each of the seven sessions the subject overheard the confederate's evaluation of him. These evaluations were either all positive, all negative, initially negative and then positive, or initially positive and then negative. After overhearing all evaluations, subjects recorded their impressions of the confederate. In this experiment the event manipulated was the overhearing of an evaluation of the subject's performance. This manipulation could also have taken place through instructions in the sense that the experimenter could have told the subjects how they performed. However, the event manipulation was more meaningful and

74   realistic to the subjects. The advantage of this increased realism or meaningfulness in experimentation is that the problems of inattentiveness and misinterpretation are minimized. Additionally, the response emitted by the subject in a situation that has realism is probably a better representation of how he or she would respond outside the experimental environment because the realism probably removes much of the artificiality created by the experiment.

In animal research the issue of realism seldom exists for two reasons. First, events are used to manipulate the independent variable. Second, the conditions that are used to motivate the animal to respond seem to create the realism. Animals are motivated to respond by doing such things as depriving them of food or water, or by administering electric shock. Such conditions seem to be real and meaningful to these subjects even though this is something about which an animal researcher rarely speculates.

That is not to say that all manipulations of events get the person involved or are as meaningful as real life. In fact, many experiments have little impact on the individual and consequently tend to have little realism. Many person perception experiments have, for example, manipulated exposure by requiring judges to predict responses of others after viewing different amounts of a filmed interview of them. The filmed interview removes the realism from the experiment. Instead the experiment could have required the judge and the others to spend either 10 minutes or a half hour together before the judge made any predictions. Such a situation would have increased the realism. Why was this situation not employed? The answer is related to the problem of control. The filmed situation enables control over variables that are not controlled in the free interaction situation. In the free interaction situation many differences would exist between the judges and the others, such as what the judge and the other talked about and how each responded. Consequently, judges would have different information upon which to base their judgments, which boils down to the fact that many uncontrolled variables exist. In the filmed interview, each judge receives the same information, resulting in control over both the type and amount of information received.

With some types of research, especially those involving social interaction, there is a difficulty created with attempting to make the event manipulations meaningful. As one attempts to make the event manipulations more meaningful, control of extraneous influences decreases. As noted with the person perception research example, use of filmed interviews increases control but decreases impact. A rule of thumb that can be followed when conducting research involving social interaction is that as realism and meaningfulness of social experiences are increased in an attempt to increase impact, control is decreased. As control over variables is increased, the impact of the experiment is decreased. This is a real dilemma for the scientist attempting to experimentally investigate social interaction. On the one hand the scientist wants control over variables. On the other hand, he or she wants to eliminate the sterile atmosphere of the experiment, for such an atmosphere may fail to involve the subject and therefore may not have any significant influence on behavior since no impact was attained. There is no simple solution to this problem. The ideal situation is one in which realism and control are maximized. However, the first concern of the experimenter should be to make sure that the experimental effect desired actually occurs, for if this effect does not occur it makes no sense to worry about other aspects of the experiment.

MEASUREMENT OF INTERNAL STATES. In reading the psychological literature one frequently encounters studies that have been conducted where the independent variable was manipulated by selecting subjects that differed in terms of some measured internal state such as self-esteem or anxiety level. The assumption is that each individual possesses a certain amount of a variety of variables commonly labeled "personality variables." One efficient means of achieving a manipulation would be to select subjects having different levels of a given variable (e.g., anxiety) and then look for its effects. The procedure typically followed is to administer an instrument to a large sample of people, measuring the internal state of interest. From the test results, two smaller groups of subjects are selected, one group that has scored high on the variable of interest and one group that has scored low. These two groups are then required to perform a task, and the two groups are compared to determine if a difference exists in the task performance. If a difference does exist, it is typically attributed to the differences in the measured internal states. Ritchie and Phares (1969) were interested in the relationship between internal-external control, communicator status, and attitude change. To examine this relationship, subjects first had to be classified as internals or externals. To accomplish this task, 152 female subjects were administered the Locus of Control Scale from which 42 *externals* and 42 *internals* were chosen. The degree of attitude change of these two groups of subjects was compared for different levels of communicator status. Results indicated that a high-prestige communicator produces more change in externals than internals. This result was attributed to the externals' higher expectancy of reinforcement.

What is wrong with such an experiment? It seems to be appropriately designed and statistically analyzable. The difficulty lies in the fact that the states, internal and external control, were *measured* and not experimentally manipulated. Consequently, subjects were not randomly assigned to conditions but were nonrandomly assigned or selected on the basis of their test scores. Since subjects were selected on the basis of their test scores, it is possible that another variable, correlated with the internal or external states, produced the differences in performance. If, in a learning experiment, motivation was highly correlated with tested anxiety, then it would be impossible to determine if a difference in performance of a high- and a low-anxiety group was due to the anxiety factor or motivation. If, in the Ritchie and Phares study, some other variable was highly correlated with the subjects' locus of control, then, in the same manner, one could not determine if the observed effect was due to one's perceived locus of control, internal or external, or to the other correlated variable. An experiment which attempts to manipulate variables in this manner is, therefore, an ex post facto type of study even though it may be conducted in a laboratory with control over other variables. In fairness to Ritchie and Phares, it must be stated that they did manipulate the communicator status variable so that the study they conducted actually included an ex post facto component and an experimental component.

INTERNAL ANALYSIS OF THE DATA.   In psychological research a fourth type of variation that is sometimes engaged in has been labeled "internal analysis." Variation by way of internal analysis of the data involves a post hoc assignment of subjects to groups. Assume, as frequently happens, that a significant difference did not exist between two groups of subjects randomly assigned to two experimental manipulations. Assume also that a check had been provided on the experimental manipulation to determine if it had the intended influence. This check revealed that the manipulation did not have the desired effect on some subjects. What are we supposed to do? One could disregard this fact and proceed with data analysis. But what if no significant difference is found between groups? Can you conclude that the hypothesized effect does not exist? Not really, because the subjects on which the intended influence did not occur may be the explanation for the failure to obtain significance.

Other alternatives are either to throw out the subjects who did not respond to the manipulation, or to reassign them to a group based on the way in which they responded to the treatment condition. If the experimental manipulation did not have any influence on the subjects, they could be reassigned to the groups that did not receive any experimental manipulation. Raven and Fishbein (1961) engaged in the reassignment technique in their study on the effect of "Acceptance of punishment and change in belief." After collecting the data they found no overall difference in the shock and no-shock groups. However, the female shock subjects responded in the predicted direction but the male subjects did not. So Raven and Fishbein made the assumption, **77** based on other data, that male shock subjects were part of a common population with the no-shock subjects, with respect to dissonance, and combined these two groups of subjects, who were then compared with female shock subjects. This comparison resulted in significance. Raven and Fishbein did, however, recognize the post hoc nature of this analysis. Brehm (1960) engaged in the throw-out technique (footnote, p. 380), when he eliminated a whole group of subjects because the experimental treatment "failed to affect" the dependent variable.

The procedure followed when conducting an internal analysis of the data has a definite weakness in common with that noted when variation was achieved through measuring internal states. Doing an internal analysis violates the principle of randomization since subjects have really assigned themselves to conditions based on their response or lack of response to the treatment condition. Consequently, the study has changed from an experimental one to an ex post facto type of study. As such it has the same disadvantages as an ex post facto study.

Relation of the Independent Variable to the Concept

After deciding upon the experimental operations that you are going to use as your manifestation of the conceptual variable and the manner in which this variable will be varied, it is a good idea to look back at these operations and ask the following questions: "Do my experimental operations represent the conceptual variable which I had in mind? Will my different levels of variation of the independent variable make subjects behave differently? What ways should they behave differently?" The reason for asking these questions is that the variables with which we experiment frequently cannot be directly translated into experimental operations. Since we must frequently deal with imperfect translations, it is possible that our operations do not represent what we had in mind. Schachter and Singer (1962), for example, attempted to generate euphoria in subjects by having a confederate waltz around a room shooting rubber bands, playing with hula hoops, and practicing hook shots into a wastebasket with wadded paper. Did the confederate generate euphoria in the subjects? Selltiz et al. (1959, p. 43) state that this is often a matter of judgment on the part of the investigators. Aronson and Carlsmith (1968), however, give several techniques for attempting to answer this question.

First, let us examine a situation in which a conceptual variable, hunger, was inappropriately translated into experimental operations. For some time it has been known that the ventromedial area of the hypothalamus is involved in eating, and some investigations have, in the past, translated hunger into the experimental operations of producing lesions in this area. More recent results (Valenstein, Cox, and Kakolewski, 1970; and Pribram, 1971) reveal that this is probably an inappropriate translation. Pribram discusses the results of experiments that indicate that the production of hunger involves the far-lateral hypothalamic feeding mechanism. This mechanism "serves as a crossroads of tracts from various parts of the brain which connect peripheral and central stations concerned in the initiation and cessation of eating" (p. 190). Lesions of the ventromedial area of the hypothalamus just do not result in the same motivational (Miller, 1957) or behavioral (Valenstein, Cox, and Kakolewski, 1970) effects as does a normal increase in hunger. Therefore, hunger cannot be considered as synonymous with the eating behavior that can be produced by lesions in the ventromedial area.

How can we be sure that our experimental operations do, in fact, represent an empirical realization of our conceptual variable? This is a difficult problem without a simple solution. Aronson and Carlsmith (1968) attempt to deal with this problem. They state that there are two necessary requirements of experiments to insure that we understand our conceptual variable. First, a number of different techniques for operationally defining the conceptual variable must be used in an experiment. If they all yield the same result then we have increased assurance that all the techniques are in fact appropriate translations of the conceptual variable. Miller (1957) reports the results of two studies in which this approach was used in investigating hunger. Three identical procedures thought to influence hunger were used in each study. These three procedures were injection of isotonic saline directly into the stomach, normal intake of milk by mouth, and injection of milk directly into the stomach. Results revealed that injection of saline resulted in the least reduction of hunger, while the other two techniques produced hunger reduction. While these studies were not directly concerned with whether or not the conceptual variable of hunger had been appropriately translated, they do illustrate the point Aronson and Carlsmith were making. If several different operations are supposed to represent a concept, then each of these ways of representing it should yield the same results.

Second, we must be able to demonstrate that the empirical representation of the independent variable produces the outcomes expected. If a rat were hungry, we would expect it to engage in such behavior as consuming more food, tolerating more quinine in the food, increasing rate of bar pressing to obtain food, and producing more stomach contractions. Miller (1957) actually conducted such a study. While all these four measures did not produce identical results, depriving the rats of food did result in the expected behavior, giving

additional evidence that food deprivation appropriately represents
hunger.

The procedures which have just been suggested are, unfortunately, used infrequently in psychological experimentation. Most of the time an experimenter operationally defines the independent variable and it is up to the reader to judge whether or not an empirical realization of the conceptual variable was actually produced. All too frequently no data are given that provide validating evidence of the fact that an adequate translation of the conceptual variable was actually attained.

There seem to be at least two reasons why the techniques discussed are rarely used. First, the techniques described are time consuming. It is much easier to select the operational definition and then proceed to investigate the problem area. Second, the techniques are often difficult to carry out. In some experiments a simple replication that changes only the operational definition of the independent variable is difficult if not impossible to perform. Aronson and Carlsmith (1968, p. 16) drive this point home when discussing the Aronson and Mills experiment.

> Thus a replication of the Aronson-Mills (1959) study might necessitate a major change in the context of the experiment. If the subjects were asked to perform 30 push-ups (instead of reading obscene words), one could hardly maintain the format of a group discussion on the psychology of sex without straining the credulity of the subjects. Even the most naive of subjects would have second thoughts about doing push-ups as a screening device for a discussion on sex. Thus, one must often redo the entire experiment, changing not only the particular operations used in setting up the independent variable, but also the general setting, the experimental instructions, the stimulus to be rated, and the measurement of the dependent variable.[1]

When using human subjects there are several additional techniques one can use to provide some evidence of whether the conceptual variable is generating the observed results.

The first approach is to conduct long and probing interviews with the subject, after the independent variable has been introduced, to determine if the construct desired was actually attained. Asch (1956), for example, in a study on conformity, wanted to create pressure on each subject to conform and say something that was obviously not correct. In constructing a situation that possibly would create such

---

1. Reprinted by special permission from Aronson-Carlsmith, "Experimentation in Social Psychology," *The handbook of social psychology*, Second Edition, Volume Two, 1968, edited by Lindzey-Aronson, Addison-Wesley, Reading, Mass., p. 16.

80 pressure, one needs to ask whether such pressure is indeed created. One means of doing so could be to generate the group pressure on several subjects and then interview them to find out if the pressure were actually created. Naturally there are difficulties with conducting these interviews. Subjects often identify the response that is wanted and then provide this response. However, if the postinterviews are appropriately conducted, this error is minimized. The appropriate means of conducting debriefing sessions or postinterviews will be discussed in a later chapter in the book. The benefits that can accrue from this interview are several, the greatest of which is that the interview can point out possible weaknesses in the operational definition of the independent variable and indicate what needs to be done to eliminate these weaknesses. It is important that these interviews follow immediately after the administration of the treatment conditions rather than after the response data is collected, for the response may influence the subjects' introspective report. Research on scapegoating supports this statement; it has revealed that variables such as aroused hostility may be diminished by giving the subjects an opportunity to displace it. Since these interviews follow the administration of the treatment conditions, they must, as you might suspect, be conducted on subjects that comprise a pilot study conducted for the purpose of investigating the influence of the experimental operations. Otherwise, the interview may affect the response data.

A second and more difficult, but superior, technique involves getting a behavioral indicator that the experimental operations are arousing the desired effect. If you want to arouse anxiety in subjects, get some indication, like a galvanic skin response (GSR), that anxiety is actually being aroused. Zimbardo et al. (1966) measured subjects' GSR to monitor anxiety through the course of their experiments. Aronson and Carlsmith (1963) attempted to create mild and severe threat in children. Intuitively, they seem to have manipulated threat. They could have verified the manipulation of the threat conditions by pretesting the children with toys of varying degrees of attractiveness and various threat conditions until they had a condition where more children disregarded the mild threat than the severe threat condition in order to play with the forbidden toy. In this way they would have had a behavioral indication that threat was actually varied.

Pretesting can also give some indication of the level of intensity of the manipulation. Suppose the problem one is investigating has a hypothesis about three levels of intensity of threat. Three levels of threat have to be created. How does one know that three levels are created and how intense they are? Either of the above methods could give some indication. A verbal report or response to a questionnaire may indicate level of intensity. In a study that attempted to generate three levels of threat, level of intensity of the severity of threat could be determined behaviorally by noting the percentage of children that disregarded the threat. If, in one condition, 10% of the children disregarded the threat, in the second condition 50% of the children disregarded the threat, and in the third condition 80% of the children disregarded the threat, one would have some evidence of the intensity of each of the threat conditions.

The Number of Independent Variables

How many independent variables should be used in an experiment? In looking through the literature in any area of psychology, you will find some studies that used only one independent variable whereas others used two or more independent variables. What criterion or rule dictated the number used in each study? Unfortunately, there is no rule or criterion that can be stated to give an answer to such a question. We do know that behavior is multidetermined and inclusion of more than one independent variable is often desirable because of the added information that it will give in the form of an interaction. Interaction refers to the differential effect which one independent variable has for each level of one or more additional independent variables. For example, Mellgren, Nation, and Wrather (1975) investigated the relationship between magnitude of negative reinforcement and schedule of reinforcement for producing resistance to extinction. As predicted, they found that the effect of magnitude of reinforcement was dependent upon the schedule of reinforcement used. The subjects (albino rats) that were performing under a partial reinforcement schedule revealed greater resistance to extinction when administered a large negative reinforcement whereas rats performing under a continuous schedule of reinforcement revealed greater resistance to extinction when administered a small negative reinforcement. In other words, the effect of reinforcement magnitude is dependent upon the schedule of reinforcement. If the second variable of reinforcement schedule had not been included, the study would probably have revealed, as demonstrated by other studies, that no difference existed between magnitude of negative reinforcement in terms of its ability to affect resistance to extinction. Inclusion of this variable revealed that magnitude of negative reinforcement did affect resistance to extinction, but its effect interacted with the schedule of reinforcement.

Experiments such as Mellgren et al. reveal the advantage and even the necessity of varying more than one independent variable because of the clarity that is added by the inclusion of additional variables. This again gets us back to the question of the number of independent variables that should be included in an experiment.

82   Theoretically and statistically there is no limit to the number of variables that can be varied. Realistically or practically there is a limit. From the subject's point of view, as the number of variables increases he or she has to do more things, such as participate in more events or take more tests. The subject is apt to become bored, irritated, or resentful, and thereby introduce a confounding variable into the experiment. From the experimenter's point of view, as the number of variables increases the difficulty in making sense out of the data increases, as well as the difficulty in setting up the experiment. Aronson and Carlsmith (1968, p. 51) give a rule of thumb that may be followed. They say that the experiment "should only be as complex as is necessary for the important relationships to emerge in a clear manner."[2] In other words, do not use the "why not" approach. This approach involves including a variable in the experiment because there is no real reason not to include it. By the same token there is no reason to include it. Only include in an experiment those variables that seem to be necessary to reveal the important relationships.

The Dependent Variable

The dependent variable has been defined as the behavioral variable designed to measure the effect of the variation of the independent variable. This definition, like the definition of the independent variable, seems straightforward and simple enough. Also, like the independent variable, it is relatively easy to identify the dependent variable in a given study. Aronson and Mills wanted to investigate the influence of severity of initiation on liking for a group. Liking for a group represented the dependent variable measure. Ritchie and Phares (1969) investigated attitude change as a function of communicator status and locus of control. Attitude change represented their dependent variable. However, there are many decisions that have to be made in securing the most appropriate measure of the effect of the variation in the independent variable. To gain an appreciation for the complexity of the decision-making process involved, let us take a look at the psychological experiment.

The psychological experiment is conducted to answer a question, "What is the effect of . . . ?" and to test the corresponding hypothesis, "A certain change in X will result in a certain change in Y." In order to

2. Reprinted by special permission from Aronson-Carlsmith, "Experimentation in Social Psychology," *The handbook of social psychology*, Second Edition, Volume Two, 1968, edited by Lindzey-Aronson, Addison-Wesley, Reading, Mass., p. 51.

answer the question and test the hypothesis, a variable—the independent variable—is varied in order to determine if it produces the desired or hypothesized effect. The issue of concern for the experimenter is to make sure that he or she actually obtains an indication of the effect produced by the variation in the independent variable. To accomplish this task, the experimenter has to select a dependent variable that will be sensitive to, or be able to pick up, the influence exerted by the independent variable. It is not infrequent that researchers conduct a study that indicates that the independent variable produces no effect. However, they know that an effect was produced because they think they saw behavioral change exhibited. Such a case may represent distorted perception, or it may mean that the dependent variable was not sensitive to the effects produced by the independent variable.

It is the task of the dependent variable to determine whether the independent variable did or did not produce an effect. If an effect was produced, the dependent variable must indicate if the effect was a facilitating one or an inhibiting one, and also be able to reveal the magnitude of this effect. If the dependent variable can accomplish these tasks, the experimenter has identified and used a good sensitive dependent variable. Here we find the first decision point for the experimenter. What specific measure should one use to assess the effect of the independent variable? Once a decision has been made on this issue the experimenter still has several problems to confront.

The experimenter must somehow insure that the subject is taking the measurement seriously and doing his or her best. The experimenter must also make sure that the subject is responding in a truthful manner rather than "cooperating" with the experimenter and responding in a manner that he or she feels will be most helpful to the experimenter. The last two problems are most crucial in human experiments.

The Response to be Used as the Dependent Variable

What response should be selected as the dependent variable? We just saw that the first and foremost criterion it must meet is sensitivity to the effect of the independent variable. There is not to my knowledge any specific rule or statement that will tell you how to select a dependent variable. Psychologists use a wide variety of responses as dependent variables ranging from questionnaire responses, to verbal reports, to overt behavior, to physiological responses. The problem is to select the best response for use as the dependent variable. Which type of response is best, or, to put it another way, which response is the most sensitive to the effect produced by the independent variable? In most, if not all, experiments there are several different measures that potentially could be used and one can choose between them. For example,

84   attitudes have and could be measured by a response to a questionnaire, by a physiological response, or by observing a response made by the subject. There seems to be no pat solution or specific rule to follow that will pinpoint the most appropriate dependent variable.

The difficulty in identifying the most appropriate dependent variable seems to be due to the fact that psychologists study processes, attributes, or outcomes of the human and/or infrahuman organism. The psychologist studies phenomena. When an independent variable is introduced, our task is one of determining the effect of the independent variable on phenomena such as learning, attitudes, or intelligence. Are these processes, attributes, or outcomes facilitated, inhibited, or affected in some other way? The difficulty is that the processes, attributes, or outcomes are not directly observable. Since direct observation is not possible, some result of the construct under study that can be observed must be selected for observation to allow inference back to the construct. Consider learning as an example. It is impossible to study the learning process directly. If, on the other hand, a student sits down and studies certain material for an hour and then can answer questions he or she previously could not, we say learning has taken place. In this case learning is inferred from an increase in performance. In such a way we can acquire information about a phenomenon. The decision that the scientist is faced with is selecting the aspect or the type of response that will provide the best representation of change in the construct as a result of the variation in the independent variable. Previous experimentation can frequently help in making such a decision. Prior research has been conducted on most phenomena and many dependent variables have been used in these studies. Results of these studies should provide clues to which responses would be most sensitive.

Aronson and Carlsmith (1968, p. 54) address the problem of selecting the dependent variable with research conducted on humans. They discuss some of the advantages and disadvantages of various measures that can be used as a measure of the dependent variable when conducting social psychological research. One very significant point they make is that the more commitment demanded of the subject by the dependent variable, the greater the degree of confidence we can have in the results of our experiment. Why is this so? First, making a commitment to a course of action reduces the probability of faking on the part of the subject because it helps insure that subjects take the dependent variable measure seriously. If we wanted to find out which person of a group of individuals is most liked by a particular individual, we could have that individual rate each of them on a liking rating scale, and pick out the one who received the highest ratings. We could also have him or her choose a member of the group as a roommate for the next year, with the contingency that the person picked will in fact be the roommate. In this case, the subject would be motivated to respond truthfully because he or she would have to live with the decision. The second advantage of requiring the subject to make a commitment is that it frequently increases one's confidence that the dependent variable of interest is really being measured. Recording the frequency with which fights are initiated is a better index of aggression than having a subject verbally state that he or she is angry or evaluate the degree of felt anger on a rating scale.

Behavior that involves a commitment is probably the best type of dependent variable to use. Frequently it is not feasible, because of cost, time, or some other constraint, to use such a dependent variable, and a questionnaire or a verbal report must be used. Questionnaires and verbal reports yield a great deal of useful data. The difficulty with these measures is that there is an increased likelihood of error because either the subjects do not take the measure seriously and/or they "cooperate" with the experimenter, thereby producing the results they think the experimenter desires.

After deciding which measure to use as the dependent variable, you must determine if that measure is *reliable* and *valid*. If the dependent variable is not valid, you will not measure what you want to measure, and if the dependent variable is not reliable, you will not consistently measure it. This is a matter in which experimental psychologists have been extremely lax and a matter in which those in the field of test construction have justifiably been extremely rigorous. In constructing a test, one of the first things the investigator does is to establish the reliability of that test, and then proceed to attempt to get evidence of its validity. The psychologist conducting experiments has, for some reason, chosen to neglect this issue. It seems as though reliability and validity are assumed to exist intrinsically if the dependent variable has been operationally defined. Such an assumption cannot and should not be made, because if the dependent variable is not reliable and valid the experiment is worthless.

Reliability of the dependent variable can, in most experiments, be established by the same techniques used by those constructing tests. Reliability could be established by determining the consistency with which responses are made to the dependent variable. If organisms consistently respond in the same way to the dependent variable, then it is reliable. In experimentation, replication is taken as a good measure of the reliability of dependent measures, because replication of an effect could not be attained if the dependent variable measure were unreliable. Establishing the validity of the dependent variable involves obtaining evidence that the dependent variable actually measures the construct we want it to measure. For example, does latency of response really represent degree of learning? Does selecting a roommate for the next year really represent the degree to which the subject likes that

86 person? As you can see, establishing the validity of the dependent variable is the more difficult task. The individuals concerned with test construction have also wrestled with this problem and have devised a number of techniques for obtaining evidence of validity. Experimenters most frequently do not even consider the validity question because, I believe, it has been obscured by operationism. For example, intelligence could be, and has been, operationally defined as what intelligence tests measure. No one can argue with this operational definition. What you can argue with is whether intelligence tests do really measure intelligence. Operational definitions are necessary to communicate between scientists, but such definitions in no way say anything about validity, even though many experimenters seem to write off the validity question once they have satisfied the criterion of operational definition.

How do we obtain an index of validity of our operationally defined dependent variable? Again there is no simple solution. The discussion of commitment alluded to the validity question. As the commitment required of the dependent variable increases, we can increase our faith in the results of the experiment because it reduces faking and it seems frequently to represent a more valid representation of the dependent variable we wanted to measure. In other words, commitment has face validity. Fighting seems to be a more valid index of aggression than a rating of anger. Commitment, therefore, seems to be related to validity. To get additional indicators of validity we must resort to the *construct* validity techniques used by test constructors. One could, for example, correlate the scores obtained on the selected dependent variable with scores obtained by the same subject on another measure that is *known* to be valid. If the correlation is high, the measure is assumed to be valid. If the correlation is low or nonsignificant, the measure is not valid. The problem that arises in such a case is that many of the constructs that we want to measure are multidimensional and the different dimensions may not be highly correlated. Strength of conditioning has, for example, been inferred from amplitude, latency, and resistance to extinction, and investigators have sometimes used these measures interchangeably. However, Hall and Kobrick (1952) have revealed that the correlations between some of these measures are very low. As you can see, the validity question is very difficult but one which must be considered in every experiment.

Reducing Subject Error

Once a decision has been made as to what the dependent variable will be, the experimenter using human subjects must insure that the subject is taking the measure seriously and not trying to fake the responses. The problem of insuring that the subject is taking the measurement seriously increases as the degree of commitment decreases. For example, in filling out a questionnaire, some subjects will undoubtedly race through it, reading questions in a haphazard manner and checking answers without putting much thought into them. One way of decreasing such errors is to disguise the measure of the dependent variable. In addition to increasing the likelihood of insuring that the subject takes the measure seriously, disguising also helps guard against the possibility of the subject cooperating with the experimenter. Aronson and Carlsmith (1968, p. 58) present a number of techniques that have been used in the past that are useful for disguising the dependent variable.

One technique is to assess the dependent variable in a setting removed from the experiment. Carlsmith, Collins, and Helmreich (1966) solicited the aid of a consumer research analyst to assess the dependent variable. Another technique is to assess behavior of significance to the subject, such as requiring selection of a roommate. A third technique is to construct the experiment in such a way that the subject does not realize that the dependent variable is being observed. Lefkowitz, Blake, and Mouton (1955) observed the frequency with which people jaywalked or disobeyed signs upon introduction of various levels of an independent variable. A fourth technique frequently used in attitude-change experiments is to imbed key items in a larger questionnaire in the hope that the key items will not be recognized and falsely reported on. A similar technique is to disguise the reason for interest in a particular dependent variable. Aronson (1961) was interested in finding out whether the attractiveness of several colors varied as the effort expended in getting them varied. To do so he needed a measure of attractiveness and asked the subjects to rate the attractiveness of colors because, as he told them, there appears to be a relationship between color preference and a person's performance. Using unsuspicious subjects such as young children is also a very useful method for reducing or eliminating cooperation. Young children are very straightforward and not motivated by more devious means. A sixth technique is to use what Aronson and Carlsmith call the family of "whoops" procedures. The typical procedure is to collect pretest data and then claim that something happened to it so posttest data can be collected. Christensen (1968) used this method in collecting test-retest reliability data on ratings of a series of concepts. A seventh procedure is to have a confederate collect the data. Karhan (1973) had the learner, a member of the experiment who had supposedly received electric shock for errors made, make a request of the subject. The dependent variable was the subject's response to the confederate's request. A last technique is to use a measure that is presumably not under the subject's conscious control. These represent the whole class of physiological measures. However, a number of individuals have

88 presented data that indicate these measures may be consciously influenced by the subject.

The Number of Dependent Variables

Should more than one dependent variable be used in a psychological experiment? This is a very reasonable question, particularly when more than one dependent variable could be used to measure the effect of variation of a given independent variable. In a learning experiment using rats, the dependent variable could be the frequency, amplitude, or latency of response. Likewise, in an attitude experiment the dependent variable could be measured by a questionnaire, observing behavior, or a physiological measure. When more than one dependent variable can be used, the scientist typically selects only one and proceeds with the experiment. If the scientist elects to use more than one dependent variable, certain problems arise. Assuming the scientist knows how to measure each of the dependent variables, he or she must be concerned with the relationship between them. If the various dependent variable measures are very highly correlated, e.g., 0.95 or above, there is reasonable assurance that they are identical measures and all but one can be dropped. If they are not so highly correlated, the experimenter must ask why not. The lack of correspondence could be due to unreliability of the measures or to the fact that they are not measuring the same aspect of the construct under study. Two different measures of learning may be measuring different aspects of the learning process. These difficulties must be resolved. However, the scientist all too often does not have the data available to solve all of these problems. As a field advances, more and more of the aspects of a phenomenon are unraveled and problems such as these are resolved. Such cases support the notion that multiple dependent variables should be used in some experiments because they contribute to the understanding of a phenomenon, and this is what science is attempting to accomplish.

The problem of the use of more than one dependent variable reveals that the constructs that we are attempting to measure, such as learning or anxiety, are multidimensional in the sense that they can be measured by several different techniques. In order to obtain a good grasp of the effect that our independent variable has on our multidimensional dependent variable we must use several different measures. Multidimensional statistical procedures have been developed to handle the simultaneous use of several dependent variables in the same study. When several independent variables and several dependent variables are manipulated in one experiment, a more elaborate statistical technique called multivariate analysis of variance must be used to analyze the results. The advantage of this approach is that it allows us to take the correlation between the dependent variables into account (Kerlinger and Pedhazur, 1973). Analyzing each dependent variable separately would violate one of the underlying assumptions of the statistical test, if a correlation did exist between the different dependent variable measures. Using several dependent variables in a study and appropriately analyzing them can, therefore, increase our knowledge of the complex relationship that exists between antecedent conditions and behavior.

Summary

In seeking an answer to a research question it is necessary to develop a design that will provide the necessary information. Two primary ingredients in a research design are the independent and dependent variables. Before the research design can be finalized it is necessary to make a number of decisions regarding these two variables.

For the independent variable, the investigator must first specify not only the number of independent variables to be used but also the exact concrete operations that are going to represent the conceptual variable or variables. For some independent variables this is easy since specific empirical referents exist, whereas others are not so easily translated. In either case the conceptual independent variable must be operationally defined. In addition to translating the independent variable the investigator must also specify how variation is to be established in the independent variable. Generally, variation is created by a presence-versus-absence technique or by varying the amount or type of the independent variable. But the investigator must determine, within the framework of one of these techniques, the exact mode for creating the variation. Will the variation be created by manipulating instructions or events, or by measuring the internal states of the organism? After these decisions are made, it is advisable to reexamine the operational definition of the independent variable to determine if the operations really represent the construct you want them to represent. There are also several ways in which concrete information can be attained regarding this issue. If several ways of defining the independent variable all produce the same experimental results, added assurance exists that the conceptual variable was appropriately translated. Also, if several empirical representations of the independent variable produce the expected outcomes, then we are more confident that the appropriate translation was made. Additional techniques that can be used with human subjects are to conduct long probing interviews and to obtain a behavioral indication that the appropriate translation was made.

The dependent variable is also complex and requires that a number of decisions be made. First, the experimenter has to decide upon what response will be used as the dependent variable and if more than one dependent variable will be used. Typically, there is a choice of a number of responses. The investigator must select the one or more dependent variables that will be most sensitive to the effects produced by the independent variable. While no hard rules can be given as to which variable to select, prior research can provide valuable clues. For human subjects, selecting a response that requires a commitment seems to be best. In addition to selecting the most sensitive dependent variable, the investigator must also select a response that is reliable and valid. This is an issue that has been neglected by most researchers. For human subjects, consideration must be given to selecting a response that is free of bias. When subject bias represents a potential source of error, a disguised measure of the dependent variable is often useful.

Key Concepts

One way to test your mastery of the material that was presented in this chapter is to see if you know the meaning of the following terms. These terms were selected because they represent the key concepts. If you can define, identify, or otherwise explain each of the following terms without referring back to the material in the chapter, you can be assured that you have mastered the basics of the material that was presented. Just in case you cannot recall the meaning of a given term, the page on which it can be found appears in parentheses beside it.

design (p. 65)
independent variable (pp. 66–67)
variation (p. 67)
translating independent variable into concrete
   operations (pp. 69–71)
instructional manipulation (pp. 72–73)
event manipulation (pp. 73–74)
internal states (p. 75)
internal analysis (p. 76)
dependent variable (pp. 82–83)
reliable (p. 85)
valid (p. 85)

Control in Experimentation

One of the most crucial tasks facing the experimenter is the need for controlling the influence of extraneous variables, because without control it would be impossible to identify causation. When the experimenter sets up his or her experiment, one of the prime objectives is to control for the variation that would be produced by these extraneous variables. The effect of attaining this control is to avoid confounding the results of the study and/or to reduce the variability in subjects' scores. Reducing the variability of subjects' scores has the effect of increasing the probability of detecting the effect of the independent variable. When the experimenter tries to avoid confounding, he or she is attempting to insure the attainment of what Campbell and Stanley

(1963) have labeled *internal validity.* Internal validity is attained when the observed effect is due to the experimental treatments and not due to some other extraneous variable.

What is really meant when one talks about controlling for the unwanted variation that is produced by extraneous variables? The neophyte may think that controlling for the effect of extraneous variables means that the influence of these variables is completely eliminated from the experiment. It is possible to eliminate totally the influence of some variables. The influence of visual or auditory stimulation could, for example, be eliminated by conducting the experiment in a lightproof, blacked-out room or a soundproof room. Conducting the experiment in such a room would totally eliminate the influence of such variables since they would be held constant at a magnitude of zero. However, most of the variables that could influence a psychological experiment are not of the type that can be eliminated. In psychological experiments variables such as intelligence, past experience, or history of reinforcement can affect the dependent variables; such variables cannot be eliminated. Somehow, it is necessary to eliminate the *influence* of these variables from the experiment. However, while it is not possible to eliminate the influence of these variables from the experiment, it *is* possible to eliminate any *differential* influence these variables may have across the various levels of the independent variable. In other words, it is possible to keep the influence of these variables constant across the various levels of the independent variable. By so doing, the effect on the dependent variable should be the same and, therefore, any differential influence noted on the dependent variable can be attributed to the levels of variation in the independent variable. To illustrate this point consider the study conducted by Wade and Blier (1974). They investigated the differential effect that two methods of learning had on the retention of lists of words (they actually used consonant-vowel-consonant trigrams). In this study they had to control for the associations that subjects had with these words, since it has been shown that association value influences rate of learning. Therefore, they chose words that had previously been shown to have an average association value of 48.4% for subjects. In this manner they held the association value of the words constant across the two groups of subjects and eliminated any differential influence this variable might have had.

Ideally, the scientist would like to keep the amount or type of each extraneous factor identical throughout the experiment. This means that the same amount and/or type of the factor must be present for all subjects. Subjects in all groups must possess identical amounts of the variable at the beginning of the experiment as well as during the entire experiment. Variables that are noncontinuous, or variables that do not vary as a function of the independent variable or progress through the experiment, can meet the criterion of ideal constancy. Ideal constancy can be obtained with variables such as sex of the subject or rate of presentation of words, but not for factors such as interest or learning ability.

Such variables cannot be held completely constant because they are distributed along a continuum ranging from some very low point to some extremely high point. Therefore, it is difficult to select subjects who have an identical amount of a characteristic such as interest because our measuring devices are too crude to get more than an approximation. Constancy requires an exact measure. For many variables that range along a continuum, this requirement cannot be met. A second reason constancy cannot be met with all variables is that a number of the variables present in an experiment may change as the experiment progresses. Fatigue, motivation, interest, attention, and many other variables fall into this category. If these factors do vary, constancy would dictate that the magnitude of these changes has to be the same for all individuals. All subjects' degree of boredom or fatigue would have to increase and decrease simultaneously. Even if this were possible, which it is probably not, it is also possible that the waxing and waning of these factors influences the behavior measured by the dependent variable. Increased fatigue could and frequently does affect performance. If the waxing and waning of a variable such as fatigue, even though it occurs simultaneously and in the same amount for all subjects, affects the dependent variable of performance, constancy is not achieved; it would be impossible to determine what caused the variation in the dependent variable of performance. The variation could be due entirely to the independent variable, entirely to the waxing and waning of fatigue, or to a combination of these two. As you can readily see, a case such as this would not allow you to unambiguously identify the cause of the variation noted in the dependent variable. Constancy requires an equal amount and/or type of a factor in all subjects throughout the course of the experiment.

The ideal type of constancy, which was just discussed, is not always possible because of the inability to accurately measure the variable and because of the inability to keep all factors constant throughout the experiment. However, in most cases it is possible to eliminate the differential effects of these variables on the dependent variable and thereby allow the scientist to relate unambiguously the variation in the independent variable to the dependent variable.

How is constancy achieved, or how do we arrange factors in such a way as to have no differential influence on the result of the experiment? The only way constancy can be achieved is through control. Control means exerting a constant influence. If one wanted to control, or hold constant, the trait of dominance, one would attempt to make sure that this trait had an equal influence on all groups of subjects. In this way constancy would be achieved by exerting a constant influence.

Control, or achieving constancy of potential extraneous variables, is often not difficult to accomplish once the extraneous variables are identified. The difficulty frequently lies in identifying these variables. Before looking at the techniques for controlling extraneous variables, one must identify the variables that need to be controlled. The variables identified in this chapter do not run the gamut of extraneous variables but do represent the more salient ones.

Extraneous Variables to be Controlled

In experimentation the desired condition that the scientist strives for is constancy of all variables except the one or more variables that are deliberately being manipulated. Constancy is necessary to enable the scientist accurately to infer that the obtained effect is due to the variation in the independent variable. Campbell and Stanley (1963) state that experiments are internally valid when the obtained effect can unambiguously be attributed to the manipulation of the independent variable. In other words, if the effects obtained in the experiment are due only to the experimental conditions manipulated by the scientist and not to any other variables, the experiment has internal validity. To the extent that other variables have possibly contributed to the observed effects, the experiment is internally invalid.

In any experiment there are always some variables, other than the independent variable, that could influence the observed effects. These potentially confounding variables have to be dealt with or held constant and, in order to deal with them most effectively, we must have some knowledge as to what they are. Campbell and Stanley (1963) list a number of classes of variables that need to be controlled for internal validity to be attained.

History

The history variable operates in an experiment that is designed in such a way as to have both a pre- and postmeasurement of the dependent variable. History refers to the specific events, other than the independent variable, that occur between the first and second measurement of the dependent variable. These events, in addition to the independent variable, could have influenced the postmeasurement and therefore these history events become plausible rival hypotheses as to the change that occurred between the pre- and postmeasurement. Consider an attitude-change experiment. One of the typical procedures followed is to pretest subjects to identify their current attitude. An experimental condition is then introduced in an attempt to change the subjects' attitude, and a postattitude measurement is given to all subjects. The difference in the pre- and postattitude scores is typically taken as a measure of the effect of the experimental variable on the attitude. The difficulty with making this automatic assumption is that a certain amount of time typically exists between the pre- and postmeasure. It is possible that the subjects experienced events during this time that had an effect on their attitude, and that effect was reflected in the postmeasurement. If such a condition actually took place, the history variable, in addition to the experimental variable, may have influenced the observed effects, creating *internal invalidity*, since the history events would be plausible rival hypotheses.

A study by Watts (1967) can be used to illustrate history events. He investigated relative persistence of attitude change induced by actively writing an argument or reading an argument for one of three selected issues. Immediately after the active (writing) or passive (reading) participation, subjects took the pretest opinionnaire to measure the change induced by these two techniques. No difference existed in the initial opinion change generated by these two techniques. Actually, Watts modified the passive messages to attempt to insure that this initial attitude change would be identical in both conditions. Watts then waited six weeks and posttested the subjects to determine which of the two techniques would induce most persistence. Results revealed that subjects in the active participation condition not only maintained the change initially induced by that treatment condition but revealed increased opinion change. The subjects in the passive participation group regressed back toward the opinion they possessed prior to participation in the passive condition. From such results it is tempting to conclude that active participation produces greater persistence. However, six weeks intervened between pre- and posttesting and many events could have taken place during this time. Watts also realized this and took a look at the activities of the subjects during this time. He found that subjects in the active participation group tended to discuss and read about the attitude topic more than subjects in the passive condition. Thus, it seems as though the active participation condition may lead to other events, which influence persistence. It is these other events, the history events, that must be identified by the sensitive and alert investigator.

Generally speaking, the longer the time lapse between the pre- and posttest, the greater the possibility of history becoming a rival explanation. However, it must be recognized that short time lapses can also generate the history effect. If group data is collected, and an irrelevant

96   unique event such as an obstreperous joke or comment occurs between the pre- and the posttest, this event can have an influence on the posttest, making it a rival hypothesis.

Maturation

Maturation, as defined by Campbell and Stanley, refers to changes in the internal conditions of the individual that occur as a function of the passage of time. The changes include both biological and psychological processes such as age, learning, fatigue, boredom, and hunger, which are not related to specific external events but reside within the individual. To the extent that such changes affect the response made to the experimental treatment, internal invalidity exists. Consider a study that attempts to evaluate the benefits achieved from a Head Start program. Assume the investigator gave the subjects a preachievement measure at the beginning of the school year, and at the end of the school year gave them a postachievement measure. In comparing the pre- and postachievement measures she found that significant increases in achievement existed and concluded that Head Start programs are very beneficial. Such a study is internally invalid because there was no control for the maturational influence. The increased achievement could have been due to the changes that occurred with the passage of time. A group of equated children that did not participate in Head Start may have increased an equal amount. In order to determine the effect of a program such as Head Start, a control group that did not receive the treatment would also have to be included to control for the potential rival influence of maturation.

Liddle and Long (1958) conducted a study that did not seem to control for the maturational variable. They identified a group of "slow learner," culturally deprived children who had been unsuccessful in the first grade, and set up an experimental room to attempt to motivate and increase the amount these children learned. The investigators gave the children an initial intelligence test and assigned them a reading grade placement score. Toward the end of the second year in the experimental room, the Metropolitan Achievement Tests were administered and revealed "an improvement of about 1.75 years in less than two school years" (p. 145). Based on such evidence the authors suggest that an experimental room such as the one they developed enhances the learning of slow learners. One of the difficulties with this study is that maturational influences were not ruled out. These slow learners were two years older at the end of the study and therefore probably more mature; and, I suspect, some learning would definitely have taken place outside this experimental room. The difficulty is that

the investigators did not isolate the effect due *just* to the experimental   97
room but allowed many other variables to enter in, one of which may
have been maturation.

Instrumentation

Instrumentation refers to changes that occur over time in the measurement of the dependent variable. This class of variables does not
refer to subject changes but to changes that occur during the process of
measurement. Unfortunately, many of the techniques that we use to
measure our dependent variable are subject to change during the course
of the study. The measurement situation that is most subject to the
instrumentation source of error is one that requires the use of human
observers. Physical measurements show minor changes but human
observers are subject to influences such as fatigue, boredom, and
learning processes. In administering intelligence tests, the tester typically gains facility and skill over time, and many collect more reliable
and valid data as additional tests are given. Observers and interviewers
are frequently used to assess the effects of various experimental treatments. As the observers and/or interviewers assess increasingly more
individuals, they gain skill on the additional occasions. The interviewers may, for example, gain additional skill with the interview schedule
or with observing a particular type of behavior, producing shifts in the
response measure that cannot be attributed to either the subjects or the
treatment conditions. This is why studies that use human observers to
measure the behavioral characteristics of interest typically use more
than one observer and have each of the observers go through a training
program. In this way some of the biases inherent in making observations can be minimized, and the various observers can serve as checks
on one another to insure that accurate data are being collected. Typically, the data collected by the various observers have to coincide
before they are considered valid to help insure that they are as free as
possible from instrumentation effects.

Statistical Regression

Many psychological experiments, such as the attitude change experiment outlined under the history factor, require pre- and posttesting on
the same dependent variable measure or some other equivalent form
for the purpose of measuring change. Additionally, these studies frequently select only the two groups of subjects who have the extreme
scores, such as high or low attitude scores or—if conducting a rat study
on learning—high or low criterion scores on, say, maze-running abil-

98 ity. The two extreme scoring groups are then administered an experimental treatment condition, and a posttest score is obtained. In the examples just given, an attitude scale would be administered a second time, or the rats would be required to learn to traverse a second equivalent maze to determine if the experimental condition changed, in the one case, the subjects' attitudes or, in the other case, the rats' maze-running ability.

A variable that could cause the pre- and posttest scores of the extreme groups to change is statistical regression. This "refers to the fact that the extreme scores in a particular distribution will tend to move—that is, regress—toward the mean of the distribution as a function of repeated testing" (Neale and Liebert, 1973, p. 38). The scores of the high groups may become lower, not because of any treatment condition introduced, but because of the statistical regression phenomenon. Low scorers could show increases upon retesting because of statistical regression and not because of any experimental treatment effect. This regression phenomenon exists because the first and second measurements are not perfectly correlated. In other words, there is some degree of unreliability in the measuring device. Campbell and Stanley (1963, p. 11) explain the phenomenon in another, more down-to-earth manner.

> The more deviant the score, the larger the error of measurement it probably contains. Thus, in a sense, the typical extremely high scorer has had unusually good "luck" (large positive error) and the extremely low scorer bad luck (large negative error). Luck is capricious, however, so on a posttest we expect the high scorers to decline somewhat on the average, the low scorers to improve their relative standing.

Regression effects are, as can be seen, different from both maturation or history. They constitute a real source of possible internal invalidity, which must be controlled if any conclusive statement is to be drawn regarding the cause of the observed effects.

Selection

The selection bias exists when a differential selection procedure is used for placing subjects in the various comparison groups. Ideally, a sample of subjects is randomly selected from a population, and then these subjects are randomly assigned to the various treatment groups. When this procedure cannot be followed and assignment to groups is based upon some differential selection procedure, then possible rival hypotheses are introduced. Assume you wanted to investigate the relative efficacy of a given type of therapy on various types of psychotic behaviors. For your subjects you selected two groups of psychotic patients. After two months of therapy, progress in therapy was evaluated and you found that the subjects exhibiting one type of psychotic reaction improved significantly more than those with the other classification. With these results one is tempted to say that the therapy technique used is the agent that produced the difference in improvement between the two groups of psychotic patients. Such an inference is unjustified because there may be other differences between the two groups that would provide a better explanation of the observed difference. The psychotic patients who improved most may possess characteristics that predispose them towards more rapid improvement with almost any type of therapy. If this is the case, then it is these characteristics and not the type of therapy that was the cause of the more rapid improvement. Such difficulties are encountered when subjects are differentially selected based on a criterion such as type of psychosis. This corresponds to the difficulty with ex post facto studies which was discussed earlier.

Mortality

Mortality refers to the differential subject loss from the various comparison groups in an experiment. Most psychological experiments, both human and infrahuman, have to contend with this potential source of bias at some time. Physiological experiments involving electrode implantation frequently, if not almost always, experience subject loss due to the complications that may arise from the surgical procedures. Human experiments must contend with subjects not showing up for the experiment at the designated time and place or not participating in all the conditions required by the study. The difficulty arises not just because subjects are lost but because the subjects that are lost may produce differences in the groups that cannot be attributed to the experimental treatment. Consider the following example. Assume you want to test the effect of a certain treatment condition upon conformity. You know that past research has demonstrated that females conform to a greater degree than males so you control for this factor by assigning an equal number of males and females to two groups. However, when you are actually running the experiment, half of the females assigned to the group that does not receive the treatment condition do not show up, and half of the males assigned to the other group, the one receiving the treatment condition, do not show up. Statistical analysis reveals that the group receiving the treatment condition conforms significantly more than the group not receiving any treatment. Can you conclude that this significantly greater degree of conformity is due to the independent variable administered? Such an inference would be incorrect because more females were in the group receiving the experimental treatment and past research indicates they exhibit greater degrees of conformity. This variable, and not the independent variable, may have produced the observed significant difference.

Subject-Experimenter Effects to be Controlled

Any human experiment involves an interaction between an experimenter and a subject. In such a situation two roles can be identified, that of the experimenter and that of the subject. Each role has specific behavioral requirements and mutual expectations, which are held by each role member. These expectations should define the behavior that is appropriate for each member. When agreeing to take part in an experiment, a person is making an implicit contract to play the role of the subject. Theoretically, this means that the subject will listen to the instructions and perform the tasks requested to the best of his or her ability and as truthfully as possible. In reality, such an idealistic situation does not always exist because the subject has certain perceptions of the experiment which may alter behavior. The subject may want to comply and participate in the experiment but, because of certain perceptions and motives, may respond in several different ways. That is to say, there is an interaction between the way a person responds in an experiment and his or her motives and perception of the experiment.

Knowledge of the potential biasing effect of this social interaction between the subject and the experimenter has been known for some time. In 1933 Saul Rosenzweig made an intensive analysis of the social nature of the psychological experiment and very insightfully pointed out potential biases resulting from both the subject and the experimenter. The potential subject biases he pointed out are three. The first is *errors of observational attitude.* This is an error arising from a Titchenerian type of introspective analysis and is of little current concern. The second error identified was *errors of motivational attitude.* This error arises from the fact that a subject seldom reacts in a naive and humble way but "he entertains opinions about the experiment—what its purpose is and what he may reveal in it—instead of simply reacting in a naive manner. The causes of the opinion error are usually certain motives, such as curiosity and pride" (p. 343). In other words, Rosenzweig realized that the subject is not a passive organism. The third error identified was *errors of personality influence.* The error arises from the potential influence of the experimenter on the outcome of the experiment. Here Rosenzweig was addressing the fact that the experimenter's attributes as well as his or her unintentional behavior may affect the outcome of the experiment. This type of bias will be discussed extensively under the next section, "Experimenter Bias."

With the realization of these potential biases, it seems as though experimenters would have conducted research on this issue. Indeed there has been some research but the interest given this topic was so modest as really to classify it as an ignored topic. Adair (1973) believes that the reason for this neglect was the zeitgeist of behaviorism that existed up until the 1950s. Investigators who did recognize the influence of subject-experimenter interactions seemed to think that recognition was sufficient because they never pursued a systematic research program on this issue. It was not until the 1960s that intense interest was given to the social aspects of the psychological experiment.

Subject Bias

In an experiment the experimenter would like to have the so-called ideal subject. In other words, the experimenter would like to have naive subjects who bring no preconceived notions to the laboratory. Once in the laboratory they should accept our instructions and be motivated to respond in as truthful a manner as possible. While such an ideal view is great and it would be wonderful if such a situation existed, it does not. The subjects bring with them certain attitudes and predispositions which can alter their behavior in the experimental task. First of all, why do subjects participate in a psychological experiment in the first place? Is it because, as we may like to think, they are interested in advancing science? Probably not, although the subjects may be curious about the experiment and curiosity may be a motivator.

Jackson and Pollard (1966) found that about half of the subjects who volunteered for their sensory deprivation experiment listed curiosity as their primary reason. Jung (1971) states that the subjects' primary interest is in learning something about themselves. Cooperation in the psychological experiment is only infrequently a result of the subject's desire to benefit science. Instead, cooperation is attained from volunteering because subjects are curious, because they are paid to participate and they need money, they are pressured by friends or their instructor, or, as frequently occurs, compulsory participation is required by the course. Some research has been conducted to investigate the consequences of compulsory participation. This research (Argyris, 1968; and Gustav, 1962) has revealed that most subjects resent the requirement. Argyris (1968, p. 188) states that "the subjects were very

102 critical, mistrustful, and hostile to the requirement. In many cases they identified how they expressed their pentup feelings by 'beating the researcher' in such a way that he never found out." As you can see, "the subject does not enter the experiment as a tabula rasa but rather with a variety of positive and negative attitudes, expectations, and suspicions, any of which can distort his performance" (Schultz, 1969, p. 220).

SUBJECT MOTIVES.   When the subjects enter the laboratory they are not passive organisms responding just to the manipulation of the independent variable, but rather active organisms responding to many cues and trying to find out what the hypothesis is, especially since the experimenter frequently does not tell them, and if he or she does it is often false. Also, the experimenter is not just any person, but a *psychologist*, and psychologists are reputed to possess an uncanny ability to explore one's mind, thoughts, and feelings. In fact, a number of people have postulated a variety of motives that subjects may possess. Orne (1962) has taken the position that subjects want to cooperate with the experimenter and be the good subject. To accomplish this, they attempt to identify the hypothesis of the study and respond in a manner that will confirm the hypothesis. Riecken (1962), on the other hand, has advocated that a subject attempts to "put his best foot forward" in the sense of trying to appear in the best light possible. The subject assumes that there are certain responses that will be evaluated more positively than others, and attempts to determine what these are so that these and not the more negatively evaluated responses can be made. Rosenberg (1969) has taken a similar but more restricted view. He assumes that subjects approach the experiment with the expectation that their emotional stability will be evaluated. Once in the experiment the subject searches for cues that will confirm this expectation. If it is confirmed, the subject experiences evaluation apprehension, which is an anxious desire to be evaluated positively or at least not negatively. Subjects who experience evaluation apprehension make hypotheses, based on cues within the experiment, about how to respond in a manner that will yield an evaluation of being emotionally stable and then respond in this manner. Fillenbaum (1966) took a completely different point of view. He stated that subjects attempt to be faithful and follow instructions scrupulously. If they have any suspicions they will avoid acting upon them. The last subject role advocated is that of the negative subject (Masling, 1966; Jourard, 1968). This is the uncooperative and/or hostile subject who attempts to respond in a manner that would lead to a failure to support the hypothesis.

As you can see from the above discussion of subject motives, **103** virtually every possible motive has been advocated at some point in time, and research has been presented to support each subject motive. However, one has to wonder if all these motives are possible. Weber and Cook (1972), in their review of the literature, concluded that the evaluation apprehension motive received the most support. Subsequent research has not supported this. In fact, recent research (Kruglanski, 1975; Christensen, 1979; McGinley, Kaplan and Kinsey, 1975; Adair and Schachter, 1972; Sigall, Aronson, and Van Hoose, 1970; Spinner, Adair and Barnes, 1977; and Christensen, 1977) has basically refuted the existence of these subject motives.

If recent research does not support the previously advocated subject roles the question becomes, "What is the proper conceptualization of a subject's motive in the psychological experiment?" Christensen (1979) has reviewed the literature relating to subject motives and has revealed that a motive of positive self-presentation can account for all the prior literature relating to subject motives. This means that all prior postulated subject motives can be subsumed under the framework of a single motive of positive self-presentation. This would afford a more parsimonous explanation of the subject's motive in psychological research and parsimony is one of the goals for which we strive.

If it is true, as the literature suggests, that positive self-presentation is the dominant subject motive, this means that subjects in experiments search for ways to enhance themselves. They use the available demand characteristics to identify the type of response that will enable them to enhance themselves or present themselves most positively. Once they have identified the type of response that will maximize the possibility of self-enhancement, they engage in this type of response. By demand characteristics, I am referring to any of the cues available in an experiment that can serve to provide the subject with knowledge as to what the response is that will satisfy the motive of positive self-presentation. According to Orne (1962, p. 779) these cues include:

> The rumors or campus scuttlebutt about the research, the information conveyed during the original solicitation, the person of the experimenter and the setting of the laboratory, as well as all explicit and implicit communication during the experiment proper.

To illustrate this self-enhancement phenomenon consider the experiment conducted by Christensen (1977). He found that subjects who interpreted verbal conditioning as an attempt to manipulate their be-

104 havior resisted any behavioral manifestation of conditioning. This resistance was due to their viewing manipulation as being negative. If they did not demonstrate any conditioning, then they would reveal that they could not be manipulated and in this way present themselves most positively. Similarly, Bradley (1978) has revealed that individuals take credit for desirable acts but deny blame for undesirable ones to enhance themselves.

Conditions producing a positive self-presentation motive. The fact that subjects would assume a role when participating within an experiment supports the conception that many people have had about the effects of being part of an experiment. Just knowing that one is part of an experiment, and consequently, being observed, alters behavior regardless of one's attitudes or motivations about supporting or refuting the experimental hypothesis. Serving as a subject in an experiment is similar to being on stage or in front of a TV camera. While in front of a TV camera, most people do not act as they normally would, but produce behavior that ranges from being silly to being stilted. Likewise, being in an experiment may generate behavior that is more socially desirable, restrained, subdued, or defiant.

When such a tendency is coupled with the behavior that may be produced by attempts to use the demand characteristics of an experiment to generate the most favorable possible impression, it is easy to see how results may be produced that are only partially a manifestation of the independent variable.

In order possibly to control the interactive effects that exist between the subjects' behavior and their role in an experiment, it would be advantageous to know the conditions that alter subjects' behavior in their attempt to attain favorable positive self-presentations. Only when such conditions are identified can one construct conditions that would control for the confounding effect that may be produced by the positive self-presentation motive.

Tedeschi, Schlenker, and Bonoma (1977) provide some insight into the general conditions that may determine whether or not the self-presentational motive will exist within an experiment. They state that the self-presentational motive arises only when the behavior in which the subject engages is indicative of the subject's true intentions, beliefs, or feelings. If subjects believe that others view their behavior as being determined by some external source not under their control, then the positive self-presentational motive is not aroused. However, our experiments are seldom constructed so that the subjects would believe that others think their behavior is externally determined. Therefore, it seems that the positive self-presentational motive would exist in most research studies.

Given this state of affairs, the research (Christensen, 1979) reveals **105**
that subjects will respond in the most desirable fashion, or practice
self-enhancement, unless the experimenter has access to information
that reveals their self-enhancement responses to be inaccurate. For
example, if the experimenter asked subjects to estimate their intelligence, they would give high estimates if they thought the experimenter or others would never find out their true intelligence. However, if the subjects knew the experimenter could, and possibly would,
check to see how accurate the subjects' estimates were, then their
estimates would be considerably lower to avoid any self-deprecating
effect.

Christensen (1977) revealed the interactive effect that may exist
between the subjects' interpretation of the experimental procedures
and their positive self-presentational drive. He revealed that if subjects
interpret an experimental procedure as an attempted manipulation,
they will respond differently than subjects who do not make such an
interpretation, in an effort to enhance their self image. Therefore, the
conditions that produce a positive self-presentational confounding
influence on data can exist not only in the experimental procedures but
also in the subjects' interpretation of these experimental procedures.
This research on the factors influencing the subjects positive self-
presentational drive is very recent. Much more research needs to be
conducted in this area before we can have a good understanding of the
factors that alter one's perception of the type of response that leads to a
positive self-presentational drive. Only when such knowledge exists
can we construct techniques for controlling this potential bias.

Experimenter Bias

We have just seen that the subjects who are used in psychological
research are frequently not apathetic or willing passively to accept and
follow the experimenter's instructions. Rather, they have motives that
can have an effect upon the experimental results. In like manner, the
experimenter is not just a passive noninteractive observer but an active
agent who can influence the outcome of the experiment. We have only
recently focused attention upon this significant component of the
experiment. Friedman (1967, pp. 3–4) has appropriately stated that
psychology has, in the past

> implicitly subscribed to the democratic notion that all *experiment-
> ers* are created equal; that they have been endowed by their
> graduate training with certain interchangeable properties; that
> among these properties are the anonymity and impersonality
> which allow them to elicit from the same subject identical data
> which they then identically observe and record. Just as inches

were once supposed to adhere in tables regardless of the identity of the measuring instrument, so needs, motives, traits, IQs, anxieties, and attitudes were supposed to adhere to patients and subjects and to emerge uncontaminated by the identity and attitude of the examiner or experimenter.

Such a conception of the experimenter is highly inappropriate because research, as we shall see, has demonstrated biasing effects that are directly attributable to the experimenter. Take a look at the motives that the experimenter brings with him or her. First, the experimenter has a specific motive for conducting the experiment. The experimenter is a scientist and is attempting to uncover the laws of nature through experimentation. In performing this task certain perceptions of the experiment and the subject are developed. Lyons (1964, p. 105) states that the experimenter wants the subject to be the perfect servant. He or she wants intelligent individuals who will cooperate and maintain their position without becoming hostile or negative. The experimenter wants so-called perfect subjects who conform to some ideal image. It is easy to see why such a perception exists. The scientist seeks to understand, control, and predict behavior. To attain this goal, bias, such as that discussed under the subject bias, must be eliminated and the ideal subject does not have such bias. This, however, is an ideal perception and experimenters realize that it does not exist. Also, the experimenter has certain expectations regarding the outcome of the experiment. He or she has made certain hypotheses and would, therefore, like to see these confirmed. While this aspect of science is legitimate and sanctioned, it can, as we shall see, lead to certain difficulties. Additionally, journals have a bias toward publishing primarily positive results, which essentially means that studies that support the hypothesis have a greater chance of being accepted for publication. Knowing this, the experimenter has an even greater desire to see the hypotheses confirmed. Can this desire or expectancy bias the results of the experiment so as to increase the probability of attaining the desired outcome? Consider the fascinating story of Clever Hans. Clever Hans was a remarkable horse that could apparently solve many types of arithmetic problems. Von Osten, the master of Clever Hans, would give Hans a problem and then Hans would give the correct answer by tapping with his hoof. Pfungst (1911) observed and studied this incredible behavior. Careful scrutiny revealed that von Osten would, as Hans approached the correct answer, look up at Hans. This response of looking up represented a cue for Hans to stop tapping his foot. The cue was unintentional and not noticed by observers who attributed mathematical skills to him.

Observations such as that made by Pfungst of Clever Hans would seem to indicate that one's desires and expectancies can somehow be communicated to the subject and the subject will respond to them.

The research has suggested that subjects are motivated to present themselves in the most positive manner. If this is true, then the subtle cues presented by the experimenter in the experimental session may very well be picked up by the subjects and influence their performance in the direction desired by the experimenter. Consequently, the experimenter may represent a demand characteristic.

The experimenter, zealous to confirm his or her hypothesis, may also unintentionally influence the recording of data to support the hypothesis. Kennedy and Uphoff (1939) investigated the frequency of misrecording of responses as a function of subjects' orientation. Subjects, classified on the basis of their belief or disbelief in ESP, were requested to record the guesses made by the "receiver." The receiver was supposedly trying to receive messages sent by a transmitter. Kennedy and Uphoff found that, of the errors that were in the direction of increasing the telepathic scores, 63% were made by believers in ESP, whereas 67% of the errors that were in the direction of lowering the telepathic scores were made by disbelievers. Such data reveals that biased recording, unintentional as it may be, exists in some experiments.

Additionally, the experimenter is an active participant in the social interaction that occurs with the subject. As stated earlier, the experiment may be considered a social situation in which two roles, that of the experimenter and that of the subject, exist. The role behavior of the subject can vary slightly as a function of the experimenter's attributes. McGuigan (1963), for example, found that the results of a learning experiment varied as a function of the experimenter. Some of the nine experimenters used to test the effectiveness of the same four methods of learning found significant differences whereas the others did not. Such research reveals that certain attributes, behavior, or characteristics of the experimenter may influence the subjects' response in a particular manner.

The preceding discussion reveals that there are several ways in which the experimenter can potentially bias the results of an experiment. These biases can be dichotomized into two types, bias arising from the attributes of the experimenter and bias resulting from the expectancy of the experimenter.

EXPERIMENTER ATTRIBUTES.   Experimenter attributes refers to the physical and psychological characteristics of experimenters, which may interact with the independent variable to cause differential performance in subjects. Currently there exists a rather large body of data that reveals the differential influence produced by various aspects of experimenters. Rosenthal (1966) has summarized a great deal of this research and has proposed that at least three categories of attributes exist. The first represents *biosocial attributes*. Biosocial attributes

108   include factors such as the experimenter's age, sex, race, and religion. The second category proposed is *psychosocial attributes.* These attributes include the experimenter's psychometrically determined characteristics of anxiety level, need for social approval, hostility, authoritarianism, intelligence, and dominance, and social behavior of relative status and warmth. The third category proposed by Rosenthal represents *situational factors.* These situational factors include such things as whether or not the experimenter and subject have had prior contact, whether the experimenter is a naive or experienced experimenter, and whether the subject is friendly or hostile. Additionally, the characteristics or physical appearance of the laboratory may influence the outcome of the research study.

A great many biasing factors have been identified. Does this mean that experimenter attributes will always affect the experiment and lead to artifactual results? McGuigan (1963) says that there are three general answers to this question. First, the attributes of the experimenters may have absolutely no effect on the outcome of the experiment. Ideally, this is the type of situation that is desired. The second probability is that the experimenter attributes affect the dependent variable but the influence is identical for all subjects. Such a case would be of no concern, because all subjects were uniformly affected and therefore all experimenters would attain the same experimental results. The third case is one where the experimenter attributes differentially affect subjects. Here the results of the experiment would be partially a function of the experimenter who conducted the study. If, for example, a black experimenter found that subjects in an attitude change experiment responded in a significantly less prejudiced manner, whereas a significant change was not found by a white experimenter, one would have to conclude that the biosocial attribute of race differentially affected subjects' responses.

Psychologists are working on the problem of the influence of the experimenter's characteristics. From this research one should ultimately be able to identify when and what attributes will influence one's experiments. Jung (1971, p. 49) has stated that "the extent to which the variable can affect results may vary with the type of experiment, being stronger in social and personality experiments and weaker with psychophysical, perceptual, and sensory experiments." Psychologists need to work toward the goal of being able to identify where, under what conditions, and in what type of experiments experimenter attributes are confounding variables, for these variables, as well as other variables, may well account for some of the controversies that arise from failure to replicate previously published studies.

About the only experimenter attribute that has been investigated in sufficient depth to begin to answer these questions is the attribute of experimenter sex. Rumenik, Capasso, and Hendrick (1977) reviewed the literature relating to this attribute and "despite the sloppy methodological state of most research . . ." (p. 874) the data suggest that young children perform better for female experimenters on a variety of tasks. For adults, male experimenters seem to elicit better performance. Within a client-counselor relation the studies suggest that male counselors elicit more information-seeking responses whereas female counselors seem to elicit more self-disclosure and emotional expression.

Before anything definitive can be stated regarding the influence of experimenter attributes on specific types of research, it is necessary that researchers conduct studies which are methodologically sound. Specifically, they must attempt to overcome the deficiencies identified by Johnson (1976). This means that future research on experimenter attributes must overcome three deficiencies. First, they must control for the confounding influence of attributes other than the ones being studied. If sex of the experimenter is being studied, researchers must control for other attributes such as age, race, warmth, and need for social approval. Second, it is necessary to take into account and study the interactive influence of subject and experimenter attributes. For example, it may be that male and female experimenters of one ethnic group obtain different responses from male and female subjects of another ethnic group. Third, it is necessary for researchers to sample a variety of types of tasks. A given experimenter attribute may have an influence on one task whereas it may not on another task. Until such methodological refinements are made about the only thing that can be said about experimenter attributes is that they "may at times affect how subjects perform in the experiment, but we can rarely predict beforehand what experimenter attributes will exert what kind of effects on subjects' performance on what kinds of tasks" (Barber, 1976).

EXPERIMENTER EXPECTANCIES.   The term experimenter expectancies refers to the biasing effects that can be attributed to the expectancies the experimenter has regarding the outcome of his or her experiment. As noted earlier, experimenters are motivated by several forces to see their hypotheses validated. Therefore, they have expectancies regarding the outcome of the experiment. These expectancies can lead the experimenter to behave unintentionally in ways that will bias the results of the experiment in the desired direction. These unintentional influences can operate on the experimenter to alter his or her behavior and/or on the subjects to alter their behavior.

Effect upon the Experimenter.   It has been well documented that the expectancies we have can color our perceptions of our physical and social world. Research in social perception has repeatedly demonstrated the biased nature of our perceptions of others. With knowledge of such research it would be rather naive to assume that the expectancies of the experimenter did not have a potential influence on his or her behavior. In fact, there are several documented ways in which these expectancies have actually influenced the outcome of the experiment. The expectancies of the experimenter can lead him or her to record responses inaccurately but in the direction which supports the expectancies, as was noted in the ESP experiment conducted by Kennedy and Uphoff (1939). Recently, Rosenthal (1978) has summarized the results of 21 studies relating to this issue. These studies have revealed that, on the average, 60% of the recording biases favored experimenter expectancies. In one study 91% of the recording biases supported the experimenter's expectancies. Impressive as these percentages are, it is important to understand that the magnitude of these recording errors, both biased and unbiased, represent only a small portion of the overall number of observations made. Generally speaking, only about one percent of all observations are misrecorded and of this about two-thirds support the experimenters expectancies (Rosenthal, 1978). Such a rate of misrecording, even if the majority of them support the expectancies of the experimenter, is so small as to affect only infrequently the conclusions reached in a given study. Just because recording errors occur infrequently does not mean that experimenters can relax regarding this issue, because when this happens we run the risk of increasing such errors. Reviews such as the one conducted by Rosenthal (1978) reveal that when we attempt to avoid recording errors we are relatively successful. At least we are successful enough to avoid reaching an unfounded conclusion that can be directly traced to recording errors.

A second type of bias falling under the category of "effect upon the experimenter" involves the effects of expectancies upon interpretation of the data collected. Once the data is collected, the experimenter attempts to interpret or explain the data obtained from the experiment. Practically any set of data can be interpreted in different ways, depending upon the orientation of the person doing the interpreting. Robinson and Cohen (1954), for example, report finding differences in the psychological reports written for 30 patients by three examiners. Barber and Silver (1968) do not agree with the conclusion Rosenthal reaches regarding experimenter bias. This disagreement does not revolve around the validity of the data collected but around the interpretation of these data. The interpreter effects, though real, are not considered to be a serious methodological problem. The reason for this is that the data recorded are considered to be indisputable, while the interpretations of the recorded data are assumed to be private, that is, a function of the experimenter and his or her specific orientation. This is supported by the fact that the debates that occur in the literature seldom involve another's observations but often involve the interpretations that are placed on the observed data.

Effect upon the subject. It is relatively easy to see and accept the fact that the experimenters' expectancies may cause them to behave in ways that support their expectancies. It is not so easy to see how these same expectancies can influence the subject to behave in a way that would support them. Yet there is a body of research which is demonstrating just this influence. Remember that subjects seem to be motivated toward positive self-presentation. How do they know what response will maximize the possibility of achieving such a positive self-presentation? Somehow they make use of the demand characteristics surrounding the experiment. One of these demand characteristics seems to be the experimenter. The experimenter has certain expectancies that lead him or her unintentionally to behave in ways which convey these expectancies. Subjects pick up these subtle cues and respond accordingly. Mr. Von Osten, for example, conveyed to Clever Hans when he should stop tapping his foot. Rosenthal and his associates have devoted a great deal of attention to this source of bias. They have conducted many studies in which they demonstrate that the experimenter definitely can influence the results of the study in the direction of their hypothesis. To put it another way, the experimenter can influence the subjects' response in such a way that they will support the experimenter's hypothesis. For example, Rosenthal and Fode (1963) found that experimenters who expected to get high success ratings on previously judged neutral photographs actually got significantly higher ratings than experimenters who were led to expect that they would get low success ratings.

Do these biasing effects exist in different types of experiments in psychology? Initially one might think that the biasing effects of the expectancies of the experimenter upon the subject's response is limited to human types of experimentation, and more specifically to human experiments in such areas as social and personality psychology. As one may expect, most of the experiments investigating expectancy have been conducted on human subjects. However, Rosenthal (1966) summarizes the results of many studies which reveal that the bias exists for a wide variety of areas including learning studies (e.g., Hurwitz and Jenkins, 1966), ability studies (Larrabee and Kleinsasser, 1967), psychophysical studies (e.g., Zoble, 1968), reaction time studies (Silverman, 1968), inkblot test studies (e.g., Marwit, 1968), structured laboratory studies (e.g., Timaeus and Luck, 1968), and person perception studies (e.g., Fode, 1967). At least eight different areas of human research have found biasing effects to exist. Such evidence would seem

112 to suggest that experimenters would be wise to attempt to control for this bias since it is a definite source of potential internal invalidity.

But what about experimenters conducting animal research? Are they spared from this bias? Studies investigating this area, unexpected as it may seem, say no. Rosenthal and Fode (1963), for example, found that experimenters who were told they had been given rats specially bred for brightness obtained superior results to those obtained from experimenters given rats that, they were told, were specially bred for dullness. The rats were, in reality, not specially bred for any purpose but were assigned to experimenters in such a way as to minimize age differences of the rats.

The evidence presented by Rosenthal and others is consistent in indicating that the problem of the biasing effects of the experimenter is serious and needs to be dealt with. To deal most effectively with such biases we must know what is causing them. In other words, just how is the experimenter transmitting expectancies? In addressing this question Rosenthal considers the possibility of recording errors, particularly those biased in the direction of the expectancy. This would seem to be a particularly important issue since several studies (e.g., Johnson and Ryan, 1976) have revealed that recording biases can account for much of the so-called expectancy effects. Rosenthal (1976) directly confronted this issue and revealed that, in some studies, recording errors can account for some of the expectancy effect. However, they cannot account for all of it. To further support the fact that the experimenter expectancy bias cannot be reduced to a recording bias Rosenthal (1976) reviewed 36 studies which employed special techniques for the control of recording errors or deliberate cheating. He found that these studies were *more* rather than less likely to demonstrate the experimenter expectancy effect.

MEDIATION OF EXPECTANCY.   If recording errors and intentional biases are insufficient to explain the occurrence of expectancy effects, then how can they be accounted for? Rosenthal (1969) suggests that experimenters may communicate their expectancy by means of a nod, a glance, or a smile. Adair (1973, p. 41) concludes, based on a survey of studies focusing on the mediation problem, that "research has consistently demonstrated that paralinguistic (verbal) cues mediate bias effects." The experimenter may emphasize different key sections of the instructions, signaling the hypothesis to the subjects. Additional research has shown that factors such as number of glances between the experimenter and the subject are positively related to expectancy (Jones and Cooper, 1971) as well as is task ambiguity (Felton, 1971). Barber (1976) concludes that experimenter expectancies are mediated by the experimenter's facial and postural cues.

Little is currently known about the precise behaviors that communicate the expectancy effects. In human studies paralinguistic cues seem to be important. In animal studies differences in animal handling (Rosenthal and Fode, 1963) seem to be important. Yet there are many variables that need to be studied as they relate to expectancy effects. Rosenthal (1969) considers the possibility that the mediation takes place prior to, rather than during, the actual experiment since the greatest expectancy effects seem to occur during the subjects' initial responses. Despite these suggestions and some evidence to back them up, there are only a few ideas as to how expectancies are communicated. One of the difficulties operating in uncovering the source of communication may be that the mediating mechanisms vary for different tasks and different experimenters.

MAGNITUDE OF THE EXPECTANCY EFFECTS.   The influence of experimenter expectancies has repeatedly been demonstrated in a wide variety of contexts. Rosenthal (1976) states that about one-third of the studies conducted reveal the expectancy effect at the .05 significance level which is "about seven times more than we would expect if there were in fact no significant relationship between experimenter's . . . expectations and their subjects' . . . subsequent behavior" (p. 441–442). In spite of such evidence, the generality and pervasiveness of the phenomenon have not gone unchallenged.

Barber and Silver (1968) and Barber (1976), the strongest critics of the expectancy effect, charge that most of the studies supporting experimenter bias are weak. Their attack is focused on both statistical and methodological grounds. Barber and Silver (1968) state that the statistics are weak or inappropriate and that intentional bias of actual fudging or doctoring of data cannot always be ruled out. Barber (1976) has extended this attack by revealing that in some cases the expectancy effect can be reduced to a "failure to follow the procedure" effect. Other studies have produced equivocal results. Barber (1976) found that only 29% of the studies he reviewed, which had been published since 1968, demonstrated that experimenters could unintentionally affect the outcome of the experiment. This is a smaller percentage than that revealed by Rosenthal.

So what can be concluded from this discussion? Rosenthal conveys the impression that the experimenter bias is extremely strong and pervasive. Investigators such as Barber and Silver seem to have helped put the phenomenon in more realistic perspective by their negative evidence. From the available evidence it seems safe and reasonable to conclude that the biasing effects of experimenter expectancy can exist but that its magnitude is not quite as great as Rosenthal would have one believe. To the extent that it does exist, time and effort should be

114 taken to make as many precautions as possible against it. What is needed, as Levy (1969) suggests, is a taxonomy of situations (tasks or experiments) revealing where and to what extent experimenter bias exists.

Sequencing Effect to be Controlled

In an experiment at least two conditions must exist in order to establish variation in the independent variable. This variation can be in the form of a presence-versus-absence type of variation, or it could be obtained by varying the amount or type of a variable. In addition to making a decision regarding the manner in which the independent variable will be varied, the investigator must make a decision regarding how the subjects are to be used in the experiment. Here there are two choices. The investigator can randomly assign subjects to the various treatment groups or he or she can administer the various levels of variation of the independent variable to the same subjects. In a drug experiment having both a placebo and a drug condition, the experimenter could either randomly assign subjects to the placebo and drug conditions or have all subjects respond under both the placebo and drug conditions. While there is a definite advantage, which will be discussed at a later time, to having the same subjects respond in both treatment conditions, there is also a definite disadvantage. The disadvantage to this type of arrangement involves a sequencing effect.

The sequencing effect occurs when participation in one condition affects the response the subject will make in a subsequent treatment condition. If subjects first participate in the drug condition and then in the placebo condition, their response in the placebo condition may partially be a function of carry-over effects of the drug. If it is, then a sequencing effect has taken place. Sequencing effects occur any time the subject's response in one treatment condition is partially determined by participation in a prior treatment condition. This is a function of carry-over effects such as may exist with a drug experiment, or the result of practice received, or fatigue incurred, or any of a number of other possible conditions.

Additional Extraneous Variables to be Held Constant

In addition to the variables already discussed there are many others that could have an influence on a given experiment. These include such things as the subject's motivation and ability, and physical variables such as noise level and lighting. For example, a number of investigations (Page, 1968, 1969; Page and Kahle, 1976; and Page and Scheidt, 1971) have revealed that subject sophistication can have a confounding influence on the results produced in our psychological experiments. By subject sophistication I am referring to subjects' "familiarity with or sophistication in the subject matter, and methods of experimental psychology" (Page, 1968, p. 60). These investigators have revealed that a number of the effects that had previously been identified could not be replicated unless sophisticated subjects were used. Use of novice subjects resulted in a failure to find the effect. Page (1968), for example, could not replicate the Schafer and Murphy (1943) experiment without using sophisticated subjects. In this experiment it was found that subjects more frequently reported a pair of ambiguous human profiles that had previously been associated with winning over a pair that had been associated with losing money. However, Page (1968) found this difference to exist only for the sophisticated group. Such findings suggest that in some of our experiments we must control for the influence of subject sophistication to eliminate the possibility of our results being due to this extraneous variable. When we gain better understanding of the reason why subject sophistication alters the results of our experiments, we will be in a better position to state which experiments should control for this extraneous variable and which ones can disregard it. At the present time it is an empirical question as to which experiments are subject to this effect.

Additionally, the materials and/or apparatus used should also be constant for all subjects. If a piece of apparatus breaks down, it should be fixed rather than using a different and inappropriate or nonequivalent piece of apparatus. It would be impossible to list all of the variables that could possibly affect the experiment. A number of the more salient ones have been discussed. Beyond this the experimenter must use his or her own knowledge and foresight to anticipate potential sources of error and build in controls for them.

Summary

One of the most important tasks confronting the experimenter is to insure that the experiment is internally valid. To attain internal validity the experimenter must control for the influence of extraneous variables that could serve as rival hypotheses for explaining the effects produced by the independent variable. Ideally, attaining the desired control involves completely eliminating the influence of all extraneous variables. However, this is impossible in most cases. Therefore,

116 control most frequently refers to holding the influence of the extraneous variables constant across the various levels of the independent variable or variables. The task of maintaining constancy is difficult for some variables since they may vary as the subject progresses through the experiment. In spite of this difficulty, providing the desired control is aided by identifying the variables that need to be controlled. Some of the more salient variables that could influence the experiment and serve as rival hypotheses are as follows:

History. Any of the many events other than the independent variable that occurs between a pre- and a postmeasurement of the dependent variable.

Maturation. Any of the many conditions internal to the individual that change as a function of the passage of time.

Instrumentation. Any changes that occur as a function of measuring the dependent variable.

Statistical regression. Any change that can be attributed to the tendency of extremely high or low scores to regress toward the mean.

Selection. Any change due to the differential selection procedure used in placing subjects in various groups.

Mortality. Any change due to a differential subject lost from the various comparison groups.

Subject bias. Any change in performance that can be attributed to the subject's motives or attitudes.

Experiment bias. Any change in the subject's performance that can be attributed to the experimenter.

Sequencing. Any change in the subject's performance that can be attributed to the fact that the subject participated in more than one treatment condition.

Key Concepts

One way to test your mastery of the material that was presented in this chapter is to see if you know the meaning of the following terms. These terms were selected because they represent the key concepts. If you can define, identify, or otherwise explain each of the following terms without referring back to the material in the chapter, you can be **117** assured that you have mastered the basics of the material that was presented. Just in case you cannot recall the meaning of a given term, the page on which it can be found appears in parentheses beside it.

internal validity (p. 92)
constancy (pp. 92–93)
history (pp. 94–95)
maturation (p. 96)
instrumentation (p. 97)
statistical regression (pp. 97–98)
mortality (p. 99)
subject bias (p. 101)
good subject (p. 102)
evaluation apprehension (p. 102)
negative subject (p. 102)
positive self-presentation (p. 103)
demand characteristics (p. 103)
experimenter bias (pp. 104–105)
experimenter attributes (pp. 107–108)
experimenter expectancies (p. 109)
paralinguistic cues (p. 112)
sequencing effect (p. 114)
subject sophistication (p. 115)

Techniques for Achieving Constancy

6

In the previous chapter a number of classes of extraneous variables were discussed. The influence of such variables must be controlled or held constant to identify causation. It is the task of the experimenter to attempt to create groups of subjects that are equivalent in all respects except for the variation in the independent variable or variables. This means that some procedure or technique must be incorporated into the study that will, in effect, reduce to zero or near zero the influence of these potentially confounding variables. There are three ways in which the desired control can be attained. First, control can be attained through appropriate design of the experiment. One of the purposes of experimental design is to eliminate the differential influence of extraneous variables. The control function of appropriate designs will become evident in Chapter 7. A second means of attaining control involves making statistical adjustments through use of techniques such as analysis of covariance. However, such techniques are beyond the scope of the present text and therefore will not be discussed. A third means of attaining the desired control is to incorporate one or more of the available control techniques into the design of the experiment. This control technique is intimately related to control through appropriate design of the experiment since any control technique must be incorporated into the design of the experiment. However, control techniques are discussed separately to be able to illustrate more effectively the variables that they control and how they control these unwanted sources of variation. These control techniques will be discussed in the present chapter.

There are a number of techniques that have been developed for attaining the desired control. One point must be kept in mind. All of these techniques cannot and should not be incorporated into one study. Indeed, it would be impossible to do so. By the same token, it is frequently possible and advisable to use more than one of the techniques. The researcher must decide which of the possible extraneous variables could influence the experiment and, given this knowledge, select from the available techniques those that will allow him or her to attain the desired control. Failure to do so will create internal invalidity.

Randomization

Randomization is the most important and basic of all the control methods. It provides a control not only for known sources of variation but also for unknown sources of variation. In fact, it is the only technique for controlling unknown sources of variation. What is randomization? Randomization is a control technique that has the purpose of providing assurance that extraneous variables, known or unknown, will not systematically bias the results of the study. As Cochran and Cox (1957) have stated, "Randomization is somewhat analogous to insurance, in that it is a precaution against disturbances that may or may not occur and that may or may not be serious if they do occur. It is generally advisable to take the trouble to randomize even when it is not expected that there will be any serious bias from failure to randomize. The experimenter is thus protected against unusual events that upset his expectations" (p. 8).

How does randomization eliminate systematic bias in the experiment? Randomization refers to use of some clearly stated procedures such as tossing coins, drawing cards from a well-shuffled deck, or use of table of random numbers. In setting up an experiment which will provide for maximum control of extraneous variables one should, *ideally*, randomly select subjects from a population. The randomly selected subjects should then be randomly assigned to the same number of groups as there are experimental treatment conditions, and the experimental treatment conditions should then be randomly assigned to the experimental treatment groups. While this is the ideal arrangement, it is recognized that only infrequently can one randomly select subjects from a population. Random selection from a population is not, however, the crucial element for providing control, whereas random assignment of the subjects and treatment conditions is crucial. Random selection of subjects provides assurance of the fact that your sample is *representative* of the population from which it was drawn. Random selection, therefore, has implications for generalization of the results of the experiment back to the population.

The key word in this whole process of selecting and assigning subjects is *random*. The term *random* "may be used in a theoretical sense to refer to an assumption about the equiprobability of events. Thus a random sample is one such that every member of the population has an equal probability of being included in it" (Ferguson, 1966, p. 133). In a random selection of a sample of 100 subjects from a population of, say, college freshman, every college freshman would have had an equal chance of being included in the sample of 100. In like manner, random assignment of subjects to the experimental groups would insure that each sample subject had an equal opportunity of being assigned to each group.

In order to provide equiprobability of events it is necessary to use one of the randomization procedures that are available for use. The one most frequently used is the table of random numbers. When such a procedure is used, maximum assurance is provided for eliminating any systematic bias in the experimental results. This is because the random selection of subjects and random assignment of subjects and treatment conditions is assumed to result in random distribution of all extraneous variables. Consequently the distribution and influence of the extraneous variables would be about the same in all experiment groups.

Consider the following example using only random assignment of subjects: Professor X was conducting a study on learning. Intelligence naturally is correlated with learning ability so this factor must be controlled for or held constant. Let us consider two possibilities, one that provides for the needed control through uses of random assignment and the other that does not. Assume first that no random assignment of subjects exists (no control) but that the first ten subjects that showed up for the experiment were assigned to treatment Group A and the second ten subjects were assigned to treatment Group B. Assume further that, after running the experiment, the results revealed that treatment Group B learned significantly faster than treatment Group A. Is this difference due to the different experimental treatment conditions that were administered to the two groups or to the fact that the subjects in Group B *may* have been more intelligent than those in Group A? Assume further that the investigator also considers the intelligence factor to be a possible confounding variable and therefore gives all the subjects an intelligence test. The left hand side of Table 6.1 depicts the hypothetical distribution of IQ scores of these 20 subjects. From this table you can see that the mean IQ score of the people in Group B is 10.6 points higher than that of those in Group A. Intelligence is, therefore, a potentially confounding variable and serves as a rival hypothesis for explaining the observed performance difference in the two groups. To state that the treatment conditions produced the observed effect, potentially confounding variables such as the IQ difference have to be controlled.

One means of eliminating such a bias would have been to assign randomly the 20 subjects to the two treatment groups. Each subject, when showing up for the experiment, could have been randomly assigned to one of the treatment groups. The right hand side of Table 6.1 depicts the random distribution of the 20 subjects and their corresponding hypothetical IQ scores. Now note that the mean IQ scores for the two groups are very similar. There is only a 0.2 point IQ difference as opposed to the prior 10.6 point difference. For the mean IQ scores to be so similar, both groups of subjects had to have a similar distribution of IQ scores that results in controlling for the potential biasing effect of IQ. The IQ scores in Table 6.1 have been rank ordered to reveal this similar distribution.

Random assignment produces control by virtue of the fact that the variables to be controlled are distributed in approximately the same manner in all groups (ideally the distribution would be exactly the same). Since the distribution is approximately equal in all groups, the influence of the extraneous variables is held constant because they cannot exert any differential influence on the dependent variable. Does this mean that randomization will *always* result in equal distribution of the variables to be controlled? The control function of randomiza-

Table 6.1. Hypothetical distribution of twenty subjects' IQ scores.

GROUP ASSIGNMENT BASED ON ARRIVAL SEQUENCE				RANDOM ASSIGNMENT OF SUBJECTS TO GROUPS			
GROUP A		GROUP B		GROUP A		GROUP B	
SUBJECTS	IQ SCORES	SUBJECTS	IQ SCORES	SUBJECTS	IQ SCORES	SUBJECTS	IQ SCORES
1	97	11	100	1	97	3	100
2	97	12	108	2	97	4	103
3	100	13	110	11	100	6	108
4	103	14	113	5	105	12	108
5	105	15	117	13	110	7	109
6	108	16	119	9	113	8	111
7	109	17	120	15	117	14	113
8	111	18	122	10	118	16	119
9	113	19	128	19	128	17	120
10	118	20	130	20	130	18	122
Mean I Q Score 106.1		116.7		111.5		111.3	

Mean difference between the two groups: 10.6

Mean difference between the two groups: 0.2

tion stems from the fact that random selection and assignment of subjects also results in the random selection and assignment of the extraneous variables. Since every subject, and therefore the extraneous variables present, had an equal chance of being selected and then assigned to a particular group, the extraneous variables to be controlled are distributed randomly. But since chance determines the distribution of the extraneous variables it is also possible that, by chance, these variables are not equally distributed among the various groups of subjects. What I am saying is that bias can still exist when one uses the randomization procedure. The smaller the number of subjects with which one deals the greater the risk of this happening. However, randomization still *decreases* the probability of creating a biased distribution even if one has access only to a small group of subjects. Since the probability of the groups being equal is so much greater when one uses randomization it is an extremely powerful method for controlling extraneous variables. It is really the *only* method for control of unknown variables. All other control techniques are useful only with known extraneous variables. This is why it is necessary to randomize *whenever* and *wherever* possible even when one is using any of the other control techniques.

Matching

Randomization is the basic technique for achieving control and is generally considered to be a sufficient guard for internal validity. While it does provide the best guard against interpreting differences in the dependent variable as being due to variables other than the independent variable, it is not the best technique for increasing the sensitivity of the experiment. In any study it is desirable to demonstrate the influence of the independent variable regardless of how small its influence may be. Assume we wanted to isolate the potential effect of televised aggression on children's behavior. Assume further that the effect is one of increasing aggressive behavior in children (this has been found in a number of studies) but the amount of increase is small. In order to detect this small effect we need to construct an experiment that will be as sensitive as possible in order to isolate the effect of this variable. What needs to be done to obtain the desired increase in sensitivity? To answer this question we need to take a brief look at the way in which statistical techniques operate in assisting us in determining the probability of an observed effect being "real" (e.g., $p < 0.05$) or due to chance (e.g., $p > 0.05$). The primary mode by which these statistical techniques operate is to pit the variation due to the indepen-

124   dent variable (the numerator) against the variation that would be expected by chance (the denominator), or the amount of error variance. If the error variance (variation due to random fluctuation) is large relative to the amount of treatment variance (variation due to the independent variable), then it is concluded that the independent variable did not produce a significant effect. However, it is also possible that the independent variable did produce an effect but this effect was masked by the large error variance.

In order to increase the sensitivity of an experiment and thereby increase the probability of detecting an effect that actually occurs, it is necessary to somehow reduce the error variance. The best way in which the error variance can be reduced is to engage in some form of matching. The reason for this is that matching creates a correlation between the various treatment groups' scores on the dependent variable measure, which means that a systematic source of variation is created. This systematic source of variation can then be isolated and pulled out, which has the effect of reducing the error variance. This is because, without matching, systematic variation cannot be isolated and therefore is treated as error variation. Since pulling the systematic variation out results in a smaller amount of error variance without affecting the treatment variance, the ratio of treatment to error variance has improved and the chances of obtaining a significant treatment effect have increased. As the correlation between the variable or variables on which subjects are matched and the dependent variable measure increases, the amount of systematic variance that can be extracted also increases. The result is a greater reduction in the error term. Therefore, when matching, it is to the benefit of the investigator to select as the matching variables those which are correlated highest with the dependent variable.

A second benefit of matching is that the variables on which subjects are matched are controlled in the sense that constancy of influence is attained. If subjects in all treatment conditions are matched on intelligence, then the intelligence level of the subjects would be held constant and therefore controlled for all groups. Here we have two definite benefits which can accrue from matching. However, it is important always to remember that matching is no substitute for randomization. Randomization should still be incorporated whenever possible because it is not possible to attain an exact match on most variables and it is impossible to identify and match on all variables that could affect the results of the experiment.

There are a number of ways in which matching can be accomplished. The sections that follow should provide a rather thorough understanding of the matching technique.

Matching by Holding Variables Constant   125

One technique that can be used to increase the sensitivity of the experiment and control an extraneous variable is to hold the extraneous variable constant for all experimental groups. This means that all subjects in each experiment group will have the same degree or type of extraneous variable. If we are studying conformity, then sex of subjects needs to be controlled because conformity has been shown to vary with the sex of the subject. The sex variable could be controlled simply by using only male or female subjects in the experiment, which has the effect of matching all subjects in terms of the sex variable. If only male subjects are used, the sex is held constant and the sensitivity of the experiment is increased because the variation of male and female responses is not included in the measure of error variation. Aronson and Mills, as cited in Chapter 2, used this technique in their study by using only females as subjects. This matching procedure creates a more homogeneous subject sample since only subjects with a certain amount or type of the extraneous variable are included in the subject pool.

The technique of holding variables constant is widely used but is not without its disadvantages. Two can readily be identified. The first disadvantage is that the technique restricts the size of the subject population. Consequently, it may, in some cases, be difficult to find enough subjects that will agree to participate in the study. To illustrate this difficulty I will cite a study that was recently completed. This study investigated the influence of assistance given to single parents, taking care of their child or children or doing household chores, on their attitudes and perceived interactions with their child or children. Since the study was limited to single parents, we had to find volunteers for this study. After two weeks of advertising, 18 single parents had volunteered to participate in the study. If the study had not been limited to single parents, the subject pool from which we could have drawn would have been much larger, with the probable effect of *more* individuals volunteering for the study.

The second disadvantage is the more serious of the two since it pertains to the generalizability of the results of the study. The results of the study can be generalized only to the same type of subject that participated in the study. The results obtained from the single parent study can be generalized only to other single parents. Assume someone wanted to know if complete families (both parents present) would derive the same benefit from receiving the same type of assistance. One would have to conduct a similar study using complete families to provide an answer to this question. Results from such a study may indeed reach the same conclusions as that attained from single parents.

126　However, it is an empirical question and not one that can be answered through study of only single persons. The only way we can find out if the results of one study can be generalized to individuals of another population is to conduct an identical study using the second population as subjects.

The control technique of holding variables constant is widely used and has much to recommend it. However, when considering its use, one should keep in mind the limitations that go along with its use.

Matching by Building the Extraneous Variable into the Research Design

A second means of increasing the sensitivity of an experiment is to build the extraneous variable into the design of the experiment. Assume that we were conducting a learning experiment and wanted to control for the effects of intelligence. Also assume that we had considered the previous technique of holding the variable constant by selecting only individuals with IQs of 110 to 120, but thought it unwise and inexpedient to do so. In such a case we could select several IQ levels (e.g., 90 to 99, 100 to 109, and 110 to 120) and treat them as we would an independent variable. This would allow us to identify and extract the variation due to the intelligence variable. Intelligence, therefore, would not represent a source of random fluctuation, and the sensitivity of the experiment would be increased.

To provide further insight into this control technique, I will cite a study conducted by Kendler, Kendler, and Learnard (1962) which investigated the influence of age of the subjects on their use of internal mediating responses. Prior research conducted on this topic revealed that a discontinuity existed between the results obtained with rats and college students. Rats did not use mediational processes whereas college students did. Prior research also revealed that three- and four-year-old children do not reveal the mediational process whereas about half of the children between ages five and seven do. Such data suggested that a developmental process was involved in the use of internal mediating responses, which must be controlled for in order to avoid attaining contradictory results from various studies. Kendler, Kendler, and Learnard realized this so they controlled for age by building it into the design of their study. Children at five chronological age levels, three, four, six, eight, and ten years of age, were required to engage in a task that would reveal the existence of mediational responses. Consequently, they controlled for the age factor by matching children for five different age groups, creating homogenous groups, and then used these age groupings as an independent variable in the design of the study. In this way the age variable was controlled and its influence upon mediational responses was also revealed.

Building the extraneous variable into the research design seems **127** like an excellent technique for accomplishing the dual purposes of control and achieving increased sensitivity. There are two conditions that guide the use of this technique. The technique is recommended only if one is interested in the differences produced by the various levels of the extraneous variable, and/or the interaction between the levels of the extraneous variable and other independent variable or variables. In the hypothetical learning experiment, one might be interested in the differences produced by the three levels of intelligence and/or how these three levels of intelligence interact with the other variables in the experiment. In the Kendler, Kendler, and Learnard study, the primary reason for conducting the study was to investigate the differences produced by subjects of different ages. If the interest does not exist in such conditions, then another control technique would probably be more efficient. When such conditions are of interest the technique is excellent since it isolates the variation due to the extraneous variable. Consequently, the experimenter has simultaneously effected control as well as obtained information regarding the effects of the variable. This control technique takes a variable that can operate as an extraneous variable that biases the experiment and makes it a focal variable in the experiment in the form of an independent variable.

Matching by Yoked Control

The yoked control matching technique is one that is employed to control for the possible influence of the temporal relationship between an event and a response. Consider the widely quoted study conducted by Brady (1958) in which he investigated the relationship between emotional stress and development of ulcers. Brady trained experimental monkeys to press a lever at least once during every 20-second time interval to avoid receiving electric shock. The monkeys learned this task quite rapidly and only occasionally would they miss a 20-second time interval and receive a shock. The experimental monkey was, therefore, under the psychological stress of having to press the lever. However, the monkeys also received electric shock, which may induce ulcers. To be able to determine whether the monkeys developed ulcers from the psychological stress rather than the physical stress resulting from the cumulative effect of the shocks, a control monkey had to be included that would receive an equal number of shocks. This was easily accomplished. There was still one additional variable that needed to be controlled—the temporal sequence of administering the shocks. It may be that one temporal sequence of shocks produces ulcers whereas another does not. If the experimental and control monkeys received a different temporal sequence of shocks this difference and not the stress variable may be the cause of the ulcers. Consequently, both monkeys must receive the same temporal sequence to control this potentially confounding variable. To control for temporal relationships Brady placed the experimental and the control monkeys in yoked chain, whereby both monkeys would receive shock when the experimental monkey failed to press the lever during the 20-second time interval. In such a situation both animals received the event, in this case shock, at the same time. However, the experimental animal is the only one that determines when the shock occurs. The control animal could not influence the situation and essentially had to sit back and accept the fact that sometimes the shock was going to occur. In other words, the control animal was yoked to the experimental animal. In such a case, the only apparent difference between the experimental and control animals was the ability to influence the occurrence of the shock. If only the experimental animal produced ulcers, as was the case in this experiment, the ulcers would be attributed to the psychological stress.

The yoked control technique appears to be excellent for controlling the biasing effects of the temporal distribution of events. Church (1964), however, has revealed a source of bias that may inadvertently confound the results obtained from a study using this technique. According to Church, individual differences could also account for the observed difference between experimental and control groups. Assume, for example, that you were conducting an avoidance conditioning study (using classical conditioning procedures to train subjects to avoid a noxious stimulus) and were using a yoked control design to control for the potential biasing effect of the temporal distribution of presentation of the conditioned stimulus (CS) followed by the unconditioned stimulus (UCS). According to Church, such a study could be confounded by the fact that the experimental avoidance subject may condition faster or slower than the yoked control subject. Assume, for example, that you were conducting an experiment in which you were training a group of subjects to make the avoidance response of blinking their eyelids at the sound of a bell (CS) to avoid receiving a puff of air (UCS) to that eye. To control for the number and pattern of times that the puff of air was administered to the eye, you incorporated a yoked control group that received the puff of air each time the experimental avoidance group received it. According to Church, some people will condition or learn this task faster than others. If the experimental avoidance group learns it faster, you would conclude that the significant variable was the fact that the experimental avoidance group received the puff of air only when they didn't make the avoidance response. However, if the yoked control subjects condition faster, the experimental avoidance subjects will still be given sufficient trials to demonstrate conditioning. This would be more trials than needed by the control subject. In this case no difference would be noted between the two groups of subjects. As you can see, the results of the experiment could be altered by the placement of subjects which happen to condition fastest in either the experimental or control group. For this reason Church believes that the yoked control design leads to results that are ambiguous.

Based on Church's 1964 arguments, one would be advised to avoid the yoked control technique. However, Kimmel and Terrant (1968) have revealed that Church bases his arguments on assumptions that seem to be unwarranted. Therefore, the yoked control technique still appears to be a legitimate control procedure. In case the investigator is unduly disturbed by Church's arguments, Kimmel and Terrant have presented what they call a "reciprocal yoked control design," which effectively deals with the possible confounding discussed by Church. Interested investigators should read this article and use this design if they feel Church's arguments are sufficiently convincing.

Matching by Equating Subjects

A third technique that can be used to control extraneous variables and also increase the sensitivity of the experiment is to equate subjects on the variable or variables to be controlled. If intelligence needs to be controlled, then you need to make sure that the subjects in each of the treatment groups are of the same intelligence level.

Matching by equating subjects is very similar to matching by building the extraneous variable into the design of the study since both techniques attempt to eliminate the influence of the extraneous variable by creating equivalent groups of subjects. The difference lies in the procedure for creating the equivalent groups. The previously discussed method created the equivalent groups by establishing categories or levels of the extraneous variable into which subjects were placed and thereby creating another independent variable. The present method does not build the extraneous variable into the design of the study but matches subjects on the variable to be controlled, where the number of subjects is always some multiple of the number of levels of the independent variable. There are two techniques that are commonly used to accomplish this matching. Selltiz et al. (1959) labeled these two matching techniques the *precision control* technique and the *frequency control* technique.

PRECISION CONTROL.   The precision control technique requires the investigator to match subjects in the various treatment groups on a case-by-case basis for each of the selected extraneous variables. Scholtz (1973), for example, investigated the different defense styles which were used by individuals who attempted suicide versus those who did

130   not attempt suicide. All subjects were neuropsychiatric patients. The suicide subjects were identified as those individuals who, among other things, had attempted suicide during the past year. Nonsuicide attempters were also neuropsychiatric patients who had evidenced "no history of a suicide attempt nor marked suicidal ideation" (p. 71). These nonsuicide attempters were selected on the basis of their being able to be paired on selected variables with the suicide attempters on a case-by-case basis. For a nonsuicide attempter to be included in the study, the subject had to be of the same age, sex, race, marital status, diagnosis, and education as a suicide attempter. In other words, a nonsuicide attempter was matched with a suicide attempter on each of these variables. Matching on these variables resulted in 35 pairs of subjects.

The Scholtz study illustrates quite well the various advantages and disadvantages of the precision control matching technique. Before discussing them it should be pointed out that the Scholtz study was an ex post facto study since the subjects assigned themselves to the various groups. Consequently subjects could not be randomly assigned after being paired. In a truly experimental study, subjects would be matched and then randomly assigned to the different groups. As stated before, matching is never a substitute for random assignment. However, the Scholtz study does illustrate the precision control matching technique.

The principal advantage of the precision control technique is that it increases the sensitivity of the study since it ensures that the subjects in the various groups are equal on at least the variables on which they were paired. For this advantage of increased sensitivity to exist, the variables on which subjects are matched must, as we discussed earlier in this chapter, be correlated with the dependent variable. How much of a correlation should exist? Kerlinger (1973) states that matching is a waste of time unless the variables on which subjects are matched correlate greater than 0.5 or 0.6 with the dependent variable. This criteria holds only for linearly related variables. This corresponds to the data Billewicz (1965) obtained from his simulation experiments.

In spite of the excellent advantage that can be derived from the precision control technique, it also has several disadvantages. First, it is difficult to know which are the most important variables to match. In most instances there are many potentially relevant variables. Scholtz in his study, selected age, sex, race, marital status, diagnosis, and education, but many others *could* have been selected. Which ones should be selected? The variables that should be selected are those that correlate highest with the dependent variable but lowest with each other. To put it another way, select those variables that show the lowest intercorrelation but the highest correlation with the dependent variable.

A second problem encountered in precision control matching is that the difficulty in finding matched subjects increases disproportionately as the number of variables increases. Scholtz matched on six variables, which must have been very difficult. His task would have been much easier if matching had been attempted on only two variables, such as sex and age. In order to match individuals on many variables, one must have a large pool of subjects available in order to obtain a few who are matched on the relevant variables. Fortunately, the relevant variables are generally intercorrelated so the number that can be used successfully to increase precision is limited. Associated with the disadvantage of limiting one's supply of subjects is the fact that matching limits the generality of the results of the study. Assume you are matching on age and education and your final sample of matched subjects is between the ages of 20 and 30 and has attained only a high school education. Since this is the type of subject included in the study, you can generalize the results only to other individuals with the same characteristics.

A third difficulty is that some variables are very difficult to match in individuals. If having received psychotherapy was considered a relevant variable, an individual who had received psychotherapy would have to be matched with another person who had also received psychotherapy. Certain variables such as this one are difficult to match. A related difficulty is the inability of obtaining adequate measures of the variables to be matched. If we wanted to equate individuals on the basis of the effect of psychotherapy, we would have to measure such an effect. To the extent that an adequate measure is not available, matching cannot be very accurate.

The matching of individuals case by case has a number of difficulties associated with it. However, this form of matching can be very effective and useful in terms of increasing the sensitivity of the experiment. The point is that the advantages and disadvantages of the matching procedure must be carefully weighed in any research project. If the advantages outweigh the disadvantages, then it should be used.

FREQUENCY DISTRIBUTION CONTROL.   The precision control technique of matching is excellent for increasing sensitivity, but many subjects are frequently lost because they cannot be matched. The frequency distribution control technique attempts to overcome this disadvantage while retaining some of the advantages of matching. This technique, as the name implies, attempts to match groups of subjects in terms of overall distribution of the selected variable or variables rather than match on a case-by-case basis. If IQ were to be matched in this fashion, the two or more groups of subjects would have to have the same average IQ as well as the same standard deviation, skewness, etc., of IQ scores. This means that, generally speaking, the investigator

132 would select the first group of subjects and determine the mean, standard deviation, etc. of their IQ scores. Then another group which had the same statistical measures would be selected. If more than one variable was considered to be a relevant variable on which to match subjects, the groups of subjects would have to have the same statistical measures on both of these variables. The number of subjects which are lost using this technique would not be as great because each additional subject would contribute to producing the appropriate statistical indices rather than requiring each subject to be identical to another subject on the relevant variables. Consequently this technique is more flexible in terms of being able to use a particular subject. Some subjects would naturally be lost when attempting to construct the matched groups; however, the number would be much less than when matching case by case.

The major disadvantage of matching by the frequency distribution control method is that the combinations of variables may be mismatched in the various groups. If age and IQ were to be matched, one group may include old subjects with high IQs and young subjects with low IQs, whereas the other group may comprise the opposite combination. In such a case the mean and distribution of the two variables would be equivalent but the subjects in each group would be completely different. This disadvantage naturally exists only if matching is to be conducted on more than one variable.

Counterbalancing

Counterbalancing is the technique which is used to control for sequencing effects. Sequencing effects can occur when the investigator elects to construct an experiment in which all subjects serve in each of several experimental conditions. Under these conditions there are two types of effects that can occur. The first type of effect that can occur is an *order effect.* Order effects arise from the *order* in which the treatment conditions are administered to the subjects. Assume you are conducting a verbal learning experiment in which the independent variable is rate of presentation of nonsense syllables. Nonsense syllables with a 50% level of meaningfulness are randomly assigned to three lists. The subject has to sequentially learn list S—the slow list where the syllables are presented at 6-second intervals, then list M—the moderate list where the syllables are presented at 4-second intervals, and finally list F—the fast list because the syllables are presented at 2-second time intervals. In such an experiment there is the possibility that practice with the equipment, learning the nonsense syllables, and/or just general familiarity with the surroundings of the experimental environment may enhance performance. Let us assume that one or more of these variables does enhance performance and that the increment due to the order effect for subjects progressing from list S to M is four units of performance and two units of performance when progressing from list M to list F. The left half of Table 6.2 depicts these order effects. As can be seen, order effects could affect the conclusions reached since performance increments occurred in the learning of these two lists that were due entirely to order effects.

You should also be aware that when the increment in performance is due to order effects, the particular sequence of the list is irrelevant. We could reverse the order of the lists and the increments in performance would still occur in the same ordinal position as is shown in the right half of Table 6.2

Increments due to order effects are strictly due to the fact that the subject is gaining familiarity and practice with the whole experimental environment. Other experimental factors, such as the time of testing (morning, noon, or night), may produce the order effect. In any event, one should be able to see that such effects must be controlled to avoid reaching false conclusions.

The second type of sequencing effect that can occur is a *carry-over effect.* Carry-over effects occur when performance in one treatment condition is partially dependent upon the conditions which precede it. D'Amata (1970) provides an excellent example of carry-over effects. He illustrated this with a simulated experiment designed to investigate the influence of monetary reward (5, 10, or 15 cents) on performance. In this type of study it is possible that when subjects serve in all three conditions, performance in a particular treatment condition would be partially a function of the conditions that precede it. A dime may be more rewarding when it is preceded by five cents than when it is preceded by fifteen cents. "Let us simplify the analysis by assuming that the carry-over effects from one condition to another will be directly proportional to the difference in the monetary rewards of the two

Table 6.2. Hypothetical order effects.

	LIST LEARNED				REVERSED ORDER OF LIST		
	S	M	F		F	M	S
Increment in Performance	0	4	2		0	4	2

134   conditions. We will assume that going from *A (5 cents)* to *B (10 cents)* or from *B* to *C (15 cents)* results in a positive carry-over (increment in performance) of two units, whereas traveling in the reverse direction results in the same amount of carry-over effect but negative in sign, i.e., leads to a decrement in performance of two units. Transitions from *A* to *C* and from *C* to *A* both result in four units of carry-over effects, positive and negative, respectively" (p. 53), [italics mine].

Table 6.3 illustrates the carry-over effects that would occur in such a case. The table illustrates that the carry-over effects for any one treatment condition are a function of the preceding treatment conditions. Such effects need to be controlled to identify unambiguously the effects due to the independent variable.

The order effects and carry-over effects are potential sources of bias in studies in which the subject partakes in several treatment conditions. In such cases the sequencing effects need to be controlled, and counterbalancing is often resorted to in an attempt to control for these effects. Therefore, we shall take a look at counterbalancing techniques. You also need to realize that the counterbalancing techniques have disadvantages associated with them in terms of statistical analysis. The more advanced student who has a rather good statistical background is referred to Gaito (1958, 1961) for a discussion of these statistical dangers.

Table 6.3. Calculation of assumed carry-over effects in six sequences. (From Experimental psychology methodology: Psychophysics and learning by M. R. D'Amato. Copyright 1970, McGraw-Hill. Used with permission of McGraw-Hill Book Co.)

	VALUE OF THE INDEPENDENT VARIABLE		
SEQUENCE	*A* (5 cents)	*B* (10 cents)	*C* (15 cents)
ABC	0	2	2
ACB	0	−2	4
BAC	−2	0	4
BCA	−4	0	2
CAB	−4	2	0
CBA	−2	−2	0
Total	−12	0	12

Intrasubject Counterbalancing: the ABBA Technique

The intrasubject counterbalancing technique attempts to control for sequencing effects by having each subject take the treatment effect first in one stated order and then in the reversed order. In an experiment that employed two treatment conditions, A and B, subjects would first respond under one order, AB, and then under the reversed order BA, providing an ABBA sequence. In other words, each subject would respond under each treatment condition twice. The results for the two A conditions and the results for the two B conditions are then combined for each subject, returning the experiment to a two-treatment condition experiment. Results obtained for each treatment condition can then be compared to determine if the responses differ. Any observed difference would not be due to the carry-over effect or order effect since they would have been equalized or held constant across groups.

To illustrate, assume that each subject increments his or her performance by one unit for each treatment condition in which he or she participates solely due to sequencing effects. If the ABBA technique is employed, these sequencing effects will be constant across treatment conditions and therefore controlled. This constant influence is illustrated in the top half of Table 6.4.

For both the A and B treatment conditions performance was increased by a constant amount of three units. Therefore, sequencing

Table 6.4. Sequencing effects for the ABBA technique.

	TREATMENT CONDITION			
Linear Sequencing Effect				
	A	B	B	A
Sequence effect	0	1	2	3
A sequence effect $0 + 3 = 3$				
B sequence effect $1 + 2 = 3$				
Nonlinear Sequencing Effect				
Sequence effect	0	4	6	8
A sequence effect $0 + 8 = 8$				
B sequence effect $4 + 6 = 10$				

136 was controlled. Note, however, that the sequencing effect was linear in the sense that a constant increment was added to performance in each successive position in the sequence. Would the *ABBA* technique control for carry-over and order effects if they were not linear? The answer is no. The *ABBA* method is based on the assumption that the sequencing effects are linear or constant for each successive position in the sequence. (This assumption also exists for the complete and incomplete counterbalancing methods to be discussed later.) If a constant effect is not attained, the sequencing effect will differentially affect the results, as is also revealed in Table 6.4. In this case the sequencing effects are not controlled because 10 units of performance increment occurred in condition *B* and only 8 units occurred in condition *A*. This was because the sequence effect was twice as powerful when progressing from the first *A* condition to the first *B* condition versus the remainder of the conditions. Can such differential sequence effects be controlled? The answer depends upon whether you are considering carry-over effects or order effects.

Differential order effects can be held constant by having each treatment condition appear in every possible position in the sequence. This means that a *BAAB* sequence in addition to an *ABBA* sequence must be included to control nonlinear order effects. Half of the subjects could then be assigned to each sequence. To illustrate, let us assume that each subject increments two units in performance after participating in the first treatment condition and one unit in performance after participating in each subsequent treatment condition due just to order effects. If both the *ABBA* and the *BAAB* sequences were employed, the results appearing in Table 6.5 would occur. The total order effect for both treatment conditions is equal, which means that the effect is held constant. Actually this represents a combining of intrasubject with intragroup counterbalancing.

Table 6.5. Control for order effects using intrasubject counterbalancing.

	SEQUENCE I				SEQUENCE II			
	A	*B*	*B*	*A*	*B*	*A*	*A*	*B*
Order effect	0	2	3	4	0	2	3	4

Total *A* order effect $0 + 2 + 3 + 4 = 9$

Total *B* order effect $2 + 3 + 0 + 4 = 9$

It is not as easy to control for differential carry-over effects, which frequently defy control. This is because the carry-over may vary as a function of the treatment conditions that precede it. Such a condition was illustrated earlier in the example of a simulated experiment designed to test the influence of monetary reward on performance. Table 6.3 shows the assumed carry-over effects. Note that the carry-over effect for any one treatment condition varied as a function of the particular treatment conditions that preceded it. Also note that the total carry-over effects for the treatment conditions are not identical. Here then is a case where carry-over effects are not controlled. When carry-over effects are linear, they can be controlled by the *ABBA* sequence, but in nonlinear cases such as this, they cannot. The investigator who suspects such a situation should consider use of some other technique, such as the precision control technique; otherwise, the carry-over effects serve as a rival hypothesis.

Intragroup Counterbalancing

Intragroup counterbalancing differs from intrasubject counterbalancing in that groups of subjects are counterbalanced rather than individual subjects. Therefore, the intragroup technique attempts to control sequencing effects over groups of subjects. As such, it represents a more efficient technique, particularly when more than two treatment conditions exist. The two approaches to intragroup counterbalancing will be discussed separately.

COMPLETE COUNTERBALANCING. The complete counterbalancing technique is distinguishable by virtue of the two requirements that it must meet. First, every possible sequence of the various treatment conditions must be enumerated. Second, every sequence that is enumerated must be used. To illustrate these two requirements, assume we were conducting an experiment in which we had three treatment conditions—A, B, and C. To meet the first requirement we would have to enumerate all possible sequences of these three values. This would yield six different sequences: *ABC, ACB, BAC, BCA, CAB,* and *CBA.* If we then proceeded to use all six sequences, we would have completed the second requirement.

If the complete counterbalancing technique were selected for use in a given study, all possible sequences of the various treatment conditions would be enumerated and a *different* group of subjects would take each sequence of treatment conditions. Herein lie two interrelated disadvantages of this technique. We have seen that an experiment that uses three treatment conditions results in six different sequences. However, as the number of treatment conditions increases arithmeti-

138 cally, the number of corresponding sequences increases factorially. With four treatment conditions 24 (4 × 3 × 2 × 1) sequences are enumerated; with five treatment conditions 120 (5 × 4 × 3 × 2 × 1) are enumerated. So the first difficulty with complete counterbalancing is that the number of enumerated sequences rapidly becomes very large. The second and related difficulty is that the number of subjects needed increases proportionately as the number of sequences increases. This is because the number of subjects needed is always some multiple of the number of sequences enumerated. In a three-treatment condition experiment six sequences are enumerated, which means that the number of subjects employed must be some multiple of 6, i.e., 6, 12, 18, 24.

How well does the complete counterbalancing technique control for sequencing effects? For an answer we need to consider order effects and carry-over effects separately. The influence of order effects is controlled very effectively because every treatment condition has occurred at each possible position in the sequence. To verify this, look at Table 6.3 and note that every condition (A, B, or C) precedes and follows every other condition for every possible combination. A, for example, has preceded and followed B and C for all combinations of A, B, and C. But what about carry-over effects? These are controlled only if they are linear for all sequences. If they are not—as illustrated in Table 6.3— then complete counterbalancing does not provide adequate control.

From the above it should be readily apparent that complete counterbalancing has several disadvantages. First, the number of subjects must always be some multiple of the total number of possible sequences. Second, the total number of possible sequences increases in a disporportionate relation to increases in the number of experimental conditions. Third, nonlinear carry-over effects are not adequately controlled. For these reasons it is frequently impractical to use the method of complete counterbalancing.

INCOMPLETE COUNTERBALANCING.   Incomplete counterbalancing derives its name from the fact that all possible sequences of treatment conditions are not enumerated. The criterion that incomplete counterbalancing must meet is that, for the sequences enumerated, each treatment condition must appear an equal number of times in each ordinal position. Also, each treatment condition must precede and be followed by every other condition an equal number of times.

To illustrate the incomplete counterbalancing method, let us assume that we have 4 experimental conditions (A, B, C, and D) and we want to counterbalance the order in which they are administered to subjects. Whenever the number of treatment conditions is even, as is the case with four experimental conditions, then the number of coun-

terbalanced sequences equals the number of treatment conditions. The
sequences are established in the following way. The first sequence is
established by the following procedure: 1, 2, n, 3, $(n - 1)$, 4, $(n - 2)$, 5,
and so forth, until we have accounted for the total number of treatment
conditions. In our example using four treatment conditions, the first
sequence would be *ABDC*, or 1, 2, 4, 3. If your experiment consisted of
6 treatment conditions, the first sequence would be *A, B, F, C, E, D*, or
1, 2, 6, 3, 5, 4. The remaining sequences of the incomplete counterbalancing technique are then established by incrementing each value in
the preceeding sequence by 1. For example, in the 4 treatment condition example the first sequence was *A, B, D, C*. The second sequence
would consist of incrementing each value by 1, with the resulting
sequence being *BCAD*. Naturally, for the last treatment condition, *D*,
you do not proceed to *E* but go back to *A*. Such a procedure results in
the following set of sequences for the 4 treatment condition example:

SUBJECT	SEQUENCE
1	A B D C
2	B C A D
3	C D B A
4	D A C D

If the number of treatment conditions is odd, as with five treatment conditions, the criterion that each value precede and follow every
other value an equal number of times is not fulfilled if the above
procedure is followed. For example, using the above procedure the
following set of sequences would exist:

SEQUENCE
A B E C D
B C A D E
C D B E A
D E C A B
E A D B C

In this case each treatment condition appears in every possible
position but, for example, *D* is immediately preceded by *A* twice but
never by *B*. To remedy this situation, 5 additional sequences must be
enumerated that are exactly the reverse of the first 5 sequences. In the
5 treatment condition example, the additional 5 sequences would
appear as follows:

SEQUENCE

D C E B A
E D A C B
A E B D C
B A C E D
C B D A E

When these 10 sequences are combined, the criteria of the incomplete counterbalancing are met. Consequently, the incomplete counterbalancing technique provides for control of order effects. Also, an economy in number of subjects is obtained because of the smaller total number of sequences. In the four treatment condition situation, the total number of subjects required is some multiple of 4 rather than 24 as would be the case with the complete counterbalancing technique.

What about carry-over effects? Are they controlled any better using this technique than using complete counterbalancing? The answer, as you may suspect, is *no* when the carry-over effects are nonlinear. Therefore, intragroup counterbalancing does not provide for control of nonlinear carry-over effects.

Randomized Counterbalancing

The randomized counterbalancing technique differs from the previous two techniques of counterbalancing in terms of the procedure used to generate the sequence of experimental conditions the subject takes. The randomized counterbalancing technique, as the name implies, randomly selects the sequence for each subject. If four experimental conditions exist in the experiment, the sequence given to each subject is determined by chance. If 20 subjects are used in the experiment, then 20 sequences are randomly selected and randomly assigned to each subject. This method assumes that the order and carry-over effects are controlled by randomly distributing them. Confidence in such an assumption is increased as the number of subjects increases. This is why Zimney (1961) states that at least 60 subjects should be included in an experiment before the randomized counterbalancing method is used.

Now that I have discussed counterbalancing techniques at some length I want to correct a misperception I may have created—that these counterbalancing techniques are widely used. The fact is that the trend seems to be away from the use of these techniques. The biggest contributor to this state of affairs seems to be due to the increased use of analysis-of-variance designs. One of these designs, the Latin Square Design, represents the counterbalancing technique and, therefore, effects maximum control over sequencing effects. In spite of this, I

believe the preceding discussion of counterbalancing illustrates more   **141**
clearly what sequencing effects are and how they need to be controlled.

Control of Subject Bias

We have seen that subjects' behavior in the experimental situation can
be a function of the perceptions and motives they bring with them in
addition to the influence of the experimental treatments. It seems as
though subjects are motivated to present themselves in the best possible light. If the demand characteristics suggest that a particular type of
response would allow them to fulfill this motive, the subjects' responses would be a function of their own motives rather than a function of the experimental treatment conditions. Such a situation would
produce internal invalidity and, therefore, the demand characteristics
that may operate within the experiment must be controlled.

There are a number of techniques that may be used to control or
minimize demand characteristics. These techniques, which will be
discussed, cannot be used in all types of experiments; they are presented so that the experimenter can choose the one or ones that will be
most appropriate for the particular study being conducted.

Double Blind Placebo Model

One of the best techniques for controlling demand characteristics is to
use the double blind placebo model. This model requires that one
"devise manipulations that appear essentially identical to subjects in
all conditions"[1] and that the experimenter does not know which group
received the placebo condition or the experimental manipulation.

If you were conducting an experiment designed to test the effects
of a given drug on reaction time, one group of subjects would receive
the drug and the other group of subjects would receive a placebo. In this
way both groups of subjects would think they had received the drug
and this would yield constant expectations. The experimenter must
not know whether a given subject received the drug or placebo to avoid
communicating the expectancy of a given response. In this way the
experimenter is blind in terms of not knowing which subjects received
the drug. Drug research has for some time recognized the influence of

1. Reprinted by special permission from Aronson-Carlsmith, "Experimentation in Social
   Psychology," *The handbook of social psychology*, Second Edition, Volume Two,
   1968, edited by Lindzey-Aronson, Addison-Wesley, Reading, Mass., p. 62.

142 patients' expectations and beliefs on their experiences subsequent to taking a drug. For this reason drug research consistently uses this model to eliminate subject bias.

Beecher (1966) used this technique and found no difference in pain alleviation between a placebo group which was administered a weak saline solution and a drug group which was administered a large dose of morphine. Such results ran counter to a large body of previous research. However, Beecher communicated with another experienced drug researcher who revealed that demand characteristics probably existed in the prior studies. This researcher said that he "found that as long as he knew what the subject had received, he could reproduce fine dose-effect curves; but when he was kept in ignorance, he was no more able than we were to distinguish between a large dose of morphine and an inert substance such as saline" (p. 841). In cases such as this the subject knows the correct response and responds accordingly.

Use of the double blind placebo model precludes any systematic subject bias on the effect of the experiment because the same demand characteristics exist for both groups. Any bias that does exist is therefore held constant across all groups so that any difference can be attributed to the independent variable. Unfortunately many types of experiments cannot use such a technique because all conditions cannot be created so that they appear identical to subjects in all respects. Such a difficulty is frequently encountered in many types of experiments and in such cases other techniques must be employed.

Deception

One of the more common attempts to solve the problem of subject bias is by use of deception in the experiment. Deception involves providing all subjects with a hypothesis that is unrelated to or orthogonal to the real hypothesis. In this sense almost all experiments contain some form of deception ranging from minor deceit to an elaborate attempt to hide the true hypothesis. Most experiments use minor deceit in the form of an omission or slight alterations of the truth. Gagné and Baker (1950), for example, in their investigation of transfer of training refrained from telling the subjects anything about the purpose of the study. The instructions given to subjects pertained directly to the task at hand. Subjects did, however, have knowledge of the fact that the experiment was concerned with learning but they did not know that it was concerned with transfer of training. At the other end of the continuum, there are experiments that use an extremely elaborate procedure to ensure that subjects not only do not know the hypothesis, but have unrelated or orthogonal hypothesis.

The previously discussed experiment conducted by Aronson and Mills is an example of such an experiment. They used deception

repeatedly in this study. At just about every stage of the experiment **143**
some type of cover for the real purpose was given. Is it better to use
deception, or just refrain from giving any rationale or hypothesis for
the tasks to be completed in the experiment, as was illustrated by
Gagné and Baker in their study? It seems as though providing subjects
with a false, but plausible, hypothesis is the preferred procedure because the subjects may have their curiosity satisfied and not try to
devise their own hypotheses. If a plausible hypothesis is not given,
each subject will probably try to figure out a hypothesis, which may
not be identical for all subjects and could create a source of subject
bias.

The rationale underlying the deception approach to controlling for
subject bias is that an attempt is made "to provide a cognitive analogy
to the placebo."[2] In a placebo experiment all subjects think they have
received the same independent variable. In the deception experiment
all subjects receive the same false information of what is being done. In
this way the subjects are all provided with an identical hypothesis
which should produce relatively constant subject biasing effects across
all levels of the independent variable. Since any subject source of bias
is held constant it could not operate as a rival hypothesis for the
differences found in the various treatment groups.

Disguised Experiment

The disguised experiment represents exactly what the name suggests.
An experiment is conducted in a context that does not communicate to
the subjects that they are in an experiment. This means that a procedure has to be established so that the independent variable as well as
the dependent variable can be administered without telling the subjects that they are in an experiment. Abelson and Miller (1967) conducted such a study in their investigation of the influence of a personal
insult on persuasion. The experimenter, disguised as a roving reporter,
approached a subject seated at a park bench. The experimenter explained to the subject that he was conducting a survey on a particular
issue. The individual was asked to give an opinion regarding the issue,
and then the person seated next to him or her—an experimental
confederate—was asked for his views on the same issue. In one treatment condition the confederate derogated the subject before expressing
an opposite point of view. The experimenter then obtained a second
measure of the subject's opinion to assess the influence of the confed-

2. Reprinted by special permission from Aronson-Carlsmith, "Experimentation in Social
Psychology," *The handbook of social psychology*, Second Edition, Volume Two,
1968, edited by Lindzey-Aronson, Addison-Wesley, Reading, Mass., p. 63.

144 erate's insult. In this study you can see that the whole experiment is disguised in the sense that the subjects have no way of knowing that they are participants. Consequently, demand characteristics are minimal if they exist at all.

The disguised experiment has much to recommend it and is an excellent way of controlling subject bias. But it is not without its limitations. First, there are numerous studies which cannot be disguised in this way. Second, most disguised experiments would have to be field studies as was Abelson and Miller's study. Associated with field studies is the difficulty of controlling extraneous variables. The third area of difficulty is an ethical one. The subject had not been informed that he or she was to participate in an experiment and therefore was not given the option of declining participation prior to being approached. This whole topic of ethical issues will be discussed in detail in a later chapter.

Independent Measurement of the Dependent Variable

This technique requires the experimenter to measure the dependent variable in a context that is completely removed from the manipulation of the independent variable. One of the typical ways this is accomplished is by manipulating the independent variable within the context of one experiment and measuring the dependent variable at some later time within the context of another unrelated experiment. Carlsmith, Collins, and Helmreich (1966) conducted a study which illustrates this procedure. They were investigating the influence of one's attitude toward a task if one were paid various amounts of money to state that the boring task performed was actually interesting. All subjects performed the tasks required of them and thought they had completed the experiment when they were asked to participate in another study conducted by a different group of individuals. This second study in which the subjects participated was actually a bogus study set up especially to measure the subjects' attitudes toward the boring task they completed in the first experiment. Such a situation would minimize subject bias because the subjects would think they were participating in another study (assuming there was nothing about the procedure that would arouse the subjects' suspicions) and would form hypotheses relative to this new study. Consequently, any biasing effects should not systematically influence one group over another.

This technique is good when it can be used. One of the major difficulties with the technique is that the dependent variable must be capable of being independently measured. For many studies, this cannot be accomplished because the independent and dependent variable are interdependent. There is also an ethical issue involved here since subjects are not told the true purpose of the experiment.

Procedural Control or Control of Subject Interpretation

The four techniques just discussed are excellent techniques for control of most of the demand characteristics present in the experiment. They control for such demand characteristics as knowledge of being in an experiment or whether one is in the experimental versus the control group. However, they do not control for the differential interpretation that different subjects may place on the experimental procedures. Under conditions such as verbal conditioning it has been shown (Christensen, 1977) that subjects respond differently to this task depending upon how they interpret the verbal reinforcer. If they interpret it as an attempt on the part of the experimenter to manipulate their behavior they will not demonstrate verbal conditioning. However, if such an interpretation is not made, they will behaviorally demonstrate verbal conditioning.

In other experiments slightly different procedures must be followed in order to vary levels of variation of the independent variable. For example, Sigall, Aronson, and Van Hoose (1970), in an attempt to vary the hypothesis that subjects held about the experiment, told one group of subjects that they expected more rapid performance during the second trial of the experiment than they had achieved during the first pretest trial. A second group of subjects was told that slower performance was expected on the second trial due to the dimly lit room they were in, the boring task they were confronted with, and so forth. The factor that Sigall et al. did not count on was that subjects in this second group did not interpret the instructions the way Sigall et al. wanted them to. Subjects, in spite of the instructions, did not view this as a justification for slowing down. Instead, with their orientation toward positive self-presentation, they interpreted the boring task and dimly lit room as challenges to rapid performance and proceeded to engage in rapid performance. As you can see, the manipulation that experimenters present to subjects is interpreted by subjects in light of their orientation toward positive self-presentation. Given such an orientation, it is necessary to eliminate a differential interpretation of how to behave to present oneself in a positive manner. If, in all levels of variation of the independent variable, the behavior used to promote a positive self-image was the same, then constancy and control would have been achieved regarding this subject motive. However, if this is not the case then control has not been achieved. What is needed is an assessment of the types of situations or instructions that would alter

146   subjects' interpretation of how to present themselves in the most positive manner. This information unfortunately is in its infancy.Therefore, at the present time, it is necessary to consider each experiment separately and try to identify if the subjects would respond differentially to the levels of variation in the independent variable in an attempt to satisfy their motive of positive self-presentation.

Orne (1969) has provided several quasi controls which can be used to assist in isolating the differential demand characteristics to which subjects may react in the different treatment combinations of an experiment. The most helpful of these quasi controls seems to be the postexperimental inquiry. The postexperimental inquiry is exactly what it say it is. After completing the experiment, the subject is questioned regarding the essential aspects of the experiment. Subjects should be questioned about their perceptions of the experiment. What did the subject think the experiment was about? What did he or she think the experimenter expected to find? What type of response did the subject attempt to give and why? How does the subject think others will respond in this situation? Such information will help reveal the factors underlying the subject's perception of his or her response. Naturally this is not a foolproof method since we generally have only a dim idea about what influenced our behavior.

Control of Experimenter Effects

Experimenter effects have been defined as the unintentional biasing effects that the experimenter can have on the results of the experiment. The experimenter is not a passive noninfluential agent in an experiment but an active, potential source of bias. This potential bias seems to exist in most types of experiments even though it may not be quite as powerful as Rosenthal purports it to be.

Page and Yates (1973) have revealed that 90% of the respondents they surveyed felt the implications of experimenter bias for psychology were serious. Additionally, 81% of the respondents felt that experimenter-related controls should be major criteria for publishability of studies. Such data suggest that psychologists in general consider the experimenter bias effect to be of importance in psychological research. The logical extension of this is that researchers would incorporate techniques to control for such potential biasing effects. Wyer, Dion, and Ellsworth (1978) have stated that problems such as experimenter bias are widely understood in social psychology and it is assumed "that most persons who submit papers to JESP avoid these problems as a matter of course" (p. 143). In spite of this Silverman (1974) concluded, from his survey, that "despite all of the rhetoric and data on experi-menter effects, it appears that psychologists show little more concern for their experimenters as sources of variance as they might for the light fixtures in their laboratories" (p. 276). Based on such data, it appears to be quite important to present and emphasize the utilization of controls for experimenter bias.

Control of Recording Errors

Errors resulting from the misrecording of data can be minimized if the person recording the data emphasizes, and consciously remains aware of, the necessity of careful observations to insure the accuracy of data transcription. An even better approach would be to use multiple ob-servers or data recorders. If, for example, three individuals were inde-pendently used to record the data, after the data had been recorded, discrepancies could be noted and resolved to generate more accurate data. Naturally all data recorders could err in the same direction which would mask the misrecording. But the probability of this occurring is remote, which results in the fact that multiple recorders would yield a greater percentage of accurate observations. This procedure could be improved even further if the data recorders were kept blind regarding the experimental conditions in which the subject was responding (Rosenthal, 1978).

The best means for controlling recording errors, although not possible in all studies, would be to eliminate the human data recorder and have responses recorded by some mechanical or electronic device. In some research laboratories the subject's responses are automatically fed into a computer.

Control of Experimenter Attribute Errors

At first glance there seems to be a simple and logical solution to the problem created by experimenter attributes. Throughout much of this text I have referred to control in terms of constancy. Most extraneous variables cannot be eliminated so they are held constant and in this way a differential influence is not exerted on the subjects' responses in the various treatment groups. In like manner, the influence of experi-menter attributes could be held constant across all treatment condi-tions. Some experimenters, because of their attributes, may obtain more of an effect than other experimenters. But this increased effect should be constant across all treatment groups. Therefore, the influence of the experimenter attributes should not significantly affect the *mean differences* between the treatment groups. To illustrate, assume a cold and a warm experimenter independently conduct the same learning study and that the warm experimenter obtains an average of three units more learning from subjects in each of the two treatment groups than does the cold experimenter as shown in the top half of Table 6.6. Note that the mean difference between Groups A and B is identical for both experimenters, indicating that they would have reached the same conclusions even though each obtained different absolute amounts of learning. In such a situation, the effects of the experimenter attributes would not have had any influence on the final conclusion reached.

Control through the technique of constancy does imply that the variable being held constant—experimenter attributes in this case—produces an equal effect on all treatment groups. If this assumption does not exist or if the experimenter's attributes interact with the various treatment effects, control has not been achieved. If, in the above example, warm experimenters obtained an average of 8 units of performance from subjects in Group A and 21 units of performance from subjects in Group B, whereas the cold experimenter obtained identical performance from subjects in both treatment groups (as shown in the bottom half of Table 6.6), we would not have controlled for the influence of the experimenter attributes. In this case the two experimenters would have produced conflicting results. Unfortunately, we do not know which attributes interact with numerous independent variables that exist within psychology. Since we do not know how much difference would be exerted by various experimenters, a number of individuals (e.g., McGuigan, 1963; Rosenthal, 1966) have suggested that several experimenters be employed in a given study. The ideal but impractical recommendation is that a random sample of experimenters be selected to conduct the experiment.

Table 6.6. Hypothetical data illustrating the mean difference in learning obtained from a warm and a cold experimenter.

EXPERIMENTERS	EXPERIMENTAL GROUPS		MEAN DIFFERENCE
	A	*B*	
Experimenter Attributes Controlled			
Warm	10	20	10
Cold	7	17	10
Experimenter Attributes Not Controlled			
Warm	8	21	13
Cold	17	17	0

If more than one experimenter were employed in an experiment, evidence could be acquired as to whether or not there was an interaction between the treatment conditions and an experimenter's attributes. If identical results were produced by all experimenters, one would have increased assurance that the independent variable and the experimenter attributes did not interact. However, if the two or more experimenters produced different results, we would know that an interaction existed, and also we might be able to identify the probable cause of the interaction. In any event, without using more than one experimenter, we would never know about the possible interaction effects that might occur.

Since such interaction effects do occur in some studies, several individuals (e.g., McGuigan, 1963) have recommended that the experimenter should be studied as an independent variable. Lyons (1964), however, feels this merely complicates the issue, since an experimenter with given attributes still has to study the influence of other experimenters' attributes and certain investigators may find an influence of certain attributes whereas others may not. How far back can we push the problem? The solution that Lyons proposes is to automate the experiment and thus get rid of the experimenter. But even if this solution is employed, some human contact is still necessary in the form of recruiting subjects and greeting them before turning them over to the automated section, for example. Also, automation is not always possible or feasible and is often expensive.

Aronson and Carlsmith (1968) believe that the experimenter is frequently necessary in an experiment to eliminate bias, as well as potentially producing it. They argue that the experimenter can help standardize the extent to which all subjects understand the instructions. Jung (1971) also states that the experimenter may be necessary to detect the occurrence of unanticipated phenomena that could affect the outcome of the experiment, and identify ways of improving the experiment. In the final analysis, the possible gains of having a live experimenter must be weighed against the possible bias that he or she may produce.

As you can see from the above discussion we do not as yet have a good means, since automation frequently cannot be used, for controlling the potential artifactual influence of the experimenter. To obtain this knowledge we must conduct experiments that systematically vary experimenter attributes, and types of psychological tasks as well as subject attributes. It may be that subject and experimenter attributes interact in some fashion to produce artifactual results (Johnson, 1976). While it is well and good to state that additional research is needed to identify the situations that require control of experimenter attributes, this provides little direction or assistance to the investigator who must use live experimenters. Johnson (1976) has provided some suggestions in this regard. Based on his review of the literature, he has found that the experimenter attributes effect can be minimized if one controls for "those experimenter attributes which correspond with the psychological task" (p. 75). In other words, if the experimenter attribute is correlated with the dependent variable, then it should be controlled. On hostility-related tasks it is necessary to hold the experimenters' hostility level constant. In a weight reduction experiment, the weight of the therapist may be correlated with the success of the program. Therefore, it would be necessary, at the very least, to make sure the therapists were of approximately the same weight to identify the relative effectiveness of different weight reduction techniques. Such an attribute consideration may not, however, have an artifactual influence in a verbal learning study. As you can see, at the present time it is necessary for the investigator to use his or her judgment as well as any available research to ascertain if the given attributes of the experimenters may have a confounding influence on the study.

Control of Experimenter Expectancy Error

Rosenthal and his associates have presented a rather strong argument for the existence of experimenter expectancy effects in most types of psychological research. In spite of the fact that certain individuals, notably Barber and Silver (1968), present arguments against Rosenthal, it would seem to be important to devise techniques for eliminating bias of this type. There are a number of techniques that can be used for eliminating, or at least minimizing, expectancy effects. Generally, they involve automating the experiment and thereby getting the experimenter out of the experimental situation so he cannot transmit cues, or keeping the experimenter ignorant of the condition the subject is in so appropriate cues cannot be transmitted. Rosenthal (1966) discusses such techniques, several of which will now be presented.

THE BLIND TECHNIQUE.   The blind technique actually corresponds to the experimenter half of the double blind placebo model. In the blind technique the experimenter knows the hypothesis but he is blind as to which treatment condition the subject is in. Consequently, the experimenter could not unintentionally treat subjects in one group differently than those in another group.

Rosenthal (1966) has even taken the blind technique one step further and suggested that what we need is a professional experimenter. The professional experimenter would be a trained data collector analogous to the laboratory technician. This person's interest and emotional investment would be in collecting the most accurate data possible and not in attaining support of the hypothesis. Even if you wanted to keep the hypothesis from this individual, it would be very difficult to do so, as revealed by Rosenthal et al. (1963). Even if we were successful in such an endeavor, these experimenters would probably develop their own. However, since this person's primary interest would be in collecting accurate data, he or she would have less incentive to bias the results and therefore would probably not be as much of a biasing agent. As Rosenthal has stated, this idea has already been implemented with survey research and may have merit for experimental psychology. However, Page and Yates (1973) have revealed that most psychologists are not favorably disposed toward this alternative.

At the present time the blind technique is probably the best procedure for controlling experimenter expectancies. However, there are many studies in which it is impossible to remain ignorant of the condition the subject is in. In such cases, the next best technique should be employed—the *partial blind technique.*

PARTIAL BLIND TECHNIQUE.   In cases where the blind technique cannot be employed, it is still frequently possible to keep the experimenter ignorant of the condition the subject is in for a portion of the experiment. The experimenter could remain blind while initial contact was made with the subject and during all conditions prior to the actual presentation of the independent variable. When the treatment condition was to be administered to the subject, the experimenter could use some technique, such as pulling a number out of a pocket, that would designate which condition the subject was in. Therefore, all instructions and conditions preliminary to the manipulations would be standardized and expectancy minimized, since the experimenter would not know which subject would be in what condition. Aronson and Cope (1968) used this procedure in investigating the attraction between two people who share a common enemy. The experimenter explained the purpose of the study and instructed each subject in the performance of a task. After the task had been completed the subject was randomly assigned to one of two experimental conditions. This was accomplished by having the experimenter unfold a slip of paper—given to him or her just prior to running the subject—that stated the subject's experimental condition. Only at this point did the experimenter have any knowledge of the subject's experimental condition. Consequently the experimenter was blind to this point.

While this procedure is only a partial solution, it is better than having knowledge of the subjects' condition throughout the experiment. If the experimenter could leave the room immediately following administration of the independent variable and allow another person, one who was ignorant of the experimental manipulations administered

152   to the subject, to measure the dependent variable, the solution would come closer to approaching completeness. Again, in many experiments this is not possible because the independent and dependent variables cannot be temporally separated.

AUTOMATION.   A third possibility for eliminating expectancy bias is to totally automate the experiment. This could operate for both animal and human research. Indeed numerous animal researchers currently use automated data collection procedures. Many human studies could also be completely automated by having instructions written, tape recorded, filmed, or televised, and by recording responses via timers, counters, pen recorders, or some similar device. These procedures are easily justified to the subject on the basis of control and standardization and minimize the subject-experimenter interaction. Johnson and Adair (1972) have provided some evidence that automation can reduce expectancy effects for male experimenters. Videbeck and Bates (1966) have demonstrated that the computer can be used to replace totally the experimenter.

Complete automation, via such approaches as the computer, are restricted by such practical considerations as cost of equipment and programming. Cost considerations would also prohibit total automation of animal research. In most cases the experimenter has to transport his animals to and from the home cages as well as feed and care for them. Seldom is this operation totally automated. With human research, Aronson and Carlsmith (1968) make the point that the experimenter is not always a biasing agent but can also operate to eliminate bias. When the experimenter's participation is considered vital, Rosenthal (1966) states that his or her behavior should be as constant as possible and experimenter-subject contact and interaction should be minimal. In spite of these limiting factors, psychological experiments are becoming increasingly automated. With each passing year we find increasing numbers of electronic devices manufactured for use in our experiments. However, at the present time, few of them totally remove the experimenter from the experimental environment.

Likelihood of Achieving Control

So far we have looked at a number of categories of extraneous variables that need to be controlled, and we have looked at a number of techniques for controlling them. Do these control techniques allow us to achieve the control that is desired? Are the control techniques effective? The answer to these questions seems to be both yes and no.

The control techniques are effective, but they are not 100% effective.   **153**
Also, we do not know exactly how effective they are. If we are controlling by equating subjects on some phenomenon then the effectiveness
of the control is dependent upon such factors as the ability of the
measure, e.g., an intelligence test, to measure intelligence. Likewise,
the effectiveness of control through randomization is dependent upon
the extent to which the random procedure equated the groups. Since
subjects were randomly assigned to groups, it is also possible that the
factors that affect the experiments were unequally distributed between
the groups, which would result in internal invalidity.

The point is that we can never be certain that complete control has
been effected in the experiment. All we can do is increase the probability that we have attained the desired control of the extraneous variables that would represent sources of rival hypotheses.

Summary

In conducting an experiment that attempts to identify a causal relationship, one of the very important tasks that must be accomplished
by the experimenter is to control for the influence of extraneous variables. One of the ways in which this can be accomplished is to use one
or more of the control techniques available to the experimenter. Of all
the available control techniques none is more important than randomization. This technique is extremely valuable because it provides
control for unknown as well as known sources of variation by distributing them equally across all experimental conditions. In this way the
extraneous variables exert a constant influence which in effect results
in control.

The matching technique represents another but less powerful control technique in terms of ability to equate groups of subjects on all
extraneous variables. The prime advantage of the matching technique
is that it increases the sensitivity of the experiment by reducing error
variance. Additionally, it provides control on those extraneous variables which are matched. There are four basic matching techniques.
One technique, matching by holding variables constant, produces control by including in the study only subjects with a given amount or
type of an extraneous variable. Certain extraneous variables are,
therefore, totally excluded from the study, which means they cannot
influence the results. A second matching technique involves building
the extraneous variable into the design of the experiment. In this case
the extraneous variable actually represents another independent variable, which means that its effect on the results is noted and isolated

154   from the effect of other independent variables. The yoked control matching technique is a very restrictive type of technique in the sense that it controls only for the temporal relationship between an event and a response. It accomplishes this by having a yoked control subject receive the stimulus conditions at exactly the same time as does the experimental subject.

The last matching technique involves equating subjects in each of the experimental groups on either a case-by-case method (precision control) or by matching the distribution of extraneous variables in each experimental group. Regardless of which approach is used, the matching technique represents an attempt to generate groups of subjects that are equated on extraneous variables which are considered to be of greatest importance.

The counterbalancing technique is one which attempts to control for both order and carry-over sequencing effects. Order effects exist where a change in performance arises from the order in which the treatment conditions are administered, whereas carry-over effects refer to the influence that one treatment condition has on performance under another treatment condition. Three counterbalancing techniques can provide some control over sequencing effects. Intrasubject counterbalancing involves counterbalancing subjects, whereas intragroup counterbalancing refers to counterbalancing groups of subjects. These two techniques are effective in controlling for all sequencing effects except nonlinear carry-over effects. The randomized counterbalancing technique involves randomly assigning a sequence of experimental conditions to each subject. Sequencing effects are supposedly controlled because they are randomly distributed, but many subjects are needed to have confidence in this procedure.

Subject bias has also been shown to be a potential source of bias in psychological experiments, as has experimenter bias. The most effective method of controlling experimenter and subject bias is to use the double blind placebo model. However, it is not possible to use this technique in most experiments. Other means of controlling subject bias include deception, disguising the experiment, and obtaining an independent measurement of the dependent variable because use of these techniques decreases the demand characteristics of the experiment, which reduces the subject's ability to bias the results of the study. Experimenter bias can be minimized by including some technique that conceals from the experimenter the treatment condition the subject is in or eliminates an experimenter-subject interaction. Such techniques include automation, the blind technique, and the partial blind technique.

After all of these control techniques have been considered for a given study and the appropriate ones used, one is still not 100% sure that all extraneous variables are controlled. The only sure thing that can be said is that more control exists after use of these techniques than would exist without their use.

Key Concepts

One way to test your mastery of the material that was presented in this chapter is to see if you know the meaning of the following terms. These terms were selected because they represent the key concepts. If you can define, identify, or otherwise explain each of the following terms without referring back to the material in the chapter, you can be assured that you have mastered the basics of the material that was presented. Just in case you cannot recall the meaning of a given term, the page on which it can be found appears in parentheses beside it.

> randomization (pp. 119–120)
> equiprobability of events (p. 120)
> matching (pp. 123–124)
> error variance (p. 124)
> systematic variation (p. 124)
> yoked control (pp. 127–128)
> precision control (pp. 129–130)
> frequency distribution control (pp. 131–132)
> counterbalancing (p. 132)
> order effect (p. 132)
> carry-over effect (p. 133)
> *ABBA* counterbalancing (p. 135)
> complete counterbalancing (pp. 137–138)
> incomplete counterbalancing (pp. 138–139)
> randomized counterbalancing (p. 140)
> double blind placebo model (p. 141)
> deception (p. 142)
> postexperimental inquiry (p. 146)
> blind technique (p. 150)
> partial blind technique (p. 151)
> automation (p. 152)

General Research Design

In Chapter 4, design was defined as the outline, plan, or strategy one conceives in an attempt to answer the research question. Consequently, research design has as one of its purposes the specification of how to proceed in seeking an answer to the research question. It helps specify such things as how to proceed in collecting data and how to analyze the data. Design also has as its purpose the control of unwanted variation. One of the ways it accomplishes this is to incorporate one or more of the control techniques discussed in Chapter 6. Another is to incorporate a control group. The significance of the control group will be discussed in detail later in the chapter, and the manner in which it assists in achieving control will be discussed in conjunction with the various research designs.

To illustrate the purposes of research design, we will look at a study by Sigall, Aronson, and Van Hoose (1970) in which they investigated some of the conditions under which a subject would demonstrate cooperation with the experimenter. They used three treatment groups and one control group (a group that received no treatment condition). The three treatment groups consisted of a group that was led to believe their performance was to increase, a group that was led to believe that their performance was to decrease, and a group that was led to believe that an increase in performance was an indication of obsessive-compulsive behavior. Forty subjects were randomly assigned to the four groups, and the number of telephone numbers copied in seven minutes was used as the dependent variable. Results revealed that subjects will alter their behavior in a manner that will make them look good. In the obsessive-compulsive condition subjects decreased performance to appear most adjusted to the experimenter. Figure 7.1 depicts this design as well as the actual mean performance scores for each experimental group.

The design selected by Sigall, Aronson, and Van Hoose was a simple one, but it illustrates how the purposes of research design are met. The design shown in Figure 7.1 indicates such factors as the number of subjects needed. Since there were four groups, some multiple of 4 was needed. Sigall et al. decided to have 10 subjects per group, which meant that 40 subjects were needed. These 40 subjects were to be tested once under the experimental conditions to which they were assigned. The design also suggests the statistical test that would be needed to analyze the data. In this case a one-way classification analysis of variance and, perhaps, post hoc tests were appropriate. This point is significant because research design is intimately linked to statistics.

Experimental Groups

Control	Increase	Decrease	Obssessive-Compulsive
(A_1)	(A_2)	(A_3)	(A_4)

Mean Dependent Variable Scores

+1.9	+5.7	+6.2	−8.0

Figure 7.1. Sigall, Aronson, and VanHoose's experimental design (1970).

Not infrequently a person designs an experiment and collects data according to the specifications of the design without attempting to determine if the design will permit statistical analysis. To their dismay these individuals frequently find that either their data cannot be analyzed or analysis would not be worthwhile. This difficulty can be traced to the fact that these individuals did not appropriately design their study; the data could not be statistically analyzed, and therefore the research problem could not be tested. As a general rule of thumb, never conduct an experiment until you have determined if your research design permits analysis that will answer your research questions.

The design also suggests the conclusions that can be drawn from the experiment. This point is closely related to the previous one, since the conclusions reached are tied in with the statistical tests that can be performed. With the design of Figure 7.1, an overall statistical test—one-way classification analysis of variance—could be computed to determine if any differences existed between the four groups. (Naturally, this assumes that the assumptions of analysis of variance are met.) If a significant F-test did result, post hoc tests could be computed between the various group combinations (e.g., A_1 versus A_2) to isolate specifically where the significant difference exists. In this way one could tell exactly which experimental conditions differed significantly.

The design in Figure 7.1 also illustrates how the controls are incorporated. The randomization control technique was incorporated by randomly assigning subjects to the four groups and thus subjects were equated on all extraneous variables. If the design had been more elaborate, additional control techniques could also have been incorporated. Christensen and Dickinson (1975), for example, conducted a modified replication of the Sigall et al. study and, in addition to using randomization, incorporated the matching technique of using an extraneous variable as an independent variable. As one component of their study they wanted to control for preexperimental attitudes, so they identified subjects with positive and negative attitudes toward participation in psychological experiments. These subjects were then randomly assigned to the various treatment groups. In this way two-control techniques were incorporated into the study, as shown in Figure 7.2.

The design of the experiment is, therefore, very important. It is crucial that the design is an appropriate one because it determines whether or not valid, objective, and accurate answers to research questions will be obtained. This is because the design suggests the observations that will be made and how these observations will be analyzed.

Designs can be good or bad in the sense that they will or will not enable one to attain the answers sought. It is generally much easier to

	Experimental Groups			
	Control (A_1)	Increase (A_2)	Decrease (A_3)	Obsessive-Compulsive (A_4)
Positive (B_1)	A_1B_1	A_2B_1	A_3B_1	A_4B_1
Negative (B_2)	A_1B_2	A_2B_2	A_3B_2	A_4B_2

Preexperimental Attitude

Figure 7.2. Christensen and Dickenson's experimental design (1975).

160 design an experiment inappropriately, because careful thought and planning are not required. However, to the extent that the design is faulty, the results of the experiment will be faulty. How does one go about conceiving a good research design that will provide answers to the questions asked? It is no simple task and there is no set way of instructing others in how to develop one. Designing a piece of research requires thought—thought about the components to include and pitfalls to avoid. One has to identify the independent and dependent variables, the best way to collect and analyze the data, and the extraneous variables that are to be controlled. Once these have been identified one must plan, outline, or design the experiment in such a way that these components are appropriately incorporated. This chapter will first discuss some faulty designs and then discuss appropriate research designs. I will be drawing heavily on material presented by Campbell and Stanley (1963), who have contributed greatly to good research design.

Throughout most of the discussion in this and the following chapter, the systematic notation presented by Campbell and Stanley will be followed. For each of the designs presented, each row will refer to a different group of subjects, and each column will refer to a different point in time. The letter X will refer to a treatment condition that is administered to a subject, and the letter Y will refer to the observations or measurements (dependent variable) taken. R will stand for the process of random assignment of subjects to the various treatment groups. The letter R will appear only when random assignment has taken place. Therefore, absence of the letter R means that subjects have not been randomly assigned to the various treatment groups. To further illustrate cases in which nonrandom assignment has occurred, a dashed line will be used to separate groups not equated by randomization.

Faulty Research Design

In seeking solutions to questions, the scientist conducts experiments, conceiving a certain plan or strategy that is to be followed. To the extent that the experiment is inappropriately conceived and therefore inappropriately designed, solutions to research questions will not be attained. Unfortunately, research is and has been conducted using designs that are inappropriate. The faulty research designs that will now be discussed are examples of ones that are defective. The purpose of presenting them is to demonstrate their weakness so they can be avoided.

One-Shot Case Study Design

The one-shot case study design is one in which a single group of subjects or a single subject is measured on a dependent variable subsequent to the presentation of some treatment that is presumed to cause change. Figure 7.3 depicts this type of design.

This design is representative of traditional case studies and an experimental type of research. To illustrate how case studies fit this design, consider "The Case of Richard Benson" (Leon, 1974, pp. 109–126). Richard Benson suffered from severe and overwhelming anxiety attacks, which had become particularly severe since his recent job promotion. These attacks manifested themselves in a fear of urinating in his pants if he was in a strange environment where he did not know of the location of the bathroom, if he was not close to a bathroom, or if for some reason he was not free to leave to go to the bathroom. Probes into his life history revealed that, as a child, he had had chronic bladder and kidney infections, which led him always to locate the bathroom in unfamiliar places. Based on this data, Richard Benson's current anxiety attacks (Y, or the dependent variable) were interpreted as a result of anxiety being classically conditioned (X, or the treatment) to bladder distention. The fear of urinating involuntarily caused the anxiety response to generalize to many other stimuli and situations in which a bathroom was not immediately available.

The experimental type of research that falls under this design can be illustrated by a hypothetical example of a situation in which an institution decides to institute a training program (X, or the treatment condition). Naturally, the institution wants to evaluate the effectiveness of the program so, upon its completion, they assess behaviors: the Y measure, such as the opinions, attitudes, and perhaps performance of the individuals who went through the program. If they are positive, and if these individuals' performance is found to be good, then the validity of the program is thought to be established.

For yielding scientific data, the design represented in Figure 7.3 is, as Campbell and Stanley (1963) state, of almost no scientific value. This is not to say that case studies are of no value or that they do not

Treatment	Response Measure
X	Y

Figure 7.3. One-shot case study design. (Adapted from Campbell, D. T., and Stanley, J. C. Experimental and quasi-experimental designs for research. Chicago: Rand McNally and Co., 1963. Copyright 1963, American Educational Research Association, Washington, D. C.)

162   serve a function, but they cannot provide evidence of causal relationships. One of the basic requirements for attaining scientific evidence is that an equated comparison be included that did not receive the treatment condition. Only in this way can you attain any degree of assurance that the treatment effect, X, was the cause of the observed behavior, Y. In the training program example, the same performance may have been attained without the training. With the case of Richard Benson, the anxiety attacks and fear of urination could have been caused by things other than classical conditioning during childhood. The point is that this design does not give any evidence of the causes of Y. Its only asset—though a valuable one—is that it can generate hypotheses about possible causal relationships that can be tested by good research designs.

One-Group Before-After (Pretest-Posttest) Design

Most researchers recognize the deficiencies in the one-shot case study design and attempt to improve upon it, at least, by including a pretest. In evaluating a curriculum or training program some measure of improvement or success is necessary. However, it seems as though some individuals assume that all that is necessary is to include a pretest that can be compared with a posttest, the latter taken after administering some treatment condition. Figure 7.4 depicts such a design, which corresponds to the one-group before-after design.

A group of subjects is measured on the dependent variable, Y, prior to administering the treatment condition. The independent variable, X, is then administered and the dependent variable, Y, is again measured. The difference between the pre- and posttest scores is taken as an indication of the effectiveness of the treatment condition. In evaluating a new curriculum, an attitude scale and an achievement test could be administered at the beginning of the school year (pretest Y). The new curriculum—X—is introduced to the students. At the end

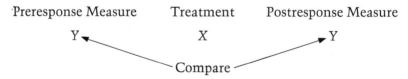

Preresponse Measure   Treatment   Postresponse Measure

Y   X   Y

Compare

Figure 7.4. One-group before-after design. (Adapted from Campbell, D. T., and Stanley, J. C. Experimental and quasi-experimental designs for research. Chicago: Rand McNally and Co., 1963. Copyright 1963, American Educational Research Association, Washington, D. C.)

of the school year the attitude scale and the achievement test (posttest Y) are again administered. The pre- and posttest scores on the attitude scale and the achievement test are examined for change. A significant change between these two scores is attributed to the new curriculum.

The Liddle and Long (1958) study, which was mentioned earlier, represents an example of the use of this design. Liddle and Long selected 18 slow learners who were administered an intelligence test and were assigned a reading grade placement score, pre Y, prior to being placed in the experimental classroom. After approximately two years in the experimental classroom the Metropolitan Achievement Tests were administered, post Y, and compared with the previously assigned reading grade placement score. This comparison revealed "an improvement of about 1.75 years in less than two school years" (p. 145). At face value such a study has intuitive appeal and seems to represent a good way to accomplish the research purpose. This appeal seems to come from the fact that a change in performance can be seen and documented. In actuality, this design represents only a small improvement over the one-shot case study because of the many uncontrolled rival hypotheses which could also explain the obtained results.

In the Liddle and Long study, almost two years elapsed between the pre- and posttest. Consequently, the uncontrolled rival hypotheses of history, maturation, and so on could creep in and produce some, if not all, of the observed change in performance. To be able to state that the observed change in performance was due to the treatment effect (the experimental classroom) and not due to these rival hypotheses, an equated group of slow learners who did not participate in the experimental room needed to have been included. This equated group's performance could be compared with the performance of the children who received the experimental treatment; if a significant difference was found between the scores attained by these two groups, the difference could be attributed to the influence of the experimental classroom. This is because both groups would have experienced any history and maturation effects that occurred and, therefore, these variables would have been held constant or controlled. The design of the study was inadequate, not so much because the sources of rival hypotheses *can* affect the results, but because we do not know *if* they did. The design does not allow us to control or to test for the potential influence of these effects.

This design, however, is not totally worthless. There are situations in which it is impossible to obtain an equated comparison group. In such cases the design can be used and it will provide some information. However, one should remain constantly aware of the possible confounding extraneous variables which can jeopardize internal validity.

Static-Group Comparison

The primary disadvantage of the previous two designs is the lack of a comparison group and the consequent impossibility of drawing any unambiguous conclusions as to the influence of the treatment condition. The static-group comparison design makes an inadequate attempt to remedy this deficiency by including a comparison group. In this design, one group of subjects receives the treatment condition, X, and is then compared on the dependent variable, Y, with a group that did not receive this treatment condition. Figure 7.5 depicts this design.

This design is used quite frequently and is quite appealing because it does include a comparison group. Brown et al. (1971) conducted a study that illustrates its use. They were attempting to evaluate the influence of a student-to-student counseling program on potential college freshman dropouts. One group of potential dropouts received the student-to-student counseling and another matched group—the comparison group—did not. Following the series of counseling sessions, all students were administered several tests designed to evaluate the effects of the counseling program. First-semester grade point averages were also obtained. Results revealed that, on all dependent variable measures, the group receiving the counseling performed in a superior manner.

The design of this study seems to be adequate. A comparison group was included to evaluate the influence of the treatment condition and subjects in both groups were matched. Why, then, is this design included as an example of a one that is faulty? The reason is that the two groups typically are *assumed* to be equated on variables other than the independent variable. Granted, Brown et al. did match on a number of variables such as age, sex, and ACT composite scores. However, matching is no assurance of having attained equated groups. As Campbell and Stanley (1963, p. 12) have stated, "Matching on back-

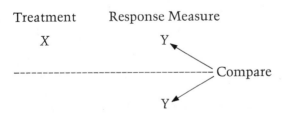

Figure 7.5. Static-group comparison. (Adapted from Campbell, D. T., and Stanley, J. C. Experimental and quasi-experimental designs for research. Chicago: Rand McNally and Co., 1963. Copyright 1963, American Educational Research Association, Washington, D. C.)

ground characteristics other than *0* is usually ineffective and misleading . . ." The only way one can have any assurance that the groups are
equated is to assign subjects randomly to the two groups. As indicated
by the dashed lines in Figure 7.5, random assignment is not included in
the static-group comparison design. Of course, matching is better than
doing nothing, since it controls for the variables on which subjects are
matched. In studies where it is not possible to assign subjects randomly, the next best technique is to match on relevant variables.
However, matching is no substitute for random assignment.

Requirements of Good Research Designs

The designs just presented are considered faulty because, in general,
they do not represent a means for isolating the effect of the treatment
condition; rival hypotheses were not excluded. If these designs are
weak and inadequate, what then is required of a good research design?
Kerlinger (1973) discusses three criteria that need to be met in a
research design. The first criterion is: "Does the design answer the
research questions, or does the design adequately test the hypothesis?"
One of the first and foremost requirements of a good design is that it is
capable of providing answers to one's questions or hypotheses. Periodically, one encounters a situation in which an investigator sets out to
seek an answer to a research question. The researcher designs the
study, collects the data, analyzes the data, and only when attempting
to interpret the data, does he or she realize that there is no answer to
the research question. Such instances could be avoided if, after the
study was designed, the researcher had asked the following question:
"What conclusion or conclusions can I draw from this experiment?"
Remember that the design of the study suggests the statistical tests
that can be performed on the data, which in turn determine the conclusions that can be drawn. If the design conceived allows one to conduct
statistical tests that will provide an answer to the research question,
the first criterion has been met.

The second criterion of a good research design is whether or not
extraneous variables have been controlled. This criterion refers to the
concept of *internal validity.* Remember that internal validity asks
whether or not the observed effects can be attributed to the independent variable. If they can, the experiment is internally valid. In order
to achieve the second criterion of internal validity, potential rival
hypotheses must be eliminated. This can be accomplished by two
means, control techniques and control group.

The first means by which control of extraneous variables can be effected is incorporation of one or more of the control techniques discussed in Chapter 6. Of these, the most important one is randomization. The importance of this technique cannot be overemphasized; it is the only means by which unknown variables can be controlled. Also, statistical reasoning is dependent upon the randomization procedure, so I emphasize again, *randomize whenever and wherever possible.*

The second means for effecting control is inclusion of a control group. In conducting a study and conversing with others, the terms *experimental group* and *control group* are frequently employed. The control group refers to the group of subjects that does not receive the independent variable, receives a zero amount of it, or receives a value that is in some sense a *standard* value. The experimental group, or groups, refers to the groups of subjects that receive some amount of the independent variable. In the study conducted by Aronson and Mills on severity of initiation, the group who did not have to take the embarrassment test represented the control group, whereas the other two groups, who had to read either embarrassing or not very embarrassing material, represented the two experimental groups. In a drug study, the subjects who received a placebo would represent the control group, and subjects receiving the drug would represent the experimental group.

A control group serves two functions. First, it serves as a source of comparison. The one-shot case study and the one-group before-after designs were primarily considered faulty because there was no way to tell if the treatment condition, X, caused the observed behavior, Y. To arrive at such a conclusion you have to have a comparison group or a control group that did not receive the treatment effect. Only by including a control group—assuming all other variables are controlled—can you get any concrete indication of whether or not the treatment condition produced results different from those which would have been attained in the absence of the treatment. Consider a hypothetical case of a father who has a daughter who always cries for candy when they go into a store. The parent does not like the behavior so, in order to get rid of it, he decides to spank the child whenever she cries for candy in the store, and also he does not let her have any candy. After two weeks the child has stopped the crying behavior and the parent concludes that the spanking was effective. Is he correct? Note that the child also did not receive any candy during the two weeks, so a rival hypothesis is that crying was extinguished. To determine whether it was the spanking or extinction that stopped the behavior, a control child who did not receive the spanking would also have to be included, and if both stopped crying in two weeks then you would know that the spanking was not the variable causing the elimination of the crying behavior.

The hypothetical example of the child and the parent illustrates the need for a comparison group in order to reach an unambiguous conclusion regarding the influence of an independent variable. The example also illustrates the second function of a control group, that is, to serve as a control for rival hypotheses. All variables operating on the control and experimental groups must be identical, except for the one being manipulated by the experimenter. In this way the influence of extraneous variables is held constant. The extinction variable was held constant across the child who did and did not receive the spanking and therefore did not confound the results. In the one-group before-after design, extraneous variables such as history and maturation can creep in and serve as rival hypotheses unless a control group is included. If a control group is included, these variables will affect the performance of both the control subjects and the experimental subjects, effectively holding their influence constant and thereby controlled. It is in this way that a control group also serves a control function.

Before leaving the discussion of the control group, one additional point needs to be made. A necessary requirement of the control group is that the subjects in the group are similar to those in the experimental group. If this condition does not exist, the control group could not act as a baseline for evaluating the influence of the independent variable. For the control group to operate as a basis for comparison, the responses of this group and the experimental group must be similar in the absence of the imposition of the independent variable. The rationale underlying this requirement seems rather obvious. The responses of the control group must stand for the responses the experimental group would have given if they had not received the treatment condition. Therefore, the subjects in the two groups must theoretically be as similar as possible to yield identical scores in the absence of the introduction of the independent variable.

The third criterion of a good research design is generalizability or external validity, as presented by Campbell and Stanley (1963). Generalizability asks the question: "Can the results of this experiment be applied to individuals other than those who participated in the study?" If the answer is yes, then we need to follow with the question: "To whom do the results apply? Can we say that the results should apply to everyone, or only females, or just females who are attending college?" In all cases we would ideally like to be able to generalize beyond the confines of the actual study; however, whether or not we can generalize and how far we can generalize our results is never completely answerable.

The above three criteria represent the ideal. Naturally, the first criterion must be met by all studies. However, the degree to which the second and third are met will vary from study to study. Basic research

168   focuses primarily on the second criterion of internal validity since its foremost concern is the examination of the relations among variables. Applied research, on the other hand, places equal emphasis on external and internal validity, since the central interest of such research is to apply the results to persons and situations.

Pretesting Subjects

The necessity of including a comparison or a control group in experimental design cannot be overemphasized. The reasoning underlying this is that one must assess the relevant state of the organism prior to the administration of the treatment condition. This is necessary to determine if the treatment condition produces a change in the organism. The control group provides information regarding this initial condition. However, another means for obtaining such information is to pretest subjects, such as was done in the one-group before-after design. One can then directly observe change in the subjects' behavior as a result of the treatment effect. But one may legitimately question the need to pretest. Is it not sufficient and appropriate to assign subjects randomly to experimental and control groups and forget about pretesting? One can then assume comparability of the subjects in the two groups, and those in the control group provide the comparison data. Hence a pretest is unnecessary. However, there are several reasons (Selltiz et al., 1959, and Lana, 1969) that are frequently given why a pretest is included in the experimental design. These are as follows:

1. *Increased sensitivity.* One can increase the sensitivity of the experiment by matching subjects on relevant variables. Such matching does, however, require pretesting. This issue was discussed at some length in an earlier chapter and therefore will not be reiterated.

2. *Ceiling effect.* Another reason for pretesting is to determine if there is room for the treatment condition to have an effect. Assume you were investigating the efficiency of a particular persuasive communication for positively increasing one's attitude toward ecology. If, by chance, all subjects in the experiment already had extremely positive attitudes toward ecology, there would be no room for the treatment condition to have an effect. Such a case could exist if, on a 10-point rating scale with 10 being the positive end, all subjects were evaluated as being 8, 9, or 10. In such a situation the effect of the persuasive communication cannot be assessed. Pretesting enables the investigator to identify the existence of a possible ceiling effect and take it into consideration when evaluating the effects of the independent variable.

3. *Initial position.* Many studies in psychology are conducted in which
it is necessary to know a person's initial position on the dependent
variable because it may interact with the experimental condition.
A treatment condition that attempts to induce hostility toward a
minority group may find that the effectiveness of this treatment
condition is a function of the subjects' initial level of hostility.
The treatment condition may be very successful with individuals
with little hostility but unsuccessful with extremely hostile individuals. With such conditions it would be very helpful to pretest
subjects. LeUnes, Christensen, and Wilkerson (1975), for example,
pretested subjects on their attitudes toward various components of
mental retardation. Subjects were then separated into a positive or
negative group to identify whether a subject's initial attitude position affected whether or not there was a change in attitude toward
the various components of mental retardation as a result of taking
an institutional tour. These investigators found that a subject's
initial attitude was a significant factor.

4. *Initial comparability.* Another reason for pretesting is to assure that
subjects are initially comparable on relevant variables. Ideally
subjects are randomly assigned to conditions. While random assignment provides the greatest assurance possible of comparability
of subjects, it is not infallible. Should there be a failure of randomization to provide comparability, comparison of the sub-
group's pretest mean scores would tell us so.

In field research it is frequently not possible to assign subjects
randomly. Rather, they have to be taken as intact groups. Educational experiments, for example, are frequently restricted to using
one intact class for one group of subjects and another class for
another group of subjects. In instances such as this, it would be
advisable to insure that subjects, because of lack of random
assignment, do not differ initially on the independent variable.
While it is recognized that failure to assign randomly departs from
the ideal requirements of a study, compromises such as this frequently have to be made. Recognition also has to be made of the
fact that the results of the experiment could be due to group
differences on characteristics other than the pretested variables.
The pretest does, however, give additional confidence that the
observed differences are due to the treatment condition.

5. *Evidence of change.* The last, and perhaps the most frequently used,
reason for pretesting is to gain an empirical demonstration of the
fact that the treatment condition did or did not succeed in producing a change in the organisms. The most direct way of gaining
such evidence is to measure the difference obtained before and
after a treatment is introduced.

A number of reasons have been given for pretesting over the use of
a design that does not include this initial measure. There is, however,
one basic confounding variable that could arise as a result of pretesting.

170   The pretest may alter the subject's response to the treatment condition in the sense of either increasing or decreasing the subject's sensitivity to it. For example, pretesting subjects' attitudes may alert them to the fact that the experiment they are participating in is an attitude experiment, and this knowledge could heighten their sensitivity to the independent variable. Subjects who were pretested may, therefore, produce results that were not representative of those obtained from an unpretested population. This potential error has been considered so real as to lead Campbell and Stanley (1963) to list it as a factor jeopardizing external validity.

Lana (1969), however, has summarized the research that seeks to document this potential source of bias and reaches some interesting conclusions. When the pretest involves a learning process such as requiring subjects to recall previously learned material, the posttest score may very well be affected. "Ordinarily, if the task of the recall demanded by the pretest procedure is properly understood by the subject, the effect on the posttest should be facilitative" (p. 132). However, the conclusion regarding attitude research is somewhat different. "In attitude research pretest measures, if they have any impact at all, depress the effect being measured; any differences which can be attributed to the experimental treatment probably represent strong treatment effects" (p. 139). The evidence presented by Lana is so convincing as to lead Campbell (1969) to retract his earlier position (Campbell, 1957) that one could not generalize the results obtained on a pretested population to an unpretested one.

Appropriate Research Designs

The designs presented in this section represent "true" experimental research designs. For a research design to be a true experimental design, it must enable the researcher to maintain control over the situation in terms of assignment of subjects to groups, in terms of who gets the treatment condition, and in terms of the amount of the treatment condition that subjects receive. In other words, the researcher must have a controlled experiment in order to have confidence in the relations he discovers between the independent variable or variables and the dependent variable. The following research designs allow one to gain the needed control.

After-Only Research Design

The after-only research design is one in which a group of subjects is randomly assigned to the experimental and the control groups. The

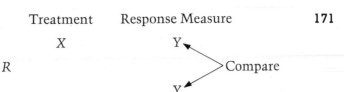

Figure 7.6. After-only design. (Adapted from Campbell, D. T., and Stanley, J. C. <u>Experimental and quasi-experimental designs for research</u>. Chicago: Rand McNally and Co., 1963. Copyright 1963, American Educational Research Association, Washington, D. C.)

experimental group receives the treatment condition and then both groups of subjects are measured on the dependent variable. The scores on the dependent variable are then compared and, if the experimental group's scores are significantly different from those of the control group, the difference is attributed to the treatment condition. Figure 7.6 depicts this design.

The design in Figure 7.6 has a similar appearance to the static-group comparison design. There is, however, one basic and important difference. Remember that the static-group comparison design was criticized primarily from the standpoint of not providing any assurance of equality between the various groups. This design provides the necessary equivalence by randomly assigning subjects to the two groups. If enough subjects are included to allow randomization to work, then, theoretically, all possible extraneous variables are controlled (excluding ones such as experimenter expectancies).

The after-only design, and particularly its extensions, which will be discussed later, is widely used in psychology. The reason for its popularity is logical because of its effectiveness from two standpoints. The first is the much-discussed virtue of randomization, which provides the needed control of extraneous variables. The second virtue is the inclusion of a control group, which provides the comparability required by science.

A means for increasing the sensitivity of the after-only design would be to match subjects on the relevant variables prior to assigning them to groups randomly as depicted in Figure 7.7. The M in front of the R reflects the fact that subjects are matched on one or more variables which are correlated with the dependent variable. Note that matching has not taken the place of randomization but merely supplemented it. Matched pairs of subjects must be randomly assigned; otherwise one loses the assurance of comparability of the two groups. When both procedures are used, the design is more sensitive, and one increases the likelihood of detecting a significant treatment effect.

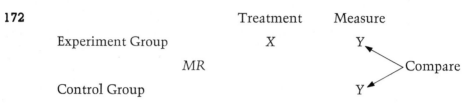

Figure 7.7. Matched after-only design.

Before-After Research Design

The before-after type of design is similar to the one-group before-after design. However, there are important basic differences between these two designs: the existence or nonexistence of a control group, and randomization. In the before-after type of design, subjects are randomly assigned to groups and then pretested on the dependent variable, Y. The independent variable, X, is administered to the experimental group, and the experimental and control groups are posttested on the dependent variable, Y. The differences between the pre- and postscores for the experimental and control groups are then tested statistically to assess the effect of the independent variable. Figure 7.8 depicts this design.

This design is also a good experimental design and very efficient in the sense that it does an excellent job of controlling for rival hypotheses such as history and maturation. The similar but faulty one-group before-after design was said to have been contaminated by extraneous variables such as history, maturation, and so forth. The before-after design neatly controls for many of these rival hypotheses. The history and maturation variables are clearly controlled, since they should be manifested to the same extent in both the control and the experimental groups. Any history events that may have produced a difference in the experimental group would also produce a difference in the control group. Since both groups would experience the same effect from the historical event, this effect is held constant and therefore controlled. Note, however, that an intragroup history effect could exist in this design or any other design that included more than one group of subjects. If all the subjects in the experimental group were treated in one session and the subjects in the control group were treated in another session, it is possible that events took place in one group that did not take place in the other group. If a differential event did take place (e.g., laughter, a joke, or a comment about the experimental procedure), there would be no way of eliminating its influence and it may have produced an effect that would be picked up by the dependent

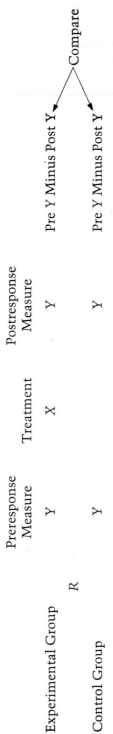

	Preresponse Measure	Treatment	Postresponse Measure	
Experimental Group	Y	X	Y	Pre Y Minus Post Y
Control Group	Y		Y	Pre Y Minus Post Y

R

Compare

Figure 7.8. Before-after design. (Adapted from Campbell, D. T., and Stanley, J. C. Experimental and quasi-experimental designs for research. Chicago: Rand McNally and Co., 1963. Copyright 1963, American Educational Research Association. Washington, D. C.)

174 variable. Such an event would have to be considered a possible cause
for any significant difference noted between the groups.

The intragroup history effect can be controlled by individually
testing subjects that are randomly assigned to the treatment groups
and by randomly determining when a control and an experimental
treatment will be administered. If group administration of each level of
variation of the independent variable is essential, then each separate
group potentially has a different intrasession history. In this case it
would be necessary to test statistically the various groups to determine
if differences exist as a function of intrasession history. In other words,
it would be necessary to include groups as another independent variable.

Maturation and instrumentation are also controlled in this design
because they should be equally manifested in both the experimental
and control group. Since the effect is equally manifested, any difference
produced by these two variables would be constant across the two
groups and therefore controlled. Equal manifestation of the testing
effect in experiments that use observers or interviewers to collect the
dependent variable data does, however, assume that the observers are
randomly assigned to individual observation sessions. This is to assure
that the instrumentation effect is randomly distributed across groups.
When this assumption cannot be met, a double-blind model should be
used with each available observer used in both experimental and control sessions.

Regression and selection variables are controlled by virtue of the
fact that subjects are randomly assigned to both the experimental and
the control groups. Randomization has assured initial equality of
groups as well as the extent to which each group will regress toward
the mean. Since subjects were randomly assigned, each group should
have the same percentage of extreme scores and, therefore, demonstrate the same degree of regression toward the mean. Selection is
naturally ruled out since random assignment has assured equality of
the experimental and control groups at the time of randomization. As
stated earlier, randomization does not provide 100% assurance, and
one will occasionally be wrong. However, it is our *best* protection
against the selection rival hypothesis.

In the past (Cronbach and Furby, 1970; Kerlinger, 1973), it has
been stated that a statistical analysis computed on pretest-posttest
difference scores was inappropriate because such gain scores may have
low reliability. However, Nicewander and Price (1978) have revealed
that the reliability of our dependent variable measures do not have any
general relationship to the power of the statistical test. According to
this recent evidence presented by these investigators, "low reliability

in a difference score is certainly not sufficient evidence to conclude that one has a faulty experiment and should in no way deter one from statistically evaluating a hypothesis stating that the average difference or gain score is zero" (Nicewander and Price, 1978, p. 408). Therefore, it appears that it is appropriate to analyze statistically differences in the gain scores achieved by the experimental and control groups to determine if the experimental groups' gains were significantly greater than that achieved by the control group.

Before-After Four-Group Design

In 1949 Solomon proposed the four-group design which has been strongly recommended by Campbell (1957). This design is indeed highly esteemed and very strong because of the potent controls it includes. In this design subjects are randomly assigned either to an experimental group or to one of three control groups. The experimental group is pretested, given the treatment condition, and then posttested. The first control group is also pretested and then posttested without receiving the treatment condition. The second control group is given the treatment condition and then posttested and the third control group is only posttested. Figure 7.9 depicts this design.

As Figure 7.9 reveals, this design represents a combination of the two designs just discussed. The experimental and first control group taken together represent the before-after type of design and the second and third control groups taken together represent the after-only type of design. The design is, therefore, very strong in the sense that the demand for comparisons is well satisfied. Also, the groups are statistically equivalent since subjects were randomly assigned, and consequently potential extraneous variables such as history, maturation, or regression are controlled. The last advantage of the Solomon four-group design is that it actually represents two separate experiments, so we have the advantage of replication for increasing the faith we have in the validity of the tested hypothesis. If both the before-after and the after-only components of the design reveal significant treatment effects, then strong evidence exists that our hypothesis was valid.

The design has many strong and important points. To illustrate how its use can facilitate understanding over and above the two previously discussed designs, the student is directed to an article written by Solomon and Lessac (1968). In this article, they reveal how the four-group design can more appropriately be employed in studies of developmental processes, because it allows one to assess the influence of pretesting and the type of effect produced by the experimental treatment.

		Preresponse Measure	Treatment	Postresponse Measure
Before-After	Experimental Group	Y	X	Y
	Control Group I	Y		Y
After-Only	Control Group II		X	Y
	Control Group III			Y

R

Figure 7.9. Before-after four-group design. (Adapted from Campbell, D. T., and Stanley, J. C. Experimental and quasi-experimental designs for research. Chicago: Rand McNally and Co., 1963. Copyright 1963, American Educational Research Association, Washington, D. C.)

In spite of the appeal and strengths of the design, it has several difficulties. The first is a practical difficulty in that it is harder to run four groups of subjects than two. As more groups are added more subjects must be located, and the time required to conduct the experiment increases. This, however, is not a weakness but merely one of the concomitants of using this stronger design. The second difficulty with using the design is a more serious one. A statistical test does not exist that simultaneously makes use of all six sets of observations. Solomon (1949) also recognized this deficiency, and Campbell and Stanley (1963) suggested the use of analysis of variance using only the four posttest scores as presented in Figure 7.10. Comparison of the column means would provide a way of determining if the treatment condition produced an observed effect. Comparison of the row means would allow one to evaluate the influence of pretesting on the posttest results. This design also allows for the testing of interaction effects or whether pretesting was influential for the groups that did not receive the treatment condition or vice versa. As you can see, when presented in this fashion the design is still capable of yielding a lot of information and now is amenable to appropriate statistical analysis.

Application of the Research Designs

The designs just described represent the basic conceptual structure of research design. However, most current research is not confined to these designs but conforms to the more complex elaboration typical of the Fisher (1935) factorial designs. These more elaborate designs are extensions of the after-only and the before-after type of designs. These variations and extensions will be described in the following section to provide the feeling for when they can appropriately be used. One cannot state explicitly when and under what conditions a particular

	Treatment Present	Treatment Absent
Pretested	Experimental	Control I
Not Pretested	Control II	Control III

Figure 7.10. Summary of four-group design capable of being statistically analyzed. (Adapted from Campbell, D. T., and Stanley, J. C. Experimental and quasi-experimental designs for research. Chicago: Rand McNally and Co., 1963. Copyright 1963, American Educational Research Association, Washington, D. C.)

178 design needs to be used. All that can be done is to present the alternatives along with their strengths and weaknesses. The investigator must consider these alternatives and weigh each one in terms of its ability to assist in providing the necessary information.

Randomized Subjects Design

The randomized subjects design is actually an after-only type of design and therefore conforms to the design depicted in Figure 7.6. As such, the design has the strength of equating the various groups of subjects through randomization. The design is also very flexible and can be applied in many situations.

Very few of the studies reported in psychological journals use a design that conforms exactly to the after-only design. Instead, most studies use several levels of variation of an independent variable and/or several independent variables. Many of these studies reflect extensions of the basic after-only design. The following section shows some general ways in which the after-only design can be extended.

SIMPLE RANDOMIZED SUBJECTS DESIGN.   The simple randomized subjects design is an after-only type of design that has been extended to include more than one level of the independent variable. There are many situations in which it is desirable to administer varying amounts or degrees of an independent variable to different groups of subjects. In drug research the investigator may want to administer different amounts of a drug to determine if the different amounts produce a differential reaction to the dependent variable. In such a case, subjects would be randomly assigned to the various treatment groups. If there were three experimental groups and one control group, subjects would be randomly assigned to the four groups as illustrated in Figure 7.11. A statistical technique known as analysis of variance would then be used, assuming all assumptions and requirements are met, to determine if a significant difference existed between the means of the four groups of subjects. To obtain information about whether each treatment group differed significantly from the control group and whether the variations in the treatment conditions produced significant differences, one would have to conduct post hoc tests. The analysis of variance would only tell you whether or not there were significant differences among the various groups but not which groups were significantly different. To determine which groups were significantly different one would have to make individual comparisons between the various groups. Kirk (1968, Chapter 3) presents a good discussion of the correct procedure for making such post hoc comparisons.

The Sigall, Aronson, and Van Hoose (1970) experiment represents an example of a study that used the simple randomized subjects design. The investigators were attempting to determine if subjects are motivated to look good or if they are motivated to cooperate with the experimenter to produce the results that he or she wants. To investigate these motives, they had a control group and three experimental groups. In one experimental group the subjects were led to believe that they should increase performance; in another group they were led to believe that they should decrease performance; and in a third group, evaluative apprehension was generated by telling subjects that increased performance was indicative of obsessive-compulsive behavior. Consequently, the design of this experiment was identical to that depicted in Figure 7.11.

Sigall et al. analyzed their data using analysis of variance, which revealed that significant differences existed between the various groups. Post hoc tests revealed that the three experimental groups differed significantly from the control group and that the evaluative apprehension group differed significantly from the other two experimental groups. From this they concluded that the subject's primary motive is to look good rather than cooperate with the experimenter. They arrived at this conclusion because the subjects in the obsessive-compulsive group performed slower than any other group, whereas the other two experimental groups performed better than either the control or the obsessive-compulsive experimental group.

The simple randomized subjects design considers only one independent variable. In psychological research, as with other types of research, one is frequently interested in the effect of several independent variables acting in concert. In conducting research on instructional effectiveness, interest lies in methods of instruction (e.g., tutorial, discussion, lecture) as well as other factors such as instructor attitude or experience. The simple randomized subjects design would not enable one to simultaneously investigate several independent variables. However, there are designs that enable one to study simultane-

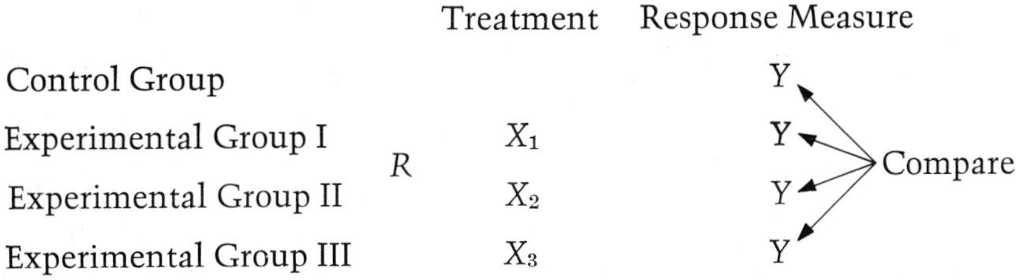

Figure 7.11. Simple randomized subjects design with four levels of variation of the independent variable.

180 ously the effects that two or more independent variables have on a dependent variable. Such designs are called *factorial designs*.

FACTORIAL DESIGNS.   A factorial design is one in which two or more independent variables are simultaneously studied to determine their independent and interactive effects on the dependent variable. To make this definition more meaningful, let us look at a hypothetical example which considers the effect of two independent variables, variable A and variable B. Assume further that variable A has three levels of variation, A_1, A_2, and A_3, and variable B has two levels of variation, B_1 and B_2. Figure 7.12 depicts this design. In this design there are six possible combinations of the two independent variables— A_1B_1, A_1B_2, A_2B_1 , A_2B_2, A_3B_1, and $A_3 B_2$. Each one of these treatment combinations is referred to as a cell. Therefore, there are six cells within this design. The subjects would be randomly assigned to these six cells. The subjects which were randomly assigned to the A_1B_1 would receive the A_1 level of the first independent variable and the B_1 level of the second independent variable. In like manner, the subjects randomly assigned to the other cells would receive the designated combination of the two independent variables.

   In an experiment that has the design shown in Figure 7.12, there are two types of effects that need to be analyzed. There are two independent variables included in this design and naturally their influence needs to be analyzed statistically to determine if the different levels of each produced significantly different results. Additionally, and of at least equal importance, there is the necessity of analyzing the data to detect any interactive effects that may have resulted from the simultaneous presentation of the two independent variables. Analyzing the independent effects of each independent variable requires that one

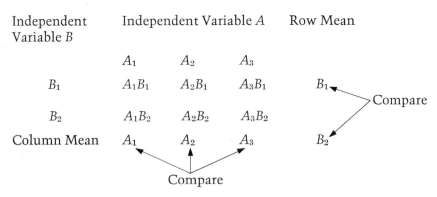

Figure 7.12. Factorial design with two independent
   variables.

analyze separately the effects of the different levels of variation of the two independent variables, A and B. In other words, it is necessary to compare the three A mean scores to determine if they differ significantly, and compare the two B mean scores to see if they differ significantly. Analyzing the interactive effects of the two independent variables requires one to determine if the difference between the means of the levels of variation of one independent variable vary as a function of the levels of variation of the other independent variable. In other words, does the difference between B_1 and B_2 depend upon whether you are at level A_1, A_2, or A_3?

The concept of interaction is sometimes difficult to grasp and, therefore, it is necessary to digress in order to add additional clarity to this issue. In attempting to accomplish this goal I will present a number of possible outcomes that could accrue from an experiment with the design shown in Figure 7.12. Some of the outcomes will represent an interaction and others will not, so that you can see the difference in the two situations. A progression will be set up beginning with a situation in which one main effect is significant to a situation in which both main effects and the interaction are significant. The term "main effect" is used to signify an independent variable. Consequently, the A independent variable represents one main effect and the B independent variable represents the other main effect. Table 7.1 and Figure 7.13 depict these various situations. For the sake of clarity, the hypothetical scores in the cells will represent the mean score for the subjects in each cell.

Illustrations (a), (b), and (d) represent cases in which one or both of the main effects were significant. In each case the mean scores for the level of variation of at least one of the main effects differ. This can readily be seen from both the numerical examples presented in Table 7.1 as well as from the graphs in Figure 7.13. Note also from Figure 7.13 that the lines for levels B_1 and B_2 are parallel in each of these three cases. When such a situation exists, an interaction cannot exist, because an interaction means that the effect of one variable, such as B, depends upon the level of the other variable being considered, such as whether one is considering level A_1, A_2, or A_3. In each of these cases the B effect is the same at all levels of A.

Illustration (c) depicts the classical example of an interaction. Neither main effect is significant, as noted by the fact that the three-column means are identical and the two-row means are identical and reveal no variation. However, if the A treatment effect is considered only for level B_1, we note that the scores systematically increase from level A_1 to level A_3. In like manner, if only level B_2 were considered, then a systematic decrement exists from level A_1 to A_3. A_3. In other words, A is effective but in opposite directions for level B_1 and B_2, or

Table 7.1. Tabular presentation of hypothetical data illustrating different kinds of main and/or interaction effects.

	A_1	A_2	A_3	MEAN
B_1	10	20	30	20
B_2	10	20	30	20
Mean	10	20	30	

(a) *A* is significant; *B* and the interaction are not significant

	A_1	A_2	A_3	MEAN
B_1	20	20	20	20
B_2	30	30	30	30
Mean	25	25	25	

(b) *B* is significant; *A* and the interaction are not significant

	A_1	A_2	A_3	MEAN
B_1	30	40	50	40
B_2	50	40	30	40
Mean	40	40	40	

(c) Interaction is significant; *A* and *B* are not significant

	A_1	A_2	A_3	MEAN
B_1	10	20	30	20
B_2	40	50	60	50
Mean	25	35	45	

(d) *A* and *B* are significant; interaction is not significant

	A_1	A_2	A_3	MEAN
B_1	20	30	40	30
B_2	30	30	30	30
Mean	25	30	35	

(e) *A* and the interaction are significant; *B* is not significant

	A_1	A_2	A_3	MEAN
B_1	10	20	30	20
B_2	50	40	30	40
Mean	30	30	30	

(f) *B* and the interaction are significant; *A* is not significant

	A_1	A_2	A_3	MEAN
B_1	30	50	70	50
B_2	20	30	40	30
Mean	25	40	55	

(g) *A*, *B*, and the interaction are significant

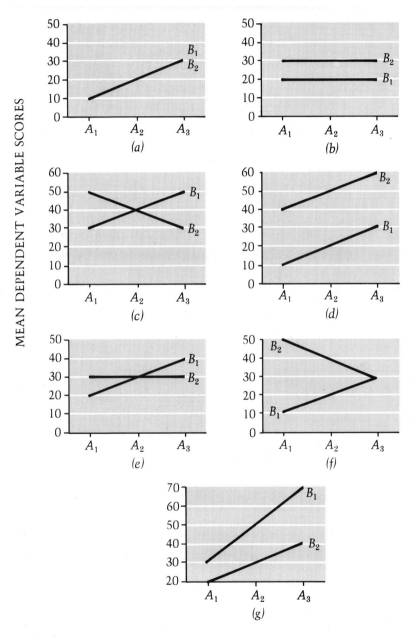

Figure 7.13. Graphic presentation of hypothetical data illustrating different kinds of main and/or interaction effects.

the effect of *A* depends upon which level of *B* one is considering. This is the definition of interaction. From my experience I have found the graphs to be more helpful in illustrating the interaction and, therefore, aiding in its interpretation. However, you should use whichever mode best conveys the information.

Illustrations (e) and (f) represent examples of situations in which a main effect and an interaction are significant; illustration (g) represents a case in which both main effects and the interaction are significant. These illustrations exhaust the possibilities that exist in a factorial design that has two independent variables. The exact nature of the main effects or the interaction may change but one of these types of conditions will exist. Before leaving this section one additional point needs to be made regarding the interpretation of significant main and interaction effects. Where either main or interaction effects *alone* are significant, you naturally have to interpret this effect. However, when *both* main and interaction effects are significant, and the main effect is contained in the interaction effect, only the interaction effect is interpreted. This is because the significant interaction effect qualifies the meaning that would arise from looking only at the main effect.

The following experiment used the design I have been discussing. Baron (1973) investigated the influence of threatened retaliation on inhibiting aggression. Specifically, he hypothesized that aggression would be inhibited by threatened retaliation only if the victim had not previously angered the person. The victim who had previously angered the person would act aggressively even if the victim could retaliate. In investigating this hypothesis Baron used three levels of probability of retaliation from the victim and two levels of prior anger arousal, giving a 3×2 factorial design which is represented in Figure 7.14. Ten subjects were randomly assigned to each of the six cells. Anger was aroused in half the subjects by a confederate. Subjects then had an opportunity to deliver shocks of varying degrees of intensity to this confederate. In the low probability of retaliation condition, subjects could not receive any shocks from the confederate. In the moderate condition the subject was told that he or she would have to change

Prior Anger Arousal	Probability of Retaliation		
	Low (A_1)	Moderate (A_2)	High (A_3)
Nonangry (B_1)	A_1B_1	A_2B_1	A_3B_1
Angry (B_2)	A_1B_2	A_2B_2	A_3B_2

Figure 7.14. Design of Baron's study (1973).

places with the confederate if time allowed, and in the high condition the subject was told he or she would definitely have to trade places with the confederate and therefore receive shocks. The dependent variable was the mean intensity of shocks delivered to the confederate by subjects.

Analysis of the data yielded significant main effects and interaction effect which revealed that "threatened retaliation from the victim was more effective in inhibiting subsequent aggression under conditions where subjects had not previously been exposed to anger arousal, than under conditions where they had previously experienced strong provocation" (Baron, 1973, p. 110).

So far, the discussion of factorial designs has been limited to two independent variables. There are times when it would be advantageous to include three or more independent variables in a study. Factorial designs enable one to include as many independent variables as one considers important. Instead of just having two independent variables, A and B, one could have three, A, B, and C, four, A, B, C, and D, or more. Mathematically or statistically there is just about no limit to the number of independent variables that can be included in a study. Practically speaking there are a number of difficulties associated with such increases. First, there is an associated increase in number of subjects required. In an experiment with two independent variables, each of which has two levels of variation, a 2×2 arrangement is generated, yielding 4 cells. If ten subjects are required for each cell, the experiment requires a total of 40 subjects. In a three variable design with two levels of variation per independent variable a $2 \times 2 \times 2$ arrangement exists, yielding 8 cells, and 80 subjects are required in order to have ten subjects per cell. Extending to four variables, 16 cells and 160 subjects are required. As you can see, the required number of subjects rapidly increases with an increase in number of independent variables. However, many studies are conducted with large numbers of subjects and this difficulty does not seem to be the most undesirable one. The second and third difficulties seem to be more severe.

A second difficulty of factorial designs incorporating more than two variables is that the ability to simultaneously manipulate the combinations of independent variables increases. In an attitude study, it is more difficult to simultaneously manipulate credibility of the communicator, type of message, sex of communicator, prior attitudes of the audience, and intelligence of the audience (a five-variable problem) than it is to just manipulate credibility of the communicator and prior attitudes of the audience.

A third difficulty with factorial designs arises when higher order interactions are significant. In a design with three independent variables it is possible to have a significant interaction between the three

186 variables *A*, *B*, and *C*. Consider a study that included the variables of age, sex, and intelligence. A three-variable interaction means that the effect on the dependent variable is a joint function of the subjects' age, sex, and intelligence. The investigator has to look at this triple interaction and interpret its meaning, deciphering what combinations produced what effect and why they produced this effect. Triple interactions can be quite difficult to interpret and interactions of an even higher order tend to become unwieldy. Therefore, it is advisable to try to keep your design at no more than a three-variable problem.

In spite of these difficulties, factorial designs are very popular and frequently used. This is because the advantages which they provide override the difficulties when these designs are used appropriately. The four advantages of factorial designs to be discussed here are ones presented by Kerlinger (1973, p. 257).

The first advantage is that more than one independent variable can be manipulated in an experiment and therefore more than one hypothesis can be tested. In a one-variable experiment only one hypothesis can be tested. Did the treatment condition produce the desired effect? In an experiment with three independent variables seven hypotheses can be tested. You can test a hypothesis regarding each of the three main effects—*A*, *B*, and *C*—and each of the four interactions—$A \times B$, $A \times C$, $B \times C$, and $A \times B \times C$.

A second advantage is that a potentially confounding variable can be controlled by building it into the design. This, as noted in the chapter on control, was one of mechanisms for eliminating the influence of an extraneous variable. Naturally, the decision to include the extraneous variable, such as sex, in the design will partially be a function of how many independent variables are already included. If three or four are already included it may be wise to effect control in another manner, as including only males or females. If only one or two independent variables exist, then the decision, in most cases, should be to include it in the design. Including the extraneous variable in the design not only controls it but may also provide valuable information regarding its effect on the dependent variable.

The third advantage of the factorial design is the greater precision it provides over the experiment with only one variable. The reasoning underlying this statement was discussed earlier and will not be reiterated.

The last advantage of the factorial design is that it enables the study of the interactive effects of the independent variables upon the dependent variable. This advantage is probably the most important since it enables one to hypothesize and test interactive effects. Testing main effects does not require a factorial design but testing interactions does. Lana (1959), for example, specifically set out to test an interactive hypothesis put forth by Solomon (1949) and Campbell (1957). They stated that pretests have a potentially sensitizing effect on attitudes. Lana used the four-group design to test this interactive hypothesis and found no significant interaction. Pretesting apparently did not have the hypothesized sensitizing effect upon attitudes.

Correlated-Groups Design

The correlated-groups (or within subject) design is a design that is structured in such a way that a correlation is introduced into the dependent variable measure. This correlation exists because there is a correlation between the various groups of subjects' scores in some variable which is related to the dependent variable. There are two basic ways in which this correlation can be introduced. One approach is to use the same subjects in each of the experimental groups included in the study. One would randomly select subjects (if this were possible) and then all of the selected subjects would respond under each treatment condition as shown in Figure 7.15. This design is very similar to the one-group before-after design. Only one group of subjects is used and they are repeatedly measured on the dependent variable, Y. Since only one group of subjects is included, this approach has all of the potential disadvantages associated with the one-group before-after design.

Haslerud and Meyers (1958) used this design in studying the transfer value of individually derived principles. All subjects were first trained on problems in which rules were given and on problems in which the subjects had to derive their own rules. After this training, *all* subjects solved problems using both the rules they had been given and the rules they had derived. Consequently, subjects served under both conditions. Results revealed that subjects initially did best on the

Treatment Conditions

X_1	X_2	X_3
S_1	S_1	S_1
S_2	S_2	S_2
S_3	S_3	S_3
.	.	.
.	.	.
.	.	.
S_n	S_n	S_n

Figure 7.15. Correlated-groups design using the same subjects in all experimental groups.

rule-given problems, but upon a second test given a week later, subjects did best on the rule-derived problems.

The second approach to the correlated-group design—and the more popular one—is to match subjects on one or more variables associated with the dependent variable and then randomly assign subjects to the experimental conditions. Figure 7.16 depicts such a design. Three subjects are first matched on the relevant variables and then are randomly assigned to the three treatment groups. This design is quite similar to the before-after design because subjects are first pretested and matched on the pretest scores, then the treatment conditions are administered and a posttest is administered.

Here we have the two means of establishing a correlated-groups design. This type of design is excellent when the sequencing effects or the disadvantages of having to match subjects, depending upon which type of correlated-groups design is used, are minimized. The strength or increased power of the design comes from the fact that it is more sensitive and therefore more capable of detecting the existence of a treatment effect. The increase in sensitivity arises from the fact that the correlated-groups design enables the investigator to isolate and eliminate the systematic effect produced by the correlated variable. When this effect is eliminated, one is left with a less contaminated dependent variable measure, increasing the probability of detecting the existence of any treatment effect. This is because the systematic effect that is eliminated is an effect that would ordinarily have been included as a source of error variance. When it is eliminated, then the magnitude of the error variance is smaller, increasing chances of detecting a difference produced by the experimental treatment effect. This issue will be discussed in more detail at a later point in the chapter.

Although the correlated-groups design is excellent means for increasing the sensitivity of your experiment, it has a number of disadvantages associated with it that make it inappropriate for use in most situations. First, if one engages in matching subjects prior to randomly assigning them to treatment conditions, there is the difficulty of having to match subjects on the variable or variables that are correlated

	Matched Subjects (a, b, and c)			
Experimental Group 1	$1a$	$2a$	$3a$	$4a \ldots n$
Experimental Group 2 MR	$1b$	$2b$	$3b$	$4b \ldots n$
Experimental Group 3	$1c$	$2c$	$3c$	$4c \ldots n$

Figure 7.16. Correlated-groups design using matched subjects in the experimental conditions.

with the dependent variable. Even if you elect to administer each experimental treatment condition to all subjects and thereby avoid the matching problem, there are other difficulties to be overcome. You must deal with the possibility of a sequencing effect influencing the outcome of the experiment. If this can be overcome by counterbalancing, then the additional problems with which you must contend are the possibilities of history, maturation, and statistical regression effects artifactually confounding the results of your experiment. Potentially confounding variables, such as the ones just mentioned, are generally more difficult to control in a correlated group design than they are in other designs. As a result of this, it is not the most frequently used design.

Combining Randomized and Correlated-Groups Designs

In conducting psychological research there are many times when one is interested in several variables, of which one or more would fit into a randomized-group design and others would fit into a correlated-groups design. Does this mean that two separate studies have to be investigated, or can they be combined into one design? As you probably have suspected, they can be incorporated into one design. Such a design is called a *factorial correlated-groups design* or a *factorial design based on a Mixed Model.* The simplest form of such a design would be a situation in which two independent variables had to be varied. However, one independent variable required a different group of subjects for each level of variation. The other independent variable was constructed in such a way that all subjects had to take each level of variation. Consequently, the first independent variable requires a randomized subjects design and the second independent variable requires a correlated-groups design. When these two independent variables are included in the same design, it becomes a factorial correlated groups design as illustrated in figure 7.17.

In such a design subjects are randomly assigned to the different levels of variation of the randomized subjects independent variable. All subjects then take each level of variation of the correlated-groups independent variable. This design has, therefore, the advantage of being able to test for the effects produced by each of the two independent variables as well as for the interaction between the two independent variables. Additionally, it has an advantage in terms of requiring fewer subjects since all subjects take all levels of variation of one of the independent variables. Therefore, the number of subjects required is only some multiple of the number of levels of the randomized subject independent variable.

RANDOMIZED SUBJECTS INDEPENDENT VARIABLE	CORRELATED-GROUPS INDEPENDENT VARIABLE		
	A_1	A_2	A_3
	S_1	S_1	S_1
	S_2	S_2	S_2
B_1	S_3	S_3	S_3
	S_4	S_4	S_4
	S_5	S_5	S_5
	S_6	S_6	S_6
	S_7	S_7	S_7
B_2	S_8	S_8	S_8
	S_9	S_9	S_9
	S_{10}	S_{10}	S_{10}

Figure 7.17. Factorial correlated-groups design with two independent variables.

The discussion of the factorial correlated-groups design has been limited to consideration of only two independent variables. This in no way is meant to imply that the design could not be extended to include more than two independent variables. As with the factorial designs, one could include as many independent variables as were considered necessary. One could include any combination of the randomized subjects with the correlated-groups type of independent variable. If one were conducting a study with three independent variables, *A*, *B*, and *C*, two of these independent variables, *B* and *C*, may be such that they require all subjects to take each level of variation of the both independent variables. Therefore, this design would have included two independent variables of the correlated-groups variety and one of the randomized subjects variety.

Choice of a Research Design

In the present chapter various types of research designs have been presented for possible use in a research study. It is your task to choose the one that is most appropriate. There are some rather straightforward factors to consider in making the design selections. As you shall see, as these factors are discussed, the appropriate choice requires a thorough knowledge of your problem and the extraneous variables you must control in your study, as well as the alternative designs available and their advantages and disadvantages.

Research Question

Naturally, when you set out to conduct a research study you want to conduct it to answer a specific research question. You may want to find out if people react to a given stimulus in the same way as animals do. Regardless of your problem, you must select the design so that it will give you an answer to your problem. There are times when investigators try to force a problem into a specific research design. This would be an example of the tail wagging the dog, and typically would not allow you to arrive at an appropriate answer. Therefore, the primary criterion for selection of a design is whether or not it will enable you to arrive at an answer to the research question.

Control

The second factor to consider in the selection of a research design is whether or not you can incorporate the control techniques that would allow you to unambiguously arrive at an answer to your research question. If you have the choice of several designs that could allow you to answer your research question, then you must select that design that will provide maximum control over variables that could also explain the results obtained from the experiment. Control therefore, appears to be the second most important criterion to consider.

Randomized vs. Correlated-Groups Design

The third factor to consider is the nature of the research design. In some cases the research problem dictates the type of research design. For example, if you were engaged in a learning study it is necessary to give subjects a number of trials to enable them to learn the material. If the research question focused on, for example, the speed of acquisition of the material, then trials have to be incorporated into the design. Therefore, a correlated-groups design is necessary. However, this does not exist in all cases. Where this does not exist the investigator is faced with the choice of manipulating the independent variable or variables with a randomized subjects (between-subjects) design or a correlated-groups (within-subjects) design. The randomized subjects design is more frequently labeled a between-subjects design because different subjects exist in each level of variation of the independent variable. In a similar manner, the correlated-groups design is labeled a within-subjects design because all subjects respond at each level of variation of the independent variable.

Where one has a choice of a between- or a within-subjects design the choice is most frequently made in favor of the within-subjects design. This is because, as I have previously pointed out, the within-subjects design provides a more sensitive test of the independent variable. To explain why this is so, you first need to have an understanding of the concept of variance.

Variance is a measure of the amount of variability that exists in a group of scores. It is calculated by computing the amount to which a set of scores deviates about their mean or average score. To obtain this measure one uses the following formula:

$$S = \frac{\Sigma x^2}{N} = \frac{\Sigma (X - M)^2}{N}$$

X = raw score
S = variance
x = raw score minus the mean score $(X - M)$
N = number of scores
M = mean score or $\dfrac{\Sigma X}{N}$
Σ = sum

Consider the following set of scores:

X	M	$X - M$	$(X - M)^2$	$\Sigma (X - M)^2$	$\dfrac{\Sigma x^2}{N}$
1	5	− 4	16	58	6.67
2	5	− 3	9		
3	5	− 2	4		
7	5	2	4		
8	5	3	9		
9	5	4	16		

For this set of scores the variance is 6.67.

The reason that variances are discussed is that a great deal of our statistical analysis of data consists of comparing variances. The most generally accepted way of classifying variances is in terms of systematic variance and error variance. Systematic variance can be defined as the variation in scores that can be attributed to some known or unknown influence that causes the scores to systematically increase or decrease. Consider the case of an honest versus a crooked gambler. An honest gambler would use fair dice in the sense that the numbers would be expected to turn up a given percentage of the time. The numbers 1 through 6 should appear about equally often. On the other hand, a crooked gambler would attempt to increase his chances of winning by loading the dice. In other words, he would fix the dice so that certain numbers would appear more often than other numbers. Once he has done this, he has introduced a source of systematic variance because he has made certain numbers systematically appear more often than other numbers. In psychological experimentation we engage in a similar procedure when we introduce the independent variable. The primary purpose of presenting the independent variable is to isolate the differential influence which it produces. If one level of the independent variable depresses scores and another level of the independent variable increases scores then it is producing a systematic influence because a given level is systematically making the scores go up or down. Consequently, the studies conducted by the research psychologist represent an attempt to isolate the variables which produce a systematic influence on behavior.

Error variance, ideally, represents the random or chance variation that exists in scores. Error variance, therefore, refers to any changes in scores that cannot be attributed to a systematic influence. It represents the changes that occur that could not be controlled because they are not systematically influenced by any given variable.

When one conducts a psychological study it is necessary to determine if the independent variable manipulation had an effect. The way this decision is typically made is to conduct a statistical test on the obtained data. If our study consisted of one experimental and one control group we would probably conduct a t test, whereas, if one control and two or more experimental groups were used we would have to perform an F test. Regardless of which statistical test we conduct the basic procedure would be the same. We would be comparing the amount of systematic variance produced by the independent variable, or the variance between the treatment groups, with the within-group variance or the variance between the scores that occurs within each treatment group. The within-group variance is typically called the error variance, but it is not error variance in the true sense of the word. True error variance consists entirely of random fluctuations in scores. Error variance that is called or equated with within-group variance typically contains true error variance plus some unidentified or unknown source of systematic variance. Consequently, in a statistical test we are actually comparing the amount of between group or systematic variance with true error variance plus uncontrolled systematic variance:

$$\frac{\text{between group systematic variance}}{\text{true error variance plus uncontrolled systematic variance}}$$

194   If the numerator is much larger (as reflected by a probability statement) than the denominator, then we conclude that the independent variable exerted a significant influence and, therefore, conclude that it caused a change in behavior. However, since a statistical test involves comparing the variation which occurs between groups of subjects with that which occurs within groups of subjects, it is possible that the independent variable did exert a significant influence even though the results of the statistical test may suggest the opposite. Such a state of affairs could exist if the amount of uncontrolled systematic variation that existed in the denominator was so large as to mask the influence of the independent variable. If such a state existed, then identifying and controlling some of the previously uncontrolled systematic variation would result in decreasing the size of the denominator and increasing the chances of detecting the potential influence of the independent variable. This is exactly what a correlated-groups design does. The correlated-groups design controls or eliminates much of the otherwise uncontrolled systematic variation by either matching subjects or having each subject participate in each level of variation of the independent variable. In this way the denominator is smaller and the possibility of detecting an effect of the independent variable is increased.

Summary

The design of a research study represents the basic outline of the study in terms of how one will collect and analyze the data as well as how unwanted variation will be controlled. Consequently, the design of the experiment determines to a great extent whether or not one will attain an answer to the research question. Inappropriately designed studies such as the one-shot case study, one-group before-after design, and static-group comparison design do not provide the desired answers because they do not control for the influence of the many extraneous variables that can have an effect on the results of an experiment.

In order to design a good study there are three criteria to be met. First, the design must test the hypotheses advanced. The second criterion of a good design focuses on the control of extraneous variables. It is necessary to meet this criterion in order to be able to attribute the observed effects to the independent variable. The third criterion is generalizability. These three criteria are the ideal; seldom will a study meet all three.

In designing a study that attempts to meet the criteria just stated, many investigators make frequent use of a pretest. There seems to be a

number of good reasons for administering a pretest. It can be used to   **195**
match subjects and thereby increase the sensitivity of the experiment.
It could also be used to determine if a ceiling effect exists, or to test a
subject's initial position on a variable to determine if the variable
interacted with the independent variable. Other reasons for pretesting
include testing for initial comparability of subjects and establishing
that subjects actually changed as a result of the independent variable.

True or good general research designs consist of the after-only,
before-after, and before-after four-group design because they have the
ability to eliminate the influence of extraneous variables that serve as
sources of rival hypotheses for explaining the observed results. The
primary reasons these designs can control for unwanted variation is
that they all include a comparison control group and subjects are
randomly assigned to the experimental and control groups. While these
three designs illustrate the basic structure of good research designs,
they do not represent the type most frequently used. Most studies use
an extension of one of these designs in the form of a simple
randomized-subjects design, a factorial design, a correlated-groups design, or a factorial correlated-groups design.

Key Concepts

One way to test your mastery of the material that was presented in this
chapter is to see if you know the meaning of the following terms.
These terms were selected because they represent the key concepts. If
you can define, identify, or otherwise explain each of the following
terms without referring back to the material in the chapter, you can be
assured that you have mastered the basics of the material that was
presented. Just in case you cannot recall the meaning of a given term,
the page on which it can be found appears in parentheses beside it.

> one-shot case study (p. 161)
> one-group before-after (p. 162)
> static group comparison (p. 164)
> control group (p. 166)
> experimental group (p. 166)
> external validity (p. 167)
> pretesting (p. 168)
> ceiling effect (p. 168)
> initial position (p. 169)
> after-only research design (pp. 170–171)
> before-after research design (p. 172)

196

intragroup history effect (p. 174)
before-after four-group design (p. 175)
simple randomized subjects design (p. 178)
factorial design (p. 180)
cell (p. 180)
interaction (p. 181)
main effect (p. 181)
correlated-groups design (p. 187)
mixed model design (p. 189)
variance (p. 192)

8

Quasi-Experimental
Designs

Throughout this text the need for conducting true experimental studies has been emphasized. This is because true experimental studies obtain the most unambiguous answers to questions asked and have the greatest capacity for reducing alternative explanations because the influence of extraneous variables that could serve as rival hypotheses is controlled. However, as one moves out of the laboratory it is more difficult to control possible extraneous variables. Also, there are many events taking place in the natural setting of the real world that need to be experimentally investigated, yet it is not possible for the experimenter to have control over the manipulation of all antecedent conditions. For example, consider child abuse. An investigator could not ethically or morally manipulate conditions that *may* cause parents to abuse their child. In spite of these restrictions such phenomena exist and need to be investigated. In such cases it is frequently possible to approximate a true experimental design. Such approximations are labeled quasi-experimental designs.

This section on quasi-experimental designs in no way minimizes the importance and necessity of increasing the use of true experimentation. However, there are many settings in which one would like to be able to assess the impact of a given treatment condition but cannot do so within the framework of a true experiment. Such settings include unplanned events—war or natural disaster—as well as planned interventions such as a specific persuasive communication designed to change some condition, policy, or behavior of individuals. In such settings one would like to isolate the effect due to the treatment. This is where the quasi-experimental designs come in.

"The phrase 'quasi-experimental design' refers to the application of an experimental mode of analysis and interpretation to bodies of data not meeting the full requirements of experimental control" (Campbell, 1968, p. 259). In natural settings where planned or unplanned effects occur, one cannot randomly assign subjects to treatment conditions, nor is it possible to control for the influence of extraneous variables through other techniques. Therefore, a quasi-experimental design is needed to obtain some index of the impact of the treatment condition.

At this point you may be somewhat skeptical of the possibility that causal inferences can be drawn without having the ability to manipulate the independent variable or control for extraneous variables. However, many causal inferences are made without use of the experimental framework. They are made by rendering other rival interpretations implausible. If a friend of yours unknowingly stepped in front of an oncoming car and was pronounced dead after being hit by the car, you would probably attribute her death to the moving vehicle. Your friend might have died as a result of numerous other causes—a heart attack, for example—but such alternative explanations are not accepted because they are not plausible. In like manner, the causal interpretations arrived at from quasi-experimental analysis are those that are consistent with the data and where other rival interpretations have been shown to be implausible. I am not trying to say that the identification of what is and is not plausible is always as apparent as this illustration suggests. If it were, we would not need to conduct the experiment. I am only demonstrating in as simple a fashion as possible the type of procedure that must be used within the framework of quasi-experimental designs.

Before-After Quasi-Research Designs

There are two quasi-research designs that fall into the category of before-after designs, so categorized because a measurement of the dependent variable is made both before and after the experimental treatment condition is imposed. These two designs are the nonequivalent control group design and the simulated before-after design.

Nonequivalent Control Group Design

There are a number of designs which have been identified by Cook and Campbell (1975) as being nonequivalent control group designs. These designs are so named because they include both an experimental and a control group. However, subjects are not randomly assigned to each group. This results in having subjects in the control and experimental groups who are not equivalent on all variables, which may affect the dependent variable. Consequently, these uncontrolled variables operate as rival hypotheses to explain the outcome of the experiment. This is what makes these designs nonequivalent control group quasi-experimental designs. However, there are instances in which these are the only kinds of designs that can be used. Where a better design cannot be used, some form of a nonequivalent control group design is frequently recommended. This design, depicted in Figure 8.1, consists of an experimental and a control group which are given a pretest and then a posttest after the treatment condition is administered to the experimental group. The pre- to posttest difference scores of the two groups are then typically compared to determine if significant differences exist. As can be seen, the design appears identical to the before-after experimental design. However, there is one basic difference that makes one a *true* experimental design and the other a *quasi*-experimental design. In the before-after design subjects are randomly assigned to the experimental and control group whereas in the nonequivalent control group design they are not. This is the component that makes this design a quasi-experimental design. The two groups of subjects represent naturally assembled groups, such as two classrooms of children or two training groups.

Consider the study conducted by Shingles (1973) in which he attempted to assess the influence of membership in a Head Start program on attitude change. The stimulus for this study was a proposition made by a number of individuals, which was based primarily on interview data, that membership in voluntary associations leads to the creation of certain attitudes, which in turn leads to increased political involvement that is beneficial to the democratic process.

The advocates of this process have primarily collected interview data to support their contention; however, as Shingles points out, this

Figure 8.1. Nonequivalent control group design. (Adapted from Campbell, D. T., and Stanley, J. C. Experimental and quasi-experimental designs for research. Chicago: Rand McNally and Co., 1963. Copyright 1963, American Educational Research Association, Washington, D. C.)

does not eliminate a number of rival hypotheses. To be able to infer causality, the rival hypotheses must be controlled. In an attempt to determine if there really is a causal link between membership in voluntary associations—a Head Start program in this study—and the creation of attitudes beneficial to the democratic process, Shingles used the quasi-experimental nonequivalent control group design.

Shingles's design, depicted in Figure 8.2, consisted of an experimental group and a control group. Actually, Shingles included one additional experimental group (oldtimers), which is not represented in Figure 8.2 because it is not needed to illustrate the nonequivalent control group design and because this experimental group represents a slight deviation from the structure of the design as presented in Figure 8.1. The experimental group of subjects consisted of female parents whose children were enrolled in the local Head Start program. Shingles chose Head Start parents because, he reasoned, members of this organization would be more likely to reveal an effect if one actually existed, and one of the stated purposes of Head Start was to generate certain types of attitudinal change. The control group consisted of a matched group of mothers whose children did not participate in the Head Start program. The mothers in both groups were pretested on a series of attitude measures designed to assess the subjects' feelings of both personal and political alienation, since the purpose of the study was to determine if these attitudes would be reduced. Additionally, several other scales were also given. After pretesting, the children in the experimental group participated in the Head Start program and the mothers of these children were encouraged to become actively involved in the program. Approximately a year and half later, the mothers in both groups were posttested and their attitudes were measured. Results of this study revealed that, contrary to prior thinking and interpretation of interview data, voluntary participation in an organization such as Head Start has little effect on the members' attitudes, and if any effect exists, it is that greater, rather than less, personal alienation is generated.

The Shingles study represents an excellent example of a quasi-experiment using the nonequivalent control group design because both

	Preresponse Measure	Treatment	Postresponse Measure
Experimental Group	Attitude Scales	Head Start	Attitude Scales
Control Group	Attitude Scales		Attitude Scales

Figure 8.2. The design of Shingles's study (1973).

202 an experimental and a control group were included in the study. However, the two groups were not randomly assigned from a common population, thus representing the quasi nature of the design, which means that all extraneous variables probably had not been controlled. This means that rival hypotheses, other than the experimental treatment, exist when attempting to explain the outcome of the experiment. As Cook and Campbell (1975) have pointed out, the rival hypotheses that exist tend to be directly related to the results obtained in the experiment. These researchers have identified several different experimental outcomes that could occur from use of a nonequivalent control group design. They have then appropriately pointed out the rival hypotheses that could also explain the obtained results. These outcomes as well as the rival hypotheses that threaten them will now be discussed.

INCREASING TREATMENT EFFECT I.   The increasing treatment effect I outcome, illustrated in figure 8.3, is a situation in which the control group scores reveal no change from pretest to posttest but the experimental group starts at a higher level and shows a significant positive change. Such an outcome appears on the surface to suggest that the experimental treatment was effective. However, such an out-

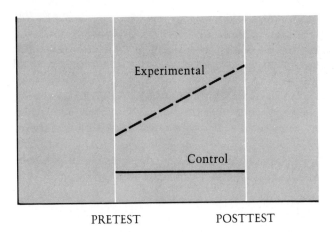

PRETEST   POSTTEST

Figure 8.3. Increasing treatment effect I. (From Cook, T. D., and Campbell, D. T., "The design and conduct of quasi-experiments and true experiments in field settings," in Handbook of industrial and organizational psychology edited by M. D. Dunnette. Copyright © Rand McNally College Publishing Company, 1976.)

come could also have occurred as a result of a selection-maturation effect or a local history effect.

A selection-maturation effect refers to the fact that one of the two groups of subjects was selected in such a way that they were growing or developing faster than the subjects in the other group. One group may be progressing faster because they are more intelligent or capable than the other group. If the Shingles study had obtained the increasing treatment effect outcome it would have indicated that the experimental treatment group had a more positive attitude during pretesting and even more positive attitude during posttesting. This increase in positive attitude could be due to the treatment effect. However, it could also be due to the fact that the experimental subjects were more receptive to having their attitudes changed. If this were the case, then the posttest increase could be accounted for by the fact that the selection procedure happened to place the more changeable or adaptable subjects in the experimental condition.

In an attempt to eliminate the potential biasing effect of such a selection-maturation effect, many investigators attempt to match subjects. Shingles, for example, matched mothers in the experimental and control groups on a series of attitude measures. This matching is supposed to equate subjects on the matched variables not only at the time of matching, but also during the remainder of the entire study. If matching is conducted during the pretest then experimental and control subjects should not differ on the dependent variable measure. If they do not, then it is assumed that they are equated. This equality is assumed to persist in time so that any difference that is observed during a posttest is attributed to the experimental treatment effect. Recent evidence (Campbell and Erlebacher, 1970; and Campbell and Boruch, 1975) has revealed that such an assumption may be an erroneous one. This is because of a statistical regression phenomenon that may occur within the two groups of subjects. This statistical regression phenomenon operates in such a way that it increases the difference between the two matched groups upon posttesting apart from any experimental treatment effect. Such a difference could erroneously be interpreted as being due to a treatment effect, or a failure to find a treatment effect, depending upon which of the matched groups of subjects operated as the experimental group and which operated as the control group.

To illustrate this potential artifact let us reconsider the Shingles study. This study attempted to equate subjects by matching on a variety of variables. For the sake of illustration, let us assume that matching was conducted on the pretest attitude measures. Actually, matching was conducted in terms of similarity of life styles. Assume further that the attitude scores obtained from mothers who did and did not have children in the Head Start program were distributed in the manner revealed in Table 8.1. From this table it is readily apparent that most of the Head Start mothers had lower attitude scores than did the non-Head Start mothers. If one matched in an attempt to equate subjects, the mothers who would be included in the study would be the high scoring Head Start mothers and the low scoring non-Head Start mothers. In other words, one would have only included subjects with extreme scores and, therefore, subjects who were most susceptible to the statistical regression phenomenon would have been included. This would not have been a serious factor if the distribution of scores of the two groups had been the same. However, they are not. Therefore, matching involved selecting for the experimental group Head Start mothers who had the highest attitude scores. The control group consisted of mothers who had the lowest attitude scores. Statistical regression would dictate that the Head Start mothers' scores, upon posttesting, would decline and regress toward the mean of their group and the control subjects' scores would regress or increase toward their group's mean, as also illustrated in Table 8.1. Such a statistical regression phenomenon could indicate that the experimental treatment was actually detrimental when it may not have had any effect. If the treatment did have a positive effect, such a statistical regression effect would lead one to underestimate the impact of the treatment effect.

Table 8.1 Hypothetical attitude scores.

HEAD START SUBJECTS	HEAD START MOTHER'S PRETEST ATTITUDE	MOTHER'S POSTTEST ATTITUDE	NON-HEAD START SUBJECTS	NON-HEAD START MOTHER'S PRETEST ATTITUDE	MOTHER'S POSTTEST ATTITUDES
S_1	5		S_{16}	25	28
S_2	7		S_{17}	27	30
S_3	9		S_{18}	29	32
S_4	11		S_{19}	31	34
S_5	13		S_{20}	33	36
S_6	15		S_{21}	35	
S_7	17		S_{22}	37	
S_8	19		S_{23}	39	
S_9	21		S_{24}	41	
S_{10}	23		S_{25}	43	
S_{11}	25	22	S_{26}	45	
S_{12}	27	24	S_{27}	47	
S_{13}	29	26	S_{28}	49	
S_{14}	31	28	S_{29}	51	
S_{15}	33	30	S_{30}	53	

Matched Subjects

Another attempt at equating subjects by eliminating the selection-maturation bias artifact is to use a variety of statistical regression techniques, such as analysis of covariance and partial correlation. Again, Campbell and Erlebacher (1970) and Campbell and Boruch (1975) have pointed out the fallacy of such an approach. Delving into the fallacy of this approach is beyond the scope of this text. Suffice it to say that these researchers as well as others (Lord, 1969, and Cronbach and Furby, 1970) have revealed that such statistical adjustments cannot equate nonequivalent groups unless there is no error in the dependent measures given to these individuals.

A second rival hypothesis existing in the increasing treatment effect I outcome is that of a local history effect (Cook and Campbell, 1975). A general history effect, such as that discussed in a previous chapter, is controlled in the nonequivalent control group design by inclusion of a control group. However, the design is still susceptible to a local history effect (Cook and Campbell, 1975). By this I am referring to some event that affects *only* the experimental or the control group. Such a local history effect could have operated in the Shingles study if enrolling their children in the Head Start program had enabled the mothers to acquire goods not available to the control mothers. If the experimental mothers, through their involvement in Head Start, made contacts that enabled them to, for example, secure a better job, such a variable might operate to influence the posttest assessment of subjects' attitudes. Since such a variable would only have operated for the experimental subjects, it would serve as a rival hypothesis for any difference observed between the experimental and control groups.

INCREASING TREATMENT AND CONTROL GROUPS.   The increasing treatment and control groups outcome is a situation in which both the control and the experimental groups show an increment in the dependent variable from pre- to posttesting, as revealed in figure 8.4. The difference between the increased growth rates could be due to an actual treatment effect but it could also be due to a type of selection-maturation interaction. Figure 8.4 reveals that subjects in both groups are increasing in performance. Note, however, that the treatment group, at the time of pretesting, scored higher on the dependent variable. This could indicate that the subjects in the experimental treatment group were just naturally increasing faster on the dependent variable than the control subjects. The greater difference between groups of subjects at posttesting may only reflect the fact that the experimental subjects continued to increase faster on the dependent variable than did the control subjects. For example, assume that the dependent variable consisted of a measure of problem solving ability and the subjects were six years old at the time of pretesting and eight years old at the time of posttesting. Assume further that the experimental subjects were brighter and therefore increasing in problem solving ability more rapidly than control subjects. If this were the case, then one would expect the two groups of subjects to differ somewhat at pretest time. However, subjects would not stop in terms of problem solving ability at age six, but would continue to develop this ability. Since the experimental subjects were already increasing faster than control subjects at age six, one would expect this differential growth rate to continue, leading to an even greater difference at posttest time, independent of any treatment effect. If such a differential growth pattern occurred one may artifactually interpret a greater posttest difference as being due to a treatment effect when it is really due to a selection-maturation interaction.

Evidence of the existence of such a selection-maturation interaction could be obtained from looking at the variability of the subjects' scores at pretest and posttest time. Random error would say that the variability of the scores should be the same at both testing occasions. However, a growth factor would suggest that the scores should increase in terms of variability. Therefore, if the variability of the scores for the experimental and control group increased from pretest to post-

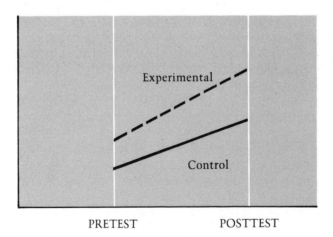

PRETEST   POSTTEST

Figure 8.4. Increasing treatment and control groups. (From Cook, T. D., and Campbell, D. T., "The design and conduct of quasi-experiments and true experiments in field settings," in Handbook of industrial and organizational psychology edited by M. D. Dunnette. © Rand McNally College Publishing Company, 1976.)

testing, this suggests the possibility of the existence of a selection-maturation interaction.

INCREASING TREATMENT EFFECT II.   The increasing treatment effect II, depicted in figure 8.5, is an outcome in which control and experimental treatment groups differ rather extensively at pretest time. However, the experimental group improves over time, presumably due to the experimental treatment, so that the posttest difference is decreased. Such an outcome would be desired when the experimental group was a disadvantaged group and the experimental treatment was designed to overcome the disadvantage. For example, Head Start was initiated in an attempt to overcome the environmental deprivation experienced by many children in the United States. The Head Start program was supposed to overcome the effects of this environmental handicap and bring the performance of these disadvantaged individuals up to the level of performance of nondisadvantaged individuals. If a study were conducted that compared the pretest and posttest performances of a group of control individuals, who had not experienced the environmental handicap, with a group of environmentally handicapped individuals who received the Head Start experimental treatment, one would hope to find the type of effect illustrated in figure 8.5. However, before one can interpret the increase in performance of the experimental treatment group as being due to the Head Start experience several rival hypotheses must be ruled out. The first rival hypothesis to be ruled out is a local history effect, which has already been discussed. This refers to events that affect only one of the two groups of subjects. The second and more likely rival hypothesis is a statistical regression effect. The statistical regression effect is a likely source of confounding because the subjects in the experimental treatment group are typically selected because of their unusually poor performance or low scores. Consequently, the regression artifact would predict that the scores of this group of subjects should increase during posttesting. Statistical regression could, therefore, produce the outcome depicted in figure 8.5. The unwary investigator would interpret this as a treatment effect. Therefore, designs that involve administering an experimental treatment to a disadvantaged group should check for the possibility of such a regression artifact.

One indicator of the existence of a regression artifact is the stability of the deprived group's scores in the absence of the experimental treatment. If the deprived group's scores consistently stay low over time this suggests that the low scores represent the true standing of the individuals. In such cases a pretest to posttest increment would probably represent a true experimental effect or at least one not confounded by the influence of a regression artifact.

208

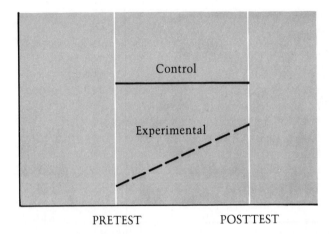

PRETEST   POSTTEST

Figure 8.5. Increasing treatment effect II. (From Cook, T. D., and Campbell, D. T., "The design and conduct of quasi-experiments and true experiments in field settings," in Handbook of industrial and organizational psychology edited by M. D. Dunnette. Copyright © Rand McNally College Publishing Company, 1976.)

CROSSOVER EFFECT.   Figure 8.6 depicts an experimental outcome in which the treatment group scored significantly lower at pretest time but significantly higher at posttest time. While this outcome represents the typical interaction effect, the important point is that the experimental treatment group started at a point significantly lower, but ended up at a point significantly higher, than the control group. Such an outcome is much more readily interpreted than the other outcomes discussed because it renders many of the potential rival hypotheses implausible. Statistical regression can be ruled out because it is highly unlikely that the experimental treatment group's lower pretest scores would regress to a point significantly higher than the control group's scores upon posttesting. Second, a selection maturation effect is highly unlikely because it is typically the higher-scoring pretest subjects who grow faster. The outcome depicted in figure 8.6 reveals that the subjects scoring lower on the pretest increased more rapidly than did the controls scoring higher on the pretest. This is the opposite of what a selection-maturation outcome would suggest.

Four different potential outcomes from use of the nonequivalent control group design have now been discussed. It has been revealed that the interpretability of this design depends on the results obtained since the obtained results basically dictate the type of rival hypothesis that may exist. Therefore, when considering use of this design it is

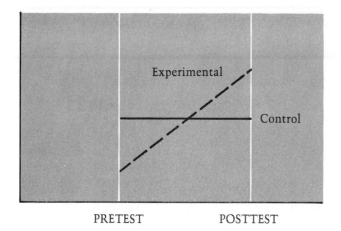

PRETEST   POSTTEST

Figure 8.6. Crossover effect. (From Cook, T. D., and
    Campbell, D. T., "The design and conduct of quasi-
    experiments and true experiments in field settings," in
    <u>Handbook of industrial and organizational psychology</u>
    edited by M. D. Dunnette. Copyright © Rand McNally
    College Publishing Company, 1976.)

advisable to ponder the potential pattern of results that may be obtained to determine whether or not the impact of the potential rival
hypotheses can be assessed. If they cannot, then it may be best to
discontinue the study.

STATISTICAL ANALYSIS OF THE NONEQUIVALENT CONTROL
GROUP DESIGN.   Statistical analyses of true experiments are easily conducted in the sense that appropriate analyses exist. However,
quasi-experimental designs such as the nonequivalent control group design do not lend themselves as readily to the standard statistical tests.
This is because subjects are not randomly assigned to treatment conditions (a general requirement of most statistical tests) and rival hypotheses that exist as a result of the biased selection may create artifactual
differences between the experimental and control groups. Ideally, there
would be a statistical analysis which would adjust for such artifactually produced difference. Campbell and Erlebacher (1970) have revealed
that matching cannot adequately adjust for such differences, and
Campbell and Boruch (1975) have shown that regression techniques
such as analysis of covariance are inadequate unless measurement is
error-free (Cronbach and Furby, 1970).
    According to Kenny (1975) the issue at hand "is whether pretreat-
ment differences should increase, decrease, or remain stable if there is

210   no treatment effect" (p. 346). From his review of the literature he has revealed that there are four modes of statistical analysis that have been used to analyze the nonequivalent control group design. These include analysis of covariance, analysis of covariance with reliability correction, raw change score analysis, and standardized change score analysis. Although different researchers (e.g., Cronbach and Furby, 1970; Werts and Linn, 1970; and Campbell and Erlebacher, 1970) have condemned various of these techniques, Kenny (1975) suggests that in different situations, each of these statistical techniques may be appropriate. More specifically, Kenny states that the correct mode of statistical analysis depends upon matching it with the way in which subjects are selected for the experimental and control groups. If the control and experimental groups are assigned on the basis of a pretest, then analysis of covariance is the appropriate statistical test. For example, if subjects scoring above a certain score on a pretest were given the experimental treatment, and subjects scoring below that predetermined score served as controls, then one should analyze the data by analysis of covariance. However, if subjects self-select into groups, then analysis of covariance with reliability correction is the appropriate statistical analysis. By self-selection I am referring to the fact that the subjects determined whether or not they wanted to participate in the treatment versus the control group. For example, subjects, for the most part, determine whether or not they want a college education. In a similar manner, smokers decide themselves whether or not they want to participate in an antismoking study. This is one type of self-selection, and in such cases analysis of covariance with reliability correction is the appropriate statistical text.

If selection for inclusion into a treatment program is based upon some sociological, demographic, or social psychological characteristics, then other statistical tests are more appropriate. For example, the government has legislated certain social programs for particular groups of individuals such as Head Start, Job Corps, and other programs aimed at individuals with specific demographic or sociological characteristics. In such cases, if the differences in the groups remain stable over time or a selection-maturation interaction does not exist then raw change score analysis is appropriate. However, if a selection-maturation interaction does exist (subjects in the two groups are naturally growing or maturing at different rates) then some type of transformation must be conducted to extract this natural differential growth factor. One such transformation is standardization. The combined control and treatment groups' raw pretest and posttest scores should be separately standardized. This would have the effect of eliminating the selection-maturation interaction. After the scores are standardized pretest-posttest change scores would be computed and analyzed. Consequently, the appropriate mode of analysis in such a situation would be a standardized change score analysis. However, standardized change score analysis should not be considered the panacea when selection-maturation interaction or growth factor exists. Bryk and Weisberg (1977) have appropriately demonstrated that the selection-maturation or growth factor can take several different forms. The choice of a statistical test should be consistent with the form of the growth parameter.

Simulated Before-After Design

The simulated before-after design is useful in a situation where it is impossible to assign subjects randomly to an experimental condition. However, it is possible to select randomly, from the larger population, two subgroups. One of these subgroups would serve as the control group and would be tested prior to administering the treatment condition, and the other group would serve as the experimental group and would be tested after the treatment condition was introduced. This design is depicted in Figure 8.7. The pretest scores of the control group would then be compared with the posttest scores of the experimental group to assess the influence of the treatment condition.

Star and Hughes (1950) used this design to assess the influence of a six-month experimental campaign program designed to inform the city of Cincinnati of facts about the United Nations. Thus the campaign was designed to be an informational campaign rather than a persuasive one. To assess the influence of the campaign, Star and Hughes interviewed a representative sample of 745 members of Cincinnati's adult

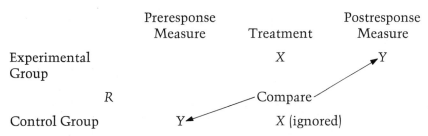

Figure 8.7. Simulated before-after design. R indicates that the two groups of subjects were randomly selected. (Adapted from Campbell, D. T., and Stanley, J. C. Experimental and quasi-experimental designs for research. Chicago: Rand McNally and Co., 1963. Copyright 1963, American Educational Research Association, Washington, D. C.)

212   population prior to the introduction of the campaign. The experimental campaign was then introduced in such a way that an attempt was made to reach *every* adult resident (1,155,703) within the retail trading zone of Cincinnati.

> In all, 59,588 pieces of literature were distributed and 2,800 clubs were reached by speakers supplied by a speakers' bureau and by circular, hundreds of documentary films were shown and the slogan, "Peace Begins With the United Nations—the United Nations Begins With You" was exhibited everywhere, in every imaginable form—blotters, matchbooks, streetcar cards, etc.[1] [p. 390]

Following this campaign a second and different representative sample of 758 adults was interviewed and the results of the interviews for the two groups compared. Results of the study revealed that the campaign had little effect, since there was very little difference between the responses of the two groups.

This design is not exceptionally strong, but it is much better than the one-group before-after design, eliminating as it does a number of rival hypotheses. Specifically, this design controls for such variables as statistical regression and selection biases. The primary disadvantage of the design is that it does not control for history effects. An effect due to history could have occurred during the intervening six-month period of time in which the campaign took place, which could explain some of the results obtained. Indeed, a real history effect did occur during the Star and Hughes study. At the time of the study, a cold war was taking place with Russia, and this event was a rival hypothesis for some of the results found. Star and Hughes did, in fact, attribute some of their findings to this variable and obtained data to support this interpretation.

Problems such as the history effect can, however, be overcome if the investigator is not restricted to testing only that group of subjects that *must* receive the treatment effect. If the investigator has the option of testing a comparable though not entirely equivalent group of subjects, which does not have to receive the treatment effect, then this group of subjects could serve as a control group. Such a separate samples simulated before-after design would take the form shown in Figure 8.8. Two different randomly selected groups of subjects are used to measure the treatment effect. Following introduction of the treatment condition, one group's pretest scores are subtracted from the other group's posttest scores. This difference is then compared with the difference between one of the control group's pretest scores and the

1. From Star, S. A., and Hughes, H. M. Report on an educational campaign: The Cincinnati plan for the United Nations. *American Journal of Sociology*, 1950, 55, 389–400. Composed and printed by the University of Chicago Press, Chicago, Illinois, USA.

	Preresponse Measure	Treatment	Postresponse Measure	Difference
Experimental Group I R		X	Y	Group I Y minus Group II Y
Experimental Group II R	Y	X (ignored)		
Control Group I R			Y	Group I Y minus Group II Y
Control Group II R	Y			

Compare

Figure 8.8. Separate samples simulated before-after design. R indicates that the two experimental and control groups of subjects were randomly selected. (Adapted from Campbell, D. T., and Stanley, J. C. Experimental and quasi-experimental designs for research. Chicago: Rand McNally and Co., 1963. Copyright 1963, American Educational Research Association, Washington, D. C.)

214   other control group's posttest scores. If a significant difference is obtained, added assurance is gained that the difference is due to the treatment condition—the history rival hypothesis has now been ruled out. Therefore, this design is much stronger than the simulated before-after design. Star and Hughes wanted to use such a design in their study but could not because they said no comparable community was available. Consequently, they were limited to the simulated before-after design.

Regression-Discontinuity Design

The regression discontinuity design is a design that can be used in a situation in which a group of individuals is selectively given some special attention. For example, educational systems frequently place students on the Dean's List if they acquire a certain level of academic achievement. Similarly, industrial organizations may give a bonus or some award to individuals who demonstrate some exceptional performance. It would frequently be desirable to know if such special attention had any beneficial effect on these individuals' subsequent performance level. Where one seeks to answer such a question one should use the regression-discontinuity design. This design, depicted in figure 8.9, consists of comparing the scores of the individuals who received the bonus, or special attention, with those who did not. This is accomplished by examining the pattern of scores before and after the award is administered. If the award did not have any influence on subjects' behavior one would expect the pattern of the no treatment scores to continue after the treatment or award was administered as illustrated by the dotted line in figure 8.9. However, if the award did have some effect then one would expect a discontinuity to exist between the no treatment and treatment scores as illustrated by the two solid lines. Consequently, the logic underlying the design is relatively simple. Individuals are classified along some continuum of merit such as grades. Those who score above a given point are given some special attention, and those scoring below the cutting point are not. If the special attention has any effect on the individual's subsequent behavior one would expect to see a discontinuity of scores between the individuals who did and did not receive the treatment effect.

Cook and Campbell (1975) cite a study by Seaver and Quarton (1973) which used the regression-discontinuity design to examine the influence of being on the Dean's List. These investigators examined the grades of 1002 students during two quarters of schooling. They

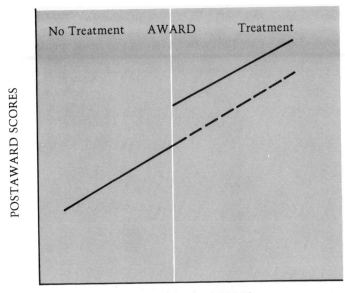

No Treatment   AWARD   Treatment

POSTAWARD SCORES

PREAWARD SCORES

Figure 8.9. Regression-discontinuity design.

found that students who made the Dean's List during the first quarter in which the study was conducted made better grades than would have been predicted during the second quarter of study. In other words, there was a discontinuity between the pattern of scores of subjects who made the Dean's List and those that did not, indicating that the Dean's List did have a positive influence on subsequent academic performance.

So far the presentation of the regression discontinuity design seems relatively straightforward and appears to be comparatively easy to interpret. However, as one should expect, there are several difficulties and problems that one may encounter (Cook and Campbell, 1975). For example, assume that an explicit discontinuity did not exist between the treatment and no treatment groups. Instead the slope of the pattern of scores changed as illustrated in figure 8.10. This could be interpreted as a pretest by treatment interaction effect. People with the higher pretest scores, e.g., grades, are more likely to profit from an award such as being on the Dean's List. It could also be a result of natural change in the pattern of scores of the more capable individuals. To determine if this is the case one would need to get independent evidence of this fact by use of some comparable group who did not receive the treatment award.

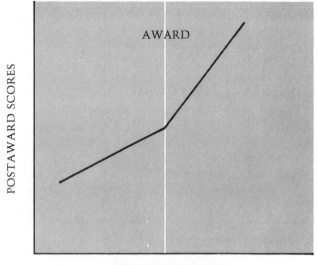

Figure 8.10. Regression-discontinuity design—change in slope of treatment scores.

A second problem with the regression-discontinuity design is that the treatment tends to be given only to the more gifted or needy individuals. This means that there will be only a narrow range of scores on the treatment side of the cutting point. For example, if individuals had to have a 3.5 grade point average to be on the Dean's List, then the scores on the treatment side of this 3.5 cutting point could only range from 3.5 to 4.0. In the no treatment side they could range from 0.0 to 3.49. This restricted range of scores on the treatment side of the cutting point makes it difficult to obtain a good measure of the pattern of these scores. Consequently, it may be difficult to tell if the treatment scores represent a discontinuity from the no treatment scores.

A third problem with the regression-discontinuity design is that the cutting score may not be rigidly adhered to. With the Dean's List example the cutting score is rather explicit and adhered to. However, assume you were in charge of distributing a bonus or some other award in an industrial organization. You may have an explicit cutting score to direct who gets the bonus or merit, but you "bend" the criterion cutting score to repay a debt, to avoid disapproval from a friend, or for some other reason. In such cases the cutting score is fuzzy (Cook and Campbell, 1975), and it is necessary to identify those individuals for whom the cutting score has been altered, and remove them from the study.

Time-Series Design

In the previous chapter, one of the faulty research designs discussed was the one-group before-after design. It was considered faulty because of the many rival hypotheses that could also explain any observed difference that might occur between the pre- and postmeasurement of the dependent variable. Also stated was the fact that the design was not totally worthless. If a better design cannot be developed, the one-group before-after design is better than nothing and will yield some information. There are research areas in which it is frequently very difficult to find an equivalent group of subjects to serve as a control group. Psychotherapy and education represent such research areas.

Is the one-group before-after design the only available design one can use in such cases? Is there no means of eliminating some of the rival hypotheses that exist in the one-group before-after design? Fortunately there is a means for eliminating *some* of these rival hypotheses, but to do so one must think of other mechanisms than the use of a control group of subjects. "Control is achieved by a network of complementary control strategies, not solely by control-group designs" (Gottman, McFall, and Barnett, 1969, p. 299). These complementary strategies are illustrated in the following design.

Interrupted Time-Series Design

The interrupted time-series design is one that requires the investigator to take a *series* of measurements both *before* and *after* the introduction of some treatment condition, as is depicted in Figure 8.11. The result of the treatment condition is indicated by a discontinuity in the recorded series of response measurements. Consider the study conducted by Caporaso (1974) in which he tried to assess the extent to which the formation of the European Economic Community (EEC) resulted in the development of internal linkage, ties, and interdependencies. Only the portion of the study concerned with the impact of the EEC on political integration will be presented here, since this is all that is needed to

Preresponse Measures	Treatment	Postresponse Measures
Y_1 Y_2 Y_3 Y_4 Y_5	X	Y_6 Y_7 Y_8 Y_9 Y_{10}

Figure 8.11. Interrupted time-series design. (Adapted from Campbell, D. T., and Stanley, J. C. Experimental and quasi-experimental designs for research. Chicago: Rand McNally and Co., 1963. Copyright 1963, American Educational Research Association, Washington, D.C.)

illustrate the interrupted time-series design. Readers interested in the overall study are referred to Caporaso (1974).

In assessing the impact of EEC on political integration, Caporaso viewed integration as a shift in orientation of key national interest groups to the more comprehensive level represented by the EEC. The question Caporaso asked was, "Did the establishment of the EEC act as a stimulus encouraging a shift in interest group activity to the European level?"[2] To answer this question he examined the pattern of interest group formation from 1950 to 1970. This is where the study represents the interrupted time-series design. The EEC was formed on January 1, 1958. However, Caporaso began his measurement of frequency of interest group formation eight years earlier—the presresponse measures—and extended them 12 years—the postresponse measure—beyond the introduction of the EEC. Consequently, the series of measurements of the dependent variable was interrupted by the formation of the EEC—the treatment condition. Graphic presentation of the data appears in Figure 8.12. As a general rule interrupted time-series data should be graphed, since this mode of presentation represents the clearest illustration of the results.

From Figure 8.12 you can readily see there was a marked rise in interest group formation at about the same time that the EEC was formed, and this marked rise sustained itself for several years. Such persistence suggests that the influence of the EEC was more than a momentary one. All this is, however, a visual interpretation. At this point it is necessary to ask two questions. First, did a significant change occur following the introduction of the treatment condition? Second, can the observed change be attributed to the treatment condition?

Let us address the first question. Did a significant change occur following the introduction of the treatment condition? One answer to this question naturally involves tests of significance since, as Gottman, McFall, and Barnett (1969, p. 301) have stated, "The data resulting from the best of experimental designs is of little value unless subsequent analyses permit the investigator to test the extent to which obtained differences exceed chance fluctuations." However, before presenting the specific tests of significance I want to follow the orientation set forth by Campbell and Stanley (1963) and Caporaso (1974) and discuss the possible outcome patterns for time series that would reflect a significant change resulting from an experimental alteration. In discussing these outcome patterns, let us first take a look at the data that would have been obtained from Caporaso's 1974 study and a study conducted by Vernon, Bedford, and Wyatt (1924) if they had used only a

2. From *The structure and function of European integration*, by James A. Caporaso, (p. 122). Copyright © 1974 by Goodyear Publishing Co. Reprinted by permission.

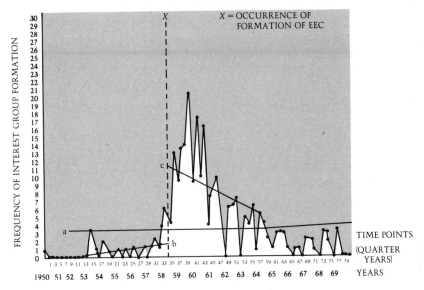

Figure 8.12. Effect of formation of EEC on interest group formation. (From The structure and function of European integration, by James A. Caporaso, (p. 123). Copyright © 1974 by Goodyear Publishing Co. Reprinted by permission.)

one-group before-after design. The Vernon et al. study was concerned with investigating the influence of introducing a rest period upon the productivity of various kinds of factory workers. These data are presented in Figure 8.13. Note that in *both* studies beautiful data seem to support the hypothesis that the experimental treatment condition produced a beneficial effect. Statistical tests may well have supported such a contention. However, remember that the one-group before-after design does not include a comparison group, so the increase in performance could have been due to many variables other than just the experimental treatment condition.

One means of eliminating many of the sources of rival hypotheses is to take a number of pre- and postmeasurements or conduct an interrupted time-series analysis. When such a study is undertaken, we find the data depicted in Figure 8.12 for Caporaso's study and the data depicted in Figure 8.14 for the Vernon et al. study. The data suggest that the experimental treatment condition investigated by Caporaso was influential but the experimental treatment condition investigated by Vernon et al. was not. The pattern of responses obtained by Vernon et al. seems to represent a chance fluctuation rather than a real change in performance. Visual inspection of a pattern of behavior can be very informative in terms of determining whether or not an experimental

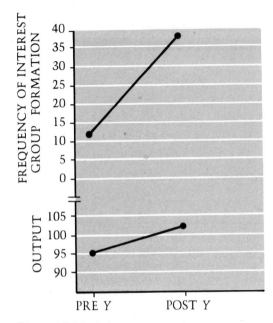

Figure 8.13. A one-group before-after representation of a portion of the Caporaso and Vernon et al. data.

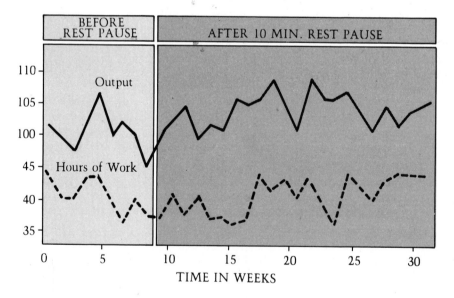

Figure 8.14. Effect of a 10-minute rest pause on worker productivity (Reprinted from Vernon et al., 1924).

treatment was a real effect. Caporaso (1974) has presented a number of additional possible patterns of behavior, shown in Figure 8.15, which could be obtained from time-series data. Note that the first three patterns reveal no treatment effect but merely represent a continuation of a previously established pattern of behavior. Lines D, E, F, and G, however, represent *true* changes (I am assuming that they would be statistically significant) in behavior although line D represents only a temporary shift.

Now let us return to our original question of whether or not a significant change in behavior followed the introduction of the treatment condition. Such a determination involves tests of significance. The most widely used and, I believe, the most appropriate statistical test is the Bayesian moving average model (Glass, Willson, and Gottman, 1975; Glass, Tiao, and Maguire, 1971; Box and Jenkins, 1970; Box and Tiao, 1965). Basically, this statistical method consists of

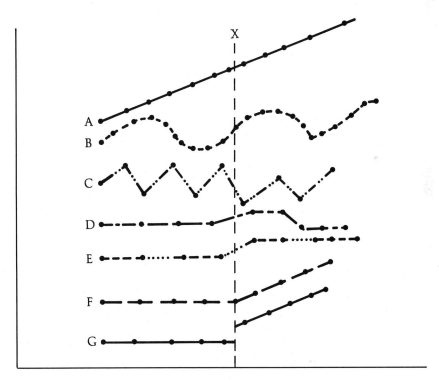

Figure 8.15. Possible pattern of behavior of a time-series variable. (From Caporaso, J. A., Quasi-experimental approaches to social science. In Quasi-experimental approaches, edited by J. A. Caporaso and L. L. Ross, Jr. Evanston, Ill.: Northwestern University Press, 1973.)

222   determining whether the pattern of postresponse measures differs from the pattern of preresponse measures. To make such an assessment using the moving average model does require many data points. Glass, Willson, and Gottman (1975) recommend that at least 50 data points be obtained. There may be situations in which enough data points cannot be collected to achieve the desired level of sensitivity. In such a situation Cook and Campbell (1975) advocate that one still use the time-series design. The data can be plotted on a graph and visually inspected to determine whether a discontinuity exists between the pre- and postresponse measures. Naturally this is an approach to be used only when one cannot use the appropriate statistical test. In such cases one of the important points to remember is that the number of preresponse data points obtained has to be large enough to identify all the plausible patterns that may exist.

Caporaso's 1974 analysis of his data revealed a significant difference between the pattern of pre- versus postresponse measures. This led him to conclude that a nonrandom change occurred following the formation of the EEC. This brings us to the second question of whether or not this significant change can be attributed to the formation of the EEC. The primary source of weakness in the interrupted time-series design is its failure to control for the effects of history. Considering Caporaso's study, assume some extraneous event occurred at about the same time the EEC was formed that could also have led to an increase in the formation of interest groups. Such an extraneous event serves as a rival hypothesis for the significant nonrandom change that occurred. Just because a significant change occurs following the introduction of a treatment condition does not automatically enable one to infer that this change was a function of the imposed treatment. Before such an inference can be made, the investigator must consider all the other events occurring at about the same time as the experimental event and determine whether or not they can serve as potential rival hypotheses. Caporaso went through such a process and rejected the notion of an historical event serving as a rival hypothesis.

The two other potential but unlikely sources of rival hypotheses that could occur in the interrupted time-series design are maturation and instrumentation. The interested reader is referred to Campbell and Stanley (1963, p. 41) for a discussion of the unique situations in which these biases may occur. Glass, Willson, and Gottman (1975) also present a discussion of sources of invalidity in the time-series experiment.

Multiple Time-Series Design

The multiple time-series design is basically an extension of the interrupted time-series design. However, it has the advantage of eliminating the history effect by including an equivalent—or at least comparable—

	Preresponse Measure				Treatment	Postresponse Measure				**223**
Experimental Group	Y_1	Y_2	Y_3	Y_4	X	Y_5	Y_6	Y_7	Y_8	
Control Group	Y_1	Y_2	Y_3	Y_4		Y_5	Y_6	Y_7	Y_8	

Figure 8.16. Multiple time-series design. (Adapted from Campbell, D. T., and Stanley, J. C. Experimental and quasi-experimental designs for research. Chicago: Rand McNally and Co., 1963. Copyright 1963, American Educational Research Association, Washington, D.C.)

group of subjects that does not receive the treatment condition. As Figure 8.16 reveals, this design has an experimental group of subjects that receives the treatment condition and an equivalent or comparable control group that does not. Consequently, the design offers a greater degree of control over sources of rival hypotheses. The history effects, for example, are controlled because any history effects would equally influence the experimental and the control groups.

Consider the study conducted by Campbell and Ross (1968) in which they attempted to assess the impact of Connecticut Governor Ribicoff's 1955 crackdown on speeding violators. In one portion of this study a multiple time-series design was used. The state of Connecticut was naturally used for the experimental group; a number of adjacent states were used as the control group. The number of traffic fatalities were plotted for the years 1951 through 1959 as shown in Figure 8.17 (the crackdown was instituted in 1955). Look just at the line representing the Connecticut fatality rate, particularly following the year of the crackdown. It seems as though there was a definite decline in fatality rate. If only this data were presented, it would represent an interrupted time-series design. Remember, however, that history effects may serve as rival hypotheses in such designs. As Campbell and Ross point out, the immediate decline occurring in 1956 may be due to such effects as less severe winter driving conditions or more safety features on automobiles. Such history effects may even persist for several years, creating the progressive downward trend revealed.

In order to state conclusively that the downward trend was due to the crackdown on speeding violators and to eliminate the rival hypothesis of history, it was necessary to use a multiple time-series design that included a comparable control group. As Figure 8.17 illustrates, this was incorporated into the study. Campbell and Ross used as their comparison group a pool of adjacent states (New York, New Jersey, Rhode Island, and Massachusetts). This comparison group re-

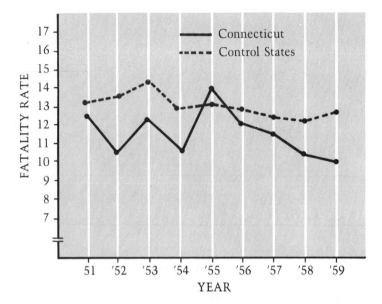

Figure 8.17. Connecticut and control states' traffic fatalities for the years 1951–1959. (From Campbell, D. T., and Ross, H. L. The Connecticut crackdown on speeding: Time series data in quasi-experimental analysis. The Law and Society Review, 1968, 3, p. 44. Reprinted by permission from Law and Society Association. The Law and Society Review is the official publication of the Law and Society Association.)

vealed no progressive decline paralleling the one depicted by the Connecticut data. Graphically, it seems as though the crackdown had a slight effect.

However, it is still necessary to determine if this slight decline is significant. This means that the data must be statistically analyzed. Again, the most appropriate approach seems to involve using the moving-average model discussed by Gottman, McFall, and Barnett (1969) and presented in considerable detail in Glass, Willson, and Gottman (1975).

Cross-Lagged Panel Design

The cross-lagged panel design is a design that makes use of cross-lagged correlations (see Figure 8.18) as a means of determining the directionality of causality. In psychology there are many issues that require and need investigation but do not lend themselves to experimental investigation in terms of enabling the investigator to manipulate antecedent

Auto-Correlation

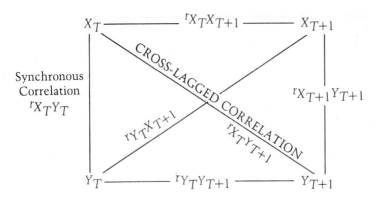

Figure 8.18. Cross-lagged design.

conditions. Parent-child relations, longitudinal studies of child development, and consumer behavior all represent such settings. For example, Crano, Kenny, and Campbell (1972) asked whether intelligence causes achievement. Other similar questions could be asked: Do teacher attitudes determine pupil behavior or does pupil behavior determine a teacher's attitudes? Does ineffective parental behavior cause children to be behavior problems or does a difficult child cause the parents to behave ineffectively? Does watching televised violence cause aggression or does aggression cause one to watch violent television programs? All these are very significant questions and require research that will reveal the causal relations. Indeed, research is providing answers to such questions, and the cross-lagged panel design is one design that is being used in these studies.

In conducting research on such questions as those just posed, there are two significant points that need to be considered. The first is that the causal relations undoubtedly exist, in many instances, in both directions. Watching televised violence may indeed cause one to become more aggressive, but being aggressive may also lead to a preference for watching violence on television. In like manner, ineffective parent behavior may cause behavior problems in a child, but a child who is difficult to handle may also cause the parent to behave more ineffectively toward the child. In other words, there may be an interactive feedback process where causality exists in both directions. In such cases the pattern of *preponderant causality* (Crano, Kenny, and Campbell, 1972) needs to be determined. In other words, it is important to determine, for example, whether the preponderant causal relation operates in the direction of ineffective parent behavior to problem behavior in the child or in the reverse direction.

226   The second point to be considered is that the causal process occurs over time (Pelz and Andrews, 1964). Consider the study conducted by Rozelle (in Rozelle and Campbell, 1969) in which he investigated the effect of class attendance on the grades made by first-year foreign language students. The effect of missing a week or two of school is not going to have an immediate effect on grades, if for no other reason than the fact that the study investigated grades at the end of the semester. Consequently there is a built-in delay or time factor. Consider another example in which the delay factor is not built in. Assume you were trying to determine whether ineffective parental behavior was the preponderant cause of child misbehavior or the reverse. Regardless of which agent, the parent or child, is the primary cause, the effect is going to be delayed. If ineffective parent behavior began at one point in time, the child, in all probability, would not simultaneously become a behavior problem. The child's misbehavior would gradually develop as the parent's ineffective behavior toward him continued. The same type of slow causal process can also be seen in the development of mental illness. The cross-lagged panel design is appropriate when the two issues discussed relate to the research question; it enables the investigator to choose between two competing hypotheses.

The cross-lagged panel design involves two or more variables measured at two or more different times on the same group of subjects. For ease of presentation discussion of the cross-lagged panel design will focus on a two variable situation, X and Y, where the two variables have been measured at two different time intervals, T and $T + 1$.

From these four measurements, six correlations can be computed, as illustrated in Figure 8.18. These consist of two synchronous correlations, the correlation between two variables measured at the same point in time, e.g., $r_{X_T Y_T}$, two auto-correlations (the correlation of one item in a series with the succeeding item), e.g., $r_{X_T X_{T+1}}$, and two cross-lagged correlations (the correlation between the two variables measured at two different points in time), e.g., the diagonal correlation, $r_{X_T Y_{T+1}}$. Of these six correlations the two cross-lagged correlations are the critical ones to be examined. If X at time T (X_T) is the preponderant cause of Y at time $T + 1$ (Y_{T+1}), then this cross-lagged correlation should be greater than the cross-lagged correlation between Y at time $T(Y_T)$ and X at time $T + 1(X_{T+1})$. On the other hand, if Y at time T is the preponderant causal agent, then the opposite relationship should exist. This is based on the assumption that a cause must precede an effect and, therefore, the correlation between an effect and a *prior* cause should be higher than the correlation between an effect and a *subsequent* cause. Pelz and Andrews (1964) elaborate on this logic and provide empirical support for it.

Eron et al. (1972) provide an example of a study that used the cross-lagged panel design. In their study they used the design as one means of determining the preponderant causal relationship between aggression and watching televised violence. This longitudinal study consisted of measuring—in addition to a number of other variables—the degree of aggression and preference for televised violence in all 875 third-grade children from a semirural county. Ten years later, 427 of these children (identified as the thirteenth grade) were again measured on these variables. Figure 8.19 depicts results of this study using the cross-lagged panel design.

When examining the correlations in a cross-lagged panel design, the critical ones on which to focus are those on the diagonals, because two rival hypotheses exist. The first hypothesis is that watching televised violence in the third grade is the preponderant cause of aggression in the thirteenth grade. The rival hypothesis is that aggression in the third grade is the preponderant cause of watching televised violence in the thirteenth grade. Since a cause *must* precede an effect which it produces, one would expect that the correlation between the prior cause and the subsequent effect would be higher than a prior effect with a subsequent cause. In terms of the Eron et al. data, if watching televised violence in the third grade was the preponderant cause of aggression in the thirteenth grade, then this cross-lagged correlation should be greater than the cross-lagged correlation between aggression in the third grade and preference for watching televised

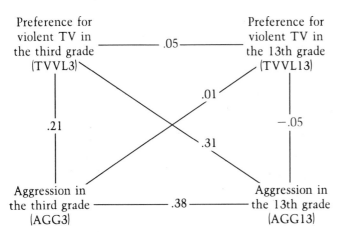

Figure 8.19. Correlation between preference for violent television and peer-rated aggression. (From Eron, L. D., Huesmann, L. R., Lefkowitz, M. M., and Walder, L. D. Does television violence cause aggression? <u>American Psychologist</u>, 1972, <u>27</u>, p. 257. Copyright 1972 by the American Psychological Association. Reprinted by permission.)

violence in the thirteenth grade. This is exactly the relationship found by Eron et al.

Although the two cross-lagged correlations are the critical ones on which to focus attention, they are the last set of correlations to which one must attend. This is because the autocorrelations and the synchronous correlations have a direct effect on the interpretability of the cross-lagged correlations. Kenny (1975) suggests that the first step in analyzing the cross-lagged panel design is to examine the autocorrelations, which measure stability and reliability and should be reasonably large but not too large. If they are too large or too small it is difficult to study a change. However, Kenny does not specify what is reasonably large. From the examples he uses it appears that autocorrelations that are significant and range from about .35 to about .70 are acceptable. If the autocorrelations are reasonably large then the next step is to examine the synchronous correlations. Ideally these correlations should be stable or the same at both measuring times. This requirement is necessary because it is one manifestation of stationarity which is necessary to interpret the cross-lagged correlations.

Stationarity refers to the fact that the causes of the measured variables under investigation do not change from one testing time to the next. For example, in the Eron et al. study this means that the causes of the measures of aggression and television watching do not change across the different times at which they are measured. Identical synchronous correlations are one manifestation of stationarity. If stationarity does not exist, then the cross-lagged correlations may differ. In such a case, the confounding rival hypothesis of a different causal model, existing at the two different times when the variables were measured, could also explain any difference in the cross-lagged correlations. There are two additional reasons one needs to inspect the synchronous correlations before moving on to the cross-lagged correlations (Kenny, 1975). First, the sign of the synchronous correlation is suggestive of the direction of the causal effect (Kenny, 1975). If the synchronous correlations are positive they suggest that X causes increase in Y, and Y causes increases in X. If they are negative they suggest that X causes decreases in Y, and Y causes decreases in X. Second, if the variables being examined in the design are measured at the same time, or synchronicity is achieved, and stationarity exists then the cross-lag correlations should always be smaller than the synchronous correlations. Consequently, a cross-lag that is larger than the synchronous correlations indicates a causal effect exists (Kenny, 1975).

After you have examined the autocorrelations and the synchronous correlations, and established that they meet the proper criteria, you proceed to examine the cross-lag correlations. When this point is reached, you must determine if these two correlations differ significantly. Kenny (1975) demonstrates how to test whether these cross-lag correlations differ significantly.

To illustrate the sequence that needs to be followed in interpreting the cross-lag panel design, let us consider the study conducted by Eron et al. on the relationship between aggression and televised violence. First one must inspect the autocorrelations. The autocorrelation depicted in figure 8.19 reveals a respectable relationship for the aggression measure but not for the measure of television. This low autocorrelation for the television measure could be due to the fact that the measure of preference for watching violent television programs was unreliable or unstable, or it could be due to low stationarity. This latter interpretation suggests that the cause of watching violent television programs has changed over time. Such an interpretation is also suggested by the lack of stability of the synchronous correlations. In looking at the synchronous correlations, you can see that they decrease rather dramatically over time and this is a significant decrease (Kenny, 1975). This suggests that a comparison of the cross-lagged correlations is not valid. However, as Kenny (1975) has pointed out, the data from the Eron et al. study is not useless, since the cross-lag correlation between grade 3 television watching and grade 13 aggression is greater than the synchronous correlation between grade 3 television watching and grade 3 aggression. This suggests that watching violent television did cause later aggression, assuming stationarity of the aggression measure.

As you can see, the cross-lagged panel design is rather complex. However, it is a valuable design that can provide insights into the causal relations that may exist between variables that cannot be experimentally manipulated. When considering the use of this design, there are at least two other points that need to be made. First, the number of subjects required is rather large. Kenny (1975) indicates that one should use over 300 subjects to obtain statistically different cross-lagged correlations, assuming that differences actually exist. Cook and Campbell (1975) suggest that one should collect data or measure the dependent variables at three or more times instead of two as Eron et al. did. Adherence to these suggestions will make the cross-lagged panel design an even more powerful design.

The cross-lagged panel design is a valuable addition to the researcher's arsenal of designs. However, one should keep in mind that it is still a passive correlational approach (Cook and Campbell, 1975). By this I mean that the design only requires one to measure variables at different points in time as opposed to the active approach used in experiments where you actively manipulate variables and note the effects. This is probably why Kenny (1975) has stated that it "is largely an exploratory strategy of data analysis" (p. 901). He suspects that its

230 main use will be to uncover simple causal relationships between uncontrolled variables. Once this relationship has been defined the variables may be refined and tested in the context of a true experiment.

Summary

This chapter has deviated considerably from the orientation taken in the previous chapters by presenting a number of quasi-experimental designs, which represent approximations of true experimental designs in the sense that they use the experimental mode of analysis in investigating areas that do not allow for complete control of extraneous variables. Consequently, quasi-experimental designs represent the best and only type of design available for use in some field studies in which one wants to make causal inferences. Of the five different quasi-experimental designs which have been presented, two were before-after designs, two were time-series designs, and one was a panel design.

Of the two before-after type of designs, the nonequivalent control group design is the one which is probably most frequently used. This design is exactly like the before-after true experimental design except that subjects are not randomly assigned to the experimental and control groups, which means that one does not have the necessary assurance that the two groups of subjects are equated. One could use the matching techniques and attempt to equate subjects on the important variables. However, this still does not assure one that the subjects are totally equated and it may produce a statistical regression effect. In spite of this, the design is very good since it may control for effects such as history and maturation.

The simulated before-after design is one that can be used where the investigator has the ability of randomly selecting, from the population, an experimental and control group, but cannot randomly assign the experimental treatment to one of these two groups. In such a case, one group serves as a control group and is tested prior to the administration of the experimental treatment condition and the other group represents the experimental group, which is tested after the administration of experimental treatment condition. This design controls for such effects as statistical regression and selection bias, but does not control for such effects as the history effect. The history effect can, however, be overcome if it is possible to include a comparable group of subjects to form a separate sample simulated before-after design.

The time-series design represents a design that, with the exception of the multiple time-series design, attempts to eliminate rival hypotheses without the use of a control group. The interrupted time-series

design attempts to eliminate rival hypotheses by taking a series of   231
measurements on the dependent variable both before and after the
introduction of some experimental treatment condition. The effect of
the experimental treatment condition is then determined by examining the magnitude of the discontinuity produced in the series of recorded responses by the experimental treatment condition. The primary source of error in this design is the possible history effect. In such
cases, if an equivalent or comparable group of subjects who have not
received the experimental treatment condition can be found, the potential history effect can be eliminated by using a multiple time-series
design.

The last type of quasi-experimental design that was discussed was
the cross-lagged panel design. This design can be used in those situations where the causal process takes place over time and where the
causal relation is not a unidirectional phenomenon. In such cases, the
pattern of preponderant causality can be determined by examining the
cross-lagged correlations. The largest cross-lagged correlation indicates
the preponderant causal relation that exists between two variables.

Key Concepts

One way to test your mastery of the material that was presented in this
chapter is to see if you know the meaning of the following terms.
These terms were selected because they represent the key concepts. If
you can define, identify, or otherwise explain each of the following
terms without referring back to the material in the chapter, you can be
assured that you have mastered the basics of the material that was
presented. Just in case you cannot recall the meaning of a given term,
the page on which it can be found appears in parentheses beside it.

quasi-experimental design (p. 198)
nonequivalent control group designs (p. 199)
increasing treatment effect I (p. 202)
increasing treatment and control groups (p. 205)
increasing treatment effects II (p. 207)

232 ·

crossover effect (p. 208)
simulated before-after design (p. 211)
regression-discontinuity design (pp. 214–215)
time-series design (p. 217)
interrupted time-series design (p. 217)
moving average model (p. 221)
multiple time-series design (pp. 222–223)
cross-lagged panel design (pp. 224–225)
preponderant causality (p. 225)
autocorrelation (p. 226)
synchronous correlation (p. 226)
stationarity (p. 228)

9

Single-Subject Research Techniques

In the previous chapters of this book, I have focused on the use of more than one subject in a given experiment. However, legitimate research can also be conducted on a single subject. Based on the material that you have already covered, it may seem impossible to conduct an experiment using only one subject because the techniques required of a true experiment could not be implemented. Two of the basic requirements of a true experiment are randomization and the inclusion of a control group for comparison purposes. However, it is not possible to assign just one subject randomly, nor is it possible to have a com-

234 parison group when dealing with only one subject. Such restrictions suggest that experimental research cannot be conducted with only one subject. On the surface it seems that single subject studies have to be reduced to case studies. Dukes (1965) revealed that this is not the case. His review of single-subject research studies revealed that only 30% of single subject studies were case studies. Such evidence suggests that a minority of the single-subject studies are of the case study variety.

If you looked at the type of research that was conducted by the pioneers of the field of psychology, you would find extensive use of single-subject studies. Wundt's method of intraspection required the use of a highly trained individual subject. Ebbinghaus (1885) conducted his landmark studies on a single subject, namely himself. Pavlov's (1928) basic findings were the result of experimentation with a single organism but replicated on other organisms. As you can see, single subject research was alive and well during the early history of psychology. However, with the publication of Fisher's work during the 1930s (Fisher, 1935), psychologists turned away from single-subject studies and toward the multisubject approach. This multisubject approach became the primary acceptable manner of doing research until recently. A notable exception to this tradition was B. F. Skinner and his students and colleagues. However, this orientation did not have much influence on methodology until the 1960s (Hersen and Barlow, 1976).

The single-subject approach used by Skinner (1953) and his colleagues in the animal laboratory, and explicated by Sidman (1960), probably would not have had the current impact that it has had without the growth in popularity of behavior therapy (Hersen and Barlow, 1976). If one looks at the history of research in psychotherapy, it is evident that the case study has been the primary method of investigation (Bolger, 1965). During the 1940s and 1950s (Hersen and Barlow, 1976), researchers grounded in experimental methodology attacked the case study method on methodological grounds. This led some investigators to focus on the percentage of clients that were successfully treated by a given psychotherapy. However, Eysenck (1952) demonstrated the inadequacy of this method by revealing that the percentage of success achieved by psychotherapy was no greater than that achieved by a spontaneous remission of symptoms. This disturbing evidence led researchers to focus even more on the multisubject design. When researchers focused on multisubject designs, they found many difficulties in applying this approach (Bergin and Strupp, 1972) and, more significantly, they found "that these studies did not prove that psychotherapy worked" (Hersen and Barlow, 1976, p. 12). Such evidence left researchers very perplexed and some wondered if psychotherapy could be evaluated (e.g., Hyman and Berger, 1966). Other researchers lapsed into naturalistic studies of the therapeutic process.

Still others engaged in process research, whereby emphasis is placed on what goes on during therapy and deemphasizes the outcome of therapy. These efforts did little to advance knowledge of psychotherapy. By the 1960s there was tremendous dissatisfaction with respect to the clinical practice and research, leading researchers to search for other alternatives. Bergin (1966) revealed that the multisubject designs were ineffective in demonstrating the effectiveness of therapy, because results were averaged. In the studies he reviewed, he noted that some clients improved and some got worse, but when results of these two types of clients were averaged the effects canceled each other out to reveal no effect of therapy. Such evidence, and the fact that process research was not beneficial in increasing effectiveness of therapy, led some researchers (Bergin and Strupp, 1970) to advocate turning back to the use of an experimental case study, which employs an experimental analogue. Consequently, research was making a change back to single-subject research. However, during the 1960s, an appropriate methodology for experimentally investigating the single subject was not apparent. It took the growing popularity of behavior therapy to provide a vehicle for the use of the appropriate methodology. Since behavior therapy involved the application of many of the principles of learning that had been identified in the laboratory, it was but a small step for these applied researchers also to borrow the methodology that was used to identify these principles. As researchers have successfully used this methodology in applied settings, it has become an acceptable and respectable methodology for use in identifying the influence of antecedents on individual behavior. This chapter will elaborate on the research designs that have been used in experimental studies on a single subject. This discussion will draw heavily on the work of Kratochwill (1978) and Hersen and Barlow (1976) as they have presented the most comprehensive coverage of these issues.

Single-Subject Designs

When designing an experimental study that uses only one subject, it is necessary to use some form of a time-series design. In the previous discussion of this design, it was revealed that the time-series design requires that repeated measurement be taken on the dependent variable both *before* and *after* the treatment condition is introduced. The repeated measurement of the dependent variable is necessary to enable detection of any effect produced by the treatment condition because it is not possible to include a control group of subjects. Now consider a single-subject study. You have only one subject and you want to know if a given treatment condition has an effect on the subject's behavior. You could administer the treatment condition to the subject and measure her response on the dependent variable. But if you followed this procedure, you would have no basis for determining if the treatment condition produced an effect because a set of "no treatment" responses does not exist. Without such a comparison, it would be impossible to infer any effect of the treatment condition.

What can one use as a basis of comparison in a single-subject design? Since only one subject exists in the study, the comparison responses have to be the subject's own pretreatment responses. In other words, the investigator has to record the subject's responses prior to and after administering the independent variable. If only one pre- and one postresponse measure were taken, we would have a one-group before-after design, which has many disadvantages. To overcome some of those disadvantages (e.g., maturation), it is necessary to obtain multiple pre- and postresponse measures. Now we have a time-series design using one subject. Such a single-subject time-series design represents descriptive experimentation because it furnishes a continuous record of the organism's responses during the entire course of the experiment. Second, it is experimental because it permits one to introject a planned intervention—a treatment condition—into the program. Consequently, it allows one to evaluate the effect of an independent variable.

Although the basic time-series design is a possible quasi-experimental strategy that could be used in single-subject research, you should remember that it is only a quasi-experimental design. The repeated pre- and postintervention measures of the dependent variable do allow one to rule out many potential biasing effects. However, you should also recall that it does *not* rule out the possibility of a potential history effect. Also, Risley and Wolf (1972) have appropriately pointed out that ability to detect a treatment effect when using the time-series design hinges on its ability to predict or forecast the behavior of the subject if the treatment condition had not been administered. When using the time-series design one collects both pre- and postintervention measures of the dependent variable. In determining whether or not the treatment or intervention had any effect on behavior, one compares the pre- and postdependent variable measures to determine if there is a change in the level and/or slope of the responses. However, in making this assessment, the underlying assumption is that the pattern of preresponse measures would have been continued if the treatment intervention had not been applied. In other words, the pretreatment responses are used to predict or forecast what the posttreatment responses would have been in the absence of the treatment. If this forecast is inaccurate, then one cannot adequately assess the effects of

the treatment intervention because the pretreatment responses do not   **237**
serve as a legitimate basis for comparison. Consequently, the basic
time-series design is truly limited in unambiguously indentifying the
influence of an experimental treatment effect.

A-B-A Design

In order to improve on the basic time-series design in an attempt to
provide unambiguous evidence of the causal effect of a treatment
condition, a third phase has been added. This third phase constitutes a
withdrawal of the experimental treatment conditions. Consequently,
the design can be represented as an *A-B-A* design. The *A-B-A* design,
depicted in Figure 9.1, represents the most basic of the single-subject
research designs. This design, as the name suggests, has three separate
conditions. The *A* condition refers to the baseline condition, which is
the target behavior as recorded in its freely occurring state. In other
words, the baseline condition refers to a given behavior as observed
prior to presenting any treatment designed to alter this behavior. In
this way the baseline behavior can serve as a kind of standard, frame of
reference, or comparison to assess the influence of a treatment condition on this behavior. The *B* condition represents the experimental
condition, or the condition where some treatment is deliberately imposed to try to alter the behavior recorded during baseline. Generally,
the treatment condition is continued for an interval equivalent to that
of the original baseline period, or until some substantial and stable
change occurs in the behaviors being observed (Leitenberg, 1973).

After the treatment condition has been introduced and the desired
behavior generated, the *A* condition is then reintroduced. There is a
return to the baseline conditions, meaning that the treatment conditions are withdrawn and whatever conditions existed during baseline
are reinstated. This second *A* condition is reinstituted in an attempt to
return the behavior to its pretreatment level. In other words, an attempt is made to determine if behavior will revert back to its pretreatment level. Reversal of the behavior back to its pretreatment level is
considered to be a very crucial element for demonstrating that the

A	*B*	*A*
Baseline	Treatment	Baseline
Measure	Condition	Measure

Figure 9.1. A-B-A design.

238 experimental treatment condition, and not some other extraneous variable, produced the behavioral change observed during the B phase of the experiment. If the design had included only two phases (A and B), such as exists with the typical time-series design, rival hypotheses, such as history, would have existed as alternative explanation for the observed change in behavior. However, if the behavior reverts back to the original baseline level when the treatment conditions are withdrawn, rival hypotheses, such as history, become less plausible. Consequently, a reversal of behavior back to its pretreatment baseline level is viewed as a rather powerful demonstration that the change in behavior was due to the experimental treatment condition and not due to some rival hypothesis.

To illustrate the A-B-A design consider the study conducted by Walker and Buckley (1968). These researchers investigated the effect of using positive reinforcement to condition attending behavior in a 9½-year-old boy named Phillip. Phillip, a bright, underachieving male, was referred to the investigator because he exhibited deviant behavior that interfered with classroom performance. Specifically, Phillip demonstrated extreme distractability, which naturally interfered with completing academic assignments. In an attempt to deal with this extreme distractability, the investigators first took a baseline measure of the percentage of time that Phillip spent attending to his academic assignment. After the percentage of attending time had stabilized or remained about the same across different observation times, the treatment condition was introduced. The treatment condition consisted of enabling Phillip to earn points if no distraction occurred during a given time interval. These points could then be exchanged for a model of his choice. When Phillip had completed three successive 10-minute distraction-free sessions, the reinforcement of being able to earn points was withdrawn. Figure 9.2 depicts the results of this experiment. During the first baseline (A) condition, attending behavior was very low. When the treatment contingency (B) of being able to earn points was associated with attending behavior, percentage of attending behavior increased dramatically. When the contingency was withdrawn and baseline conditions were reinstated (A), attending behavior dropped to its pretreatment level.

As should be apparent from this illustration, the A-B-A design seems to provide a rather dramatic illustration of the influence of the experimental treatment conditions. However, there are several problems with this design (Hersen and Barlow, 1976). The first of these is that the design ends with the baseline condition. From the standpoint of a therapist or other individual who desires to have some behavior changed, this is unacceptable because the benefits of the treatment condition are denied. Fortunately this limitation is easily handled by

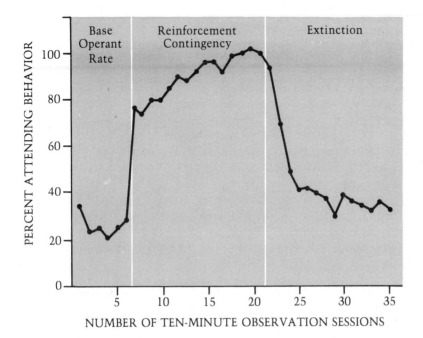

Figure 9.2. Percentage of attending behavior in successive time samples during the individual conditioning program. (From Walker, H. M., and Buckley, N. K. The use of positive reinforcement in conditioning attending behavior. Journal of Applied Behavior Analysis, 1968, 1, p. 136. Copyright 1968 by the Society for the Experimental Analysis of Behavior, Inc.)

adding a fourth phase to the *A-B-A* design. This fourth phase would involve reintroducing the treatment condition, so that we now have an *A-B-A-B* design as illustrated in Figure 9.3. Now the subject in the experiment leaves the experiment with the full benefit of the treatment condition.

Tate and Baroff (1966) provide a good illustration of the design in a study in which they investigated a means for reducing the self-

A	*B*	*A*	*B*
Baseline Measure	Treatment Condition	Baseline Measure	Treatment Condition

Figure 9.3. ABAB design.

injurious behavior of a 9-year-old boy named Sam. Sam, diagnosed as autistic, frequently engaged in such self-injurious behavior as banging his head against hard objects, hitting his face with his hands, and kicking himself. In spite of such behavior, Sam also exhibited a series of social behaviors such as clinging to others, climbing in other people's laps, and trying to wrap other people's arms around himself. Such behavior suggested that Sam desired physical contact, and the investigators decided to try to use withdrawal of this physical contact as a means of reducing the frequency of Sam's self-injurious behavior. This was accomplished by withdrawing physical contact immediately following any self-injurious outburst.

The experiment was divided into 4 5-day periods with each set of 5 days corresponding to one of the four conditions in the reversal design. The first 5 days represented the first baseline period during which the two adult investigators, while taking Sam for his daily walk around the campus, simply ignored any self-injurious behavior in which he engaged. (The investigators always held Sam's hands and talked to him during their walk.) During the second 5 days, the experimental treatment condition was instituted and consisted of immediately jerking their hands away from Sam to eliminate any physical contact when he engaged in any self-injurious behavior, and the investigators continued to withhold any physical contact for 3 seconds past the last self-injurious behavior. The third set of 5 days represented a return to the original baseline conditions; the fourth set of 5 days represented a reinstatement of the experimental treatment conditions. The frequency of occurrence of the self-injurious behaviors is depicted in Figure 9.4. It is readily apparent that there was a dramatic decline in frequency over baseline during each of the 5-day periods in which the experimental treatment conditions were introduced. It is also apparent that Sam left the experiment with the full benefit of the experimental treatment.

A second problem of the *A-B-A* design is not so easily handled. As I have previously stated, one of the basic requirements of the *A-B-A* design is that a reversal to baseline conditions exists when the experimental treatment condition is withdrawn. This requirement is necessary in order to rule out rival hypotheses such as history, since if the behavior did not revert to baseline we have only an *A-B*, or time-series, design. In the Tate and Baroff study, it was necessary to demonstrate that the self-injurious behavior returned once the contingent withdrawal of physical contact no longer occurred to reveal that the behavior was altered by the experimental treatment. As Gelfand and Hartmann (1968, p. 211) have stated:

> After substantial and apparently reliable behavior modification
> has taken place, the . . . contingencies should be altered temporar-

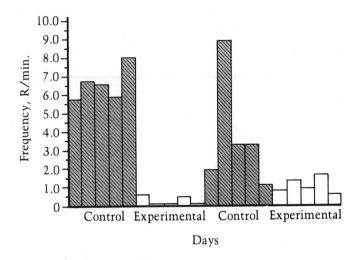

Figure 9.4. Effect of withdrawal of physical contact upon frequency of self-injurious behavior. (Reprinted with permission from Tate, B. G., and Baroff, G. S. Aversive control of self-injurious behavior in a psychotic boy, Be-havior Research and Therapy. 1966, Pergamon Press.)

ily, for example, reversed, so the problem behavior is once again ... instated ... Correlated changes in the observed response rate provide a convincing demonstration that the target behavior is unmistakably under the therapist's control and not due to adven-tious, extratherapeutic factors.

In other words, the reversal is necessary to rule out rival hypotheses such as history.

The problem with the *A-B-A* design is that a reversal to baseline does not occur with all behavior. Figure 9.4 reveals that a complete reversal did not occur in the Tate and Baroff study. Hewett, Taylor and Artuso (1969), for example, found that removal of a token program increased the target behaviors rather than returning them to baseline as is necessary to eliminate rival hypotheses. Without this reversal, the change in behavior following introduction of the experimental treat-ment condition could just as easily be due to some other extratreat-ment factor. The failure to reverse may also be due to a carry-over effect across phases, whereby the experimental treatment condition was maintained so long that a relatively permanent change in behavior took place. In fact, Bijou et al. (1969) have recommended that short experimental periods be used to facilitate obtaining a reversal effect. This is in line with Leitenberg's (1973, p. 98) statement that "single-case experimental designs are most pertinent to the discovery of short-term effects of therapeutic procedure while they are being carried out." One who has demonstrated the influence of the experimental treatment can then focus on the persistence of the experimental treatment.

While the argument for shortening the experimental treatment to facilitate reversal, and thereby demonstrating cause of the change in behavior, is valid, it is still valid only for behaviors that will in fact reverse. When the investigator is interested in nontransient effects, none of these arguments is valid because a relatively permanent change is instated. In such cases Gelfand and Hartmann (1968) have suggested the use of a yoked control subject. However, Church (1964) has strongly attacked this approach even though Kimmel and Terrant (1968) have tempered this attack and suggested a "reciprocal yoked control" method. There are other approaches that have been used to overcome the reversal problem more effectively.

A last issue concerns a distinction between a reversal and a withdrawal A-B-A design. In discussing the A-B-A design, I have used the term withdrawal to refer to the fact that the treatment condition was withdrawn during the third (second A) phase of the design. While this is appropriate, Leitenberg (1973) states that it should be distinguished from an A-B-A reversal design. The distinction occurs in the third phase (second A) of the A-B-A design. In the withdrawal design the treatment condition is withdrawn, but in the reversal design the treatment condition is applied to an alternate but incompatible behavior. For example, assume you were interested in using reinforcement to increase the play behavior of a socially withdrawn 4½-year-old girl as were Allen et al. (1964). If you followed the procedure used by these investigators, you would have recorded the percentage of time the girl spent interacting with both children and adults during the baseline phase. During treatment, or the B phase, praise would be administered whenever the girl interacted with other children, and isolated play and interaction with adults would be ignored. During the third phase of the experiment, or the second A phase, the true reversal would take place. Instead of withdrawing the contingent praise, it was shifted to interactions with adults so that any time the child interacted with adults, she was praised, and interactions with other children were ignored. This was implemented to see if the social behavior would reverse to adults and away from children as the reinforcement contingencies shifted. As you should be able to see, there is a difference between an A-B-A withdrawal and reversal design. Although the A-B-A reversal design can reveal rather dramatic results, it is more cumbersome and is used much more infrequently than the more adaptable withdrawal design. Therefore, most of the single-subject A-B-A designs that you encounter will be of the withdrawal variety.

Interaction Design 243

In surveying the literature on single-subject designs, it is readily apparent that researchers have not been content to stick to the basic *A-B-A* design, but instead have extended this basic design in an attempt to accomplish a variety of purposes. The most intriguing and valuable extension represents an attempt to identify the interactive effect of two or more variables. In discussing multisubject designs, I presented the concept of interaction as the situation that exists when the influence of one independent variable depends upon the specific level of the second independent variable. This definition of interaction was presented because multisubject designs allow one to include several levels of variation for each independent variable being investigated. In a single-subject design, one does not have that degree of flexibility. One of the cardinal rules in single-subject research (Hersen and Barlow, 1976) is that only one variable can be changed when proceeding from one phase of the research to another. For example, in the *A-B-A-B* design, one can introduce a specific type or level of reinforcement when changing from the baseline phase to the treatment phase of the experiment. However, only one level of reinforcement can be implemented. Therefore, when discussing interaction effects in single-subject research, I am referring to the combined influence of two or more specific levels of two or more different independent variables. For example, one could investigate the interaction effect of a concrete reinforcement (giving of tokens), and the verbal reinforcement of praise (the experimenter saying, "good"). One could not practically investigate the interaction of different forms of material reinforcement (e.g., tokens, points, and candy) with different forms of praise. Therefore, interaction typically refers to the combined influence of two specific variables.

In order to isolate the combined influence or interactive effect of two variables over that which would be achieved by only one of these two variables, it is necessary to analyze the influence of each variable separately and in combination. To complicate the issue further, one must do this by changing only one variable at a time. In order to accomplish this you must test for the influence of each variable separately and in combination, but the sequencing of making these tests must be such that the combination of variables or interaction effect can be compared with each variable separately. To illustrate this design further, look at figure 9.5. In sequence 1, the effect of treatment *B* is independently investigated, and then the combined influence of treatments *B* and *C* are compared to the influence of treatment *B* alone. In like manner, sequence 2 enables the investigation of the influence of

244 treatment C independently, and then the combined influence of treatments B and C against treatment C. In this way, it is possible to determine if the combined influence of B and C was greater than that of B or C. If it was, then an interactive effect exists. However, if the combined effect was greater than one of the treatment variables, C, but not the other, B, then an interactive effect does not exist because it can more parsimoniously be attributed to the effect of treatment B.

Perhaps one of the more adequate illustrations of a test of an interaction effect is represented in the combined studies of Leitenberg et al. (1968) and Leitenberg (1973). In the first study, Leitenberg et al. (1968) used feedback and praise in an attempt to overcome a severe knife phobia in a 59-year-old woman. The dependent variable measure was the amount of time the subject could maintain looking at an exposed knife. Following the completion of a trial the subject was given feedback regarding the amount of time spent observing the knife and/or praise. Praise consisted of verbally reinforcing the subject when she would look at the knife for a progressively longer period of time. The specific design of this study is depicted in figure 9.6. As you can see, the design does not correspond exactly to the requirements of an interaction design. However, it is close enough to demonstrate the essential components of this design.

The results of this study appear in figure 9.7. Feedback resulted in an increase in mean viewing time. This increase does not appear to have been altered by the introduction of praise, suggesting that praise had no effect upon the knife phobia. During the third phase of the experiment, when praise was withdrawn, the same increase continued to persist, lending even more support to the notion that praise was ineffective. Therefore, feedback seems to have been the controlling agent. The second half of the study, where feedback is presented independently and in combination with praise, provides additional support for the notion that feedback is the controlling agent.

Although the apparent conclusion of the Leitenberg et al. (1968) study is that feedback is the sole agent responsible for the reduction in the knife phobia, this is only one of two possible conclusions. As Hersen and Barlow (1976) have pointed out, an alternative interpretation is that praise had an effect but it was masked by the effect of feedback. Feedback may have been so powerful that it enabled the subject to progress at her optimal rate. If such were the case, then there would have been no room for praise to manifest itself, which would lead one to erroneously conclude that praise was ineffective when it actually did have some effect. This is one reason why both of the sequences depicted in Figure 9.5 have to be incorporated in order to isolate an interaction effect.

	BASELINE	SINGLE TREATMENT	BASELINE	SINGLE TREATMENT	COMBINED TREATMENT	SINGLE TREATMENT	COMBINED TREATMENT
Sequence 1	A	B	A	B	BC	B	BC
Sequence 2	A	C	A	C	BC	C	BC

Figure 9.5. Single-subject interaction design.

	EXPERIMENTAL CONDITION					
STUDY	B	BC	B	A	B	BC
Leitenberg et al. (1968)	Feedback	Feedback and Praise	Feedback	Baseline	Feedback	Feedback and Praise
Leitenberg (1973)	Praise	Feedback and Praise	Praise	Baseline	Praise	

Figure 9.6. Design of two studies used to test the interaction of feedback and praise.

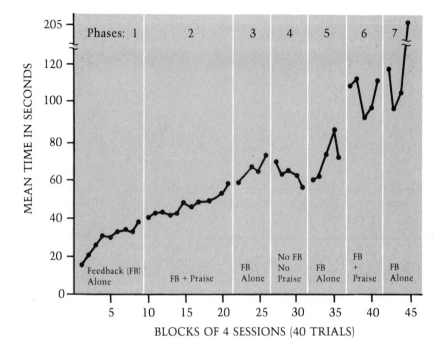

Figure 9.7. Time in which a knife was kept exposed by a
phobic patient as a function of feedback, feedback plus
praise, and no feedback or praise conditions. (From
Leitenberg, H., Agras, W. S., Thompson, L. E., and Wright,
D. E. Feedback in behavior modification: An experi-
mental analysis in two phobic cases. Journal of Applied
Behavior Analysis, 1968, 1, p. 136. Copyright 1968 by the
Society for the Experimental Analysis of Behavior, Inc.)

In accordance with this requirement, Leitenberg (1973) conducted
another experiment on a second knife phobic patient. In this study,
praise was presented independently and then in combination with
feedback as illustrated in Figure 9.6. Otherwise, the procedure of the
study was identical to that of the Leitenberg et al. (1968) study. Figure
9.8 depicts the results of the second study. As you can see, the subject
made no progress when only praise was administered. When feedback
was combined with praise, progress was made. Interestingly, this progress was maintained even when feedback was subsequently discontin-
ued in the third phase of the study. In the fifth and sixth phases of the
study, again, no progress was made unless feedback was combined
with praise.

Taken together, these two studies reveal that feedback alone was
the primary agent in helping the patient overcome the knife phobia,

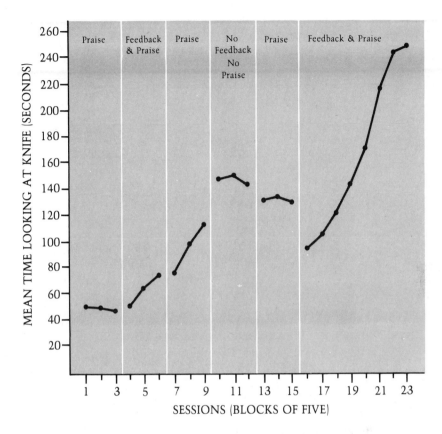

Figure 9.8. Mean time looking at phobic stimulus as a function of praise and feedback plus praise condition: Subject 1. (From Leitenberg, H., Agras, W. S., Allen, R., Butz, R., and Edwards, J. Feedback and therapist praise during treatment of phobia. Journal of Consulting and Clinical Psychology, 1975, 43, p. 397. Copyright 1975 by the American Psychological Association. Reprinted by permission.)

because praise alone had no appreciable effect, and adding praise to feedback did not reveal a marked increase in progress toward overcoming the phobia. These two studies also reveal the necessity of testing each variable (e.g., feedback and praise) separately and in combination in order to isolate any combined or interactive effect of the two variables. Herein lie what may be considered the disadvantages of testing for an interaction effect. First, it typically will require at least two subjects since a different subject will have to be tested on each of the two sequences depicted in figure 9.5. Second, the interaction effect

248   can be demonstrated only under conditions where each variable alone (e.g., feedback) does *not* produce maximum increment in performance on the part of the subject. As pointed out in the 1968 Leitenberg et al. study, it was possible that praise was effective in overcoming knife phobia but the feedback variable was so potent that it enabled the subject to respond at the maximum level, thus precluding any possibility of demonstrating an interactive effect. In such cases, the proper conclusion would be that either of the two variables being tested was equally effective, and addition of the second variable was not beneficial. Note that a conclusion could not be drawn regarding the possible interactive effect of the two variables, since this effect could not be tested. Where such a condition does not exist, then the interaction design is quite effective in demonstrating the continued effects of two or more variables.

Multiple-Baseline Design

In discussing the *A-B-A* design, it was stated that one of the primary limiting components of this design was a failure to obtain a reversal back to baseline when the treatment condition was withdrawn. In such cases, the primary rival hypothesis of history is not eliminated and one cannot unambiguously attribute the behavior change to the treatment condition. When such a condition arises, or when one suspects that such a condition may exist, then the multiple-baseline design is a logical alternative since it does not entail withdrawing a treatment condition. Therefore, its effectiveness does not hinge upon a reversal of behavior to baseline level.

The multiple-baseline design, depicted in Figure 9.9, is one in which baseline data are collected on several different behaviors for the same individual, on the same behavior for several different individuals, or on the same behavior across several different situations for the same individual. After the baseline data are collected, the experimental treatment is successively administered to each target behavior. If the

	T_1	T_2	T_3	T_4	T_5
A	Baseline	Treatment			
B	Baseline	Baseline	Treatment		
C	Baseline	Baseline	Baseline	Treatment	
D	Baseline	Baseline	Baseline	Baseline	Treatment

Behaviors, people, or situations $\left\{ \begin{array}{l} \\ \\ \\ \end{array} \right.$ (for rows A–D above)

Figure 9.9. Multiple-baseline design.

behavior exposed to the experimental treatment changes while all others remain at baseline, the efficacy of the treatment condition is enhanced. This is because it becomes increasingly implausable that rival hypotheses would contemporaneously influence each target behavior at the same time as the treatment was administered.

Marks and Gelder (1967) provide an example of the multiple-baseline design in a study in which they investigated the use of aversion therapy in treating transvestism and fetishism. One of the subjects in their study was a 21-year-old male who reported that he became sexually excited by dressing as a woman. Baseline data taken on this subject revealed that he had maximum erection when looking at or feeling a woman's panties, slip, skirt, and pajamas. He also responded maximally when viewing a photo of a nude woman. Therapy consisted of shocking the patient's forearm or leg during cross dressing with each individual garment. Figure 9.10 depicts the results of this study. The top half of the figure reveals the number of seconds, up to a maximum of three minutes, required for obtaining an erection, and the bottom half of the figure reveals the magnitude of the erection for each target object at the end of treatment for a given garment. When treatment was successively directed to each of these target objects, the erectile response disappeared until it occurred only in the presence of the nude photo. Note also that it disappeared only in conjunction with the object being treated. The results convincingly demonstrate that aversion therapy changed the subject's erectile response to each of the garments, and follow-up reports revealed that the subject was achieving a better heterosexual relationship.

While the multiple-baseline design avoids the problem of reversibility, it has another basic difficulty. For the multiple-baseline design to be effective in evaluating the efficacy of the treatment condition, the target behaviors must not be dependent or highly interrelated. This means that the behaviors being investigated must not be interdependent in such a way that a change in one behavior changes the other behaviors. Looking at Figure 9.10 reveals that this requirement existed in the Marks and Gelder study—the erectile response occurred only to the article not being treated. However, this is not always the case. Kazdin (1973), for example, noted that the classroom behaviors of inappropriate motor behavior, inappropriate verbalizations, and inappropriate tasks are interrelated, and a change in one of these responses can result in a change in one of the other responses. In like manner, Broden et al. (1970), using a multiple-baseline design across individuals, found that contingent reinforcement not only changed the inattentive behavior of the target subject but also that of an adjacent peer.

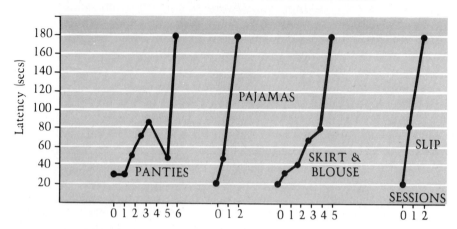

Erection latency at end of each aversion session

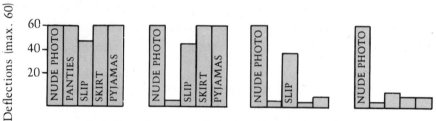

Erections after one-minute exposure to stimulus

Figure 9.10. Effect of aversion therapy on erection in a transvestite. (From Marks, I. M., and Gelder, M. G. Transvestism and fetishism: Clinical and psychological changes during Faradic aversion. British Journal of Psychiatry, 1967, 113, p. 714. Copyright 1967 by The British Journal of Psychiatry. Reprinted by permission.)

The problem of interdependence of behaviors is real and needs to be considered before selecting the multiple-baseline design because, if it does exist, it destroys much of the power of this design, resting as it does on its ability to demonstrate change whenever the treatment condition is administered to a given behavior. If administering the experimental treatment to one behavior results in a corresponding change in all other behaviors then, when the experimental treatment is administered to the remaining behaviors, it will have less impact and produce less change because the behavior had previously been altered.

Consequently, a clear-cut demonstration of change in behavior contingent upon presentation of the treatment condition does not exist. When such a case exists, it is not clear what caused the change in behavior. Therefore, it would be advantageous to know what behaviors are interrelated, so that when they are being investigated this design could be avoided. It is an empirical question as to which behaviors are interrelated. In some cases there exist data on this interdependence, but where none exists the investigator must collect his or her own.

As you can see, the multiple-baseline design rests on the assumption of independence of behavior. It is also apparent that such independence cannot be achieved at all times. When independence cannot be achieved the results are ambiguous, since it is not possible to determine if the effect was due to an extraneous variable such as history or to the treatment condition. In such cases, Kazdin and Kopel (1975) provide several recommendations that will allow one to attenuate such an ambiguous state of affairs. The first recommendation is to select behaviors that should be as independent as possible. Since it may be difficult to predict in advance which behaviors are independent, one should consider using different individuals or situations since they will probably be more topographically distinct than different behavior of the same individual.

In attempting to select independent behaviors, the investigations may correlate the baseline behaviors. If a low correlation is obtained, then it may be inferred that the behaviors are independent. While this could be taken as an indication of independence, it may also be spuriously low and suggest a level of independence that doesn't exist. If the baseline behaviors are quite stable or do not change much, a low correlation could result from this limited fluctuation in behavior. In such cases one may conclude that the behaviors are independent when they really are not. Even if one does have good valid evidence that baseline behaviors are independent, this does not provide any assurance that they will remain independent after implementation of the treatment condition. For example, implementing a time out procedure on one child in a classroom for disruptive behavior could affect other children's behavior. Therefore, consideration of independence should take place during the treatment phase as well as the baseline phase.

A second recommendation made by Kazdin and Kopel (1975) for decreasing ambiguity in the multiple-baseline design is to use several baselines. Specifically, they recommend using four or more because use of a large number of baselines decreases the possibility of dependence across all baselines. Therefore, even though some baseline behaviors will be dependent, others will be independent. Those that are independent can demonstrate the treatment-effect relationship.

A third recommendation in cases where ambiguity exists is to implement a reversal on one of the baseline behaviors. If the reversal on one of the baseline behaviors leads to a generalized reversal effect (reversal on other behaviors), then one has added evidence for the effect of the treatment. One also has evidence for a generalized treatment effect.

Multiple Schedule Design

The multiple schedule design, depicted in Figure 9.11, is a design in which the same behavior is subjected to different treatments under different stimulus conditions. Following baseline measurement, different treatment conditions are administered under different stimulus conditions. These stimulus conditions could be different points in time, different physical locations as home or school, different therapist, or different family members. The treatment condition administered under a given stimulus condition changes across time, requiring the subject to discriminate not only between the different treatment conditions but also between the different stimuli. If the subject's response changes as the treatment conditions are introduced under different stimulus conditions, then one has evidence of the fact that the treatment has an impact on the subject's behavior. For example, assume that one wanted to assess the impact of reinforcement on claustrophobic behavior. Following baseline measurement of the length of time the patient could remain inside a closed room without feeling anxious, one therapist would reinforce the patient when she remained in the closed room and the other would just maintain a pleasant relationship with her. On subsequent sessions the other therapist would verbally reinforce the claustrophobic patient while the previously reinforcing therapist would withhold praise and only maintain a pleasant relationship. If verbal reinforcement had any effect on the claustrophobic behavior, the length of time which the patient could stay in the closed room should vary with the therapist who was providing the reinforcement. This study was actually conducted by Agras et al. (1969). The results, which appear in Figure 9.12, reveal that the amount of time which the patient actually spent in the closed room was greater in the presence of the reinforcing therapist. This suggests that verbal reinforcement was having an influence on the subject behavior.

   As you should be able to see from this illustration, the power of the multiple schedule design in identifying a treatment effect comes

	T_1	T_2	T_3	T_4	T_5
Stimulus 1	Baseline	Treatment A	Treatment B	Treatment A	Treatment B
Stimulus 2	Baseline	Treatment B	Treatment A	Treatment B	Treatment A

Figure 9.11. Multiple schedule design. T_1–T_5 refer to five different time periods.

254 from its being able to demonstrate that behavior changes from one stimulus to the other as the corresponding treatment condition changes. If the behavior remained the same for each stimulus, regardless of the changes in the treatment condition, then one would have to infer that the treatment condition was not having a perceptible impact on behavior. In the Agras et al. (1969) experiment, if the behavior of the claustrophobic patient remained the same regardless of which therapist was doing the reinforcing, one would have to infer that verbal reinforcement was not having a significant impact on the claustrophobic behavior.

The multiple schedule design is one that is capable of isolating a treatment effect if one actually exists. However, it does have a number of difficulties associated with it. As Hersen and Barlow (1976) have pointed out, it requires quite a bit of control over the staff, requiring

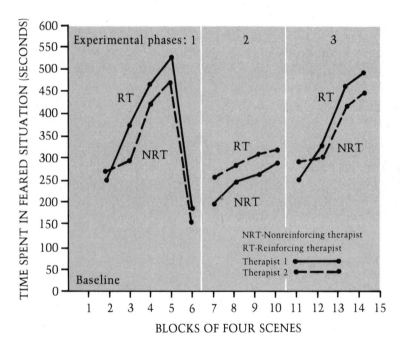

Figure 9.12. Comparison of effects of reinforcing and nonreinforcing therapists in the modification of claustrophobic behavior. (From Agras, S., Leitenberg, H., Barlow, D. H., and Thompson, L. E. Instructions and reinforcement in the modification of neurotic behavior. American Journal of Psychiatry, vol. 125, p. 1438, 1969. Copyright 1969, the American Psychiatric Association. Reprinted by permission.)

two different therapists to work with one patient. Second, the condi- **255** tions under which it is implemented tend to be artificial. In spite of such difficulties, it can be used successfully to isolate treatment effects and has the advantage of not requiring a withdrawal of treatment. It can also be used where the investigator cannot achieve complete independence of behaviors.

Changing-Criterion Design

The changing-criterion design is a relative newcomer to the area of single-subject designs. It was described by Sidman (1960, pp. 254–256) but not labeled until 1971 (Hall, 1971). More recently it has undergone rather extensive discussion (Hall and Fox, 1977; Hartman and Hall, 1976). The changing-criterion design, depicted in Figure 9.13, is one which requires an initial baseline measure on a single target behavior. Following this baseline measure, a treatment condition is implemented and continued across a series of intervention phases. During the first intervention or treatment phase, an initial criterion of successful performance is established. Following successful achievement of this performance level across several trials, or having achieved a stable criterion level, the criterion level is increased. Therefore, the experiment moves to the next successive phase. Here a new and more difficult criterion level is established, while the treatment condition is continued. When behavior reaches this new criterion level and is maintained across trials, the next phase, with its more difficult criterion level, is introduced. In this manner, each successive phase of the experiment requires a step-by-step increase in the criterion measure. "Experimental control is demonstrated through successive replication of change in the target behavior, which changes with each stepwise change in criterion" (Kratochwill, 1978, p. 66).

Hall and Fox (1977) provide a good illustration of the changing-criterion design in a study of a child named Dennis who refused to complete arithmetic problems. To overcome this resistant behavior the investigators first obtained a baseline measure of the average

T_1	T_2	T_3	T_4
Baseline	Treatment and Initial Criterion	Treatment and Criterion Increment	Treatment and Criterion Increment

Figure 9.13. Changing-criterion design. T_1–T_4 refers to four different phases of the experiment.

256 number of assigned arithmetic problems (4.25) that he would complete during a 45-minute session. Following this baseline measure, Dennis was told that a specified number had to be completed correctly during the subsequent session. If he correctly completed them, he could take recess and play with a basketball. If he did not complete the specified number correctly, he would have to miss recess and remain in the room until they were correctly completed. During the first treatment phase the criterion number of problems to be solved was set at 5, which was one plus the mean number completed during baseline. Following completion of successfully achieving the criterion performance on three consecutive days, the criterion was incremented by the addition of one problem. The recess and basketball contingencies were maintained. The results of this experiment, depicted in Figure 9.14, reveal that Dennis's peformance increased as the criterion level increased. When a change in behavior parallels the criterion change so closely, it rather convincingly demonstrates the relative effects of the treatment contingency.

Hartmann and Hall (1976) indicate that successful utilization of the changing-criterion design requires attention to three factors: paying attention to the length of the baseline and the treatment phases, the magnitude of change in the criterion, and the number of treatment phases or changes in the criterion. With regard to the length of the treatment and baseline phases, Hartmann and Hall (1976) state that the treatment phases should be of different lengths, or if they are of a constant length, then the baseline phases should be longer than the treatment phases. This consideration is necessary to ensure that the step-by-step changes in the subject's behavior are due to the experimental treatment, and not to some history or maturational variable that occurs simultaneously with the criterion change. Additionally, the baseline data should be stable or changing in a direction opposite to that achieved by the treatment condition so as to establish unambiguously that the treatment condition, and not some other extraneous variable, produced the observed change. With regard to the actual length of each treatment, only a rule of thumb can be given. Each treatment phase must be long enough to allow the behavior to change to its new criterion level and then stabilize. In other words, it must consistently achieve the new criterion level across trials. If the behavior continues to fluctuate between the new and the old criterion level stability has not been achieved.

The second consideration is the magnitude of the criterion change. Naturally, it must be large enough so that a detectable change can occur. However, creating a detectable change is directly related to the variability in the subject's behavior and ease of changing the behavior. If the behavior is difficult to change the criterion change should be

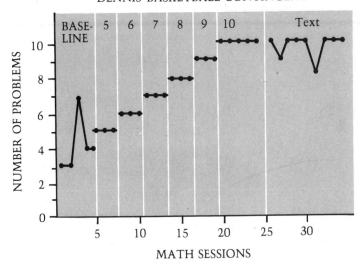

DENNIS BASKETBALL CONTINGENT

Figure 9.14. Number of math problems solved in a
changing-criterion design. (From Hall, R. V., and Fox, R.
W. Changing-Criterion Designs: An alternative applied
behavior analysis procedure. In <u>New Developments in
Behavioral Research: Theory, Method, and Application</u>,
In honor of Sidney W. Bijou, edited by C. C. Etzel, G. M.
LeBlanc, and D. M. Baer. Hillsdale, N. J.: Lawrence
Erlbaum Associates, 1977.)

small so that it can be achieved, but still large enough to be detected. If
the behavior varies wildly from trial to trial then the criterion change
must be rather large in order to detect any change.

Hartmann and Hall (1976) state that two criterion changes may be
adequate. This issue is, however, directly dependent on the number of
replications that are required to convincingly demonstrate that the
behavioral change is due to the treatment condition. For this reason,
Kratochwill (1978) recommends at least four criterion changes. When
the subject's behavior is quite variable, Hall and Fox (1977) suggest that
one include a reversal in one of the treatment phases. This reversal
could consist of reverting back to baseline or to a former criterion level.
Such a reversal would provide additional evidence of the influence of
the treatment condition.

The changing-criterion design has not been used extensively and
all of its uses or limitations have yet to be identified (Kratochwill,
1978). It seems to be a useful design in studies that require shaping of

258   behavior over a period of time (Hall and Fox, 1977) or where problems in which step-by-step increases in accuracy, frequency, duration, and/ or magnitude are the therapeutic goals (Hartmann and Hall, 1976), as may exist with learning to write or read.

Methodological Considerations in the Use of Single-Subject Designs

The single-subject research designs that have just been discussed by no means represent an exhaustive survey of such designs. They do, however, represent the most basic and frequently used designs. Regardless of which design is used, there are several common issues which must be considered when attempting to conduct a single-subject study.

Baseline

Baseline has been defined as the recording of target behaviors in their freely occurring state. Repeatedly, investigators (e.g., Gelfand and Hartmann, 1968) have emphasized the importance of the baseline data in single-subject research. Of prime importance is the necessity of obtaining a *stable* baseline, because the baseline data serve as the standard against which change induced by the experimental treatment condition is assessed. The essential question is, "When has a stable baseline been achieved?" This is a very difficult question, and has no final answer. As Sidman (1960, p. 258) states:

> There is, again, no rule to follow for the criterion will depend upon the phenomenon being investigated and upon the level of experimental control that can be maintained . . . By following behavior over an extended period of time, with no change in the experimental conditions, it is possible to make an estimate of the degree of stability that can eventually be maintained; a criterion can then be selected on the basis of these observations.

What criteria should be selected? One criterion that has been used involves continuing the baseline behavior until it is stable within a 5% range of the overall mean response. Bijou et al. (1969, p. 200) say, "Stability is defined as a trend which is more or less horizontal or slightly in the opposite direction to that anticipated during experimental manipulation."

Obtaining a stable baseline is an ideal rather than a practical consideration. It should also be recognized that the degree of variability that will be found will, in most cases, be greater when using human subjects than with animals. Naturally, this is because a much greater degree of control can generally be exercised over the animals. McCullough et al. (1974), for example, found that the frequency of irrelevant comments made by high school students during a 50-minute class period ranged from 17 to 104 during an 8-day period. While this may be somewhat atypical, it does illustrate the extent to which baseline data can fluctuate with humans. With such extreme fluctuations or unsystematic variation, Bijou et al. (1969) suggest that all components of the study be assessed and checked before proceeding.

There is one additional problem that frequently has to be considered when obtaining baseline frequencies on humans. This is the potential reactive effect of the assessment on the behavior being assessed (Webb et al., 1966). The fact that one is taking baseline data may have an effect on the behavior. This was vividly demonstrated in the classic Hawthorne studies and has more recently been demonstrated by McFall (1970) and Gottman and McFall (1972), who revealed that monitoring of one's own behavior can have a significant influence on that behavior. If one monitors frequency of smoking, one then increases the number of cigarettes smoked, whereas if one monitors the frequency of not smoking, then one smokes less. Such research demonstrates that there exists a potential reactive effect of just taking baseline data.

Changing One Variable at a Time

One of the cardinal rules in single subject research is that only one variable can be changed when proceeding from one phase of the experiment to the next (Barlow and Hersen, 1973). The rule exists because only when adhering to it can you isolate the variable that produced a change in behavior. Assume, for example, that you wanted to test the effect of reinforcement on increasing the number of social responses emitted by a chronic schizophrenic. In an attempt to employ an *A-B-A* design, you first measure baseline performance by recording the number of social responses. Following baseline, you give the schizophrenic a token, which can be redeemed for cigarettes, and say "good" after each social response. At this point you would have violated the rule of one variable because two types of reinforcements were administered. If the number of social responses had increased, you would not know which type of reinforcement was responsible for changing the behavior. In fact, it may not have been either reinforcer independently but the combined or interactive influence that was

260   responsible for the change. The point is that you would have no idea as to specifically what was producing the behavioral change. To isolate the separate and combined influence of the two types of reinforcers would require an interaction design of the variety that was previously discussed.

Length of Phases

One of the issues that must be given consideration when designing a single-subject study is the length of each phase of the study. While this is an issue with which every investigator conducting a single-subject study must contend, it is also an issue for which there are few guidelines. Most experimenters would advocate that each phase should be continued until some semblance of stability has been achieved. Johnson (1972), for example, has advocated, with regard to the study of punishment, that each phase should be continued until stability, in terms of lack of trend and a constant range of variability, is achieved. While this would be the ideal, in many clinical studies it is not feasible. Additionally, following this suggestion would lead to unequal phases, which Barlow and Hersen (1973) consider to be undesirable. According to these investigators, unequal phases, particularly when the treatment phase is extended in time to demonstrate a treatment effect, increase the possibility of a confounding influence of history or maturation. For example, if the baseline phase consisted of recording responses for 7 days and the treatment phase consisted of 14 days, one would have to entertain the possibility of a history or maturation variable affecting the data if a behavioral change did not take place until about the seventh day of the treatment phase. Because of such potential confounding influences Hersen and Barlow (1976) advocate the use of an equal number of data points for each phase of the study.

There are two other issues that relate directly to the issue of length of phases. These include carryover effects and cyclic variations (Hersen and Barlow, 1976). Carryover effects in single-subject *A-B-A-B* designs would usually appear in the second baseline phase of the study as evidenced by a failure to reverse to its original baseline level. When such carryover effects do occur, or are suspected, many single-subject researchers (e.g., Bijou et al., 1969) advocate the use of short treatment condition phases (*B*-phases). Such effects become even more problematic when conducting a single-subject drug study.

The second issue related to length of phases is cyclic variations. Hersen and Barlow (1976) consider this a most neglected issue in the applied single-subject literature. This issue is of paramount concern when using subjects that are influenced by cyclic factors such as the estrus cycle in females. Where the data may be influenced by such cyclical factors, it is advisable to extend the measurement period during each phase to incorporate the cyclic variation in both the baseline and treatment phases of the study. If it is not possible to extend the measurement period for the length of time required to include the cyclic variation, then one must replicate the results across subjects which are at different stages of the cyclic variation. If identical results are achieved across subjects regardless of the stage of the cyclic variation, then one can still derive meaningful conclusions from the data.

Statistical Analysis of the Data

In the past when single-subject research studies were conducted predominately at the infrahuman level, statistical analysis of the data was shunned. It was deemed to be an unnecessary component of a study because sufficient experimental control of extraneous variables could be established to enable the determination of the experimental effect. As single-subject designs have become more popular in the applied research areas, there has been an increased emphasis on the need for statistical analysis of the collected data. This increased emphasis has not, however, been readily accepted by researchers using the single-subject designs. McNamara and MacDonough (1972) stated that single-subject designs typically assessed the effect of the experimental treatment condition merely by presenting graphs of data or by using raw gain scores reflecting differences in the baseline and treatment scores. Michael (1974) has pointed out the harmful effects that could accrue from utilization of statistical analysis of single-subject data; Leitenberg (1973, p. 100) has even gone so far as to state that:

> It should be noted that experimenters employing single-case designs seldom apply statistical tests as criteria for evaluating whether alterations in a therapeutic procedure had demonstrable effects on an individual patient's behavior ... The "up and down" changes in patient behavior that coincide with different experimental phases are usually so substantial that statistical tests are hardly needed.

On the other side of the coin, several individuals have revealed the necessity of including statistical analysis of data obtained from single-subject designs. Bandura (1969, p. 243) points out:

> There are no difficulties in evaluating findings when large successive changes in behavior occur rapidly and consistently across different subjects. In many instances, however, not only are the accompanying behavioral changes less dramatic, but some individuals remain essentially unaffected by repeated exposure to the same treatment conditions. Replicative failures are usually attributed to inadequacies in the reinforcers employed, whereas suc-

cesses are assumed to result from the manipulated reinforcement variables. It is entirely possible, however, that in successful cases the behavioral changes are largely due to the influence of unobserved variables that happen to co-vary with the reversal of treatment conditions. The evaluative problem is further complicated by the fact that, in cases where successful behavioral control is achieved, no statistical criteria have been developed to evaluate whether the magnitude of change produced by a given treatment exceeds the variability resulting from uncontrolled factors operating while the treatment condition is not in effect.

Interpretation difficulties of the results of a given study exist in cases where the behavioral change is not dramatic or where the variability of the baseline data is so great that it could account for even a rather dramatic change in behavior. Gottman (1973) has provided an excellent example of a case in which graphic presentation of data seemed to illustrate rather dramatically an experimental treatment effect, but statistical analysis did not support such an interpretation. More recently Gottman and Glass (1978) have provided an even more dramatic illustration of the interpretative difficulties that may arise from relying only on visual analysis of data. These investigators gave 13 experienced judges two sets of previously published data from a single-subject experiment and asked them to assess, based only on a visual analysis, whether any treatment effect existed. For the first set of data 7 of the 13 judges said a treatment effect existed and 6 said one did not. This demonstrates the rather extreme unreliability that can exist when one relies only on visual analysis of data.

As you can see, there seem to be two opposing groups of individuals when it comes to the issue of statistical analysis of single-subject data. Both groups make a definite case for their point of view.

ARGUMENT AGAINST USE OF STATISTICAL ANALYSIS.   The case against the use of statistical analysis in single-subject research seems to center around two basic issues. The first of these involves the criteria for the evaluation of a treatment effect. There are two criteria that have been proposed for evaluating applied single-subject research (Kazdin, 1977; Risley, 1970). These consist of an experimental and a therapeutic or clinical criterion. The experimental criterion refers to determining whether or not the treatment condition had a significant impact on the dependent variable. The clinical criterion refers to achieving a level of change that enables the individual to function adequately in society (Hersen and Barlow, 1976; Risley, 1970). For example, a 50% reduction in the magnitude of deviant behavior exhibited by a child may represent a significant impact on behavior and thus meet the experimental criterion. However, from a clinical criterion standpoint the behavior has not changed enough because it still does not approximate "normal social interaction" (Hersen and Barlow, 1976, p. 267). To reach the clinical criterion a further reduction in the deviant behavior has to be achieved. In other words, the behavior must achieve social validation (Kazdin, 1977).

Single-subject researchers who object to the necessity of using statistical analysis argue that statistical significance is an ancillary and irrelevant criterion because it would frequently not achieve the clinical significance to which they strive. That is why applied behavioral researchers have argued that their goal is to produce large dramatic effects that do not require statistical analysis for assessment of results. This does not mean that the experimental criterion is not important, but rather that the clinical criterion exceeds the demands of the experimental criterion.

The second argument against statistical analysis of single-subject data is that statistical tests hide the performance of the individual subject. Statistical tests lump subjects together and focus on the average performance of individuals, hiding the performance of specific individuals. For example, a given treatment condition may have helped only 5 of 10 people to whom it was administered. If the 5 people who were not helped got worse the beneficial effect of the 5 who were helped would be masked if one averaged the overall improvement level of the 10 individuals. Essentially, one would reach the conclusion that the treatment effect was not effective when it actually was for half the individuals.

ARGUMENTS FOR USE OF STATISTICAL ANALYSIS.   In spite of the arguments made against use of statistical analysis there are situations for which investigators believe statistical analyses are appropriate. For example, if a stable baseline cannot be established, it becomes more difficult to assess validly the impact of the treatment condition by relying entirely on visual analysis. Similarly, as Jones, Vaught, and Weinrott (1977) point out, most single-subject research studies contain serial dependencies. By serial dependencies, I mean that the sequential responses emitted by a subject are correlated. This means that two responses emitted by a subject, be they adjacent or separated by time, will be correlated with one another. Therefore, the higher they are correlated, the greater one's ability to predict one from the other. The result of this serial dependency is to reduce the variability in the observed scores and otherwise bias the "estimates of behavioral score properties like stabilities, variabilities, or averages . . ." (Jones, Vaught and Weinrott, 1977, p. 155). These are the properties that are used to determine visually if the treatment condition produced a significant impact on behavior. Jones, Vaught, and Weinrott (1977) suggest that these serial dependencies cannot be incorporated in a visual appraisal of data.

RESOLUTION OF THE STATISTICAL ANALYSIS CONTROVERSY. As you have just seen, the proponents for and against statistical analysis each have valid points to make. However, such doctrinaire positions that unequivocally advocate one strategy to the exclusion of the other would seem to do more harm than good. The statistical and visual means of analyzing data "should be partners in the analytic endeavor" (Elashoff and Thoresen, 1978, p. 291). Statistical analysis should be used in addition to visual analysis. Visual inspection can be quite unreliable at times and the serial dependencies in the data are hard to assess by visual inspection alone. Such components suggest the necessity of including statistical analysis. Additionally, statistical tests are designed to assist in determining if the observed effects are due to chance and if they are likely to stand up to replication (Elashoff and Thoresen, 1978).

If one decided that it is appropriate to supplement visual analysis (Parsonson and Baer, 1978) with statistical analysis there are several options available. Gottman and Notarius (1978) discuss the use of Markov methods and Levin, Marascuilo, and Hubert (1978) focus on the use of randomization tests. Perhaps the most widely known and advocated approach is the autoregressive moving average model as applied to time series data. Therefore, there are several statistical approaches that can be used to supplement the visual analysis.

This brings one to the question of which statistical technique should be used. According to Elashoff and Thoresen (1978), the single most crucial question in deciding how to analyze the results is whether the experiment is the first of its type to be conducted or if other similar experiments have been conducted. If the experiment is the first of its type, then one must collect data to answer the following questions:

1. "What are the relevant response measures?"

2. "What is the baseline pattern in terms of level, variability, or trend?"

3. "What is the correlation between successive responses (Lag I, Lag 2, etc.)?"

4. "What is the pattern likely to be without intervention (if baseline were continued)?"

5. "What is the desired or expected pattern due to an intervention effect?" (Elashoff and Thoresen, 1978, p. 309).

Answers to these questions are necessary to develop a model for describing the structure of the data which is the basis for choosing a statistical test (Elashoff and Thoresen, 1978). Once you have answered these questions you can choose an appropriate test and then another experiment can be conducted and the selected statistical test can be used to assess the intervention effect. For a more detailed analysis of the selection of the appropriate model you are referred to Kratochwill (1978).

Rival Hypotheses

When discussing single-subject designs, and when reading literature on single-subject designs (e.g., Leitenberg, 1973), one gets the distinct impression that these designs can effectively identify causal relationships. However, it seems wise to heed Paul's 1969 claim that only multisubject designs are capable of establishing causal relationships: "This is the case because the important classes of variables for behavior modification research are so closely intertwined that the only way a given variable can be 'systematically manipulated' alone somewhere in the design is through the factorial representation of the variables of interest in combination with appropriate controls" (p. 51). Paul does, however, admit that the reversal and multiple-baseline designs do provide the strongest evidence of causal relationships that can be attained from single-subject designs.

What types of rival hypotheses exist in the single-subject designs presented? The issues of nonreversible changes and interdependence of behavior have already been discussed and therefore will not be repeated. A number of studies (e.g., Packard, 1970) have shown that instructions alone can change behavior. If different instructions are given for the baseline and experimental treatment phases, it is difficult to determine whether the effect was due to the treatment, the instructions, or some combination of the two. The best one can do is to maintain constant instructions across the treatment phases while introducing, withdrawing, and then reintroducing the therapeutic treatment condition (Hersen et al., 1972). Experimenter expectancies are another viable source of error in single-subject designs. In the majority of studies the experimenter is acutely aware of the time periods devoted to baseline and to the experimental treatment, which may lead to differential reactions on his or her part. These differential reactions may lead the subject's behavior to change in the desired direction. A last possible biasing effect has to do with sequencing effects (for an extended discussion of such effects in actual research the reader is referred to Poulton and Freeman, 1966). Since the same subject must perform in all phases of the experiment, order effects and/or carry-over

266   effects may exist. It is difficult to separate out the effects of the particular sequence of conditions from the effect of the treatment condition. If a change in behavior occurs, it could be due to the sequence
effect, the treatment effect, or some combination of these two.

Multisubject or Single-Subject Designs

Since both single-subject and multisubject designs have been presented, one might, at this point, wonder which of the two categories of
designs is better or which should be used in a given study. In multisubject research the basic strategy is to assign a group of subjects
randomly to various treatment conditions. The independent variable
is then manipulated and statistical tests are used to determine if there
is a significant mean difference in response of the subjects in the
various treatment groups. Single-subject research, on the other hand,
attempts to assess the effects of a given independent variable by comparing the subject's performance during presentation of the independent variable with that which exists when the independent variable is
not present. Control over a behavior is demonstrated if the behavior
can be altered at will by altering the experimental operations. Which of
these two designs is the best one to use?

Traditionally, psychological research has conformed to a multisubject strategy, and most psychologists have accepted this as the
research strategy to use. However, as Dukes (1965) has pointed out,
single-subject research has always been with us even though its impact, with a few notable exceptions, has traditionally not been great.
With the publication of Sidman's 1960 book and the proliferation of
behavior therapy research, single-subject experimentation has come
into its own. Yet, in spite of this, its proponents seem to feel compelled
to justify its existence as a viable alternative. This may have been
necessary to be accepted, since in many respects it represented a
reaction to the formalized multisubject research methodology. Perhaps
the most frequently cited advantage of the single-subject research
design over the multisubject research design is that it bypasses variability due to the intersubject differences found in multisubject designs.
As Kazdin (1973) has noted, this is desirable because intersubject variability is a function of the research design and not a feature of the
behavior of the individual subject. Related to this is the fact that
dealing with group averages frequently misrepresents individual behavior. All subjects do not behave in the same way as the average
subject.

Almost two decades ago Cronbach (1957) advocated the integration of the experimental and correlational approaches to research in

psychology. Experimental multisubject research was dedicated to identifying nomothetic laws of behavior. One of the big obstacles in the path of experimental psychology was individual difference or error variance, which was to be reduced by any possible device. Cronbach (1957, p. 674) then proceeded to identify various ways in which this could be accomplished. One device he advocated was the use of the correlation approach: studies should include the aptitudes of the subjects in an experiment to determine how they interacted with the experimental treatments. In other words, he advocated a science of aptitude by treatment interactions. In a more recent article Cronbach (1975) reported that this science was flourishing but, at the same time, stated that it was no longer sufficient. In order to reduce the error variance and explain and predict behavior, dimensions of the situation and the person had to be taken into account.

Another approach that Cronbach (1957) said could be used to eliminate error variance or individual difference was to follow B. F. Skinner's lead and use only one subject. This is the approach advocated strongly by Sidman (1960). There is a definite advantage to studying the individual organism. Variables affecting the behavior of this one organism can be more highly controlled so the effect of the treatment condition in isolation can be seen. However, the results of the study can be generalized only to another identical organism in the same controlled setting. Cronbach (1975) has argued and documented the fact that behavior is an interactive function of the situation, the subject, and the experimental treatment.

There are advantages and disadvantages to both multisubject and single-subject research, and it is impossible to state that one is the preferred mode. Rather, it seems as though the two techniques should be integrated, just as Cronbach (1957) advocated the integration of the correlational and experimental approaches. This is particularly true when one realizes that the results obtained also seem to be dependent upon the research design one uses. For an extended discussion of this issue, see Grice (1966) and D'Amato (1970, pp. 29–30). The question is, how should the two be integrated? A number of individuals (Paul, 1966; Leitenberg, 1973; Kazdin, 1973; and Shine, 1975) have suggested that the single-subject approach may be the best means for starting an investigation because of its economy in research time and costs. The single-subject approach could be used as an initial probing process to investigate promising experimental treatment conditions to determine if they are functionally related to behavior. However, this serves only as a probing or mapping device and not as a final indication of causality because of the possibility of confounding effects from extraneous variables that cannot be controlled in the single-subject approach. It is also important to realize that if a promising hypothesis is not supported with this initial probe, this does not discredit it. It must be remembered that there is often a great deal of variability in the behavior of different individuals, and an experimental treatment condition that does not work on one individual may be effective on another. Therefore, if the hypothesis does not receive support on the one individual on which it was tested, it should be tested on other, different individuals before it is discarded.

Following the single-subject approach, Paul (1966), Kazdin (1973), and Shine (1975) suggest that the experimental treatment should be investigated from a multisubject approach. Switching to the multisubject approach allows one to control for competing rival hypotheses, providing the needed assurance that it actually is the experimental treatment condition that is causing the change in behavior. This switch also allows one to examine the degree of generality of the findings: is the experimental treatment condition effective when administered to others? If a significant effect is found using the multisubject approach, generality is established.

Use of the multisubject approach does, however, bring up the objections voiced by single-subject researchers. Multisubject research focuses on mean differences between groups of subjects, which are not representative of individual performance. Seldom, if ever, does an experimental treatment change the behavior of all subjects and in the same way. This individual difference is considered to be error in the system. This is where the single-subject approach should again be used—Shine's (1975) detection and identification function—to attempt to identify what is causing the individual variation in response to the experimental treatment. This means analyzing each subject's data to determine the magnitude of effect that the experimental treatment had on each subject. Once the subjects have been clustered according to the effectiveness of the experimental treatment on their behavior, the experimenter must attempt to identify what is common to the subjects that are clustered, but differs across clusters of subjects. Once the experimenter has identified what he or she thinks is the variable or variables, they must be verified in a multisubject research design.

The process that has just been advocated consists of a continuing interaction between the multi- and single-subject approaches. It seems that this interactive approach will ultimately lead to greater prediction and explanation of behavior.

Summary

In attempting to conduct an experimental research study that uses only one subject you must reorient your thinking, because extraneous variables cannot be controlled by using a randomization control technique, nor can they be handled by the inclusion of a control group. To begin to rule out the possible confounding effect of extraneous variables, some form of a time-series approach must be taken. This means that multiple pre- and postmeasures on the dependent variable must be taken to exclude potential rival hypotheses such as maturation. The most frequently used single subject design is the A-B-A design. Utilization of this design requires the investigator to take baseline measures before and after the experimental treatment effect has been introduced. The experimental treatment effect is demonstrated by a change in behavior when the treatment condition is introduced and a reversal of the behavior to its pretreatment level when the experimental treatment condition is withdrawn. The success of this design does, however, depend upon the reversal of behavior to its pretreatment level upon withdrawal of the treatment condition.

Many extensions of the basic A-B-A design have been made; however, the most valuable one attempts to assess the combined or interactive effect of two or more variables. To accomplish this task, it is necessary to assess the influence of each variable separately and in combination. Additionally, the combination of variables, or the interaction of the two or more variables, must be compared with each variable separately. This typically means that at least two subjects must be used in the study. Even with this restriction, it provides an opportunity to assess the interactive effect of two or more variables.

A third type of single subject design is the multiple-baseline design. This design avoids the necessity of reversibility that was required of the A-B-A design by successively administering the experimental treatment condition to different target behaviors or individuals. The influence of the treatment condition is revealed if a change in behavior occurs simultaneously with the introduction of the treatment condition. While the multiple-baseline design avoids the problem of reversibility, it requires an independence of the behaviors under study to demonstrate the experimental treatment effect.

The multiple schedule design is one in which the same behavior is subjected to different experimental treatments under different stimulus conditions. The effect of the experimental treatment is demonstrated if the subject's behavior changes from one stimulus to the other as the experimental treatment conditions change.

The changing-criterion design is a relative newcomer to the area of single-subject designs. However, it is useful in studies that require a shaping of behavior over a period of time. This design requires, following baseline, a treatment condition to be implemented and continued across a series of intervention phases. Each intervention phase has a progressively more difficult criterion that must be met in order to advance to the next intervention phase. In this way, behavior can gradually be shaped to a given criterion level.

In addition to acquiring a basic knowledge of the single-subject designs, you must also have a knowledge of some of the methodological considerations required for appropriately implementing them. These include the following:

1. *Baseline.* A stable baseline must be obtained, but it is difficult to identify what constitutes a stable baseline since some variation will always occur in the freely occurring target behaviors.

2. *Change one variable at a time.* A cardinal rule in single subject research is that only one variable can be changed when proceeding from one phase of the experiment to the other.

3. *Length of phases.* While there is some disagreement, the rule seems to be that the length of the phases should be kept equal.

4. *Statistical analysis of the data.* How can one statistically analyze the data of a single subject to provide evidence of a significant change in behavior?

5. *Rival hypotheses.* This includes the effect of variables such as instructions, experimenter expectancies, and sequencing effects.

Since both single-subject and multisubject designs are available for use, one has to decide which type of design one should use in a given study. The best approach seems to be an integration of the two approaches, with the single-subject approach being an efficient means of identifying possible causal relations that can be validated by the multisubject approach.

Key Concepts

One way to test your mastery of the material that was presented in this chapter is to see if you know the meaning of the following terms. These terms were selected because they represent the key concepts. If you can define, identify, or otherwise explain each of the following terms without referring back to the material in the chapter, you can be assured that you have mastered the basics of the material that was presented. Just in case you cannot recall the meaning of a given term, the page on which it can be found appears in parentheses beside it.

A-B-A design (p. 237)

baseline (p. 237)

A-B-A-B design (p. 239)

reversal (p. 242)

interaction design (p. 243)

multiple-baseline design (p. 248)

interdependence of behavior (pp. 249–251)

multiple schedule design (p. 252)

changing-criterion design (p. 255)

magnitude of criterion change (p. 257)

length of treatment phase (p. 260)

cyclic variations (pp. 260–261)

clinical criterion (pp. 262–263)

serial dependencies (p. 263)

10

Evaluation Research

During the decades of the 1960s and the 1970s, we have seen a tremendous growth in the number of social or human service programs that have been undertaken by the federal government. Programs have been undertaken to improve public education and health care, to reduce poverty and crime, to promote mental health, and to provide public housing. Perhaps one of the most widely known social programs is Head Start. The increased attention to social programs had its start during the depression when Franklin D. Roosevelt initiated his New Deal social programs. However, major impetus was not taken until the 1960s. According to Guttentag (1977), this focus on social programs is characteristic of a social change from an industrial to a postindustrial society. An industrial society focuses on producing goods whereas a postindustrial society focuses on human, professional, and technical services. The increased focus on social programs results from this social change.

With this increased emergence of social programs has come the increased realization that some assessment or evaluation of these programs must also take place. Although this requirement was first advocated by Stephen (1935) with reference to the New Deal social programs, it went virtually unheeded until the late 1960s. By the early 1970s something called *evaluation research* was "being regularly required of health, education, and welfare programs" (Patton, 1978, p. 15). Evaluation research has been defined by Freeman (1977, p. 25) "as activities which follow the general mandates of social research, compromising these as minimally as possible because of the realities of the political and pragmatic environment in which investigators work." Therefore, evaluation research attempts to employ the basic scientific methodology in the assessment of social programs so as to provide an empirical basis of the utility of these programs. However, it should always be kept in mind that evaluation research is first and foremost a political decision-making tool. Evaluation research emerged as a result of decision makers' desire to have information not only about the effectiveness of the social programs that were implemented, but also about how to improve on existing programs. They want and need to know if programs such as Head Start are meeting their goals, or how they should be changed to meet their goals. Given such information, decision makers should be capable of taking a more rational approach to policy making. However, the experience of evaluation researchers has not revealed this to be the case. On the contrary, the typical experience is that the results of the evaluation research go unheeded (Patton, 1978 and Weiss, 1972). One of the basic issues in evaluation research is, therefore, solving the problem of how to enhance the usefulness and utilization of research. Patton (1978) has revealed that the solution to this problem appears to reside partially in what he called the personal factor. This refers to the presence of a person or a group of people who are interested in and care about the evaluation because they want to use it to make decisions about programs. When users of evaluation research are involved in the evaluation, it enhances the probability of the results being used. Therefore, evaluation research should begin by identifying not only the people and organization that need the evaluation research information, but also those individuals who are interested in it. Once these individuals are identified, it is absolutely necessary that they take part in each step of the evaluation. Without this involvement, one runs the risk of conducting a program evaluation that, when completed, is put on a shelf to gather dust. Only

274   by including interested individuals in each step of the study does one maximize chances of having the results used by decision makers. Therefore, in the following discussion of each of the phases of evaluation research, emphasis will be placed on the inclusion of the personal factor.

Types of Evaluation Research Activities

Before elaborating on the various phases involved in evaluation research, it would be useful to have an idea of the types of evaluation research activities that are carried on by investigators. Such information is useful because different people request program evaluations for different reasons. Assume, for example, that a school district appropriated money for the development and implementation of a new curriculum. The school board may want to know if the new curriculum should be continued or dropped. The principal, however, may want to know not only if the new curriculum is attaining the desired goals of improved learning, but also which components of the new curriculum are most effective and how can it be altered to become even more effective. The teachers, on the other hand, are concerned with the practical day-to-day concerns about techniques. They want and need to know such things as how to present material to students and which topics should receive greatest emphasis. From this it should be evident that different people in the overall organizational structure have slightly different goals. The evaluation researcher must identify the primary goal toward which to divert his or her activities. This is important because the goal of the evaluation dictates to a great extent the activities in which the researcher engages. In this regard, Freeman (1977) described evaluation activities as consisting of process evaluation, impact or summative (Scriven, 1967) evaluation, and comprehensive evaluation. An examination of these three types of evaluation activities should reveal that different goals require different activities.

Process Evaluation

The primary issue of concern in process evaluation is whether or not the particular program, intervention, or treatment was implemented in the manner dictated in its stated guidelines. As stated by Bernstein and Freeman (1975), process evaluation is focused on determining whether the program was directed at the people to whom it was intended and if the program was implemented in the way it was designed. Assume, for example, that a program was funded to provide counseling with the parents of children with a prior history of juvenile delinquency. Process evaluation would focus on determining whether or not such parents were identified and whether or not they received any counseling. A naive evaluator may overlook the stage of process evaluation and proceed with some other form of evaluation based on the assumption that the funded program was carried out in the manner prescribed. However, with social programs there are many uncontrolled variables which could operate to preclude the implementation of a given program. The above-mentioned program, designed to provide counseling to parents of juvenile delinquents, may falter because the courts may not provide the data necessary to identify the delinquents, or the parents may refuse counseling. Therefore, one of the obvious steps of any evaluation should involve determining if the social program was undertaken in the prescribed manner. If it was not, then one has to determine if it conformed close enough to the mandates of the program to warrant evaluation. If it did not, then one must possibly make the decision to terminate evaluation, since it would provide no useful information.

Since process evaluation should actually precede or run concurrently with any subsequent evaluation activity, the techniques for conducting this part of the evaluation will be elaborated at this point. Attention will be directed toward assessing whether or not the program was implemented in the prescribed manner and whether or not it reached the prescribed target audience.

PROGRAM IMPLEMENTATION.   Freeman (1977) states that program implementation can most effectively be studied if the specific aspects of the program are operationally defined. If a program is designed to increase the public's awareness of the hazards of driving during the Christmas vacation period, and it consists of TV announcements, radio announcements and the distribution of brochures to the public, it is possible to use a variety of approaches to determine if the program was implemented as specified. If a program is not so specifically operationalized, the task of assessing whether or not it was implemented in the prescribed manner becomes more difficult.

Initially one may think that the logical and natural approach would be for programs to be specified in such a manner that each component was operationally defined. Freeman (1977) has pointed out at least two reasons that preclude the operational specification of the elements contained in social programs. First, program planners and decision makers typically do not conceive the programs in sequenced parts. Rather, they view, and attempt to develop, an overall program such as reduction of smoking or crime prevention. Second, the inputs to many of the programs are frequently so-called professional know-how, which runs counter to specifying the exact operations that should be promoted. Physicians, for example, practice in the privacy of their examination room and there is a great deal of pressure to inhibit anyone from invading it (Freidson, 1972). Any social program that required a physician's examination would, therefore, experience a conflict between the need for specifying program elements (the components of the examination) and the physicians' demand for lack of specification as to what they are to do in the examining room.

In spite of the apparent difficulties that may arise in operationally specifying the elements of a program, it should be done, since this will strengthen the evaluation. If the program elements can be operationally specified, this has the benefit of providing additional clarity to the program rather than leaving it fuzzy and unspecified. A program that is designed to increase community members' awareness of political issues is fuzzy and nonspecific. However, one that attempts to do this with a coordinated set of TV programs and discussion groups, each of which has a well-defined content and outline of activities, is well-specified and clear in its goals and orientation.

Once the elements of the program have been specified, one must collect data to determine if the program was implemented in the manner specified. There are typically three procedures by which one collects process data (Freeman, 1977). One procedure is observational. Here the researcher would observe the program in action and take notes, or record in some other fashion, the type of activities in which the individuals implementing the program engaged. A second approach would be to interview the individuals who participated in the program and/or the persons delivering the program, to obtain their accounts of what took place in the program. A third approach would be to use available records representing the activities of the program. This would involve the use of computerized records of attendance and activities, notes made by the individuals implementing the programs, or any other records that would reveal the manner in which the program was implemented. Once this information was attained the evaluation researcher would have to evaluate this information and make an assessment as to whether or not the program was being implemented in the prescribed manner. To assist in this evaluation the discrepancy evaluation model (Provus, 1971) is recommended. This is a model which allows for a comparison of the actual program with the ideal program. From this model one can, therefore, get some rather objective idea of the degree to which a given program is operating as desired. It must be recognized that all programs will deviate to some extent from the ideal. The important issue is determining whether or not a given program is deviating too far from the ideal. This is a judgment by decision makers and evaluators. They have to determine if the program represented a sufficient realization of the ideal program, even though it was modified to meet the unique needs of the local community in which it was implemented.

TARGET IDENTIFICATION.   Process evaluation involves the assessment of not only whether or not the program was implemented in the prescribed manner but also whether or not it was administered to the population to which it was targeted. If a program was designed to assist children with learning disabilities, it would naturally be inappropriate to administer it to all children within a given school system. At first glance it may appear that target identification is an easy task. Most programs are targeted toward individuals that share common characteristics as fifth to eighth grade children who have failed one or more grades, or toward aggregates of individuals such as male prison inmates who are first offenders under the age of 25. In such cases target identification is relatively easy, since they are identified in fairly well-defined operational terms. However, many social programs do not include a target population that is so easily defined. Assume, for example, that the target population was children suffering from child abuse. In such cases it becomes much more difficult to determine validly and reliably if the target population is being reached. Such difficulties may, therefore, enhance the possibility of implementing the program on a group other than those targeted by the program. In such cases the deviation from the targeted population must be noted since it can greatly influence the assessment of the impact of the program.

It is also important to remember that social programs are frequently oriented toward rare events and conditions. Programs are oriented toward the hard-core unemployed, or the mildly retarded individual. These individuals represent a minority of individuals within a given geographic area. Therefore, it is necessary to estimate the number of individuals who are available to participate in the program. This step is important for several reasons. Decision makers and program planners frequently tend to overestimate the prevalence of such target groups. Without determining beforehand the actual prevalence of, for example, physically handicapped individuals in a given area, funds may be allocated to implement a program, and then it is realized that there is an insufficient number of available individuals. This insufficient number of individuals may stem from several sources. First, there may actually be an insufficient number of individuals in a given area to fulfill the requirements for determination of the success of the program. Second, there may be a sufficient number of individuals in a given area, but for a variety of reasons they elect not to participate in the program. Third, a sufficient number of individuals may exist in an area and they do elect to participate, but drop out before completion of the program. If a sufficient number of individuals do not participate in a social program, it is naturally doomed to failure.

To identify whether or not an adequate target population exists, one must first identify the specific social and demographic characteristics of this population and then identify them in terms of the problems, difficulties, and conditions that they share. For example, one may define the target population as male adolescents residing in a given geographic location who have demonstrated learning disabilities as defined by test X. Then one must conduct a survey to determine the size of the population available in a given area for participation in the program. If target identification requires assessment of special problems or conditions, then the survey must include special diagnostic and screening procedures. Only when it has been determined that an adequate target population exists should one implement the social program under consideration.

Impact or Summative Evaluation

Impact, or summative, evaluation has as its goal the determination of whether or not the program had the desired and predicted effect. If a program was designed to reduce recidivism among first offenders, then impact, or summative, evaluation would assess the success with which this goal was attained. Impact, or summative, evaluation implies, therefore, that there is a set of prespecified goals and a criterion of success or impact that the program attempts to achieve, such as reduction in rate of admissions to mental hospitals, or increase in frequency with which crimes are reported. The design of impact evaluation does, therefore, seem to resemble an experiment. Indeed, impact evaluation does frequently correspond to some variant of experimental or quasi-experimental design. In fact, Freeman (1977, p. 26) states that "most evaluation researchers take the position that experimental designs are the most appropriate way of measuring impact, since they provide known means of controlling external bias." However, you should be aware of the fact that not all researchers advocate the experimental approach to evaluation research. This issue will be taken up at a later point.

Conceptualizing evaluation research as an experiment does, however, seem to give it a degree of finality that it does not really have. As Weiss (1972) has pointed out, evaluations are most often called upon to help with decisions about improving a program. Decision makers seldom make do or die decisions. Rather, they tend to patch up programs that were revealed to be failures in an attempt to make them effective. This is a point of which the evaluation researcher must be aware. He or she must evaluate the impact of the program, but must also include recommendations for its improvement, or recommendations for how **279** to make an ineffective program an effective one.

In some cases the evaluator is told that his or her task is to provide information during its development that would help improve it. This type of evaluation is referred to as formative evaluation (Scriven, 1967). In a sense, one can view this type of evaluation as a series of impact evaluations. One assesses the impact of a program up to a given point. Recommendations are then made for improving the program. These recommendations are then incorporated and the revised program is evaluated. This process continues until the program goals are met or a satisfactory level of achievement has been reached.

Comprehensive Evaluation

A comprehensive evaluation "refers to studies that include both a process and an impact evaluation" (Freeman, 1977, p. 26). This is actually the ideal of all evaluations, since it would provide information not only on whether the program was implemented as planned, but also on whether the program had any desirable impact. It has frequently been noted that few evaluations demonstrate positive findings (e.g., Weiss, 1972). That is, it is frequently demonstrated that social programs do *not* have their intended benefit. To take an extreme example, the Great Society programs administered from the Office of Economic Opportunity were aimed at nothing less than the elimination of poverty. As we all know, this is a program that definitely did not achieve its goal. On a lesser scale, many other programs have met with a similar fate. Freeman (1977) believes that one of the major reasons for this failure to demonstrate positive findings is that the programs were not implemented in the proper manner. If this is actually the case, it clearly reveals the necessity of including process evaluation along with impact evaluation.

Phases of Comprehensive Evaluation

Evaluation research, as stated earlier, is a political decision-making tool. Decision makers typically want to know more than whether or not the social program that they have initiated is meeting or not meeting its goals. More frequently they want to know, in addition to whether it is achieving its goals, how to modify the existing program to enhance its effectiveness, should it be extended to other sites, and what

280 components were most effective. This is because decision makers seldom think in go-no-go terms. As Weiss (1972) has pointed out, only infrequently do decision makers completely abandon a program. Rather, they search for ways of improving an existing one. Therefore, evaluators frequently have "to be diagnosticians as well as judges" (Weiss 1972b, p. 6). Evaluators, in their role as diagnosticians and judges, would like to see the results of their labors utilized. In the past it has been relatively common for an evaluator to assess a given program and report the results to the proper decision makers only to find that the results are placed on a shelf to gather dust. This is quite discouraging to the evaluator, who would like to see his or her efforts put to some use in subsequent policy making. To accomplish this, evaluation researchers have had to identify procedures that must be followed to maximize assurance of utilization.

The following elaboration of the phases of comprehensive evaluation will focus on the basic steps that must be taken to maximize the possibility that the evaluation will answer the questions that decision makers want answered. Following these steps will also maximize the possibility that the evaluation will be used by the decision makers.

Formulating the Research Question

To the naive evaluator, formulating the research question seems like a simple task. A program should be initiated with a specific goal in mind and the evaluator's task is to determine if that goal was met. If an educational program was initiated to improve reading, then the goal is clear-cut and the evaluator's task is somewhat simplified. However, this step is seldom as simple as it seems. Programs are seldom stated in the neat framework of objectives and goals required by the evaluation researcher. More frequently, they have multiple and diffuse goals such as crime prevention, or teaching good citizenship. Therefore, the first task of the researcher is to identify, in a clear and specific manner, the exact goals and objectives.

Before one begins this goal-specification process, one must identify the relevant decision makers and information users. By this, I am referring to the identification of the individuals who can, and want to, use the information that will be obtained from the research. These are the people who have a genuine interest in the research and, therefore, will take the time and make the effort to assist the evaluators in producing the most effective and useful research study. Remember that utilization is one important facet of evaluation research, and is enhanced by the personal factor or the presence of individuals who care about the evaluation and the information that it will generate. Identification of these relevant decision makers and information users is the means by which one incorporates the personal factor, which thereby enhances the possibility of utilization.

Once the relevant decision makers and information users have been identified, the evaluation researchers must interact with these individuals in each of the phases of the comprehensive evaluation. First, they must interact to identify the purpose of the evaluation. This means that a decision has to be made as to whether the primary purpose of the evaluation is to be a summative or formative evaluation (Scriven, 1967). In other words, should the evaluation be oriented toward assessment of its effectiveness (summative), or toward collecting information that can be used to develop and improve the program (formative)? Making such a distinction, and determining which of these two approaches is the primary goal of the evaluation, is quite important since these two approaches involve significantly different research emphases.

Determining whether the primary and initial goal of the evaluation is formative or summative is, however, a rather difficult task in most cases. Weiss (1972a), for example, has noted that the attainment of a clear and concise statement of program goals is often complicated. Decision makers and program administrators most typically do not have a specific set of goals in mind when they propose and implement a social program. When pinned down as to the goals of a given program, they typically respond by giving a global and unrealistic response such as to reduce crime, enhance learning, or improve interpersonal skills. Such statements are of little help to program evaluators because they are not specific enough to guide the evaluator in determining what to assess about the program. Such fuzziness about program goals probably derives from decision makers' and program implementors' concentration on the more mundane matters of program implementation (Weiss, 1972a) or to the fact that the program does not as yet have any specific goals over and above the general fuzzy ones that are stated (Patton, 1978).

To begin to obtain information about program goals from interested and concerned decision makers and program planners, Patton (1978) suggests that the evaluation researcher should begin by having these individuals complete the sentence "I would like to know _____ about program X." This incomplete sentence should be completed ten times to reflect the ten things that the decision makers and planners want to know. Engaging in this task provides a body of information that can operate as an initial framework for discussion that can lead to the formulation of a specific set of program goals. This does not mean that a clear set of agreed-upon goals will necessarily evolve from such a discussion. In fact, in the typical case there is some degree of conflict over the program goals and especially over the priority of each of these goals. For example, in a criminal justice program there may be conflict over whether the goal of the program is to punish offenders, incarcerate them, or rehabilitate them. Even if there is agreement on the goals of the program, there will probably not be agreement on priority ordering of these goals.

To overcome the conflict that may arise in the establishment of program goals, evaluation researchers have resorted to the use of a variety of techniques. These include the Delphi technique (Dalkey, 1969), multiattributes utility measurement (Gardiner and Edwards, 1975), the decision-theoretic approach (Edwards, Guttentag, and Snapper, 1975), fuzzy set theory (Zadeh et al., 1975) and goal-free evaluation (Scriven, 1972).

As you can see from the above discussion of program goals, most evaluation researchers consider the identification and clarification of goals to be of paramount importance. However, Patton (1978, p. 121) points out that this is only one of the options available in evaluation research. He states that the identification and clarification of program goals is "neither necessary nor appropriate in every evaluation." Whether or not one focuses on the identification of clear and concise program goals and objectives depends upon the organizational dynamics of a given program. This means that the evaluation researcher must assess a given program to determine whether or not identification and clarification of program goals is appropriate. Based on Emery and Trist's 1965 work, it seems apparent that the more uncertain or unstable, turbulent, and less established a program is, the more unlikely it is that the evaluator will be able to identify specific program goals that will remain consistent over time. Suppose for example that a new moral development program was funded by the department of Health, Education, and Welfare. Four pilot schools in four different geographic areas were selected to implement the program. Although the program had the global objective of enhancing the level of moral development among school age children, the procedures for accomplishing this had to be developed. Although guidelines could be specified by the funding agency, and they could provide consultants to assist in the process, the school personnel had to engage in the implementation process as well as integrate it into the total school system. This means that different approaches and procedures have to be tried out, that uncertainty tends to exist in terms of staffing, procedures for implementing moral development, reactions of the students, parental support, and relationship to the overall school system. As you can see, new programs such as this are often unstable and turbulent. If an evaluation researcher attempted to focus on program goals identification and clarification, he or she would be focusing on the wrong issue. At this stage of a program the decision makers and program planners are interested in gaining information that will assist them in program development or formative evaluation. This means obtaining information for the program implementers that will assist them in developing the program.

After a program has gone through this development stage and has developed some stability in terms of the way it is run, one can focus on identification and clarification of program goals to assess the outcome of the program or summative evaluation.

It should be clear at this point that the organizational dynamics of a program, or the degree of turbulence, uncertainty, or instability it is experiencing, in part determines the type of evaluation that is needed. The evaluator must understand that different kinds of evaluations are needed for different types of programs, or programs in different stages of development. He or she must interact with the decision makers and program planners to determine the type of evaluation, formative or summative, that is needed, and then work within the framework of the program, and with the decision makers and program planners, to provide the most beneficial type of information.

Process Evaluation

Process evaluation, as it was defined previously, is concerned with determining whether or not the program was implemented as it was designed to be implemented. This is a procedure that should take place prior to, or concurrent with, formative or summative evaluation. Since process evaluation was elaborated on at an earlier point, only brief reference will be made to it here.

It has been revealed by many sources (e.g., Weiss, 1972a), that social programs are frequently lacking when subjected to an evaluation study. Past evaluation studies have, however, been primarily focused on summative evaluation. This means that programs focused primarily on outcome. Did a criminal justice program produce a decrease in recidivism rates? Was drug addiction decreased by a drug abuse treatment program? Little attention was focused on whether the program was carried out in the prescribed manner. Lynne and Salasin (1974) considered the gap between what was expected of human services programs and what was delivered to be due to two shortcomings. One of these was the failure to implement the program properly.

As the field of evaluation research grows in terms of sophistication, it is becoming clear that more emphasis has to be placed on process evaluation. Not only can process evaluation help explain the results of a summative evaluation, but it can, in some instances, provide information on how to alter a program to improve it. Consider the example of the case of the drug treatment program discussed by Patton (1978). Summative evaluation revealed that all programs except one had a mediocre success rate. This one program had a 100% success rate over a two-year period, so funds for this one program were tripled, allowing it to expand and serve a larger population. Evaluation of readdiction rates a year later revealed a mediocre success rate similar to the other program. The only type of evaluation that was done with this program was to perform a summative evaluation. Consequently, there was no feedback regarding how the program was conducted to assess why the one program was highly successful until it was expanded. As it turned out a process analysis was conducted at a later point, which revealed that the successful program was successful because it was small and had a dedicated staff. One staff counselor kept such a close relationship with each addict that he knew how to keep them straight. However, when the program was enlarged this counselor was elevated to the level of administrator of three halfway houses and the intimacy and dedication of the staff declined, leading to a mediocre program. From this example, it should be obvious that process evaluation can frequently provide invaluable information and should always be undertaken unless there is data revealing that the implementation of a given program deviates little from the prescribed program.

Formative Evaluation

The methodology to be followed in conducting a formative evaluation has to be relatively flexible due to the nature of the evaluation one is attempting to conduct. In formative evaluation, the researcher is attempting to provide the program staff with information that will enable them to improve their program. The very nature of this type of progress does, therefore, require a great deal of interaction with the program staff. The evaluation researcher must interact with the program staff at various intervals during the development of the program to determine the information needed to make short-run adaptive decisions. This may necessitate conducting interviews to determine staff and/or participants' perceptions or opinions about the program. It may require observations of staff and/or participants' behavior or measurement of their attitudes. To conduct a formative evaluation, the evaluator must bring with him or her an arsenal of techniques for data collection and then utilize the ones that will provide information needed by the program staff to improve their program. This arsenal may include interviews, questionnaires, observation techniques, rating scales, psychometric tests of attitudes, values, personality, and beliefs, as well as records and documents such as minutes of board meetings.

Summative or Impact Evaluation

In conducting an impact or summative evaluation, one is attempting to determine the outcome of the social program. The dominant approach used to conduct such an evaluation is the scientific method.

This means that the evaluation researcher attempts to conduct a true, **285** or controlled, experiment according to the procedures outlined in the previous chapters of this book. The evaluation researcher strives to design an outcome study that includes both an experimental group, which received the social program, and a control group, which did not receive the social program or received some traditional program. Potentially extraneous variables are controlled through techniques such as randomization. When the rigors of a true experimental study cannot be conducted, then the evaluation researcher resorts to one of the less formalized quasi-experimental designs such as a time-series design (Weiss, 1972a). Most individuals, however, seem to agree that a true experiment is the most desirable approach to take in conducting an impact, or summative, evaluation. Bernstein and Freeman (1975) conducted a study that attempted to assess the quality of evaluation research as it was currently practiced. In their assessment, quality was depicted as a study that conformed to a true experiment, which yielded quantitative data analyzed with sophisticated statistical techniques. Bernstein and Freeman cited Suchman (1967), Caro (1971), and Rossi and Williams (1972) in support of their assessment of quality.

Issues in Conducting Summative or Impact Evaluation

When attempting to conduct the most desirable impact or summative evaluation, an evaluation researcher will strive to achieve a true experimental design. This means that subjects will be randomly assigned to the various treatment groups and statistical analysis will be used to determine if the treatment groups differ at the .05 level. Herein lie two basic difficulties that have plagued evaluation researchers: the issue of randomization and the issue of statistical significance.

Randomization

One of the basic requirements for conducting a true experiment is that subjects be randomly assigned to the various treatment groups. Such a requirement is considered necessary because it provides control for both known and unknown sources of variation. Experiments that have attempted to incorporate random assignment have, however, been criticized by program managers, developers, and supporters on the basis of their feasibility, scope, usefulness, and ethicality (Boruch, 1976). Boruch has explicated these criticisms and then very appropriately shown that they have little substance. For example, advocates against the feasibility issue state that randomized experiments are

286   virtually impossible to conduct in the real world because in many programs, individuals must volunteer for the program and/or because assigning people to an untreated control group is unethical. Randomization is too expensive and time-consuming, and unnecessary because other techniques can be used to eliminate bias. Yet Boruch (1976) has shown that such arguments do not hold up. Volunteers, for example, can be randomly assigned just as easily as nonvolunteers. The ethical problem of assigning people to a control group can be handled merely by delaying their treatment until after data is collected. True experimental studies requiring randomization are not necessarily more expensive and overly time-consuming, and much evidence reveals that techniques other than random assignment are seldom as effective in counteracting bias.

Evidence such as this continues to reveal that random assignment is a desirable and necessary feature of a quality evaluation study. It is, however, well known by evaluation researchers that randomization is more difficult to achieve effectively when one is operating in the field. Conner (1978) has examined the randomization process in twelve social reform projects to determine the procedures that evaluation researchers need to follow to maximize the possibility of performing randomization successfully. He has revealed that the following steps need to be taken to achieve greatest assurance that randomization has been accomplished. In planning randomization, it is important that the evaluation researcher maintain control over the randomization process. It is tempting to turn this process over to the program staff because it seems to be a rather simple and straightforward process. Doing this, however, frequently results in nonrandom assignment, because the staff does not fully understand the importance of randomization and they make exceptions to this process. One must also determine if random assignment is to be fixed or variable. If random assignment is fixed then no exceptions to the random procedure are permitted. If it is variable then exceptions are permitted. For example, in a drunk drivers study, Blumenthal and Ross (1973) attempted to compare the effectiveness of three types of sanctions on drivers found guilty of driving while under the influence of alcohol. The researchers assigned the penalties on a random basis with one exception. Judges could vary the penalty in special cases. This exception, which was to have occurred infrequently, actually occurred quite frequently. Based on data such as this, the random assignment procedures should be fixed. If exceptions are to be made they must be under the control of the researcher. Once these two issues are solved, one must then decide whether to group or block subjects on certain characteristics, in other words, whether subjects should be grouped into those with different traits such as intellectual abilities and socioeconomic status before being randomly assigned to conditions. While random assignment provides greatest assurance of distributing subjects across treatment groups equally, it is not 100% effective. Berman (1973), for example, conducted a parolee study in which he randomly assigned ex-offenders to a treatment or control group. However, the random assignment procedure assigned, by chance, all narcotics offenders to the control group. Therefore, he could not assess the influence of the treatment on this group of subjects. If subjects had been grouped into types of offenses before random assignment, this would not have happened.

The last consideration in planning for random assignment is to decide if subjects are to be informed about the random assignment procedure. From the experience of the evaluation researchers conducting the studies reviewed by Conner (1978), it seems that clients understand and accept randomization as a necessary condition to determine program effectiveness. It would seem, therefore, that subjects should be informed of this process. However, if one is dealing with scarce resources such as jobs during a depression, individuals may not be as understanding if they are assigned to a control group that does not receive a job.

Once the above issues have been settled, and randomization is planned, then one must determine how randomization is to be implemented. If a social program, such as a drug abuse program, consisted of treating individuals in many centers across the country, one has the option of letting each center do the randomization or having a control station do the randomization. Experience has revealed that in such cases it is necessary to have a control station where random assignment is carried out; otherwise, it is not properly implemented. Once one has decided where randomization is to be carried out, one must have as few people as possible actually doing the randomization. Conner (1978, p. 148) states that "one person should be identified in each site to implement the procedure and under no circumstances should other staff, who do not have this responsibility, make the assignments."

After the staff who are to handle randomization have been identified, they must be trained about the requirements for valid randomization. This means that the staff must have a complete understanding and explanation of not only how randomization takes place but also why the procedure is necessary. After the staff has been trained and randomization has been initiated it is necessary to have a monitoring system that checks on the validity of the assignment procedure. All the training and explanation in the world will not insure the proper implementation of randomization. Therefore, it is necessary to monitor the procedure as it is implemented to detect and correct deviations that are made.

Statistical Significance and Policy Significance

When an evaluation researcher conducts a summative or impact evaluation he or she attempts to design a research study that conforms as closely as possible to a true experiment. This, as you already know, is necessary in order to eliminate the potential confounding influence of rival hypotheses. After the data is collected, the evaluation researcher analyzes the data to determine whether or not statistically significant differences exist between the individuals who received the social program (e.g., a drug abuse program) and those who did not. If a significant difference existed, then the evaluation researcher may be prone to conclude that the program was beneficial and should be continued. From a statistical point of view this is true. However, from a policy-making point of view, statistical significance is only one factor that determines whether or not a program is significant enough to be continued.

SIGNIFICANCE OF STATISTICAL SIGNIFICANCE.   When an evaluation researcher finds a statistically significant difference between individuals given the social program and those who were not, he or she can safely conclude that the program was significant from a statistical point of view. However, remember that evaluation research must be conducted with the decision maker and program planner in mind. These individuals are concerned not only with statistical significance but also with the absolute level of difference produced by a social program. Assume, for example, that an antismoking program was conducted in the junior high schools of a given school district. Their goal was to decrease the number of teenagers who started smoking during this vulnerable period of time under the assumption that if these individuals did not start smoking during this period of time they would be less likely to do so later on in life. An evaluation revealed that the program achieved a statistically significant 1% reduction in the number of individuals who started smoking later on in life. Although the program was statistically significant, one also has to decide whether or not the magnitude of the impact, a 1% reduction, was large enough to be of practical significance. The point is that a program may have reached statistical significance but the absolute magnitude of improvement gained by the program is so limited that it has little practical significance.

The problem becomes one of deciding when an effect is large enough to have practical significance. This is clearly a judgmental activity on the part of decision makers and policy planners. However, in making this judgment it is advisable to incorporate other information inputs such as cost-effectiveness analysis, which will be discussed now.

COST BENEFIT AND COST-EFFECTIVENESS.   Cost benefit refers
to an analysis in which the cost of implementing a social program is
pitted against the benefits accrued from it, to ascertain whether or not
the benefits outweigh the costs. For example, if cost benefit analysis
were applied to a water resources project one could compare the costs
of dredging, construction of dams, and maintenance, against such
benefits as hydroelectric power and water for agricultural, industrial,
and domestic use (Levin, 1975). However, cost benefit analysis has the
limitation of trying to put everything in monetary terms (Freeman,
1977). This is particularly true when attempting to apply it to social
programs, since they frequently have no market counterpart. For
example, how would one assess the monetary benefit of reducing
hydrocarbons emitted into the air, or the benefit of saving a member of
an endangered species? Because of objections such as this, Levin (1975)
advocates the use of cost-effectiveness analysis instead of cost benefit
analysis. Levin (1975, p. 89) states that "cost-effectiveness analysis in
evaluation research is to determine that strategy or combination of
strategies that maximize the desired result for any particular resource
or budget constrained." In other words, cost-effectiveness analysis is
oriented toward the assessment of the costs of alternative programs
that achieve the same outcome. Cost-effectiveness analysis could determine, say, which of three equally effective drug abuse programs was
implemented at the least cost to the taxpayer, organization, or other
funding agency. Conducting a cost-effectiveness analysis means that
one must conduct an impact evaluation on several alternative programs that attempt to achieve the same objective. For those alternative
programs that are equally effective in terms of impact, one must then
assess their respective costs to determine which can be implemented
at the least cost. Levin (1975) provides a more detailed elaboration of
this procedure.

Side effects.   An additional consideration that is incorporated by
decision makers and policy planners is the possibility of undesirable
side effects created by implementation of the social program. Consider,
for example, the global program directed at reducing school segrega-
tion. Many individuals have directly attributed the white flight from
the inner cities to this program (Freeman, 1977). This in turn has
produced economic hardships within some of these cities as well as
decreased chances for successful integration.

As can be seen, there are many considerations other than statistical significance that must be considered when evaluating the impact of
a social program and deciding whether or not it should be continued.
As much of this type of data as possible must be fed to the decision
maker to assist him or her in making the most appropriate decision.

Dissemination and Utilization of Evaluations

Following the completion of an evaluation study, the researcher is typically required to write a final report and turn it in to the program administrators and sponsors of the study. Frequently when this procedure is followed the final report is placed on a shelf to gather dust. This nonutilization of the disseminated results is one of the very frustrating components of evaluation research. The researcher knows that the study was conducted to answer a question and that evaluation research is first and foremost a political decision making tool. Consequently he or she cannot understand why the results are not used. Weiss (1972a) has listed at least five reasons which limit the use of evaluation results. These include such things as the organization's resistance to change and the failure to find positive effects. However, lack of utilization is not an inevitable consequence of evaluation research.

In order to maximize the potential for utilization, it is necessary to have the decision makers and policy planners engage in and assist in each phase of the evaluation. It is important that decision makers do more than just approve the initial evaluation research proposal. This means involving the decision makers in all aspects of the evaluation from beginning to end. They are to be included in the decisions regarding the design of the study, the measurement of characteristics or behaviors of the subjects, and the identification of the target population. In each of these situations it is the evaluation researcher's responsibility to point out the advantages and disadvantages of each alternative. After he or she has done this, the final decision must be a joint product of the decision maker and the evaluation researcher. Engaging decision makers in each phase of the evaluation study has the advantage of enhancing their understanding of the project and involving them "in the painstaking process of making decisions about what data to collect, how to collect it, and how to analyze it" (Patton, 1978).

After the data is analyzed it must be interpreted to try to make some sense out of it. From a utilization point of view, Patton (1978) advocates giving the decision makers and program planners an opportunity to study the data and make their interpretations before seeing the evaluator's interpretations. This means presenting the data to the decision makers in a format that is easily understood. Their task is then to attempt to interpret the data and make recommendations based on it. Since decision makers are frequently pressed for time and would not undertake this task if they were sent the data and asked to interpret it while at their desk, the best approach is to convene a meeting at a designated time and place and have decision makers perform this task there. The recommendations and conclusions emerging from this meeting should then be incorporated into the final report. If the evaluation researcher has additional conclusions and recommendations to make, they should also be included. The important point from a utilization point of view is that the decision makers also spend some time attempting to interpret the data. This will generally operate not only to increase their understanding and commitment to the data, but also to enhance the possibility of their using the data.

Summary

Evaluation research is a form of research that utilizes the basic scientific methodology in an attempt to assess the utility of social programs. Evaluation research is, however, more than just a social science research activity. It is first and foremost a political decision-making tool. Consequently, the evaluation researcher must constantly attempt to incorporate procedures that will increase the probability that decision makers and program planners will use the results of the evaluation in making their subsequent decisions about social programs. Increasing the probability of such utilization generally means involving the decision maker in each stage of the evaluation from goal identification through design of the evaluation to interpretation of the data.

There are basically three types of evaluation research activities. The first is process evaluation, which consists of determining whether or not the social program, intervention, or treatment was implemented in the prescribed manner. This means assessing whether or not the program was implemented as it was supposed to be and whether it was implemented on the target population for which it was designed. The second type of evaluation research activity is impact, or summative, evaluation. Impact, or summative, evaluation attempts to assess whether or not the program had the desired or predicted effect. Impact, or summative, evaluation requires the evaluation researcher first to identify the specific goal or goals of the social program. After the goals of the program are identified, the evaluation researchers, in conjunction with the decision makers and program planners, develop a design that will assess the goals of the social program. This may involve collecting data that will help the decision makers improve the program (formative evaluation) or it may involve collecting data for a summative evaluation after the program has reached some stability and is not going through developmental growing pains. After being collected according to the design that was conceptualized, the data is analyzed and interpreted by the evaluator in conjunction with the decision makers.

The third type of evaluation research is a comprehensive evaluation. This is the most complete and recommended form of evaluation.

Comprehensive evaluation refers to an evaluation that combines both process and impact, or summative, evaluation. Most evaluations in the past have been of the summative, or impact, variety. These evaluations have frequently produced negative results. One of the reasons for these negative results may be the failure to implement the program in the prescribed manner and not the fact that the program was ineffective. To determine if the results obtained are due to failure to implement the program in the prescribed manner, it is necessary to combine process evaluation with impact, or summative, evaluation.

Key Concepts

One way to test your mastery of the material that was presented in this chapter is to see if you know the meaning of the following terms. These terms were selected because they represent the key concepts. If you can define, identify, or otherwise explain each of the following terms without referring back to the material in the chapter, you can be assured that you have mastered the basics of the material that was presented. Just in case you cannot recall the meaning of a given term, the page on which it can be found appears in parentheses beside it.

> evaluation research (p. 273)
> process evaluation (pp. 274–275)
> program implementation (pp. 275–276)
> target identification (p. 277)
> summative evaluation (p. 278)
> comprehensive evaluation (p. 279)
> formative evaluation (p. 284)
> policy significance (p. 288)
> cost-benefit (p. 289)
> cost-effectiveness (p. 289)

11

Data Collection and Hypotheses Testing

Once the research study has been designed, the beginning researcher may think that he or she is now ready to begin collecting data. It seems as though all decisions have been made once the researcher has specified the concrete operations that will represent the independent and dependent variable and has specified the control techniques to be used. However, a great deal of work lies ahead—work which entails making additional decisions. What type of subjects should be used—human or infrahuman? How many subjects should be used and where does one get them? How should one prepare the instructions

294 given to the subjects? Should the researcher say anything to the subjects after the experiment has been completed? These are some of the most significant questions which now must be answered. An attempt will be made to provide an answer to each of these questions.

In this chapter these questions will of necessity be answered in a general way since each study has its own unique characteristics. Additionally, there will be no attempt to answer questions such as "How do I schedule the subjects?" or "What apparatus do I use and where do I get it?" Scheduling of subjects involves a consideration of not only when the researcher has time available but also the type of subject that he or she is using. With rats, for example, there is one type of problem. As Sidowski and Lockard (1966, p. 10) have stated:

> Rats and other nocturnal animals are most active in the dark phase of the lighting cycle and do most of their eating and drinking then. From the animal's point of view, the light portion of the day is for sleeping and inactivity but may be interrupted by an experimenter who requires him to run or bar-press for food. It is unfortunate that the amount of lighting and the timing of the cycle are usually arranged for the benefit of the caretaker and not the animals or the experimenter.[1]

When considering human subjects there is a whole different set of problems. First, one has to contact and schedule them not only when the researcher can conduct the experiment but also when the subjects can or will participate. Once they are scheduled, there are other problems. The subjects one wants may not want to participate, subjects may not show up at the scheduled time, or subjects may not show up at all.

When considering apparatus or materials needed for use in the experiment, one has the option of constructing them if one has the ability, or purchasing them if they are commercially produced. If a piece of equipment has been frequently used in the past in psychological studies, it is highly probable that the apparatus is produced commercially and the psychology department may have purchased it. If not, most departments have a shop for the construction of equipment.

Subjects

Since psychologists are investigating the behavior of organisms, there exist a wealth of organisms that can potentially serve as subjects. What

1. From *Experimental methods and instrumentation in psychology*, by Sidowski and Lockard. Copyright © 1966 by McGraw-Hill, Inc. Used with permission of McGraw-Hill Book Co.

determines which organism will be used in a given study? In some cases the question asked dictates the type of organism used. If, for example, a study is to investigate imprinting ability, then one must select a species, such as ducks, which demonstrates this ability. However, the primary determining factor of most studies is precedent. Most investigators do not seem to be plagued by deciding upon the type of subject to use, since they most frequently use those subjects that typically have been used in previous studies. If most prior studies of a given topic used rats, then, because of the precedent, there seems to be an unquestionable acceptance by most researchers that rats are the subjects to use. As Sidowski and Lockard (1966, p. 7–8) state:

> Most of the common laboratory animals are mammals; man, several species of monkey, numerous rodents, a few carnivores, and one cetacean, the porpoise. Other than mammals, teleost fishes and one species of bird, the pigeon, have mainly represented the other classes of chordates; amphibians and reptiles have been rare. The 21 phyla below the chordates have been underrepresented. . . [2]

Other than man, precedent has established the albino variant of the brown rat as the standard laboratory research animal. The concentrated use of the albino rat in infrahuman research has not gone without criticism. Beach (1950) and Lockard (1968) have eloquently criticized the fact that psychologists have focused too much attention on the use of the albino rat as a research animal. As Lockard (1968) has argued, rather than using precedent as the primary guide for selecting a particular organism as a subject, one should look at the research problem and select the type of animal that is best for its study.

Once a decision has been made regarding the type of organism that is to be used in the investigation, the dual question of "Where do I get the subjects?" and "How many subjects should I use in my study?" arises. The albino rat and humans are two types of subjects most commonly used in research studies. Researchers who select rats as their subjects can order them from one of several commercial sources which are covered in the publication, *Animals for Research*, ninth edition, 1975, available from the Office of Publications, National Academy of Sciences, 2101 Constitution Ave., N.W., Washington, D.C. 20418. There are three strains that seem to be favored by researchers. These are the Long-Evans hooded, the Sprague-Dawley albino, and the Wistar albino. The researcher must decide upon the strain, sex, age, and supplier of the albino rats since each of these variables can influence the results of the study. The reader might refer

---

2. From *Experimental methods and instrumentation in psychology*, by Sidowski and Lockard. Copyright © 1966 by McGraw-Hill, Inc. Used with permission of McGraw-Hill Book Co.

296   to Sidowski and Lockard (1966), who present a limited discussion of the potential influence of each of these variables.

Once the albino rats have been selected, ordered, and received, they must be maintained in the animal laboratory, and it is typically the experimenter who must care for these animals. Few beginning researchers have the knowledge required to maintain the animals properly. For this reason, a number of publications are available through several sources to acquaint the researcher with the appropriate guidelines. The Institute of Laboratory Animal Resources, National Academy of Sciences–National Research Council, 2101 Constitution Avenue, N.W., Washington, D.C., publishes a number of manuals on the care of laboratory animals. The U.S. Department of Health, Education, and Welfare, Public Health Service, National Institutes of Health has a manual titled, *Care and use of laboratory animals,* publication No. 73–23, revised 1972, which is available from the U.S. Government Printing Office, Washington, D.C., 20402. Either of these sources will provide the necessary maintenance information.

Researchers selecting humans as their subjects find varying degrees of ease in finding subjects for use in their study. In most university settings, the psychology department has a subject pool consisting of introductory psychology students. These students typically are motivated to participate in a research study because it is a requirement of the course, or they are offered an improved grade or grade points for participating, or they are offered the alternative of participating in an experiment in lieu of some other requirement such as writing a term paper. Disregarding the ethical issue of such coerced participation, and the possible biasing factors which it may produce (e.g., Cox and Sipprelle, 1971), such a subject pool provides a readily available supply of subjects for the researcher. However, for many types of research studies introductory psychology students are not appropriate. A child psychologist wishing to study kindergarten children will typically try to solicit the cooperation of a local kindergarten. In a similar manner, investigation of incarcerated criminals requires seeking the cooperation of prison officials.

When one has to seek subjects from sources other than a departmental subject pool, a new set of problems arises because many individuals other than the subject become involved. Assume a researcher is going to conduct a study using kindergarten children. The first task is to find a kindergarten that would allow her to collect the data needed for the study. This means that she has to seek out the individual in charge of this kindergarten to solicit his cooperation. In doing so, the researcher has to be as tactful and diplomatic as possible because others are frequently not receptive to psychological research and often are skeptical of it. Assume the person in charge agrees to allow the researcher to collect the data. The next task is to obtain the parents' permission to allow their children to participate in the study. This frequently involves having parents sign a permission slip, which has explained the nature of the research and the task or tasks required of their child. As you can see, the task of obtaining subjects is frequently not an easy one. Other agencies such as an institution for mentally retarded persons frequently require a research proposal, which their research committee can review, before they will grant permission to allow anyone to collect data.

After identifying the subject population, the researcher must select individual subjects from that group. Ideally, this should be done randomly. This means that a study investigating kindergarten children should randomly select a sample from the population of kindergarten children. While this is the ideal, it is very impractical for most studies, not only in terms of cost and time but also in terms of the availability of the children for the study. Not all kindergartens, nor all parents, will allow their children to participate in a psychological study. Therefore, human subjects are generally selected on the basis of convenience and availability. The kindergarten children used in a study are the ones closest to the university and who cooperate with the investigator.

Because of this restriction in subject selection, the researcher may have a built-in bias in the data. For example, the children whose parents allow them to participate may perform differently than children whose parents restrict their participation. Rosenthal and Rosnow (1975) have summarized research revealing the differences in the responses of volunteer and nonvolunteer subjects. The next best solution to the random selection problem is to assign subjects randomly to treatment conditions. In this way the investigator is at least assured that no systematic bias exists between the various groups of available subjects. Because of the inability to select subjects randomly, the investigator *must* report the nature of subject selection and assignment in addition to the characteristics of the subjects to enable other investigators to assess the comparability of their results.

It is similarly inappropriate to assume that any sample of albino rats represents a representative sample of the population of rats. As Sidowski and Lockard (1966, pp. 8–9) point out,

> Freshly received animals are not uniform products from an automatic production line, nor are they a random sample from the world's population of rats. Animal suppliers differ greatly in such environmental practices as the ambient temperature, light-dark cycle, type of food, cage size and animal density, and the physical arrangements of food and water devices.... To further complicate the picture, two shipments from the same firm may not be equivalent. Most companies use tiers of cages, with some high and some almost on the floor. The high animals may be in as much as ten times the illumination as the low ones because of ceiling and light

fixtures. Vertical gradients of temperature are also common, with the high animal's warmer. .... Since shipments of animals tend to be drawn by the supplier from the same cage, a given shipment is not a random sample but rather an overly homogeneous subset not representative of the range of conditions within the colony.[3]

After you have obtained access to a sample of subjects, even though it may not be a random sample, you need to decide how many subjects will be used in the study. Naturally, such a consideration exists only in studies that use more than one subject. In multisubject research studies there are few guidelines to use. The primary guide used by most investigators is the number of subjects used by other investigators within an area. If most researchers have used 10 subjects in each experimental treatment condition, it is typically assumed that this is the proper number to use. Precedent, which may be just as inappropriate as the concentrated use of the albino rat, is used as the criterion (Beach, 1950; Lockard, 1968).

There should be some more objective criteria that suggest the number of subjects needed in a research study. I am aware of only two sources that attempt to provide such objective criteria. The NEA Research Division (1960) developed the following formula which allows one to determine the sample size needed to be representative of a given population.

$$n = \chi^2 NP(1 - P) \div d^2 (N - 1) + \chi^2 P(1 - P)$$

where n = the required sample size
x^2 = the table value of chi-square for 1 degree of freedom at the desired confidence level (3.89)
N = the population size
P = the population proportion that it is desired to estimate (assumed to be .50 since this would provide the maximum sample size)
d = the degree of accuracy expressed as a proportion (.05)

This formula is appropriate and excellent when one has the capability of randomly selecting subjects from a population, and it would be very useful in determining how many subjects should be included in the study for achieving a given level of accuracy.

Krejcie and Morgan (1970) have computed the sample size required for populations up to 1,000,000 when the .05 confidence level is desired. The results of these calculations appear in Figure 11.1.

3. From *Experimental methods and instrumentation in psychology,* by Sidowski and Lockard. Copyright © 1966 by McGraw-Hill, Inc. Used with permission of McGraw-Hill Book Co.

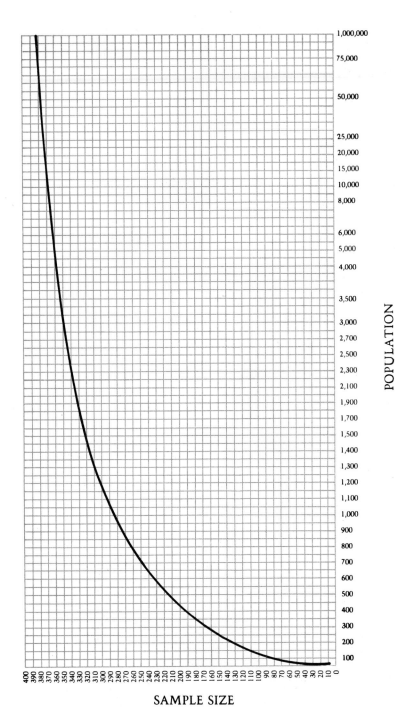

POPULATION

SAMPLE SIZE

Figure 11.1. Relationship between sample size and total population. (From Krejcie, R. V., and Morgan, D. W. Determining sample size for research activities. Educational and Psychological Measurement, 1970, 30, p. 609. Copyright 1970 by Frederick Kuder. Reprinted by permission.)

There are, however, several difficulties in attempting to use the above formula or the results appearing in Figure 11.1 when conducting an experimental study. The most serious difficulty is that it is typically not possible or practical to select subjects randomly from a given population. While this is a procedural difficulty and not one inherent in the formula, it still leaves one with the problem of determining sample size for a study that cannot randomly select from the population.

Cox (1958) has given a formula which will provide a good estimate of the approximate number of subjects needed for each treatment condition in an experimental study. This formula applies only when an equal number of subjects are to be included in each experimental treatment condition. Also, the presentation and explanation of the formula will of necessity be of a statistical nature. Those who have difficulty in following the presentation should review the meaning of the statistical concepts used in this presentation. For this purpose books such as Guilford (1965) and Edwards (1967) are helpful. The formula to be used for estimating the number of subjects needed is as follows:

$$n = 2 \times \left(\frac{\text{residual standard deviation}}{\text{required standard error}}\right)^2$$

n = the number of subjects required for each treatment condition or cell of the experiment

Residual standard deviation. A measure of the amount of uncontrolled variation in responses which exists in the experiment. This is measured by the error term in the computed F test, Mean Square error.

Required standard error. Since the standard error under consideration is a measure of the extent to which the difference between the mean experimental treatment scores can vary by chance, the required standard error represents how much you will allow the difference between the mean experimental treatment scores to vary about the *true* difference scores.

In order to use this formula, it is necessary to have knowledge of the residual standard deviation and have decided upon how large a standard error of difference between means one is willing to accept. Cox (1958) has presented five different techniques for determining the residual standard deviation. However, the only one that seems to be generally useful in psychological research studies involves using the results of previous studies to estimate the residual standard deviation. In most areas of psychology, prior experimental work has been conducted, and the random variation in the response of subjects' receiving the same experimental treatment condition can be computed. This

estimate of the residual standard deviation can then be used in the
above formula to calculate the number of subjects needed in the study
you are planning to conduct. For example, if prior experimentation had
estimated the residual standard deviation to be four units, and we had
decided that the standard error which we required was two, then the
required number of subjects would be $2 \times (^4/_2)^2 = 8$ subjects per
treatment condition.

When it is not possible to attain an estimate from prior work, a
sequential technique (Cox, 1958) can be used to estimate the residual
standard deviation. This technique involves working through a series
of steps whereby the decision regarding the final number of observations to be used is dependent upon the actual outcome of the experiment. The simplest form of the sequential technique involves a two-
stage procedure. The first stage involves conducting the experiment
using a small number of subjects, say five in each treatment condition,
and then calculating the estimate of the residual standard deviation
from this data. This estimated residual standard deviation could then
be used to determine the appropriate number of subjects needed in
each treatment condition of the experiment. The second stage involves
collecting data from additional subjects until the appropriate number
of subjects per condition had been reached.

Either the sequential technique or prior research can be used to
attain an estimate of the residual standard deviation. However, to be
able to use the formula for determining the appropriate number of
subjects to be used in an experiment, it is also necessary to make a
decision regarding the required standard error. Determining the magnitude of the required standard error that will be accepted is usually a
judgmental matter, particularly since the magnitude of the standard
error is also dependent on the number of subjects used in the experiment. Assume, for example, that you wanted a small standard error so
that you would increase your chances of detecting a significant difference if one actually existed. Therefore, you decided that your required standard error should equal one unit. If, from one of the
techniques mentioned above, the residual standard deviation was
found to be 4, then the number of subjects required for each experimental treatment would be 32 since $n = 2 \times (^4/_1)^2 = 32$.

After finding out how many subjects are needed for the level of
precision identified, a standard error of one unit, you may decide that
this represents an intolerably large number of subjects. In order to
reduce the number of subjects needed in the experiment, it is necessary
to weaken the requirements on the level of precision by allowing for a
larger standard error. In fact it would be desirable to compute the
number of subjects required for different levels of precision as follows:

Number of Subjects	Required Standard Error
32	1.0
14	1.5
8	2.0
5	2.5

Once this has been done the experimenter can consider the relationships between the level of precision and the number of subjects required to attain a given level of precision. Now it is a judgmental matter as to what to do. The experimenter must now select that number of subjects that will provide a balance between what is considered to be an acceptable level of precision and an acceptable number of subjects in each treatment condition.

Cowles (1974) has been slightly more definitive in his suggestion as to the required number of subjects. Based on such considerations as the power of the statistical test, the significance level (.05), and strength of relationship between the independent and dependent variable, Cowles suggests that 35 subjects should be used for most preliminary studies. If one is using an analysis of variance design with several levels of the independent variable, then one should use 15 subjects per cell.

Instructions

In addition to securing subjects, the investigator conducting an experiment using human subjects must prepare a set of instructions. This brings up such questions as "What should be included in the instructions?" and "How should they be presented?" Sidowski and Lockard (1966) state that instructions serve the purposes of defining the task, directing attention, developing a set, and perhaps motivating the subject. Instructions are quite important, and considerable care must be exercised in their formulation. They must include a clear description of the purpose, or disguised purpose, and the task that the subjects are to perform. Instructions should be clear, unambiguous, and specific, but at the same time they should not be too complex because of the possibility of risking a memory overload (Sutcliffe, 1972). In writing such instructions, beginning researchers often think that the instructions should be extremely terse and succinct. While this style is

good for writing the research report, in writing instructions one runs   **303**
the risk of the subject not grasping important points. Instructions
should be very simple, down to earth, and at times even redundant.
Frequently this will provide added assurance that the subjects understand all parts of the instructions.

Debriefing or Postexperimental Interview

Once the data has been collected there is the tendency to think that
one's job has been completed and the only remaining requirement,
other than data analysis, is to thank the subjects for their participation
and send them on their way. However, the experiment does not, or
should not, end with the completion of data collection. Following data
collection there frequently should be a postexperimental interview
with the subject which allows him or her to comment freely on any
part of the experiment. This interview is very important for several
reasons. In general, the interview can provide information regarding
the subject's thinking or strategies used during the experiment, which
can help explain the subject's behavior. Orne (1962), for example, used
this interview to assess why subjects would persist at a boring, repeti-
tive task for hours. Martin, while conducting learning studies with
extremely bright subjects, found that these subjects could, for example,
learn a list of nonsense syllables in one trial.[4] Upon seeing such a
performance he essentially asked them, "How did you do that?" They
relayed a specific strategy for having accomplished this task, which led
to another study (Martin, Boersma, and Cox, 1965) investigating
strategies of learning.

Tesch (1977) has identified three specific functions of debriefing.
First, debriefings have an ethical function. In many studies research
participants are deceived regarding the true purpose of an experiment.
Ethically, one must undo such deceptions, and the debriefing session is
the place to accomplish this. Other experiments generate some negative affect in the subject or in some other way create some type of
physical (e.g., electric shock) or emotional (e.g., lowered self-esteem)
stress on the part of the subject. Again, ethically one must attempt to
return the subjects to their preexperimental state, or attempt to eliminate any stress that the experiment has generated. Second, debriefings
have an educational function. Frequently, the rationale used to justify
requiring experimental participation of introductory psychology stu-

4. C. J. Martin 1975: personal communication.

dents is that they learn something about psychology and psychological research. The third function of debriefing is methodological. Debriefings are frequently used to provide evidence regarding the effectiveness of the independent variable manipulation or the deception. They are also used to probe the extent and accuracy of subjects' suspicions as well as to give the experimenter an opportunity to convince the subject not to reveal the experiment to others.

Given these functions of debriefing, how does one proceed? Two approaches have been used. Some investigators have used a questionnaire approach, in which subjects are handed a postexperimental questionnaire to complete. Others have used a face-to-face interview, which seems to be the best approach because it is not as restrictive as the questionnaire approach.

If you want to probe for any suspicions that the subject may have had about any aspect of the experiment, this is the first order of business. Aronson and Carlsmith (1968) state that one should begin by asking the subject if he or she has any questions. If so, they should be answered as completely and truthfully as possible. If not, then the experimenter should ask the subject if all phases of the experiment, both the procedure and the purpose, were clear. Next, depending upon the study being conducted, it may be appropriate to ask the subject to "comment on how the experiment struck him, why he responded as he did, how he felt at the time, etc. Then he should be asked specifically whether there was any aspect of the procedure that he found odd, confusing, or disturbing" (p. 71).[5]

If the experiment contained a deception and the subject suspected that it did, he or she is almost certain to have revealed this fact by this time. If no suspicions have been revealed, one can ask the subject if he or she thought there was more to the experiment than was immediately apparent. Such a question cues the subject that there must have been. Most subjects will, therefore, say "yes," which should be followed with a question trying to assess what the subject thought was involved and how this may have affected his or her behavior. Such questioning will give the investigator additional insight into whether or not the subject did have the experiment figured out, and also provides a perfect point for the experimenter to lead into an explanation of the purpose of the experiment. The experimenter could continue "the debriefing process by saying something like this: 'You are on the right

---

5. Reprinted by special permission from Aronson-Carlsmith, "Experimentation in Social Psychology," *The handbook of social psychology*, Second Edition, Volume Two, 1968, edited by Lindzey-Aronson, Addison-Wesley, Reading, Mass., p. 71.

track, we *were* interested in some problems that we didn't discuss with you in advance. One of our major concerns in this study is . . .' '' (Aronson and Carlsmith, 1968, p. 71).[6] The debriefing should then be continued in the manner suggested by Mills (1976). If the study involved deception, the reasons for the necessity of deception should be included. The purpose of the study should then be explained in explicit detail, as well as the specific procedures for investigating the research question. This means explaining the independent and dependent variables and how they were manipulated and measured. As you can see, the debriefing requires explaining the total experiment to the subjects.

The last part of the debriefing session should be geared to convincing the subject not to reveal any components of the experiment to others, for obvious reasons. This can be accomplished by asking the subjects not to reveal the experiment to others, at least until after the date of completion of the data collection. This point can be emphasized to subjects by telling them that communicating the results to others may invalidate the study. Since the experimenter would not know if the results were invalid and the subjects would probably not tell (Altemeyer, 1971), the experimenter would be reporting inaccurate data to the scientific community. Aronson (1966) has revealed that we can have reasonable confidence in the fact that subjects will not tell others, but Altemeyer (1971) has shown that if subjects do find out they will probably not tell the experimenter.

At this point you might wonder whether or not the preceding debriefing procedure accomplishes the three functions it is supposed to accomplish. As you shall see in the chapter on Ethics, the ethical function seems to be accomplished quite well if these procedures are adhered to. Utility and completeness are lacking in the educational function. Most investigators seem to think, or rationalize, that the educational function is served if the subjects participate in the experiment and are told of its purpose and procedures during debriefing. However, Tesch (1977) believes that this function would be served better if the researcher also required the subject to write a laboratory experience report, which would relate the experimental experience to course material. The methodological function generally seems to be served quite well, since the validity of the experiment is frequently dependent upon this. The investigator frequently has done extensive pilot study work to insure such things as that the manipulation checks do verify the manipulations.

6. Reprinted by special permission from Aronson-Carlsmith, "Experimentation in Social Psychology," *The Handbook of social psychology,* Second Edition, Volume Two, 1968, edited by Lindzey-Aronson, Addison-Wesley, Reading, Mass., p. 71.

306   Procedure

After the instruction and the debriefing interview have been written, you must specify the procedure that you are going to use in data collection. This means that the sequence of events that are going to take place in conducting the experiment must be arranged so that they flow in a smooth manner. Awareness of what is to take place is not sufficient. The investigator must very carefully and thoughtfully think through the whole experiment and specify the sequence in which each activity is to take place. He or she must lay down the exact procedure that is going to be followed during data collection. For animal research, this means not only specifying the conditions of the laboratory environment and how the animals are going to be handled in the laboratory, but also specifying how they are to be maintained in their maintenance quarters and how they are to be transferred from the maintenance quarters to the laboratory. This is very important since these variables can have an influence on the subjects' behavior in the laboratory. For an extended discussion of transient and environmental factors that can influence animals' behavior, you are referred to Sidowski and Lockard (1966, pp. 10–14).

With human subjects this means specifying not only what the subject is to do, but also how he or she is to be greeted and the type of nonverbal behavior (e.g., looking at the subject, smiling, tone of voice in reading instructions, etc.) as well as verbal behavior in which the experimenter is to engage. Friedman (1967) has shown the wide variety of ways in which the same experimenter may react to different subjects, both verbally and nonverbally. Ideally, these variations should not exist and every attempt should be made to eliminate them.

Once each of the above phases has been specified, the investigator must then conduct a pilot study. A pilot study represents a run through the experiment with a small number of subjects. This actually represents a pretest of the experiment and should be conducted in as conscientious a manner as if data were actually being collected. The pilot study is a very important phase because it can provide a great deal of information. If the instructions are not clear and/or do not communicate the expected points, this will typically reveal itself either in the debriefing session or by virtue of the fact that the subject does not know what to do after you have read the instructions to him or her.

The pilot study can also help assess whether or not the independent variable manipulation produced the intended effect. Debriefing could help determine if, for example, fear, surprise, or some other state had actually been generated. If none of the pilot subjects reported this intended emotion, then their help could be solicited to try to assess why it was not generated, after which a change could be made until the intended state was induced. In a similar manner, the sensitivity of the dependent variable can be checked. Pretesting may suggest that the dependent variable is too crude to reflect the effect of the manipulation and that a change in a certain direction would make it more appropriate.

The pilot study also gives the experimenter experience with the procedure. The first time the experimenter runs a subject, he or she is not yet wholly familiar with the sequence, and therefore probably does not make a transition from one part of the study to another as smoothly as should be made. With practice, these steps are carried out in a smooth experienced fashion, which is necessary for constancy to be maintained in the study. Also, when running pilot subjects, the experimenter tests the procedure. Too much time may be allowed for certain parts and not enough for others, the deception (if used) may be inadequate, etc. If so, the experimenter identifies problems *before* any data is collected, and the procedure can be altered at this time.

There are many subtle factors that can influence the experiment, and the pilot phase is the time to identify them. Pilot testing involves testing all parts of the experiment to determine if they are working appropriately. If a malfunction is isolated, it can be corrected without any resulting damage. If the malfunction were not spotted until after data were being collected, it *may* have had an influence on the results of the study. The point is that we do not know *if* it did, and therefore all malfunctions should be spotted before data collection and this is the purpose of the pilot study.

Data Collection

Once the procedure has been laid out and the pilot study has tested the various phases of the experimental procedure and eliminated the bugs, you are ready to run subjects and collect the data. The primary rule to follow in this phase of the experiment is to adhere as closely as possible to the procedure that has been laid out. The procedure was specified for the purpose of enabling you to conduct a well-controlled study which would provide the data needed to answer a specific question. A great deal of work has gone into developing this procedure. If it is not to be followed, there was no need for going through all the preliminary steps. More important, if the procedure is not followed exactly, you run the risk of introducing contaminants into the experiment. Consequently, you would not have the well-controlled study you worked so hard to develop, with the possible consequence of not attaining an answer to the research question.

308 Hypothesis Testing

Once you have collected the data you are now ready to analyze your data statistically to obtain an answer to the research question and to determine if the stated hypothesis has been validated. At this point I should make a distinction between a *scientific* hypothesis and the *null* hypothesis. Throughout this text I have been talking about a scientific hypothesis, which refers to the predicted relationship that the investigator hopes that the data will support. The *null* hypothesis *always* represents a statement of *no* relationship between the variables being investigated. In most cases the null hypothesis and the scientific hypothesis are at odds because the investigator wants to find a stated relationship. Therefore, if a null hypothesis were stated the investigator would want to be able to reject it because this would mean support was found for the scientific hypothesis.

In order to determine if the data supports or fails to support the scientific hypothesis, it is necessary to analyze the data statistically in the manner suggested by the design of the experiment. No attempt is being made to elaborate on the numerous statistical techniques available for data analysis since this is beyond the scope of the text and separate statistics courses cover these techniques. (This omission in no way attempts to minimize the importance of the interrelationship between experimentation and statistics.) Some beginning researchers question the necessity of conducting a statistical analysis. It may not be readily apparent why statistical analysis needs to be conducted. If you asked a naive person how you could determine if the experimental treatment condition had an effect on the subjects' performance, he or she would probably tell you to compare the performance of the experimental and control groups. In other words, compute the mean performance score for each group and see if the experimental groups's score was greater than (or less than) the control group's score. This would be sufficient to describe the performance of the two groups. But remember that you want to determine if the experimental treatment condition produced a real effect. It is possible that the difference between the two group's mean scores could have occurred by chance. This is because no two subjects are alike, which means that the different subjects in the two groups would respond differently. It would be a rare occurrence to find two groups of subjects with the same mean performance scores.

Knowing that there is variability in behavior and that one should expect some difference between the groups' performance on this basis, how can one assess whether or not the observed difference in the experimental and control groups is a real difference or just one of these chance differences due to the variability in subject performance? At this point the beginning researcher may say that the necessary information could be attained by repeating the experiment with different subjects, and seeing if the same results occurred again. This would give evidence of the reliability of the obtained findings. The more often the study was repeated with identical results, the more faith we would have in the fact that the experimental treatment produced the results, meaning that a real difference existed. This is because, if the difference were not real but were chance, the difference between the two groups, averaged over many replications of the experiment, should be zero. Sometimes the experimental group's scores would by chance be greater than the control group's scores; but, by the same token, the control group's scores would sometimes be greater than the experimental group's scores. Therefore, a reliable finding would not exist, suggesting that a given control versus treatment group difference was due to chance.

While it is possible to determine if the obtained difference between the experimental and control groups' scores are real or chance findings, by repeating the study many times on different groups of subjects, this is not a very economical approach. Statistical tests enable us to accomplish the same thing by allowing us to estimate or infer what would have happened if we followed the repetition procedure. Statistical procedures estimate the amount of difference that we could expect between the groups' scores by chance and then they pit this against what was actually found. If the difference that was actually found is much greater than that which would be expected by chance, we say that the difference which we found was a real difference.

Is there a guideline that determines how large a difference has to be to be considered real? Such a question is a good one because only rarely can one be *absolutely* sure that the obtained difference is not due to chance. Even very large differences could occur by chance, though the probability of this happening would be very low. Figure 11.2 illustrates the distribution of mean differences that would be expected to occur by chance. Note that the tails of the distribution approach the baseline but never touch it. Therefore, a very large difference *could* occur by chance, which means, except in rare cases with a restricted and finite population, one can never be completely sure that a difference is real and not due to chance. We can, however, determine the probability of a given difference being due to chance. Between the dashed lines of Figure 11.2 we would find 95% of all chance difference scores, and between the solid lines in Figure 11.2 we would find 99% of all the chance difference scores. Therefore, if the difference that we found in our experiment was so large that it fell on one of the two dashed lines,

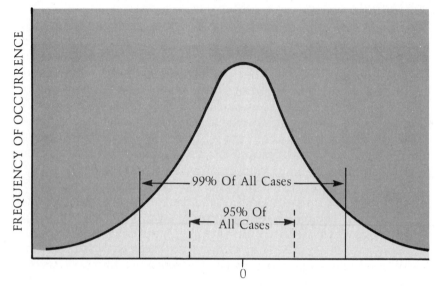

Figure 11.2. Sampling distribution of mean difference scores.

it could have occurred only 5 times in 100 by chance. In like manner, if our obtained difference was so large that it fell on one of the two solid lines, it could have occurred only 1 time in 100 by chance.

How certain do we have to be before we will say that the obtained difference between groups is a real difference and not one that could be produced by chance? The most common current practice is to state a significance level that has to be reached. A significance level is a statement of the probability of an observed difference being a chance difference. The most typically used significance levels are the .05 and .01 levels. If you have decided, prior to calculating your statistical tests, that the .05 significance level is to be used, this means that you will accept as a real difference one that is so large that it could have occurred by chance only 5 times in 100. If the .01 significance level is selected, then the differences can be expected to occur only 1 time in 100 by chance.

The above should give some appreciation of the necessity of performing statistical tests on the data. If the statistical tests reveal that a significant difference (one that has reached the specified significance level) exists between the scores of the various groups, then the scientific hypothesis is accepted as real. If the obtained difference has not reached the specified significance level, then the experimenter *fails* to reject the null hypothesis. The expression "fails to reject" is used because it is logically impossible to accept the notion of zero difference, since all things in nature presumably differ to some degree. While it is logically impossible to accept the null hypothesis of no difference, "practical concerns demand that we sometimes have to provisionally act as though the null hypothesis were true" (Cook et al., 1977). As Greenwald (1975) has pointed out, there is pervasive anti-null-hypothesis prejudice, which could lead to a variety of behavioral symptoms, as "continuing research on a problem when results have been close to rejection of the null hypothesis ("near significant"), while abandoning the problem if rejection of the null hypothesis is not close" (Greenwald, 1975, p. 3). Such undesirable behavioral manifestations have led Greenwald to conclude that we should do research in which any outcome, including a null hypothesis outcome, is possible. This does, however, mean that the research has to be conducted in such a manner as to allow for the tentative acceptance of the null hypothesis. Explication of such a procedure is beyond the scope of this text. However, Greenwald (1975) and Cook et al. (1977) present guidelines that one should follow when conducting research that may lead to support for the tentative acceptance of the null hypothesis.

Potential Errors in the Statistical Decision-Making Process

In the preceding section, primary concern was given to determining when one should accept a difference as being significant and saying that it was real. When doing so, the commonly accepted significance levels were .05 and .01, which meant that a wrong decision would occur only 5 times or 1 time in 100. In setting this stringent level we are being very conservative, making sure that the odds of being correct are definitely in our favor. It is somewhat like going to the horse races with the intention of maximizing the possibility of winning. In doing so, you would increase your chances of winning if you bet on a horse that had only a 5% chance of losing versus one that had, say, a 50% chance of losing. In like manner, scientists have set the odds so that we are quite sure of making the correct decision. Note, however, that even with this stringent significance level we will be wrong a given percentage of the time; 5% of the time if we operate at the .05 significance level, and 1% of the time if we operate at the .01 significance level. A Type I error refers to accepting the scientific hypothesis when in fact it is not correct.

Type I error is controlled by the significance level that one sets. If the .05 significance level is set, you run the risk of being wrong and committing Type I error five times in 100. At first you might think

312   that there is an easy solution to the Type I error problem: simply set a more stringent significance level such as the .0001 level. There are two difficulties with this approach. First, it is not possible to eliminate Type I error since, by definition, there will always be some possibility of attaining a chance finding as large as the observed difference. Second, and of more importance, is an error which is inversely related to Type I error. As one decreases the probability of accepting the scientific hypothesis when it is false (Type I error), one automatically increases the probability of rejecting the scientific hypothesis when it is true (Type II error). This is another reason why one fails to reject the null hypothesis, rather than accepts the null hypothesis, when the .05 or .01 significance levels are not reached. It is still possible that the experimental treatment had an effect but was not large enough to reach the required significance level.

One who makes a Type I error is believing falsely that the scientific hypothesis is true, and one who makes a Type II error believes that the scientific hypothesis was not true when in fact it was. Since decreasing one of these errors increases the other, the researcher is faced with a serious dilemma. Where should one place the significance level? As stated earlier, the accepted level is .05 or .01, which means that we generally believe that Type I error is more serious than Type II. This does not mean that Type II error is of no consequence. It is and should be considered. There may be times when the significance level needs to be dropped to the .10 or .15 level because it is more important to detect a difference if it really exists (avoid Type II error) than to increase the risk of Type I error. This requires a value judgment on the part of the researcher. He or she must consider the consequences of making each type of error and set the prescribed significance level based on this value judgment. If the researcher, based on such a consideration, deviates from the accepted .05 and .01 levels, he or she should specify as explicitly as possible the reasons for doing so. The evaluation of the relationship between these two types of errors is quite important, and the researcher should not blindly rely upon the 5% and 1% significance levels (Helmstadter, 1970).

Summary

Following the completion of the design of the study the investigator must make a number of additional decisions before being ready to collect data. One of the first decisions to be made concerns the subjects. The investigator must first decide upon the type of organism that should be used in the study. While precedent has been the primary determining factor guiding the selection of a particular organism, the **313** research problem should be the main determinant. The organism that is best for investigating the research problem should be investigated.

Once the question regarding the type of organism has been resolved, one needs to determine where one can attain these organisms. Infrahumans, particularly rats, are available from a number of commercial sources. Most human subjects used in psychological experimentation are obtainable from the departmental subject pool, typically consisting of introductory psychology students. If the study calls for subjects other than those represented in the subject pool, the investigator must locate an available source and make the necessary arrangements for their use.

In addition to identifying the source of subjects, one needs to determine how many subjects should be used in the study. For studies in which one has the ability randomly to select from the population, the NEA Research Division has published a formula that can be used for this purpose. However, most experimental studies do not have this capability. The alternative is to estimate the number of subjects needed in each cell by use of a formula that requires knowledge of both the residual standard deviation and the required standard error. The residual standard deviation can be estimated from prior research or from pilot work. The required standard error represents the amount of error which you will tolerate. Consequently, this is usually a judgmental matter.

You must also prepare instructions and a postexperimental interview for studies using human subjects. The instructions should include a clear description of the purpose, or disguised purpose, of the task required of the subject. During the postexperimental interview with the subject, the experimenter attempts to detect any suspicions that the subject may have had. Additionally, the experimenter explains the reasons for any deceptions that may have been used and explains the total experimental procedure and purpose to the subject. Following the completion of this, the investigator must specify the procedure to be used in data collection. This means specifying the exact sequence in which all phases of the experiment are to be carried out from the moment the investigator comes in contact with the subject until the subject and investigator terminate contact. In making this specification it is helpful to conduct a pilot study to iron out unforeseen difficulties. Once the procedure has been specified, you are ready to collect your data according to this procedure.

After the data is collected, you must statistically analyze the data to determine if your hypothesis has been validated. While it is not possible to determine absolutely if the hypothesis is validated, it is possible to determine the probability of the hypothesis being true. The

314   most common practice is to say that the hypothesis has been validated if there is only a 5% or a 1% chance of the hypothesis not being true. These levels are rather stringent, indicating the conservative nature of science. Note, however, that we will still be in error either 1% or 5% of the time. This is referred to as a Type I error, the probability of accepting a hypothesis that is false. The Type I error could be decreased by setting a more stringent level for acceptance of the hypothesis, but then one increases the probability of rejecting the hypothesis when in fact it is true (Type II error). There needs to be a balance between these two types of error, and the typical balance is obtained by use of the .05 and .01 significance levels.

Key Concepts

One way to test your mastery of the material that was presented in this chapter is to see if you know the meaning of the following terms. These terms were selected because they represent the key concepts. If you can define, identify, or otherwise explain each of the following terms without referring back to the material in the chapter, you can be assured that you have mastered the basics of the material that was presented. Just in case you cannot recall the meaning of a given term, the page on which it can be found appears in parentheses beside it.

subject pool (p. 296)
residual standard deviation (p. 300)
required standard error (p. 300)
debriefing (p. 303)
pilot study (p. 306)
scientific hypothesis (p. 308)
null hypothesis (p. 308)
significance level (p. 310)
Type I error (p. 312)
Type II error (p. 312)

12

Generalization

In conducting a research study, the investigator is attempting to find an answer to a question that he or she has raised. The procedure that is followed is to design a study adequately, and then to analyze the data collected on a sample of subjects. The results of this analysis should provide an answer to the research question. Seldom, however, is the investigator *only* interested in the sample of subjects on which the data were collected. Typically, one would like to state that the results of the study hold not only for the sample of subjects that participated in the study, but also for the much larger population of organisms from which the sample was drawn. For example, if we conducted a study on 20 college students we would like to say that the results that we found

316   on those 20 students also hold true for the total population of college students. This process of extending one's findings from the sample to the population is referred to as *generalization.* To the extent that the findings can be generalized to the larger population, external validity has been achieved (Campbell and Stanley, 1963).

Generalization is an inferential process because it involves making broad statements based on only limited information. However, this is a necessary component of the scientific process since only infrequently is it possible to study *all* members of a defined population. In order for one to generalize the results of a study back to the population of individuals, the sample subjects must be *representative* of the larger population. The problem of insuring that you have a representative sample is concerned with sampling techniques. Generally speaking, one has obtained a representative sample if one has *randomly* selected that sample from the defined population. If you were trying to find out whether introductory psychology students responded best to a lecture or a group discussion format, then, in order to be able to state that the results of your study would hold for all introductory students (the population), you would have to randomly select your sample from the population of introductory psychology students. However, most studies, for a variety of reasons such as cost, time, and accessibility, have not randomly sampled from the population. This failure to sample randomly represents a threat to the external validity of the experiment. While this is the most obvious threat to external validity, there are a number of others that also exist. Campbell and Stanley (1963) initially elaborated on these, and Bracht and Glass (1968) have extended this pioneering work. Because of the completeness of this extension, the issues discussed in this chapter will tend to conform to the issues presented by Bracht and Glass. Bracht and Glass consider the threats to external validity to fall into two broad classes, which "correspond to two types of external validity: population validity and ecological validity" (p. 437). These two classes are the ones that will be elaborated upon in detail. They should provide knowledge of some of the factors that limit the generalizability of the results of a study. With this knowledge in hand, it is often possible to design a study that circumvents these difficulties.

Population Validity

Population validity refers to the ability to generalize from the sample on which the study was conducted to the larger population of individuals in which one is interested. Bracht and Glass (1968) have reiterated Kempthorne's 1961 distinction between the *target* population and the experimentally accessible population. The target population is the larger population (e.g., all college students) to whom the experimental results are generalized and the experimentally accessible population is the one which is available to the researcher (e.g., the college students at the university at which the investigator is employed). In generalizing from the results of the study to the larger population, two inferential steps are involved. First, one has to generalize from the sample to the experimentally accessible population. This step can be easily accomplished if the investigator *randomly* selects the sample from the experimentally accessible population. If the sample is randomly selected it should be representative, which means that the characteristics of the experimentally accessible population can be inferred from the sample. If you conduct an experiment on a sample of 50 subjects randomly selected from a given university, then you can say that the obtained results are characteristic of students at that university.

The second step in the generalization process requires moving from the experimentally accessible population to the target population. While this is the ultimate generalization that we would like to make, this is the step that seldom can be made with any degree of confidence, because only rarely is the experimentally accessible population representative of the target population. For example, assume you were conducting a study using college students as the target population. Ideally, you would want to be able to say that the results of the study would hold for all college students. To be able to make such a statement you would have had to select randomly from the target population, and seldom can an investigator accomplish this. Therefore one has to settle with randomly selecting from the nonrepresentative experimentally accessible population.

One can readily see that it is difficult to select randomly from the target population. However, for most studies it is also very difficult to select randomly from the experimentally accessible population. This is why experimenters select subjects based on availability or precedent. The two categories of organisms that have most often been used in psychological studies are the albino rat and the college sophomore taking the introductory psychology course. A number of individuals have attacked the use of these two categories of organisms. Beach (1950, 1960), Boice (1973), Ehrlich (1974), Eysenck (1967), Kavanau (1964, 1967), Richter (1959), and Smith (1969) have all questioned the utility of using the laboratory rat as the model research animal. These individuals have questioned the degree to which the research results produced from this animal can be generalized to other animals of the

318   same or of a different species. Also, as Sidowski and Lockard (1966) point out, the ones that are used in a given study are definitely not a random sample of the experimentally accessible population.

Even more attention has been directed toward the research conducted on human subjects. Much of the research that has been conducted with human subjects has been directed toward identifying laws governing human behavior. Implicit in such an objective is the notion that the results from the sample of subjects on which the research was conducted would generalize to all humans, the target population. There is an increasing suspicion among behavioral researchers that the subjects in our research studies are not representative of humans in general. As far back as 1946, McNemar (1946, p. 333) issued a warning regarding the biased nature of our human subject research pool. He stated that "the existing science of human behavior is largely the science of the behavior of sophomores." However, it has not been until recently that attempts have been made to document such a statement.

In the last decade a number of studies illustrated the fact that psychology was predominantly a science of the behavior of college students. Table 12.1 reveals the results of these studies, which indicate that, at least for the journals surveyed, there was an increased use of college students in psychological studies up to the 1960s. Since then, about three-fourths of all studies have continued this practice in spite of the existence of the knowledge that the results obtained from these studies may have little application for the rest of the human subject population. In fact, Oakes (1972) has demonstrated that he could not replicate, using a noncollege student population, a reinforcement effect that had reliably been demonstrated on college students. He does, however, make an interesting point in defense of research using the college student. Oakes (1972) states:

> The point I am suggesting is that research with college students is just as valid as research drawing on any other subject population. A behavioral phenomenon reliably exhibited is a genuine phenomenon, no matter what population is sampled in the research in which it is demonstrated. For any behavioral phenomenon, it may well be that members of another population that one could sample might have certain behavioral characteristics that would preclude the phenomenon being demonstrated with that population. Such a finding would suggest a restriction of the generality of the phenomenon, but it would not make it any less genuine. No matter what population a researcher samples, whether it be psychology students, real-people volunteers, public school students, or whatever, there are probably some behavioral phenomena that would be manifested differently in that popula-

Table 12.1. Percentage of studies using college students as subjects.

AUTHOR	SOURCE	YEAR(S)	PERCENTAGE USING COLLEGE STUDENTS
Christie (1965)	*Journal of Abnormal and Social Psychology*	1949	20
Christie (1965)	*Journal of Abnormal and Social Psychology*	1959	49
Smart (1966)	*Journal of Abnormal and Social Psychology*	1962–1964	73
Smart (1966)	*Journal of Experimental Psychology*	1963–1964	86
Schultz (1969)	*Journal of Personality and Social Psychology*	1966–1967	70
Schultz (1969)	*Journal of Experimental Psychology*	1966–1967	84
Carlson (1971)	*Journal of Personality and Social Psychology and Journal of Personality*	1968	66
Higbee and Wells (1972)	*Journal of Personality and Social Psychology*	1969	76
Levenson, Gray and Ingram (1976)	*Journal of Personality and Social Psychology*	1973	72
Levenson, Gray and Ingram (1976)	*Journal of Personality*	1973	74

tion due to an interaction effect of the particular characteristics of that subject population.

This suggests, then, that the generalizability of the results of behavioral research is not a function of the population sampled, but rather that the external validity of the research depends on the interaction of subject characteristics and the particular behavioral phenomenon with which one is concerned. For some behavioral phenomena, probably those closer to the reflex level of response, there may be no interaction with subject characteristics. Thus, it might make no difference what population one sampled in a study of critical flicker fusion frequency. For other behavioral phenomena, however, especially those beyond the reflex level, one might well expect interactions with subject characteristics.

Thus, I would suggest that our "science of the behavior of sophomores," to the extent that it has discovered reliable behavioral phenomena, is just as valid as a science of behavior based on the sampling of any other population one could tap. The generalizability of any particular finding, however, may be limited by interaction with behavioral characteristics peculiar to any population to which one is attempting to generalize. But this would be true no matter what population one sampled in the original research.[1]

Bracht and Glass (1968) reach the same conclusion. The important issue regarding generalization of the results or external validity is whether the differences in the sample and the target population interact with the experimental treatment *condition*.

The above boils down to the fact that if a "selection by treatment" interaction (Campbell and Stanley, 1963) exists, the experiment is externally invalid or cannot be generalized to the target population. This means that the particular sample of subjects that are selected for use in a study may respond differently to the experimental treatment condition than would another sample of subjects with different characteristics. Rosenthal and Rosnow (1975), for example, have summarized the wealth of literature that reveals that volunteer and nonvolunteer subjects respond differently to many experimental treatment conditions. Kendler and Kendler (1959) have found that kindergarten children did not achieve results consistent with those obtained from college students. Their results suggest that perhaps a maturational variable exists, causing subjects at different maturational levels to respond differently to selected tasks. Such research reveals that one of our goals should be the identification of selection variable by treatment interactions similar to that done on the volunteer subject. However, I believe this emphasis is taking place and is the subject of the research focusing on the interaction of the person, situation, and the experimental treatment. Cronbach (1957) stressed the need for the study of aptitude by treatment interactions, since it involves determining the type of person for which a given treatment condition is effective. This attempt to identify treatment by selection (person) interaction is actively being pursued but has to be extended to include situational variables (Cronbach, 1975).

At this point it seems important to discuss the issue of when a generalization can be made regarding the effect of an experimental treatment effect. Naturally, one can generalize the demonstrated effects of a treatment if it does not interact with persons or situations.

However, such conditions do not exist with, perhaps, the exception of a reflexive type of condition. When interactions do exist, Lindquist (1953) has pointed out, and Lubin (1961) has expanded on, the important distinctions between ordinal and disordinal interactions. An ordinal interaction is one where the rank order of the treatment effects remains the same across persons and/or situations. Figure 12.1 illustrates an ordinal treatment by persons' interaction. Note that the rank order of the treatments remains the same for both categories of persons with treatment C producing the highest dependent variable scores, and treatment A producing the lowest dependent variable scores.

Disordinal interactions, on the other hand, are interactions where the rank order of the treatments changes across persons and/or situations as illustrated in Figure 12.2. Here treatment A is most effective for low-ability persons, whereas treatment C is most effective for high-ability persons, and treatment B is equally effective for both types of persons. What do these two types of interactions say about generalizations? Ordinal interactions do not limit generalizability of the results whereas disordinal interactions do. For ordinal interactions the one best or superior treatment condition can be prescribed for all individuals. As Figure 12.1 illustrates, treatment condition C is superior for both types of individuals. The ordinal interaction does reveal the differential effectiveness of the three treatments, and this lends support to the meaningfulness of interpreting the data; however, it does not limit the ability to generalize the data. Consequently, if the lines of the graph do not cross, in spite of the fact that a significant interaction exists, generalization of the data is not limited.

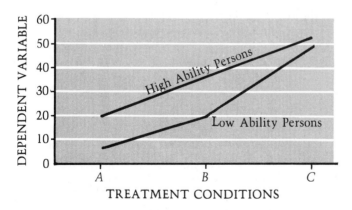

Figure 12.1. Ordinal interaction.

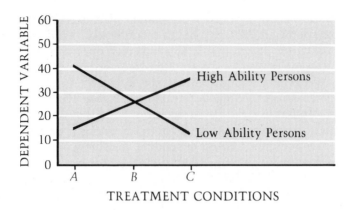

Figure 12.2. Disordinal interaction.

If a statistically significant interaction exists, and the lines of the graph cross as illustrated in Figure 12.2, a disordinal interaction exists and generalizability of the data is limited. From this figure it is readily apparent that one of the three treatment conditions is not superior for both types of individuals, but the *most* effective treatment depends upon the type of person (high or low ability) being considered. There is, however, one qualification that should be made in labeling an interaction disordinal. The differences between groups of persons must be statistically significant. For example, the scores of the high- and low-ability persons must be significantly different for treatments A and C to qualify as a disordinal interaction. This is because the lines of a graph may cross as a function of random variation in response, whereas a true disordinal interaction would represent a real difference suggested by statistical tests.

Ecological Validity

Population validity is the most frequently cited and discussed topic when the issue of generalization is brought up. However, ecological validity is just as important when considering the topic of generalization, because now the environment of the experiment is being considered. Whereas population validity referred to the ability to generalize from the sample to the larger population of individuals, ecological validity refers to the ability to generalize the results from the environmental conditions under which the study was conducted to other environmental conditions. Environmental conditions include such things as the physical setting of the experiment, the time of the day during which the treatment was administered, and the type of experimenter that was in charge of the experiment. To the extent that the experimental treatment effect is independent of such environmental effects, one can generalize the results of the experiment to other settings with different environmental conditions. Naturally, both population and ecological validity must exist for complete generalizability of results. The remainder of this chapter will be devoted to various environmental conditions within the experiment that can limit the ability to generalize the results to situations that are not similar to the experimental setting.

Multiple Treatment Interference

The multiple treatment interference phenomenon refers to the effect that participation in one treatment condition has upon participation in a second treatment condition. Consequently, the multiple treatment interference phenomenon represents a sequencing effect and, therefore, impedes direct generalization of the results of the study because it is difficult to separate the effect of the particular order of conditions from the effect of the treatment conditions. Any generalization that is made regarding the results of the study is restricted to the particular sequence of conditions that was administered.

There are at least two situations in which the multiple treatment interference phenomenon may occur. Multiple treatment interference may occur in an experiment in which the subject or subjects are required to participate in more than one treatment condition. Fox (1963), for example, found such an effect in his investigation of reading speed as related to typeface. In an incomplete counterbalanced design, one group of subjects first read material typed in Standard Elite and then in Gothic Elite, whereas the second group of subjects took the reversed order. When the data from the reading of the Standard Elite and Gothic Elite were combined across groups, no reliable difference related to typeface was found. However, when the two typefaces were compared for the first reading, it was found that the Standard Elite typeface was read reliably faster than the Gothic Elite. When the two groups switched to material typed in the other typeface, they continued to read at the average speed they had previously established. Thus, the reading rate established when reading the first typeface transferred over to the second treatment effect, and thus affected the reading rate for the second typeface. Consequently, the order of presentation of the typeface determined reading speed.

Multiple treatment interference may also occur between experiments. The effect of participation in a previous experiment may affect the subject's response to the treatment condition in a current experi-

324   ment. Underwood (1957), for example, has demonstrated that recall of serially presented adjective lists is to a great extent a function of the number of previous lists that have been learned. If a subject had previously been required to recall serial adjective lists, the current one would be more difficult to recall. More recently, Holmes (1967) and Holmes and Applebaum (1970) have found that prior participation in psychological experiments affects performance in verbal conditioning experiments. However, Cook et al. (1970) found no such effect in one of their experiments. It may be that a subject's history of experimental participation affects performance only in certain types of experimental studies. Such preliminary indicators need to be pursued to determine what types of data are affected by a subject's prior experimental history, and how they are affected, so that such effects can be taken into consideration when attempting to generalize one's experimental data.

Investigators using albino rats in their studies also must consider the potential effects of using the same albino rats in more than one study. The generally accepted procedure is to use the rats in *only* one study. When another study is being conducted, a new sample of albino rats must be purchased. In this way, the investigator assures that the rats are naive in the sense of not having previously participated in a psychological study.

The Hawthorne Effect

The Hawthorne effect refers to the fact that one's performance in an experiment is affected by knowledge of the fact that one is in an experiment. It is similar to being on television. Once you know the camera is on you, you shift to your television behavior which is typically not the same as your nontelevision behavior. Similarly, if you know that you are participating in an experiment, you may shift to your experimental behavior. This could cause a subject to take on any of a number of the roles discussed in an earlier chapter, possibly affecting performance on the dependent variable.

In addition to the motives discussed earlier in the text under the topic of subject bias, Bracht and Glass (1968) suggest several additional reasons why subjects may respond differently when they have knowledge of the fact that they are participating in an experiment. Subjects may, for example, display a high degree of compliance and diligence in performing the experimental task because they are motivated by a high regard for the aims of science and experimentation. Consequently, subjects who know they are in an experiment may comply with a request and perform on a task that they otherwise would not do. For example, if you walked up to a person and asked her to do 10 pushups, she might tell you where to go. However, if you added that you are conducting an experiment on physical fitness, you would probably find **325** that many people would now comply because you are conducting an experiment. To the extent that such effects alter the subject's performance, the experimental results cannot be accounted for by just the treatment effect.

A phenomenon similar to the Hawthorne effect is a novelty or disruption effect. If the experimental treatment condition involves something new or unusual, a treatment effect may result by virtue of this fact. When the novelty or disruption diminishes, the treatment effect may disappear. Van Buskirk (1932), for example, found that placing a red (novel) nonsense syllable in the most difficult position in a serial list of black on white nonsense syllables greatly facilitated its original learning and later recall. Brownell (1966) also provides an example of a novelty treatment effect. He set out to compare two different instructional programs in England and Scotland. However, results of the study from the two countries conflicted. This conflict was attributed to the novelty effect which existed in Scotland but not in England. Teachers and pupils in England were accustomed to innovation and new programs whereas those in Scotland were not. Consequently, the new program was enthusiastically inaugurated in Scotland, whereas it was just a continuation of an established pattern in England. Studies such as these reveal that conditions such as novelty and the Hawthorne effect limit one's ability to generalize the results of a given study to populations where such an effect does not exist.

The Experimenter Effect

Chapter 5 discussed in detail the potential biasing effects that the experimenter can have on the results of the experiment; consequently, they will not be reiterated here. Regarding generalization of results, experimenter effects are a limiting factor to the extent that experimenter bias is not controlled and the results of the experiment interact with the attributes or expectancies of the experimenter. In other words, if the results of the experiment are partially dependent upon the particular attributes or expectancies which the experimenter possesses, then the results are generalizable only to other similar situations.

The Pretesting Effect

The pretesting effect refers to the influence which administering a pretest may have on the experimental treatment effect. Administering a pretest may sensitize the subject in such a way that he or she approaches the experimental treatment differently than does the subject who does not receive the pretest. Consequently, the pretested

326   subject may respond differently to the dependent variable than does the unpretested subject, suggesting that the results of a study that pretests subjects can be generalized only to a pretested population. However, in Chapter 7, Lana's 1969 conclusion is quoted regarding a summary of research studies designed to investigate this pretest sensitization effect. The conclusion was that pretesting did not have the sensitizing effect that others had previously postulated. However, Rosenthal and Rosnow (1975), based on Rosnow and Suls (1970) research, have suggested that the failure to find a pretest sensitization effect was due to the failure to distinguish between the motivational sets among volunteer and nonvolunteer subjects, volunteers being the willing and eager subjects and nonvolunteers being the unwilling subjects. Rosnow and Suls found a pretest sensitization effect operating among volunteers and the opposite or dampening effect among nonvolunteers. This suggests that the pretest sensitization variable may be specific to the type of subject that is used in the study (a selection by treatment interaction). However, it seems that these results should be replicated before a firm conclusion can be drawn regarding the volunteer status by pretest sensitization interaction.

Time Span Effects

Time span effects are the possible interaction between length of time and the effectiveness of the experimental treatment condition. It is possible that a given treatment effect may diminish or change in some way over time. In attitude change research such an effect has been found by a number of investigators. This effect seems to be quite reliable and has been designated the sleeper effect, which refers to a delayed reaction of the treatment effect. McNamara and MacDonough (1972, p. 366) emphasize the need for a follow-up, or investigation of the persistence of a treatment effect over time. They state the case very effectively as follows:

> Although a significant change in behavior may be readily demonstrated at the termination of treatment (as in implosion therapy) it may mean very little in a practical sense if the new behavior cannot be maintained in the face of intercurrent life experience.

Although this statement was made in reference to behavior therapy research, it is just as true for most psychological research.

There are several surveys of the literature which have attempted to demonstrate the extent to which research takes the time span variable into consideration. Carlson (1971) found that 78% of the studies published in *Journal of Personality* and *Journal of Personality and Social Psychology* were based on only a *single* session. Levenson, Gray, and Ingram (1975) found five years later that the situation had

taken a turn for the worse, revealing that 89% of the articles published   **327**
in these two journals were based on a single session. If these two
journals are at all representative of work being conducted in other areas
of psychology, then we may be severely restricting the faith we can
have in making statements regarding the persistence of our treatment
conditions. The point is that we need to investigate experimentally the
extent to which we can expect our treatment effects to persist over
time.

Summary

When conducting a psychological study, we would like to have the
results hold not only for the subjects on which the study was conducted but also for the larger population of subjects from which the
sample was drawn. In other words, we would like to be able to
generalize the results of the study. In order to generalize back to the
larger population, one must randomly select subjects from this population. Seldom, however, are our subjects randomly selected from the
population. Most animal research has been conducted on a nonrandom
sample of albino rats and most human research has been conducted on
the college sophomore taking the introductory psychology course. In
spite of this the behavioral phenomena manifested in these nonrandom
samples are real, and whether or not they will generalize depends upon
whether or not there is an interaction between this behavioral
phenomena and subjects with characteristics different from those who
participated in the study. Consequently, generalization boils down to
determining if there is a subject characteristic by treatment interaction. More specifically, generalization is limited only if this interaction
is of a disordinal variety.

In considering the topic of generalization, it is also necessary to
determine if the behavioral phenomena identified generalized to other
experimental environments. If they will not, then the manifestation of
the treatment is limited to the experimental environment under which
they were demonstrated. There are a number of experimental environmental conditions that can limit one's ability to generalize the
results to other situations. The multiple treatment interference
phenomena are a sequencing effect. If the experimental effect occurs
only when a particular order of conditions exists, then generalization is
limited to this order of conditions. The Hawthorne effect refers to the
alteration that occurs in the subject's behavior when the subject knows
he or she is in an experiment. If the experimental effect is a function of
this fact, then generalization is limited to similar environments. Other

328   limiting factors include the potential influence of the experimenter, of pretesting, and of having conducted the study over only a single session. To the extent that these variables affect the results, then the results can be generalized only to other environments that include these factors.

Key Concepts

One way to test your mastery of the material that was presented in this chapter is to see if you know the meaning of the following terms. These terms were selected because they represent the key concepts. If you can define, identify, or otherwise explain each of the following terms without referring back to the material in the chapter, you can be assured that you have mastered the basics of the material that was presented. Just in case you cannot recall the meaning of a given term, the page on which it can be found appears in parentheses beside it.

generalization (pp. 316–317)
representative sample (p. 316)
population validity (pp. 316–317)
target population (p. 317)
experimental accessible population (p. 317)
selection by treatment interaction (p. 320)
ordinal interaction (p. 321)
disordinal interaction (p. 321)
ecological validity (p. 322)
multiple treatment interference (p. 323)
Hawthorne effect (p. 324)
pretesting effect (p. 325)
time span effect (p. 326)

13

Ethics

Many unanswered questions have always existed. The most respected method for obtaining answers to these questions is the scientific method, which necessitates gathering empirical data. Since many of the questions asked refer to the human organism, it is necessary to use this organism in a scientific investigation. If all scientific investigations consisted of innocuous studies that had no potentially detrimental side effects, there would be little concern for the welfare of the human subject and little need for a consideration of a code of ethics for conducting research on humans. This, however, is not the case. Consider, for example, the study in which live cancer cells were injected into hospitalized patients for the purpose of measuring the speed with which the body would reject the injected substance (Langer, 1966). This study may not have been so objectionable if the patients knew exactly what the researchers were doing and had volunteered to participate after having been given this knowledge. Instead, the patients were told that they were being given a test to discover their resistance to disease. These instructions were misleading and deceptive regarding the true nature and purpose of the study.

Individuals have the right to privacy and to protest surveillance of their behavior without their consent. Individuals also have the right to know if their behavior is being manipulated and, if so, why. While it is recognized that individuals have these rights, these same individuals are asking the scientific community to come up with answers to many significant questions. Scientists are asked for answers to problems such as cancer, arthritis, alcoholism, child abuse, and penal reform; the list is almost endless. Additionally, psychologists and many others are trained in research techniques, and most of these individuals consider a decision *not* to do research a matter of ethical concern.

In order to advance knowledge and to find answers to questions, it is often necessary to impinge on well-recognized rights of individuals. For example, it is very difficult to investigate topics like child abuse without violating certain rights such as privacy, since it is necessary to obtain information about the child abuser or the child being abused. Such factors create the ethical dilemma of whether to conduct the research and violate certain rights of individuals for the purpose of gaining knowledge or to sacrifice a gain in knowledge for the purpose of preserving human rights. The ethical dilemma is the potential contribution of the research versus the cost to the individual research participant.

In considering this ethical dilemma it is impossible to state rules or specific conditions as to when a researcher should or should not proceed with a given study. Rather, it is a judgmental process whereby the researcher must weigh the potential benefits of the study against the potential costs. If the potential benefits outweigh the costs then one should proceed, but if the costs outweigh the potential benefits then one should not conduct the research study.

Such ethical concerns have been the focus of a great deal of attention since the 1960s. This does not mean that ethical dilemmas did not exist or were not considered prior to this time. In fact, Edgar Vinacke commented on the ethics of deceiving subjects as far back as 1954. However, either the zeitgeist was not right or a sufficient number of studies posing a significant ethical dilemma had not been conducted up to that time for the scientific community to spend much time considering the ethical bounds of experimentation. A decade later the time was ripe and numerous individuals were voicing ethical concerns over both medical and psychological experimentation. In the medical field Pappworth (1967) cited numerous examples of research conducted on human subjects which violated their ethical rights. One issue of *Daedalus* (1969) was devoted to the ethics of human experimentation particularly as it related to medical research. With regard to psychological research there was an equal concern for the rights of human subjects. Kelman (1967, 1968, 1972) has by far been the most outspoken on this issue although others, e.g., Seeman (1969) and Beckman and Bishop (1970) have also contributed. This concern expressed over the ethics of the use of human subjects in psychological research led to the development of a code of ethics to be used by the psychologist for the purpose of guidance in the conduct of research using human subjects.

Before presenting the 10 principles which comprise this code of ethics, I want to elaborate briefly on the procedure that was followed in its development, hoping to give you an appreciation of the work and thought that went into it. A committee on Ethical Standards in Psychological Research was appointed by the Board of Directors of the American Psychological Association to revise the 1953 code of ethics for research using human subjects. This committee patterned its work after that developed by the previous ethics committee. There were two distinctive features of the previous method. The first feature was that the members of the profession were to supply ethical problems to serve as the raw material for the formation of the ethical principles. In meeting this first objective, two samples of 9,000 members of the American Psychological Association, and the entire membership of selected groups such as the Division of Developmental Psychology, were sent a questionnaire requesting a description of research studies that posed ethical problems. From these massive surveys, 5,000 research descriptions were obtained that comprised the raw material for the committee. While this served as the raw material from which to work, the committee members also interviewed 35 individuals who had either demonstrated a high level of concern for ethical issues or had a great deal of exposure to a variety of research projects.

With this wealth of information in hand, the committee began the process of drafting the proposed principles. Once the initial draft was completed, the second distinctive feature used by the 1953 ethics committee was initiated. This involved distributing the proposed principles throughout the profession so they could be reviewed and criticized by its members. City, state, regional, and national meetings and conventions, as well as psychology departments and individual psychologists interested in research ethics, discussed these principles. Additionally, the draft of the proposed principles appeared in the APA *Monitor* to ensure that all members had the opportunity to review the

332   principles. From this wide dissemination, numerous reactions were received as well as reactions to the reactions. Baumrind (1971, 1972), Kerlinger (1972), Pellegrini (1972), Alumbaugh (1972), and May (1972) represent interesting examples of such reactions and should be read, since they are thought-provoking.

With these many reactions in hand the committee prepared a new draft of the principles and subjected them to the same type of review process that the older draft underwent. This review of the revised ethical principles received a general level of acceptance from the APA membership. In view of this, the committee recommended adoption of the 10 principles. These 10 principles were adopted by the American Psychological Association and distributed to its membership in 1973.

Ethical Principles to Follow in Conducting Human Research

The American Psychological Association has adopted a code of ethics consisting of 10 principles which were published in *Ethical principles in the conduct of research with human participants,* by the American Psychological Association. These 10 principles will be presented in this section. Each principle will first be presented and then will be discussed briefly.[1]

> PRINCIPLE 1. In planning a study the investigator has the personal responsibility to make a careful evaluation of its ethical acceptability, taking into account these principles for research with human beings. To the extent that this appraisal, weighing scientific and humane values, suggests a deviation from any principle, the investigator incurs an increasingly serious obligation to seek ethical advice and to observe more stringent safeguards to protect the rights of the human research participant.

The first principle states that it is the investigator's moral responsibility to evaluate his or her study in light of each of the following ethical principles. If, in the investigator's opinion, any aspect of the study suggests a deviation from one or more of the principles, then the investigator must weigh the potential risks and costs to the subjects. If the risks and costs are too great the project must be abandoned. However, the risks and costs to the subject are not the only factors which must be considered. The investigator must also consider the potential benefits which could be derived from the research. If the potential

---

1. Ethical principles in the conduct of research with human participants. Copyright 1973 by the American Psychological Association. Reprinted by permission.

benefits outweigh the costs and risks to the subject the investigator may decide to proceed. If the costs are greater, the research project should be terminated.

If the investigator decides that there is an ethical question regarding the proposed research, he or she is advised to seek the counsel of others. This is because the investigator often tends to see the potential results of a study as being much greater than others do because of his or her investment in the study. Others can frequently provide a more accurate and objective assessment of the potential benefits and risks of the study. To whom should one turn for such advice and counsel? Colleagues can be very helpful in these cases, but because they may share some of one's own biases, it is frequently advisable to turn to others such as members of the subject's target group, e.g., college students or the elderly, or to ethics advisory groups for a better assessment of the costs and benefits of the research project.

> PRINCIPLE 2. Responsibility for the establishment and maintenance of acceptable ethical practice in research always remains with the individual investigators. The investigator is also responsible for the ethical treatment of research participants by collaborators, assistants, students, and employees, all of whom, however, incur parallel obligations.

The second principle states that the responsibility for maintaining ethical practice throughout the research study *always* remains the province of the investigator. This issue becomes particularly significant when there is more than one person involved in conducting the study. With more than one person involved there often is the tendency to let the other person take the responsibility for insuring ethical conduct. Principle 2 states that this should never be the case. In *no* case does the addition of individuals dilute one's ethical responsibility; instead, it merely multiplies it. Each coprincipal investigator is responsible for the ethical conduct of the study and, where students or assistants are involved, it is the principal investigator's responsibility to train them to be ethically responsible and supervise them to insure that they act in an ethical manner.

> PRINCIPLE 3. Ethical practice requires the investigator to inform the participant of all features of the research that reasonably might be expected to influence willingness to participate, and to explain all other aspects of the research about which the participant inquires. Failure to make full disclosure gives added emphasis to the investigator's responsibility to protect the welfare and dignity of the research participant.

Principle 3 states that the investigator has the ethical responsibility to inform the subject of all aspects of the research that might influence willingness to participate, and to answer any other questions

334   regarding the research project. No one can argue with such a practice since it would, ideally, enable each subject to evaluate the research and come to a free decision regarding whether or not to participate. The problem is that this ideal principle cannot always be attained. Some potential subjects, e.g., children, do not have the competence to make the necessary decision and provide informed consent. In such cases the legal as well as ethical practice is to obtain the informed consent from a person whose primary interest is the subjects' welfare, generally the parent or legal guardian. Even with such consent the subject should also provide consent before participating.

There are many other cases which conflict with Principle 3. Many types of psychological research would be invalidated if subjects were fully informed. In other situations the information may be too technical, complex, or unfamiliar for the subject to evaluate. As Principle 3 states, if one or more of these conditions exist the investigator must accept the responsibility of weighing the potential benefits of the research against the costs to the individual.

> PRINCIPLE 4. Openness and honesty are essential characteristics of the relationship between investigator and research participant. When the methodological requirements of a study necessitate concealment or deception, the investigator is required to ensure the participant's understanding of the reasons for this action and to restore the quality of the relationship with the investigator.

Principle 4 is actually an extension of Principle 3. Principle 3 states that one should obtain informed consent from the subject and Principle 4 states that one should maintain an open and honest relationship. However, it was noted that this is not always possible since informing subjects of all aspects of the research project may produce misleading results. Principle 4 extends this to cases in which the subject is not only not informed but in fact may be *misinformed* or deceived regarding the study and its various components. Here the investigator is not only not being open but is actually being dishonest. Consequently, the ethical issues are more serious. Because of the more serious ethical issue involved in giving misinformation or using deception, the issue has been widely debated. Most investigators do, however, feel that deception is necessary in some studies. APA (1973, p. 37) gives five conditions that *may* make deception more acceptable. These are:

> (a) The research problem is of great importance; (b) it may be demonstrated that the research objectives cannot be realized without deception; (c) there is sufficient reason for the concealment or misrepresentation that, on being fully informed later on (Principle 8), the research participant may be expected to find it

reasonable, and to suffer no loss of confidence in the integrity of   **335**
the investigator or of others involved; (d) the research participant
is allowed to withdraw from the study at any time (Principle 5),
and is free to withdraw the data when the concealment or misrep-
resentation is revealed (Principle 8); and (e) the investigator takes
full responsibility for detecting and removing stressful aftereffects
(Principle 9).

PRINCIPLE 5. Ethical research practice requires the investigator
to respect the individual's freedom to decline to participate in
research or to discontinue participation at any time. The obligation to protect this freedom requires special vigilance when the
investigator is in a position of power over the participant. The
decision to limit this freedom increases the investigator's responsibility to protect the participant's dignity and welfare.

Principle 5 states that it is ethically unacceptable to coerce a
subject to participate in research. One of our human rights is freedom
of choice and this extends to participation in psychological research.
One runs into two related problems when attempting to implement
this principle. The first difficulty is, as Kelman (1972) has eloquently
discussed, the power relationship that exists between the researcher
and the subject. Typically, the subject is in a less powerful position
that places him or her at a perceived disadvantage in feeling free to
decline participation. An investigator, in attempting to implement
Principle 5, may ask the group of potential subjects for volunteers to
participate in the research and tell them that they do not have to
volunteer. If these potential subjects are children, the investigator's
students, or patients, they may not feel free *not* to volunteer without
encountering some penalty. Investigators must be aware of the power
relationship they hold relative to their subjects and incorporate this
when trying to implement Principle 5.

The second difficulty one runs into when trying to fulfill Principle
5 is that the psychologist also is obligated to conduct research and
advance the segment of behavioral science in which he or she is
interested. To accomplish this one needs an available supply of subjects. For those studying humans there is a need for a supply of warm
bodies. This means that somehow a supply of humans needs to be
motivated to volunteer for psychological research studies. This has led
many psychology departments to form the subject pool consisting of
all introductory psychology students in which a course requirement is
to participate in one or more psychology experiments. In doing so, a
number of individuals feel that Principle 5 is being violated. The APA
ethics committee (APA, 1973, pp. 44–46) has provided a suggested set
of procedures a department can follow, enabling Principle 5 to be
maintained in spirit while still providing a pool of subjects to serve as
research participants. These suggestions are as follows:

336   1. Students are informed about the research requirement before they enroll in the course typically by an announcement in an official listing of courses. In addition, during the first class meeting, a detailed description of the requirement, frequently in written form, is provided covering the following points: the amount of participation required; the available alternatives to actual research participation; in a general way, the kinds of studies among which the student can choose; the right of the student to drop out of a given research project at any time without penalty; any penalities to be imposed for failure to complete the requirement or for nonappearance after agreeing to take part; the benefits to the student to be gained from participation; the obligation of the researcher to provide the student with an explanation of the research; the obligation of the researcher to treat the participant with respect and dignity; the procedures to be followed if the student is mistreated in any way; and an explanation of the scientific purposes of the research carried on in the departmental laboratories.

2. Prior approval of research proposals is required, sometimes by a single faculty member but more often by a departmental committee, that takes into account many of the considerations presented below:

   Will physical or mental stress be employed? If so, what precautions have been taken to protect the participants from the possibly damaging effects of the procedure? Will the research involve withholding information or deception? If so, what plans have been developed for subsequently informing the participants? What plans have been made for providing the participants with an explanation of the study? In general, what will the participants gain? Have the procedures been evaluated by representative participants in a pilot study?

3. Two types of alternatives are commonly available to increase the student's freedom of choice in meeting the requirement:

   A variety of opportunities for research participation is provided. This lets the student choose the type of research experience and (often of more consequence to him) the time and place where he will participate.

   Options are provided that do not require service as a research participant. The student may submit a short paper based upon the reading of research reports or observe ongoing research and prepare a report based upon this experience.

4. Before beginning his participation, the student receives a description of the procedures to be employed and is reminded of his option to drop out without penalty later on if he so desires. At this point some investigators have the student sign a form indicating informed consent.

5. Steps are taken to insure that the student is treated with respect and **337** courtesy. The concept that the participant is a "colleague in research" is widely accepted. In the service of this concept, the term "subject" has been abandoned in some universities and the expression "research participant" has replaced it.

6. Participants receive some kind of reward for their participation. At a minimum this involves as full an explanation of the purposes of the research as is possible. In addition, some departments still reward research participation with better grades although many critics would question the educational propriety of this practice. The assignment of a grade of "incomplete" as a sanction against nonfulfillment is common, although some regard this as too coercive. Where this sanction is used, procedures exist for allowing the student to fulfill the requirement later on.

7. There is a mechanism by which students may report any mistreatment. Usually this involves reporting questionable conduct on the part of a researcher to the instructor, the departmental ethics committee, or the chairman of the department.

8. The recruiting procedure is under constant review. Assessments of student attitudes toward the requirement are obtained at the end of each course having such a requirement each time it is offered. These data, together with evaluations of the workability of the procedures by the researchers, provide the basis for modifying the procedures in subsequent years.[2]

> PRINCIPLE 6. Ethically acceptable research begins with the establishment of a clear and fair agreement between the investigator and the research participant that clarifies the responsibilities of each. The investigator has the obligation to honor all promises and commitments included in that agreement.

There are three basic components to Principle 6. The first component is that a clear and explicit statement is made of the responsibilities of both the researcher and the participant. This is met by adhering to the principles requiring informed consent and freedom from coercion, although it was also noted that there are times when it seems necessary to violate such principles.

The second component of Principle 6 states that the agreement between the researcher and the participant should be fair and not exploitive. In order to meet this component, it is necessary that the participant's potential benefits be commensurate with the research demands made of him or her. Benefits include such things as monetary rewards, feeling of satisfaction, and added knowledge of self. Demands

2. Copyright 1973 by the American Psychological Association. Reprinted by permission.

338   include such things as loss of time and freedom, and any potential stress. In order for the participant to adequately evaluate such costs and benefits, he or she must be fully informed regarding the research. The problem is that this is frequently not possible. Therefore, the investigator must make such a judgment. The ethics committee (APA, 1973) gives three suggestions to guide the investigator's decision. First, the investigator can try to place himself or herself in the position of the participant and try to imagine how the participant would react. Second, the investigator can conduct a pilot study with a few participants and get their feedback regarding the fairness of the agreement. Third, the investigator can turn to colleagues for advice and suggestions regarding the degree to which the agreement is equitable.

The third component of Principle 6 states that the investigator *must* honor the agreement. This component seems to be rather implicit but needs to be stressed. The researcher must treat the participant with courtesy, consideration, and respect, and comply with all other terms stated in the *implicit* contract between the participant and researcher.

> PRINCIPLE 7. The ethical investigator protects participants from physical and mental discomfort, harm and danger. If the risk of such consequences exists, the investigator is required to inform the participant of that fact, secure consent before proceeding, and take all possible measures to minimize distress. A research procedure may not be used if it is likely to cause serious and lasting harm to participants.

Principle 7 begins by stating the ideal: The research participant should be protected from *any* physical or mental harm or discomfort. While this is true, a survey of the psychological literature would reveal that many studies have violated this ideal in order to investigate important psychological processes. These studies have induced physical stress in the form of such things as pain, drugs, or electric shock. Mental stress has taken the form of inducing such things as anxiety, fear, and frustration. Principle 7 recognized this fact and added that in such cases, the investigator had the explicit responsibility of requiring informed consent and must take all possible means of minimizing the distress. Informed consent is generally possible in studies using physical stress such as electric shock but is not always possible in studies using mental stress. If one were investigating failure, it would be necessary for the research participants to believe that they actually failed to generate valid data. In such cases the investigator has an even greater ethical responsibility and should consult with others (discussed under Principle 1) to check his or her own judgment on such ethical matters. Also, the investigator should consider and search for alternative procedures which would avoid subjecting participants to the stressful experiences. Such alternative procedures include use of animals, identification of people undergoing the stressful conditions as part of their life experiences and use of them as subjects, or perhaps use of a role-playing technique. If these alternative procedures are not acceptable, the investigator *must* take every precautionary measure to minimize the dangers to the research participants and set the level and duration of the stress at the lowest possible level even at the risk of not finding an experimental treatment effect. In all cases where an *enduring* negative after-effect exists, the research should not be conducted.

> PRINCIPLE 8. After the data are collected, ethical practice requires the investigator to provide the participant with a full clarification of the nature of the study and to remove any misconceptions that may have arisen. Where scientific or humane values justify delaying or withholding information, the investigator acquires a special responsibility to assure that there are no damaging consequences for the participant.

When discussing several of the preceding ethical principles in certain sections throughout this text, it has been stated that good research design sometimes necessitates deceiving the research participants. Where such a situation exists, Principle 8 applies and states that the investigator has the responsibility of debriefing the subject or providing the full details of the study, including why the deception was necessary. The investigator must also ensure that no damaging consequences exist for the participant.

A number of difficulties can often be encountered in trying to satisfy Principle 8. The debriefing may anger or disillusion the research participants because they were deceived. Aronson and Carlsmith (1968) discuss this issue at length and propose a debriefing procedure which should minimize this possibility. This is the debriefing procedure I have outlined in Chapter 11. A related difficulty is the fact that the debriefing may not be believed. This is a particularly difficult problem where the study involves a double deception (two consecutive deception procedures in the same study). The subject has been deceived once, and may think that this may be another deception. In cases where children are the research participants, the primary objective of debriefing should be assuring that they leave with no undesirable side effects because of their limited ability to understand the complex explanations that are frequently necessary.

The timing of debriefing can also pose a problem in some studies. The investigator may feel that the debriefing should occur en masse after completion of data collection, or, in a multiple-session study, the research design may call for delaying debriefing until the end of the second or third session even though deception occurred in the first session. From the standpoint of the welfare of the subject the inves-

340   tigator should debrief as soon as possible after the deception occurred. Where this is not possible, the investigator should seek the counsel of others regarding the proper procedure to follow.

A last issue that needs to be considered is the benefit that may be served by the debriefing. In some studies it is possible that the debriefing may be distressing to the individual instead of beneficial. Where such a possibility exists it may be the best practice *not* to debrief if the individual runs *no* risk of discovering the deception at a later date.

> PRINCIPLE 9. Where research procedures may result in undesirable consequences for the participant, the investigator has the responsibility to detect and remove or correct these consequences, including, where relevant, long-term after effects.

In psychological research, stress is sometimes either deliberately or inadvertently imposed upon the research participant. Principle 9 states that, regardless of the source of the stress, the investigator has the responsibility of detecting and removing it. Potentially harmful aftereffects must be removed immediately and in some conditions a long-term follow-up may be necessary to assure that the effects have not persisted.

> PRINCIPLE 10. Information obtained about the research participants during the course of an investigation is confidential. When the possibility exists that others may obtain access to such information, ethical research practice requires that this possibility together with the plans for protecting confidentiality, be explained to the participants as a part of the procedure for obtaining informed consent.

Principle 10 states that the investigator has the responsibility of keeping confidential the data collected on the research participants so that they remain anonymous. This principle seems straightforward and, at first glance, may appear to be easy to fulfill. However, there are several situations in which the investigator is pressured to release such data to others, posing a threat to confidentiality. Parents, friends, or an organization to which the subject belongs (e.g., school) may request the information. In such cases the investigator is obliged not to disclose the information without the consent of the subject. Other situations pose a greater threat to Principle 10. The confidentiality of psychologists' data is not protected by law and, therefore, the courts could demand that the psychologist reveal the data. Also, there is the situation where the psychologist obtains information suggesting that the subjects may be harmful to themselves or others. What is the investigator to do in such cases? When these situations arise, it is the investigator's responsibility to inform the research participant about the limits of confidentiality that can be achieved by the investigator.

Possible Consequences of Adopting the Code of Ethics

The above represents a summary of the final product produced by the ethics committee (APA, 1973). The 10 principles developed by the committee have been adopted by the American Psychological Association as its official position and, therefore, are to be used by psychologists conducting human research. The question that must be asked now is "What are the potential consequences of adopting this particular ethical posture?" West and Gunn (1978) have revealed that research proposals are receiving increased scrutiny. In some cases independent variable manipulations that previously would have been used and considered appropriate are having to be altered. For example, anger manipulations traditionally used in aggression research are being altered so that a less severe anger manipulation is used (Baron, 1976). This means that the ethical guidelines are creating a shift in the procedures used by some researchers in order to comply with the stated ethical guidelines. This shift seems to be toward the use of milder and less deceptive manipulations. The implications of this, according to West and Gunn (1978), are that the number of subjects used in a given experiment will have to be increased in order to detect a difference between treatment conditions, and there will be an accelerated trend toward nonmotivational theories. This is because the experimental manipulations generated by psychologists will be so mild that it is unlikely that they will arouse motives that will support a motivational interpretation.

Gergen (1973, p. 912) has summarized his position as follows:

> I have argued that from a research standpoint, there is little to merit the promulgation of the proposed ethical principles. Not only have we failed to demonstrate that our present procedures are detrimental to human subjects, but there is good reason to suspect that the principles would be detrimental to the profession and to the enhancement of knowledge should they be adopted. It has further been maintained that great danger lies behind our attempts at moralizing. What is needed is factual advice about the possible harmful consequences of various research strategies. Such advice could be embodied in a series of advisory statements for researchers. While these statements would primarily be conjectural at this point in time, we should ultimately be able to replace conjecture with fact.

Gergen's 1973 position is that we should have, from a research standpoint, determined the effects of each of the principles before incorporating them into a set of ethical standards for everyone to use. We should have determined the effects of such components as deception and informed consent. As Gergen (1973, p. 907) states:

342   If subjects remain unaffected by variations along these dimensions, then the establishment of the principles becomes highly questionable. If subjects are generally unconcerned about what is to happen to them, if they find experimental deceptions rather intriguing, if they do not generally care about the rationale of the research, and if their attitudes about life and themselves remain untouched regardless of whether the ethical principles are experimentally realized, then establishing and reinforcing the principles simply pose unnecessary hardships for the scientist. The life of the research psychologist is difficult enough without harnessing him with research restrictions that have little real-world consequence.

Unfortunately, we seem to have put the cart before the horse. We have adopted the ethical principles and now, after the fact, a number of researchers are actually investigating the effect of these ethical principles. However, it is better to do so now than not at all. I shall now attempt to summarize the results of such research endeavors.

The research that has been conducted on the ethical principles has focused on Principles 3 and 4, or the aspects of informed consent and deception. Principle 3 states that the investigator has the ethical responsibility of informing the subject of all aspects of the experiment about which he or she may inquire and any aspect that may influence the subject's willingness to participate. Carried to its extreme, this means informing the subject of *all* aspects of the study including its purpose and procedure. Resnick and Schwartz (1973) conducted a study that attempted to determine the impact of following Principle 3 to its logical extreme in a simple but widely used verbal conditioning task developed by Taffel (1955). The control, or noninformed, group was given typical instructions, which gave them a rationale for the study and informed them of the task that they were to complete. The experimental, or informed, group received *complete* instructions regarding the true reason for conducting the experiment and the *exact* nature of the Taffel procedure. Figure 13.1 depicts the results of the data obtained from the 14 subjects in each treatment condition. The uninformed subjects performed in the expected manner demonstrating verbal conditioning. However, the informed group revealed a reversal in the conditioning rate. Such data reveal that maintaining maximum ethical conditions alters the knowledge that we would accumulate. This alteration would possibly represent inaccurate information which would create a *lack* of external validity.

In addition to finding a drastic difference in response on the part of the informed subjects, Resnick and Schwartz also found that informing subjects of the entire experiment apparently destroys any incentive to participate in the experiment. Uninformed subjects were enthusiastic and appeared at the scheduled time but the informed subjects were

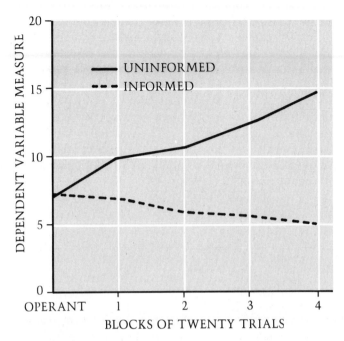

Figure 13.1. Verbal conditioning data obtained by Resnick and Schwartz. (Adapted from Resnick, J. H., and Schwartz, T. Ethical standards as an independent variable in psychological research. American Psychologist, 1973, 28, p. 136. Copyright 1973 by the American Psychological Association. Reprinted by permission.)

generally uncooperative and "often haughty, insisting that they had only one time slot to spare which we could either take or leave" (p. 137). It actually took Resnick and Schwartz *five* weeks to collect the data on the 14 informed subjects for such reasons. Completely informing subjects makes some subjects very suspicious, according to Resnick and Schwartz, and may cause them to stay away. However, for most subjects, fully disclosing the research to the subjects causes them to lose interest, which "suggests that people enjoy an element of risk and nondisclosure and become bored rapidly with the prospect of participating in something of which they already have full knowledge" (Resnick and Schwartz, 1973, p. 137). This view is also supported by a survey of student opinion conducted by Epstein, Suedfeld, and Silverstein (1973). They found that more than 70% of the college students they surveyed did *not* expect to be told the purpose of the experiment and that deception, though not desirable, was not an inappropriate feature of the research setting.

Based on the evidence just presented, it seems that a certain amount of deception is necessary in some types of psychological studies. A number of investigators have attempted to determine the extent to which deception is used in psychological studies. Table 13.1 summarizes the results of such studies. Two things are quite obvious from these surveys. First, deception has been steadily increasing since 1948; and second, this increase in deception studies, as one would probably expect, primarily resides within the personality and social areas. The point raised by these studies is that there seems to be little attempt on the part of most investigators to adhere to the openness and honesty characteristics specified in Principle 4.

The large number of studies that incorporate deception have led a number of investigators (e.g., Kelman, 1967) to suggest the possible use of role-playing as an alternative to use of deception. Use of role-playing procedure would allow the investigator to be open and honest in terms of telling them about the experiment. Then the subjects would be required to role-play the experimental situation. A number of investigators have taken this suggestion and attempted to determine its effectiveness as an alternative procedure. Miller (1972) reviewed these studies and concluded that the prospects for using role playing in the place of deception were very poor. Holmes and Bennett (1974), in a later investigation, also concluded that role playing was not a viable alternative.

Given the fact that role playing cannot be substituted for deception, most investigators, e.g., Miller (1972), seem to agree that deception is here to stay, at least for the time being. Given this reality we need to look at two other considerations. First, is it possible to incorporate a compromise between the need for deception and the ethical principle of openness and honesty? This compromise could take the form of informing all potential subjects in, say, the departmental subject pool that some of the experiments which they engage in will include some form of deception. Campbell (1969, p. 370) suggests the following as a possible procedure:

> Announce to all members of the subject pool at the beginning of the term, "In about half of the experiments you will be participating in this semester, it will be necessary for the validity of the experiment for the experimenter to deceive you in whole or in part as to his exact purpose. Nor will we be able to inform you as to which experiments these were or as to what their real purpose was, until after all the data for the experiment have been collected. We give you our guarantee that no possible danger or invasion of privacy will be involved, and that your responses will be held in complete anonymity and privacy. We ask you at this time to sign

Table 13.1. Use of deception in psychological research.

AUTHOR(S)	JOURNALS	YEAR	PERCENTAGE OF DECEPTION STUDIES
Seeman (1969)	Journal of Abnormal and Social Psychology	1948	14.3
Seeman (1969)	Journal of Personality	1948	23.8
Seeman (1969)	Journal of Consulting Psychology	1948	2.9
Seeman (1969)	Journal of Experimental Psychology	1948	14.6
Menges (1973)	Journal of Abnormal and Social Psychology	1961	16.3
Seeman (1969)	Journal of Abnormal and Social Psychology	1963	36.8
Seeman (1969)	Journal of Personality	1963	43.9
Seeman (1969)	Journal of Consulting Psychology	1963	9.3
Seeman (1969)	Journal of Experimental Psychology	1963	10.8
Menges (1973)	Journal of Personality and Social Psychology	1971	47.2
Menges (1973)	Journal of Abnormal and Social Psychology	1971	21.5
Menges (1973)	Journal of Educational Psychology	1971	8.3
Menges (1973)	Journal of Consulting Psychology	1971	6.3
Menges (1973)	Journal of Experimental Psychology	1971	3.1
Carlson (1971)	Journal of Personality and Journal of Personality and Social Psychology	1968	57.0
Levenson, Gray and Ingram (1976)	Journal of Personality	1973	42.0
Levenson, Gray and Ingram (1976)	Journal of Personality and Social Psychology	1973	62.0

the required permission form, agreeing to participate in experiments under these conditions." This would merely be making explicit what is now generally understood, and probably would not worsen the problem of awareness and suspicion that now exists.[3]

3. From Campbell, D. Prospective: Artifact and Control. In *Artifact in behavioral research*, edited by R. Rosenthal and R. L. Rosnow. New York: Academic Press, 1969. Used with permission of the author and publisher.

Again one must ask if this procedure is a legitimate alternative that would still enable one to obtain unbiased data. Holmes and Bennett (1974) provided data on this question. One of their groups of subjects, the informed group, was told that deception was involved in some psychological experiments. They found that giving this group of subjects such information in no way affected their performance. These subjects performed in the same manner as did the deceived subjects. Consequently, it seems that subjects can be informed that they may be deceived but not of the exact nature of the deception.

A second consideration on which the investigator must focus is the effect of the deception upon the subject. There are times when the deception and the experimental treatment condition cause the subject stress, and under such conditions the investigator has the responsibility of eliminating this stress. The primary mode that most investigators have used to accomplish this is to engage in a debriefing session or postexperimental interview with the subject. Is such a debriefing effective? There are several studies which have investigated this question. Milgram (1964), in his reply to Baumrind's 1964 criticism of his earlier (Milgram, 1963) study, which investigated the extent to which subjects would obey instructions to inflict extreme pain upon confederates, found that upon extensive debriefing only 1.3% of his subjects reported any negative feelings about their experience within the experiment. Such evidence would indicate that the debriefing was probably effective in eliminating the extreme anguish that these subjects apparently experienced.

Ring, Wallston, and Corey (1970) lend considerable support to Milgram's 1964 findings. In their quasi replication of Milgram's 1963 experiment, they found that only 4% of the subjects who had been debriefed indicated they regretted having participated in the experiment and only 4% indicated that the experiment should not be permitted to continue. On the other hand, about 50% of the subjects who had not been debriefed responded in this manner. Berscheid et al. (1973) have found similar ameliorative effects of debriefing upon consent-related responses. Holmes (1973) and Holmes and Bennett (1974) have taken an even more convincing approach and demonstrated that the arousal produced in a stress-producing experiment (expected electric shock) was reduced to the prearousal level through debriefing as measured by both physiological and self-report measures.

All of the above suggest that debriefing is quite effective in eliminating the stress produced by the experimental treatment condition. However, Holmes (1976a,b) has appropriately pointed out that there are two goals of debriefing and both must be met for debriefing to be maximally effective. These two goals are *dehoaxing* and *desensitizing*. Dehoaxing refers to any deception that may have been used by the experimenter. In the dehoaxing process the problem is one of convincing the subject that the fraudulent information they were given was, in fact, fraudulent. Desensitizing refers to the subject's behavior. If the experiment has made subjects aware of some undesirable feature of themselves (e.g., that they could and would inflict harm on others), then the debriefing procedure has as one of its tasks helping the subject deal with this new information. This is typically done by suggesting that the undesirable behavior exhibited by the subjects was due to some situational variable rather than some dispositional characteristic of the subject. Another tactic used by experimenters is to point out that the subjects' behavior was not abnormal or extreme. The big question regarding such tactics is whether or not they are effective in desensitizing or dehoaxing the subjects. In Holmes's 1976 (a,b) review of the literature relating to these two issues, he concluded that they were effective. However, it is very important to realize that this only means that effective debriefing is *possible.* It *must* be remembered that these results hold *only* if the debriefing is carried out properly. A sloppy or improperly prepared debriefing session may very well not have the same effect.

There is one additional point that needs to be made regarding debriefing. Perhaps debriefing should not be universally applied in all experiments. Both Aronson and Carlsmith (1968) and Campbell (1969) have discussed the potentially painful effects that debriefing can have if the subject learns of his or her own gullibility, cruelty, or bias. It is for this reason that Campbell (1969) has suggested that debriefing be eliminated in those situations in which the experimental treatment condition falls within the subject's range of ordinary everyday experiences. Such a recommendation has also been supported by survey data collected by Rugg (1975).

So far I have discussed ethics from the investigator's point of view, revealing that he or she is highly concerned with ethical issues. However, there is also the research participant's point of view. Are participants equally as concerned about how we researchers are using them in our studies? There are a couple of studies (Sullivan and Deiker, 1973; and Rugg, 1975) that have investigated this question and both studies find that, of the individuals they surveyed, the research participants were much more lenient in their perceptions of the ethical issues of human research than were the researchers. Rugg (1975) extended this survey to include additional significant groups such as ethics committee members and law professors and, with no exception, found these individuals to be much stricter in their interpretation of the ethics of human research than were the research participants (college students). It appears that individuals conducting human research constitute a strict self-regulating force that is sensitive to the rights and welfare of their research participants. Wilson and Donnerstein (1976) do, however, make the point that the research participants' attitudes toward a given research procedure should be considered, since they found that some research procedures did elicit a negative reaction from a substantial minority of the individuals they surveyed.

Ethics of Animal Research

There is and has been considerable attention focused on the ethics of human research. It is not infrequent that a project is judged to be too dangerous for one reason or another to conduct on humans. Where does this leave the investigator? In such cases the investigator, rather than scrapping the research project, redesigns the study so that it can be investigated using infrahumans as research subjects. This does not mean that there are no ethics in the use of infrahumans as subjects. Rather, it reflects the fact that some types of research are permissible with infrahumans that are not with humans.

The ethical issues surrounding the use of infrahumans are primarily concerned with the proper care and treatment of the animals. In Chapter 10, this concern was presented together with sources that could be contacted for the proper care and handling of the laboratory rat, since this is the most common laboratory animal. Additionally, in the fall of 1977 the APA approved a revision of its *Principles for the care and use of animals.* The revised principles are as follows:

1. The acquisition, care, use, and disposal of all animals shall be in compliance with current federal, state or provincial, and local laws and regulations.

2. A scientist trained in research methods and experienced in the care of laboratory animals shall closely supervise all procedures involving animals and be responsible for insuring appropriate consideration of their comfort, health, and humane treatment.

3. Scientists shall insure that all individuals using animals under their supervision have received explicit instruction in experimental methods and in the care, maintenance, and handling of the species being used. Responsibilities and activities of individuals shall be consistent with their respective competencies.

4. Scientists shall make every effort to minimize discomfort, illness, and pain to the animals. A procedure subjecting animals to pain, stress, or privation shall be used only when an alternative procedure is unavailable and the goal is justified by its prospective scientific, educational, or applied value. Surgical procedures shall

be performed under appropriate anesthesia; techniques to avoid infection and minimize pain must be followed during and after surgery. Euthanasia shall be prompt and humane.

5. Investigators are strongly urged to consult with the Committee on Animal Research and Experimentation at any stage preparatory to or during a research project for advice about the appropriateness of research procedures or ethical issues related to experiments involving animals. Concerned individuals with any questions concerning adherence to the *Principles* should consult with the committee.

6. Apparent violations of these Principles shall be reported immediately to the facility supervisor whose signature appears below:

Name:_____
Position:_____Phone:_____

If a satisfactory resolution is not achieved, a report should be made to the responsible institutional authority designated below:

Name:_____
Position:_____Phone:_____

Unresolved allegations of serious or repeated violations should be referred to the APA Committee on Animal Research and Experimentation.

7. These Principles shall be conspicuously posted in every Laboratory, teaching facility, and applied setting where animals are being used. All persons in each laboratory, classroom, or applied facility shall indicate by signature and date on the attached sheet that they have read these Principles.

By signing and dating this sheet, I signify that I have read the *Principles for the care and use of animals* of the American Psychological Association and affirm that my use of animals in research, teaching, and practical applications will conform with them.

Name	Date	Name	Date
_____	_____	_____	_____
_____	_____	_____	_____
_____	_____	_____	_____
_____	_____	_____	_____

These regulations govern the care and treatment of animals. It is necessary that these be followed if one is to conduct research using animals as the research subject.

Summary

A great deal of psychological research requires the use of humans as subjects. These individuals have certain rights, such as the right to privacy, which must be violated if we are to attempt to attain answers to many significant questions. This naturally imposes a dilemma on the researcher as to whether to conduct the research and violate the rights of the research participant, or abandon the research project. Such ethical concerns have continued to receive increased attention which has resulted in the development of a code of ethics, which has been published by the American Psychological Association. This code of ethics consists of 10 principles to be followed by the research psychologist in the conduct of his or her research.

A great deal of time, effort, and thought went into the code of ethics developed by the APA ethics committee. However, the potential consequences of adopting and adhering to these principles were not assessed prior to their adoption. Since this time a number of investigators have attempted to assess their consequences. Most of this research has been focused on the principles dealing with informed consent and deception. The research investigating informed consent reveals that completely informing subjects about the research not only would alter the results obtained, but also would create tremendous difficulties in obtaining research participants.

The studies focusing on deception have, first of all, revealed that it is a widely used procedure. This widespread use of deception has led a number of individuals to suggest alternatives to deception, such as role playing. Research studies have, however, revealed that such alternatives are poor substitutes, and therefore deception will remain as part of numerous psychological studies. Therefore, consideration must be given to the potential effects of deception. When deception creates undue stress, most investigators have used a debriefing session or postexperimental interview to eliminate this effect. This procedure has been demonstrated to be quite effective.

Many investigators have expressed considerable concern over ethical issues in the conduct of human research. This concern is, however, much greater than that revealed by the research participants themselves, suggesting that researchers are a fairly strict self-regulating group.

The Research Report

Throughout the course of this book I have attempted to present the various steps involved in the research process and to discuss in detail the intricacies of each of these steps. It is hoped that this presentation has enabled you to conduct a scientific study. If it has, then I have accomplished my goal. However, you, as a scientist conducting a scientific study, have the responsibility not only for conducting a well-designed and executed study, but also for communicating the results of your study to the rest of the scientific community. You have conducted it for the purpose of answering a specific question. While the study may have answered the question for you, this gain in knowledge is of no scientific worth until it is made public. In other words, it must somehow be communicated to others, and the primary source of such communication takes place through the professional journals in one's field. In the field of psychology the American Psychological Association publishes 18 journals in various areas of psychology. Additionally, there are numerous other journals that publish psychological material. In an attempt to facilitate clear communication of the results of research studies, the American Psychological Association has published a manual (American Psychological Association, 1974) that presents a standardized format for authors to follow in preparing their research reports. Since numerous journals, in addition to the APA journals, instruct their authors to prepare their manuscripts according to the style specified in the APA manual, this is the format I will present for writing the research report.

When reading through each of the following sections of the research report, and particularly when writing the research report, you should keep its purpose in mind. The primary purpose of the research report is to do exactly what its title suggests. You are to report as precisely as possible what you did, including a statement of the problem investigated, the methods used to investigate the problem, the results of your investigation, and any conclusions you reached as a result of your investigation. Is there any criterion you can use to determine whether or not you have clearly and explicitly reported your study? The criterion of replication is possibly the most important. If another investigator could read your research report and precisely replicate your study, then you have, in all probability, made a clear and complete report. Also, if the criterion of replication has been satisfied, another researcher can read the research report and reach his or her own conclusions regarding the adequacy of the study.

The APA Format

The structure of the research report is very simple and tends to follow the steps one takes in conducting a research study. In presenting the format of the research report I will be coordinating my presentation with an actual research report published in an APA journal. You can read the section stating the material to be included in each part of the manuscript and, adjacent to it, read an actual published study that includes this material.[1] When reading the sample article, you will note

1. From Melamed, B. G., and Siegel, L. J. Reduction of anxiety in children facing hospitalization and surgery by use of filmed modeling. *Journal of Consulting and Clinical Psychology*, 1975, *43*, 511–521. Copyright 1975 by the American Psychological Association. Reprinted by permission.

that all parts do not include all the material that I will be specifying, **353** and may not conform to the format I am specifying. This is because journal editors recognize and accept some alternatives to the recommended style. I will present the explicit style recommendations, whereas the actual article will, at times, show some deviation from the recommended style.

REDUCTION OF ANXIETY IN CHILDREN FACING HOSPITALIZATION AND SURGERY BY USE OF FILMED MODELING

Title. The title is to inform readers about the study. It should, by itself, be able to inform the reader about the contents of the study. One of the best ways to accomplish this is to state the relationship between the independent and dependent variable which has been investigated.

Barbara G. Melamed and Lawrence J. Siegel
Case Western Reserve University

Author(s) name and institutional affiliation. The author or authors who have made significant contributions to the study should appear as they customarily sign their name. Institutional affiliation appears directly under the name of the author(s). In case of multiple institutional affiliation, the separate institutional affiliation appears under the name of the respective author.

Sixty children about to undergo elective surgery for hernias, tonsillectomies, or urinary-genital tract difficulties were shown on hospital admission either a relevant peer modeling film of a child being hospitalized and receiving surgery or an unrelated control film. Both groups received extensive preparation by the hospital staff. State measures of anxiety, including self-report, behavioral observation, and Palmar Sweat Index, revealed a significant reduction of preoperative (night before) and postoperative (3–4 week postsurgery examination) fear arousal in the experimental as compared to the control film group. The parents reported a significant posthospital increment in the frequency of behavior problems in the children who had not seen the modeling film. Trait measures of anxiety did not reflect the group differences due to the hospital experience.

Abstract. The abstract represents a 100–175 word summary of the purpose and content of the research report. It should include a brief statement of the problem; a summary of the method, including a description of the subjects, research design, instruments or apparatus, or any other significant data-gathering devices; a summary of the results of the data analysis; and any conclusions that can be drawn from these results.

354

The literature on hospitalized children suggests that there is a consensus that all children need some kind of psychological preparation for the hospital experience, particularly when accompanied by surgery. The need for such preparation is predicted on the belief that hospitalization and surgery are stressful and anxiety-producing experiences that can lead to transient or long-term psychological disturbances in most children. A number of behavior problems have been observed in children who have been hospitalized for surgery (Chapman, Loeb, & Gibbons, 1956; Gellert, 1958) with estimates for the incidence of these problems ranging from 10% to 35% (Jessner, Blom, & Waldfogel, 1952; Prugh, Staub, Sands, Kirschbaum, & Lenihan, 1953; Schaffer & Callender, 1959). Cassell (1965) reported slight psychological upset in as many as 92% of the hospitalized children studied.

Skipper and Leonard (1968) noted that the hospital experience itself may produce anxiety for the child irrespective of the reason for the hospitalization. In addition to its role in the development of physical and emotional problems, anxiety is of particular interest to the hospital staff because of its influence on the patient's reaction to surgery and its adverse effects on postoperative recovery. Several authors have suggested that preoperative anxiety is a significant factor in impeding recovery from surgery (Dumas, 1963; Giller, 1963; Janis, 1958).

Introduction. The introduction, which is not labeled, is funnel shaped in the sense that it begins broad and ends narrow. It should begin with a very general introduction to the problem area and then begin to narrow by citing the results of prior works that have been conducted in the area and that bear on the specific issue that you are investigating. In citing prior research, do not attempt to make an exhaustive review of the literature. Cite only those studies that are directly pertinent and avoid tangential references. This pertinent literature should lead directly into your study and thereby show the continuity between what you are investigating and prior research. After you have cited the prior pertinent literature and shown how it leads into your topic, you should then state, preferably in question form, the purpose of your study. As you can see, the introduction attempts to give the reader the rationale for the given investigation and how it fits in with, and is a logical extension of, prior research. It accomplishes these two purposes by starting with a broad statement of the problem area and then narrows to a brief, concise summary of the pertinent literature which leads directly into a statement of the variables to be investigated in the present study.

The project was supported by funds provided by the Cleveland Foundation and the Health Sciences Communications Center of Case Western Reserve University.

Requests for reprints should be sent to Barbara G. Melamed, Mather Memorial Building, Case Western Reserve University, Cleveland, Ohio 44106.

Portions of the data reported in this study were included in an unpublished doctoral dissertation submitted by the second author in partial fulfillment for the doctoral degree at Case Western Reserve University, 1974.

In an attempt to alleviate the stressful effects of hospitalization, several methods of psychological preparation have been utilized. Vernon, Foley, Sipowicz, and Schulman (1965) have suggested that the major purpose of preoperative preparation is to (a) provide information to the child, (b) encourage emotional expression, and (c) establish a trusting relationship with the hospital staff.

The most frequently used method of preparing children for the hospital and surgery is preoperative instruction (Heller, 1967; Mellish, 1969). While a number of different procedures have been used to impart information to the child about the hospital and his operation, they are similar in that they attempt to correct any misinformation that he might have and to help him master the experience by enabling him to anticipate events and procedures and to understand their meaning and purpose.

Puppet therapy (Cassell, 1965) and play therapy (Dimock, 1960; Impallaria, 1955) have also been used as preoperative preparation techniques with children. The child is given the opportunity to act out, draw, or describe the events that he will experience in the hospital. It is believed that such activities permit the child to resolve his fears and concerns with the assistance of a supporting adult.

Several studies have investigated the effectiveness of various methods of preoperative preparation with children (Cassell, 1965; Jackson, Winkley, Faust, & Cermack, 1952; Lende, 1971; Prugh et al., 1953). The results of these studies, however, are equivocal in demonstrating differences between prepared and unprepared subjects on a variety of criterion measures. Most of the measures that purport to measure the child's anxiety are interview questionnaires with the parents or global ratings of the child's response to the treatment procedures. Reliability data on the use of these ratings are not reported. In addition, these investigations suffer from a number of methodological problems that make interpretation of the data difficult. Such factors as previous hospitalizations, age of the child, and prehospitalization personality, which are cited (Vernon et al., 1965) as major determinants of psychological upset, are often uncontrolled.

Recent demonstrations of the therapeutic use of modeling to effectively reduce anxiety-mediated avoidance behavior in children (Bandura, Grusec, & Menlove, 1967; Bandura & Menlove, 1968; Ritter, 1968) suggest that this procedure might also be useful for reducing children's anxiety and fears concerning the hospital and surgery. Vicarious extinction of emotional behavior is typically achieved by exposing the child to a model's approach responses toward a fearful stimulus that does not result in any adverse consequences or that may, in fact, produce positive consequences.

The purpose of this study was to investigate the efficacy of filmed modeling in reducing the emotional reactions of children admitted to the hospital for elective surgery and in facilitating their emotional adjustment during a posthospital period. While several investigations have demonstrated the successful application of therapeutic modeling in alleviating children's fears of dental treatment (Johnson & Machen, 1973; Melamed, Hawes, Heiby, & Glick, 1975; Melamed, Weinstein, Hawes, & Katin-Borland, 1975; White, Akers, Green, & Yates, 1974), there has been only one systematic investigation of this procedure in a hospital setting. Vernon and Bailey (1974) found that children who observed an experimental modeling film exhibited significantly less disruptive and fearful behaviors during induction of anesthesia than a control group that did not observe the modeling film. However, since children in the control group did not observe any film, it is not possible to determine whether the mere act of watching a movie or the content of the movie itself was the critical variable. In addition, the only measure of the film's effectiveness was a "global mood scale" that was used to rate the child's behavior during various phases of the anesthesia-induction procedure.

The current investigation attempts to avoid the methodological flaws of previous research by controlling for the age, sex, and prior hospitalization history of the subjects. The prehospital personality was assessed through measures of chronic anxiety and behavior maladjustment. The effectiveness of a peer-modeling hospital film in reducing anxiety of the experimental group was compared against a group of children matched in age, sex, and type of surgery who were also exposed to a preadmission film that was not related to the hospitalization. Both groups of children also received preoperative preparation by the hospital staff. Thus the effectiveness of the film was evaluated for its potency above that of procedures already thought to effectively reduce anxiety in these children.

Since anxiety is generally regarded as a multidimensional construct expressing itself in several response classes including physiological, skeletal–muscular, and verbal (cognitive) behavior, a number of dependent measures were used in the present study to assess the children's emotional responses to hospitalization and surgery (Cattell & Scheier, 1961; Lang, 1968). The measures were further selected in order to differentiate between the child's anxiety in specific situations (state anxiety) and his characteristic level of anxiety (trait anxiety) (Cattell & Scheier, 1961; Spielberger, 1966). In addition, these measures were assessed throughout the hospital experience and not just during certain medical procedures. A follow-up assessment of the children was conducted 3–4 weeks after discharge when they returned to the hospital for a postoperative examination by the surgeon.

METHOD

Subjects

The subjects were 60 children between the ages of 4 and 12 years old who were admitted to Rainbow Babies and Children's Hospital, Cleveland, Ohio, for elective surgery. They had no prior history of hospitalization. The subjects were selected from the Division of Pediatric Surgery and were scheduled for either tonsillectomies, hernia, or urinary–genital tract surgery.[1] The length of stay in the hospital for the children ranged from 2 to 3 days.

Thirty matched subjects were assigned to the experimental or control group. Group assignment was conducted in order to counterbalance for age, sex, race, and the type of operation.

Measures of Anxiety

In order to assess the various response classes considered to reflect the multidimensional nature of anxiety, a number of indices of the child's emotional behavior were employed including self-report, behavioral, and physiological measures.

Three measures were used to assess "trait" anxiety, or the long-term effects of the hospital experience. The first measure was the Anxiety scale (Klinedinst, 1971). The 30 items that comprise this scale were rationally derived from the Personality Inventory for Children (Wirt & Broen, 1958). Items on the scale, which the mother rates as true or false about her child, are intended to measure more chronic and stable anxiety.

The Children's Manifest Anxiety Scale (Castaneda, McCandless, & Palermo, 1956) was a second measure of the long-term effects of the hospital experience. The Human Figure Drawing Test (Koppitz, 1968) was the third index of trait anxiety. Koppitz has developed a set of norms for 30 "emotional indicators" that were used to score the subjects' drawings. Average interrater agreement for scoring the drawings, which was computed by dividing the number of agreements of two independent raters by the total number of agreements and disagreements, was 97%.

Situational, or "state," anxiety was assessed by

---

[1] Acknowledged is the cooperation and support of Robert Izant, Jr., Howard Filston, Robert Crumrine, Dennis Drotar, Anne Godfrey, Lester Persky, Walter Maloney, Patricia Rutherford, Cindy Chessler, and Carol Cook, who provided direct patient service, as well as guidance, in the project development. The staff of Rainbow Babies and Children's Hospital and the Ethan Stein family made a significant contribution to this study.

Method. The primary purpose of the method section is to tell the reader exactly how the study was conducted. This is the section of the research report that must directly satisfy the criterion of replication. If another investigator could read the method section and replicate the study which you conducted, then you adequately described it. An offshoot of exactly stating how you conducted the study is that the reader can evaluate the adequacy of the research.

In order to facilitate communication the method section is typically divided into the subsections of subjects; apparatus, materials, or instruments; and procedure. This is the typical subdivision, but is deviated from at times. Such a deviation is illustrated in the adjacent Melamed and Siegel (1975) study where they included a subsection labeled design.

Subjects. The subjects subsection should tell the reader not only who the research participants were, but should also tell how many there were, their characteristics (age, sex), and how they were selected. Additionally you should give any other pertinent information regarding the subjects such as how they were assigned to the experimental condition, the number of subjects that were selected for the study but did not complete it and why, and any inducements that may have been given to encourage participation.

Apparatus, materials, measures or instruments. In this subsection you need to describe to the reader what apparatus or materials you used, in sufficient detail to enable the reader to obtain comparable equipment. Additionally, you need to tell the reader why you used the

TABLE 1

Sample Characteristics of the Experimental
and Control Groups

Variable	Experi-mental	Control
Age in months		
M	90.4	86.9
SD	26.85	24.97
Sex		
Male	18	19
Female	12	11
Race		
White	23	23
Black	7	7
Type of operation		
Hernia	13	13
Tonsillectomy	4	5
Urinary-genital tract	13	12
No. mothers staying overnight	16	15

equipment. Commercially marketed equipment should be accompanied by the firm's name and model number or, in the case of a measuring instrument such as an anxiety scale, a reference that will enable the reader to obtain the same scale. Custom-made equipment should be accompanied by a description and, in the case of complex equipment, a diagram or photograph may need to be included.

the Palmar Sweat Index, the Hospital Fears Rating Scale, and the Observer Rating Scale of Anxiety.

The Palmar Sweat Index (Johnson & Dabbs, 1967; Thomson & Sutarman, 1953) is a plastic impression method that permits enumeration of active sweat gland activity of the hand. Since the sweat glands of the hand are primarily affected by emotional factors and not other variables such as temperature, the number of active sweat glands provides a measure of transitory physiological arousal. The Palmar Sweat Index was recorded from the index finger of the child's left hand. Rater reliability for two persons independently scoring the same area of the print, as determined by the Pearson product-moment correlation coefficient was .93.

The second measure of situational anxiety was the Hospital Fears Rating Scale. This is a self-report measure comprised of 8 items from the Medical Fears subscale, factor analyzed from the Fear Survey Schedule for Children (Scherer & Nakamura, 1968). Another 8 items with face validity for assessing hospital fears were also included. The Hospital Fears Rating Scale is compromised of these 16 items and 9 nonrelated filler items. Each subject rated his degree of fear for each item on a fear thermometer ·that ranged from 1 (not afraid at all) to 5 (very afraid). The sum of the ratings

360

on the 16 medical fear items was the subject's score for this measure.

A third measure of situational anxiety was the Observer Rating Scale of Anxiety. This behavioral observation scale was constructed of 29 categories of verbal and skeletal–motor behavior thought to represent behavioral manifestations of anxiety in children. A time sampling procedure was used in which an observer indicated the presence or absence of each response category during three intervals of time in a 9-minute observation period. Examples of items indicative of anxiety include "crying," "trembling hands," "stutters," and "talks about hospital fears, separation from mother, or going home." The frequency of responses observed during the total period of observation was the subject's score on the Observer Rating Scale of Anxiety. Rater reliability was assessed throughout each phase of experimental procedure. Average interrater reliability, which was computed by dividing the number of observer agreements by the total number of categories of behavior that were observed, was 94%.

Procedure

Each subject was asked to report to the hospital 1 hour prior to his scheduled admission time.[2] Upon their arrival, the child and his parents were escorted to a research area of the hospital. The parents and child were separated and taken to adjoining rooms. The parents were questioned to obtain information regarding the child's age and grade, whether he was taking medication, number of previous hospitalizations, whether other siblings had been hospitalized, and whether the mother was planning to remain overnight with the child (the hospital permitted the mother to sleep in the child's room during his stay in the hospital). A consent form was signed by the parents indicating their agreement to have their child participate in a study investigating better methods of preparing children psychologically for hospitalization and surgery.

The mother then completed the Parents' Questionnaire, which asked her to rate 10 statements pertaining to her own anxiety about being a hospital patient, how her child had reacted to past medical procedures, and how she felt her child would respond to the current hospital experience on a 5-point scale. In addition, the mother completed the Behavior Problem Checklist (Peterson, 1961; Peterson, Becker, Shoemaker, Luria, & Hellmer, 1961; Quay & Quay, 1965; Quay & Peterson, Note 1), a 55-item rating scale of behavior prob-

Procedure. In the procedure subsection you are telling the reader exactly how you executed the study from the moment the subject and the experimenter come into contact, until their contact is terminated. Consequently, this subsection represents a step-by-step account of what both you and the subject did during the study. This section should include any instructions and/or stimulus conditions presented to the subjects and the responses that were required of them. In other words, you are to tell the reader exactly what both you and the subject did and how you did it.

---

[2] Michael Ike, Neil Haymes, and Raymond Meyer were responsible for primary data collection. Lawrence Melamed and Nancy Martin assisted in analysis.

lems frequently observed in children. She was instructed to rate the child's behavior during the last 4 weeks. Finally, the mother filled out the Anxiety scale from the Personality Inventory for Children.

The child was taken to a separate room by an experimenter dressed in a white laboratory coat who introduced himself to the child as a doctor. As soon as the child was seated, a second experimenter began observing him with the Observer Rating Scale of Anxiety. The "doctor" placed electrodes on the child's left hand and chest in order to record galvanic skin response and heart rate.[3] The subjects were told that the purpose of the "wires" was to enable the doctor to listen to their heart while they watched a movie. In addition to recording electrophysiological activity, the placement of electrodes provided a sample of behavior with which to measure the subjects' response to an anxiety-evoking situation that closely resembled actual medical procedures encountered by the child in the hospital.

Following the attachment of the electrodes, the doctor left the room to begin the electrophysiological recording. A third experimenter administered the Children's Manifest Anxiety Scale, the Hospital Fears Rating Scale, and the Human Figure Drawing Test. Finally, the Palmar Sweat Index was recorded.

After the measures were completed, the subject was shown the experimental or control film depending on his group assignment. Each film was in the form of an 8-mm cassette that was shown on a Technicolor projector. The experimenter who recorded the behavioral observations left the room prior to the start of the film in order to remain unaware of the treatment condition to which the subject had been assigned. The third experimenter remained in the room with the child during the film.

The experimental film, entitled *Ethan Has an Operation,* depicts a 7-year-old white male who has been hospitalized for a hernia operation.[4] This film, which is 16 minutes in length, consists of 15 scenes showing various events that most children encounter when hospitalized for elective surgery from the time of admission to time of discharge including the child's orientation to the hospital ward and medical personnel such as the surgeon and anesthesiologist; having a blood test and exposure to standard hospital equipment; separation from the mother; and scenes in the operating and recovery

---

[3] These data were not available for presentation in this article.

[4] *Ethan Has an Operation* may be obtained from the Health Sciences Communication Center, Case Western Reserve University, Cleveland, Ohio 44106.

rooms. In addition to explanations of the hospital procedures provided by the medical staff, various scenes are narrated by the child, who describes his feelings and concerns that he had at each stage of the hospital experience. Both the child's behavior and verbal remarks exemplify the behavior of a coping model so that while he exhibits some anxiety and apprehension, he is able to overcome his initial fears and complete each event in a successful and nonanxious manner. Meichenbaum (1971) has shown that film models who are initially anxious and overcome their anxiety (coping models) result in greater reduction in anxiety than models who exhibit no fear (mastery models).

The subjects in the control group were shown a 12-minute film entitled *Living Things are Everywhere.*[5] The control film was similar in interest value to the experimental film in maintaining the children's attention but was unrelated in content to hospitalization. It presents the experiences of a white preadolescent male who is followed on a nature trip in the country.

Immediately following the experimental or control film, the second experimenter returned to the room to observe the subject with the Observer Rating Scale of Anxiety. The Palmar Sweat Index was recorded, and the Hospital Fears Rating Scale was readministered.

Following the postfilm assessment, the child and his parents were escorted to the hospital lobby. The child was formally admitted to the hospital in the usual manner and taken to the surgical ward.

Later in the afternoon, both the experimental and control subjects were given preoperative instruction by the hospital staff, a standard procedure at the pediatric hospital. This instruction involved a nurse who explained to the child, through pictures and demonstration, what would happen to him the day of surgery, including the things he would observe and experience. The child was also visited by the surgeon and/or anesthesiologist who explained to the child and his parents what his operation would involve, what he would see in the operating room, and the method of anesthesia that would be used. A preoperative teaching communication sheet was completed by the nurse in order to provide a record of the kind of information given to the child to insure that all subjects received similar preoperative instructions.

The subject's level of anxiety was again assessed the evening before he was scheduled for surgery and after preoperative instructions had been completed.

---

[5] Appreciation is expressed to *Encyclopaedia Britannica* for use of their film *Living Things are Everywhere* as a control in this study.

Observations of the child with the Observer Rating Scale of Anxiety were made in the child's hospital room while the following took place: first, the child's Palmar Sweat Index was recorded; then Hospital Fears Rating Scale was readministered, a game about hospitalization and surgery called "operation" was played with all subjects. All children were premedicated with Seconal and Atropine. A xylocaine patch was routinely placed on the hand for intravenous induction.

All subjects returned to the hospital for a postoperative physical examination by the surgeon. A follow-up assessment of the child was made at this time. The follow-up session was 20–26 days after the child had been discharged from the hospital. The parents and child were asked to report to the hospital 15 minutes prior to the appointment with the surgeon. After the parents and child were separated, the mother again completed the Anxiety scale from the Personality Inventory for Children and the Behavior Problem Checklist. She was instructed to rate the child's behavior since he left the hospital.

The child was observed with the Observer Rating Scale of Anxiety. Following measurement of the Palmar Sweat Index, the subject was readministered the Children's Manifest Anxiety Scale, the Hospital Fears Rating Scale, and the Human Figure Drawing Test. After all of the measures were completed, the subject was taken to the surgeon's office for his appointment.

Design

A mixed design was employed to evaluate the results of the between-subjects variable and the within-subjects variable. The type of film was the between-subjects variable, with matched groups of children receiving either the hospital-relevant film or an unrelated control film. The within-subjects variable was the time of measurement. Situational measures of anxiety were assessed at four points: prefilm—as the subject was being hooked up to the polygraph; postfilm—immediately after the film viewing was completed; preoperative—the night before surgery (after all preoperative preparation had been concluded a game called operation was played with the child in an attempt to elicit his concern about the impending surgery); postoperative—immediately prior to the surgeon's follow-up examination when the child returned to the hospital 3–4 weeks after discharge. The measures of chronic anxiety and the Behavior Problems Checklist were obtained at the prefilm and postoperative assessments.

The variation in the routine time of preparing the child and the use of premedication immediately prior to surgery made assessment during preoperative medical procedures and the morning of surgery impractical. Also, since the child was discharged prior to full recovery from anesthesia and pain medication, the effect of immediate recovery from the operation was obtained on a global postoperative recovery questionnaire.

RESULTS

The state measures of anxiety consistently reflected differences between the experimental and control groups. Differences between groups were also found on the prehospitalization to posthospitalization parental ratings of the child's behavior. Measures of trait anxiety did not demonstrate a significant effect of the treatment conditions.

Trait Anxiety Measures

There were no significant differences between prefilm and postoperative assessments between the experimental and control groups on the Children's Manifest Anxiety Scale, the Anxiety Scale of the Personality Inventory

PALMAR SWEAT INDEX

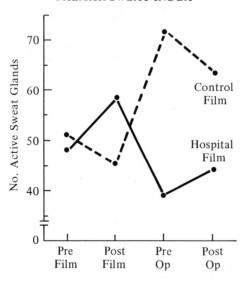

FIGURE 1. Number of active sweat glands for the experimental and control groups across the four measurement periods.

Results. The purpose of the results section of the research report is to tell the reader exactly how you analyzed the data which you collected and what the outcome of this analysis was. Consequently, the results section should tell what statistical tests were used. Significant values of the test should be accompanied by the magnitude of the obtained value of the test, along with the accompanying degrees of freedom, probability level, and direction of the effect, as illustrated in the adjacent article. In reporting and illustrating the direction of a significant effect (nonsignificant effects are not elaborated on for obvious reasons) you need to decide upon the medium that will most clearly and economically serve your purpose. If a main effect consisting of three groups is significant, your best approach is probably to incorporate the mean scores for each of these groups into the text of the report. If the significant effect is a complex interaction, then the best approach is to summarize your data by means of a figure or in a table. If you do use a figure or table (a decision which you must make) be sure to tell the reader, in the text of the report, what data it depicts, and then give a sufficient explanation of the presented data to make sure that the reader interprets it correctly.

In writing the results section there are several things you do not include. Individual data is not included unless a single-subject study is conducted. Also, statistical formulas are not included unless the statistical test for Children, or the Human Figure Drawing Score for anxiety. Because of the wide range of ages, the data were reanalyzed with sex and age taken into account. The children were divided into two age groups defined as younger than 7 years or 7 and older.

The Children's Manifest Anxiety Scale revealed a significant effect of age, $F(1, 52) = 8.39$, $p < .005$, with the younger children having higher scores on the measure. The significant Sex $\times$ Age $\times$ Time interaction, $F(1, 52) = 4.54$, $p < .04$, further revealed that young females reported more anxiety on this measure following hospitalization, whereas older females become slightly less anxious. Males reported slightly less anxiety after the hospital experience for both age groups.

On the Anxiety Scale of the Personality Inventory for Children, the main effect of the film condition was significant, $F(1, 52) = 6.21$, $p < .02$. The mean anxiety rating for the group that viewed the hospital film (5.75) was significantly lower than that of the control group (8.02). The Sex $\times$ Type of Film interaction, $F(1, 52) = 5.08$, $p < .03$, further revealed that females had significantly lower anxiety scores in the experimental (hospital film) than in the control (unrelated film) group. The difference between conditions was not significant for the males. There was no significant Sex $\times$ Film $\times$ Time of Measurement interaction.

There were no significant differences found with the Human Figure Drawing Task even when age and sex were evaluated.

Behavior Problems Checklist and Parent Questionnaire

There was a significant Film $\times$ Time of Measurement interaction, $F(1, 58) = 5.05$, $p < .03$. Subsequent t tests revealed that the children in the control group showed a significant increase in the degree of behavior problems from the prehospital to postoperative periods, $t(29) = 2.23$, $p < .05$. These children showed a mean rating of 10.63 prior

is new, unique, or in some other way not a standard or commonly used statistical test.

to the hospital experience and a mean rating of 12.5 at the postoperative assessment. The experimental subjects did not show any significant increase or decrease in behavior problems across the two assesments. When the data were further evaluated for sex and age, the Film × Time interaction remained significant, $F(1, 52) = 4.4$, $p < .03$. The significant Age × Sex × Film interaction, $F(1, 52) = 9.13$, $p < .004$, revealed that the younger females and older males exhibited the most behavior problems in the experimental group, whereas older females had the highest number of behavior problems in the control condition. The Behavior Problem Checklist score (postoperative) correlated significantly with the Anxiety scale of the Personality Inventory for Children ($r = .446$, $p < .02$). Although there were no group differences, $t(58) = .67$, $p > .20$, of initial statement of parental anxiety, the Parents' questionnaire, a measure of parental concern, correlated significantly with the Behavior Problem Checklist (postoperative $r = .36$, $p < .05$).

Situational "State" Anxiety Measures

There were no initial differences between groups for either the Palmar Sweat Index or the Observer Rating Scale for Anxiety. Repeated measures analysis of variance were used to assess the main effect of type of film and the effect of time of measurement and the interactions between these two variables. Since there were group differences on the initial self-report ratings of anxiety on the Hospital Fears Rating Scale, a covariance analysis was employed with this dependent measure. Neuman-Keuls analyses were performed to reveal differences between group means.

Palmar Sweat Index. Figure 1 illustrates the significant Film × Time of Measurement interaction, $F(3, 174) = 12.72$, $p < .0001$. The groups were significantly different the night before surgery (preoperative, $p < .01$) and at the postoperative examination ($p < .05$). The children who viewed the hospital film (experimental group) showed lower levels of sweat gland activity than those who had been exposed to an unrelated control film. Looking at the within-group differences for this same interaction, a Neuman-Keuls analysis revealed that the children who viewed the hospital film showed a significant increase ($p < .05$) in sympathetic arousal (Palmar Sweat Index) from the prefilm to postfilm assessment. However, the experimental group also showed a significant decrease ($p < .01$) in arousal from postfilm to the preoperative assessment. The significant decrease was maintained from the postfilm to the postoperative assessment ($p < .05$).

The control group (unrelated film) on the other hand, showed significant increases in physiological arousal on this measure from

HOSPITAL FEARS–RATING SCALE

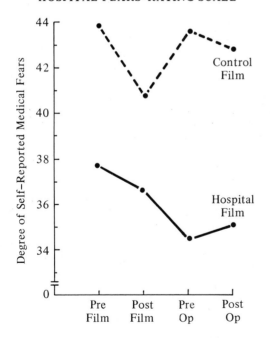

FIGURE 2. Degree of self-reported medical fears for the experimental and control groups across the four measurement periods.

368 prefilm to preoperative ($p < .01$) and from postfilm to preoperative assessment ($p < .01$). The means within the control group were also significant (with increased palmar sweating) when the comparisons between prefilm and postoperative assessment ($p < .05$) and postfilm and postoperative assessment ($p < .01$) were examined. When the analysis was made to investigate age and sex variables, the Film × Time interaction remained significant, $F(3, 156) = 14.48$, $p < .00001$, despite a significant Sex × Age interaction, $F(1, 52) = 5.28$, $p < .02$. Older males exhibited more overall arousal than younger males ($p < .01$), while younger females displayed more arousal than older females ($p < .01$).

Hospital Fears Rating Scale. Figure 2 illustrates the significant Film × Time interaction, $F(2, 115) = 4.74$, $p < .05$, that resulted when a covariance analysis was performed on this scale to statistically control for the initial difference that existed between groups. The control group had a higher fear rating than the experimental group at all assessment times.

OBSERVER RATING SCALE OF ANXIETY

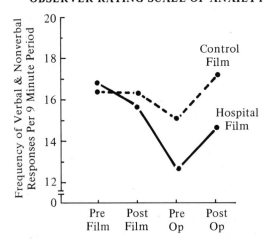

FIGURE 3. Frequency of observer-rated verbal and nonverbal anxiety responses for the experimental and control groups across the four measurement periods.

Statistical significance was achieved at the preoperative ($p < .01$) and postoperative ($p < .01$) measurement across groups. The self-report measure did not yield significant within-group effects across measurement times. There was a significant effect of age, $F(1, 52) = 4.47$, $p < .04$, with the younger children reporting greater fear regardless of film condition. This, however, did not change the significant interaction described above.

Observer Rating Scale of Anxiety. The significant differences in the frequency of observer-rated verbal and nonverbal anxiety responses that resulted between groups across the times of measurement is illustrated by Figure 3, for the Film × Time interaction, $F(3, 174) = 3.33$, $p < .02$. The groups did not differ from each other at prefilm or postfilm assessments. The group that viewed the hospital film exhibited significantly fewer ($p < .05$) anxiety-related behaviors than the control group at both the preoperative and postoperative assessments.

In further evaluating the Film × Time interaction by examining the changes within each group on subsequent measurement trials, it was revealed that the experimental subjects showed a significant reduction in this measure of anxiety from both prefilm ($p < .01$) and postfilm ($p < .01$) to the preoperative measurement. There was also a significant reduction on this scale for the comparison of prefilm to postoperative assessment ($p < .05$). It should be noted that although the prefilm to postoperative assessment showed a reduction, there was a significant increase in anxiety-related responses from preoperative to postoperative assessment ($p < .05$). Both the experimental and control groups showed a significant increase in anxiety-related behavior from preoperative to postoperative assessment ($p < .05$). It is interesting to note, however, that the experimental group evidenced a significant reduction in observed anxiety from the prefilm to postoperative assessment period

370 ($p < .05$), whereas there was no significant reduction in anxiety for the control group. There was no significant effect of age or sex on this dependent measure.

DISCUSSION

The efficacy of preoperative preparation using a film of a child undergoing hospitalization for surgery was demonstrated on all measures of transitory, situational anxiety. The experimental subjects who had viewed the hospital peer-modeling film showed lower sweat gland activity, fewer self-reported medical concerns, and fewer anxiety-related behaviors than the control subjects at both the preoperative and postoperative assessments. Since pretreatment assessment revealed that the experimental and control groups were relatively equivalent on the dependent variables, including group characteristics, any differences between groups can be attributed to the treatment conditions that were provided.

The preoperative assessment that took place the night before surgery, and only after all of the children received the typical preoperative counseling and demonstration procedures, reflected the success of the film in reducing anticipatory and situational anxiety beyond that of the staff's efforts. In fact, there was no significant reduction in anxiety for children receiving hospital-initiated preparation. The maintenance of these group differences at the postoperative examination, 3–4 weeks following discharge, further supports the need for more preparation than is ordinarily received once the child is in the hospital.

The 4-week posthospital examination by the surgeon also provided a test of generalization of the film's effectiveness since it presented the child with a similar anticipatory stressful situation that was not specifically depicted in the hospital film. Group differences were maintained on all measures of situational anxiety.

Discussion. The purpose of the discussion section of the research report is to interpret and evaluate the results obtained giving primary emphasis to the relationships between the results and the hypotheses of the study. In attempting to fulfill this purpose, it is recommended that you begin the discussion with a statement that summarizes the results obtained. Following this summary statement, you should interpret the results and tell the reader what you think they mean. In doing so you should attempt to integrate your research findings with past research and show how your results relate to the results of prior research. Note that this is the only place in the research report where you are given any latitude for stating your own opinion and then you are limited to stating your interpretation of the results and what you think the major shortcomings of the study are. When discussing the shortcomings of the study, you should discuss only the flaws that may have had a significant influence on the results obtained. In like manner, a negative finding should be accepted as such and interpreted as a negative finding rather than attempting to explain it as being due to some methodological flaw, unless, as may occasionally occur, there is a very good and documented reason why a flaw did cause the negative finding.

Furthermore, experimental subjects showed a significant reduction in anxiety-related behaviors as compared with their initial (pre-film) hospital experience. This would support generalization of the film's effectiveness. There was, however, a significant increment in behaviorally rated anxiety in both groups from the preoperative to postoperative assessments and a trend toward a similar increase, although not significant, in self-reported medical fears and physiological arousal, for the experimental group during this same measurement period. These results may reflect the greater potency of the film under the arousal condition that was present during the initial hospitalization. Another interpretation is that the content of the film, which is specific to procedures during hospitalization, may be a major influence in the reduction of anxiety since the film did not show the child what to expect at the follow-up visit with the surgeon. Finally, the time delay between the viewing of the film and the stress condition (postoperative follow-up) may have attenuated the generalization effects that were obtained.

The specific components that made the film effective will be explored in further parametric investigation. Perhaps the film oriented the child to the hospital procedures, therefore making later preparation more meaningful. Whether the use of a peer coping model enhanced the film's effectiveness must be investigated using appropriate control groups. For instance, one may question whether the film merely familiarized the child with the experiences he would most likely encounter. An experiment comparing peer model, adult model, and demonstration–no-model conditions should be undertaken.

Although the use of the film alone was not possible in the present investigation because of the ethical considerations involved in denying a child preoperative preparation, the research is being replicated in a hospital in which staff–patient ratio does not allow for preoperative preparation. Thus the effectiveness and generalizability of this particular film will be evaluated. In addition, the effectiveness of this film with children who have already been hospitalized needs to be investigated. It would seem that children with one or more hospital experiences may differ sufficiently from the subjects employed in this study since one cannot automatically assume that the film will be equally effective with children having a prior history of hospitalization for surgery.

The increase in arousal level, as measured by the Palmar Sweat Index, for the experimental group from prefilm to postfilm lends some support for the contention of Janis (1958) that a moderate amount of arousal may facilitate response to stress in those facing impending surgery. Therefore, another variable of interest would be the time of presentation of the hospital film. In the present investigation, the children seeing the film immediately prior to admission to the hospital showed an initial increase in arousal. However, their scores on this somatic index as well as the behavioral and self-report measures of situational anxiety decreased from the initial level throughout their hospital and posthospital experiences. Similar results are reported by Florell (1971), who found an increase in transitory anxiety in hospitalized patients immediately following treatment (emotional support and information about the hospital routine) and a decrease in anxiety following surgery, as compared with a control group who exhibited higher transitory anxiety scores after surgery. Schachter and Singer (1962) and Bandura and Rosenthal (1966) provided data that are particularly relevant to the present discussion. They found that moderate levels of physiological and emotional arousal increased imitation of a model's behavior by an observer. Taken together, these results suggest that a particular level of arousal may enhance the modeling effect, and in the case of the present investigation, it may further facilitate attention to the instructions and demonstrations provided by the hospital staff the day before surgery.

One shortcoming of the current investigation was the failure to assess the children's degree of anxiety during actual medical procedures, such as the blood test, the surgeon's examination, etc. However, the time at which these procedures took place was quite variable. In addition, the analysis would not clearly show the effectiveness of the film manipulation since the preoperative teaching by the hospital staff took place throughout the day of admission.

The measures of trait anxiety did not demonstrate a significant effect of the film manipulation. Thes findings are not surprising in view of the definition of trait anxiety as a stable consistent characteristic of the individual. These results are consistent with Kaplan and Hafner (1959), who found no changes on subjects' scores on the Children's Manifest Anxiety Scale during their hospitalization for surgery. Spielberger, Auerbach, Wadsworth, Dunn, and Taulbee (1973) and Auerbach (1973), using the State-Trait Anxiety Inventory, provided further data indicating the stability of trait measures of anxiety (A-Trait) wih hospitalized surgical patients. A-State scores, however, were found to change from presurgery to postsurgery assessments and again during the posthospitalization period.

When the variance due to age and sex was examined in additional analyses of variances, some interesting facts were revealed. Younger children reported higher anxiety on the measure of children's manifest anxiety. Younger females in particular appeared to be more vulnerable to the hospital experience since they reported increased anxiety on this measure at the postoperative examination. When sex is also significant as a factor contributing to the variance on the Anxiety scale of the Personality Inventory for Children, it was found that lower scores for females on

374 anxiety did occur in the experimental group. Therefore, viewing a male model did not hinder the effectiveness of this film manipulation.

It is interesting that the parents' report of behavior problems occurring 4 weeks following discharge does correspond with how the children reacted to stress during their hospitalization. The children in the control group had an increase in behavior problems during the 3–4 week posthospitalization period before they returned to the hospital for their postoperative examination by the surgeon. They also showed higher physiological arousal, greater concern about medical fears, and increased anxiety-related behaviors the night prior to surgery and at the follow-up examination. This again supports the contention that in order to avoid posthospital traumatization as observed in psychological disturbances, extensive preoperative preparation is essential.

The use of a multidimensional approach to the measurement of the anxiety proved valuable in understanding the relationships and changes between subjective (self-report), physiological, and behavioral subsystems of human fear response. At least for this sample of children between the ages of 4 and 12, the self-report measure of hospital fears was least sensitive to changes in response at various times during and after hospitalization.

The implications of the research for the measurement and alteration of the stress reaction of normal children to hospitalization and surgery are numerous. The film *Ethan Has an Operation,* which demonstrates a child going through the experiences of being hospitalized for an operation, was more effective in alleviating anxiety than simple verbal, pictorial, or actual demonstration of hospital procedures by the concerned staff. The need for a multidimensional approach to the evaluation of children's responses to stress is supported in view of the differences reflected by trait and state measures of anxiety, as well as between the measures of situational anxiety.

REFERENCE NOTE

1. Quay, H. C., and Peterson, D. R. *Manual for the Behavior Problem Checklist.* Unpublished manuscript, University of Illinois, 1967.

REFERENCES

Auerbach, S. M. Trait-state anxiety and adjustment to surgery. *Journal of Consulting and Clinical Psychology,* 1973, *40,* 264–271.

Bandura, A., Grusec, J. E., & Menlove, F. L. Vicarious extinction of avoidance behaviors. *Journal of Personality and Social Psychology,* 1967, *5,* 16–23.

Bandura, A., & Menlove, F. L. Factors determining vicarious extinction of avoidance behavior through symbolic modeling. *Journal of Personality and Social Psychology,* 1968, *8,* 99–108.

Bandura, A., & Rosenthal, T. L. Vicarious classical conditioning as a function of arousal level. *Journal of Personality and Social Psychology,* 1966, *3,* 54–62.

Cassell, S. Effects of brief puppet therapy upon the emotional responses of children undergoing cardiac catheterization. *Journal of Consulting Psychology,* 1965, *29,* 1–8.

Castaneda, A., McCandless, B. R., & Palermo, D. S. The children's form of the Manifest Anxiety Scale. *Child Development,* 1956, *27,* 317–326.

Cattell, R. B., & Scheier, I. H. *The meaning and measurement of neutroticism and anxiety.* New York: Ronald Press, 1961.

Chapman, A. H., Loeb, D. G., & Gibbons, M. J. Psychiatric aspects of hospitalization of children. *Archives of Pediatrics,* 1956, *73,* 77–88.

Dimock, H. G. *The child in hospital: A study of his emotional and social well-being.* Philadelphia: Davis, 1960.

Dumas, R. G. Psychological preparation for surgery. *American Journal of Nursing,* 1963, *63,* 52–55.

Florell, J. Crisis intervention in orthopedic surgery. (Doctoral dissertation, Northwestern University, 1971). *Dissertation Abstracts International,* 1971, *32,* 3633B. (University Microfilms No. 71-30799, 204)

Gellert, E. Reducing the emotional stress of hospitalization for children. *American Journal of Occupational Therapy,* 1958, *12,* 125–129.

Giller, D. W. Some psychological factors in recovery from surgery. *Hospital Topics,* 1963, *41,* 83–85.

Heller, J. A. *The hospitalized child and his family.* Baltimore: Johns Hopkins Press, 1967.

Impallaria, C. The contribution of social group work: The hospitalized child. *American Journal of Orthopsychiatry,* 1955, *55,* 293–318.

References. The purpose of the reference section, as you might expect, is to provide an accurate and complete list of all the references cited in the text of the report. In listing these references a distinction is made between a reference note and a reference. Reference notes consist of cited material that is not readily available, such as unpublished reports or papers presented at meetings or conventions. These notes appear together and are followed by the references, as illustrated in the adjacent article.

376

Jackson, K., Winkley, R., Faust, O. A., & Cermack, E. The problem of emotional trauma in the hospital treatment of children. *Journal of the American Medical Association,* 1952, *149,* 1536–1538.

Janis, I. L. *Psychological stress.* New York: Wiley, 1958.

Jessner, L., Blom, G. E., & Waldfogel, S. Emotional implications of tonsillectomy and adenoidectomy in children. In R. S. Eisslen (Ed.), *The psychoanalytic study of the child.* New York: International Universities Press, 1952.

Johnson, R., & Dabbs, J. M. Enumeration of active sweat glands: A simple physiological indicator of psychological changes. *Nursing Research,* 1967, *16,* 273–276.

Johnson, R., & Machen, J. B. Behavior modification techniques and maternal anxiety. *Journal of Dentistry for Children,* 1973, *40,* 272–276.

Kaplan, A. M., & Hagner, A. J. Manifest anxiety in hospitalized children. *Journal of Clinical Psychology,* 1959, *15,* 301–302.

Klinedinst, J. K. *Relationship between Minnesota Multiphasic Personality Inventory and Personality Inventory for Children data from mothers of disturbed children.* (Doctoral dissertation, University of Minnesota, 1971). *Dissertation Abstracts International,* 1971, *32,* 4860B. (University Microfilms No. 72-05545, 116)

Koppitz, E. M. *Psychological evaluation of children's human figure drawings.* New York: Grune & Stratton, 1968.

Lang, P. J. Fear reduction and fear behavior: Problems in treating a construct. In J. M. Shlien (Ed.), *Research in psychotherapy* (Vol. 3). 1968.

Lende, E. W. *The effect of preparation on children's response to tonsillectomy and adenoidectomy surgery.* (Doctoral dissertation, University of Cincinnati, 1971) *Dissertation Abstracts International,* 1971, *32,* 3642B. (University Microfilms No. 72-01440, 95)

Meichenbaum, D. Examination of model characteristics in reducing avoidance behavior. *Journal of Personality and Social Psychology,* 1971, *17,* 298–307.

Melamed, B. G., Hawes, R. R., Heiby, E., Glick, J. The use of filmed modeling to reduce uncooperative behavior of children during dental treatment. *Journal of Dental Research,* 1975, in press.

Melamed, B. G., Weinstein, D. Hawes, R., & Katin-Borland, M. Reduction of fear-related dental management problems using filmed modeling. *Journal of the American Dental Association,* 1975, *90,* 822–826.

Mellish, R. W. Preparation of a child for hospitalization and surgery. *Pediatric Clinics of North America,* 1969, *16,* 543–553.

Peterson, D. R., Behavior problems of middle childhood. *Journal of Consulting Psychology,* 1961, *25,* 205–209.

Peterson, D. R., Becker, W. C., Shoemaker, D. J., Luria, Z., & Hellmer, L. A. Child behavior problems and parental attitudes. *Child Development,* 1961, *32,* 151–162.

Prugh, D. G., Staub, E., Sands, H. H., Kirschbaum, R. M. & Lenihan, E. A. A study of the emotional reactions of children and families to hospitalization and illness. *American Journal of Orthopsyciatry,* 1953, *23,* 70–106.

Quay, H. C.. & Quay, L. C. Behavior problems in early adolescence. *Child Development,* 1965, *36,* 215–220.

Ritter, B. The group desensitization of children's snake phobias using vicarious and contact desensitization procedures. *Behaviour Research and Therapy,* 1968, *6,* 1–6.

Schachter, S., & Singer, J. E. Cognitive, social, and physiological determinants of emotional state. *Psychological Review,* 1962, *69,* 379–399.

Schaffer, H. R., & Callender, W. H. Psychological effects of hospitalization in infancy. *Pediatrics,* 1959, *24,* 528–539.

Scherer, M. W., & Nakamura, C. Y. A fear survey schedule for children (FSS-FC): A factor analytic comparison with manifest anxiety (CMAS). *Behaviour Research and Therapy,* 1968, 173–182.

Skipper, J., & Leonard, R. Children, stress, and hospitalization: A field experiment. *Journal of Health and Social Behavior,* 1968, *9,* 275–287.

Spielberger, C. D. Theory and research on anxiety. In C. D. Spielberger (Ed.), *Anxiety and behavior.* New York: Academic Press, 1966.

Spielberger, C. D., Auerbach, S. M., Wadsworth, A. P., Dunn, T. M., & Taulbee, E. S. Emotional reactions to surgery. *Journal of Consulting and Clinical Psychology,* 1973, *40,* 33–38.

Thomson, M. L., & Sutarman. The identification and enumeration of active sweat glands in man from plastic impressions of the skin. *Transactions of the Royal Society of Tropical Medicine and Hygiene,* 1953, *47,* 412–417.

Vaughan, G. F. Children in hospital. *Lancet,* 1957, *272,* 1117–1120.

Vernon, D. T. A., & Bailey, W. C. The use of motion pictures in the psychological preparation of children for induction of anesthesia. *Anesthesiology,* 1974, *40,* 68–72.

Vernon, D. T. A., Foley, J. M., Sipowicz, R. R., & Schulman, J. L. *The psychological responses of*

378

children to hospitalization and illness. Springfield, Ill.: Charles C Thomas, 1965.

Wirt, R. D., & Broen, W. E. *Booklet for the Personality Inventory for Children.* Minneapolis: Authors, 1958.

White, W., Akers, J., Green, J., & Yates, D. Use of imitation in the treatment of dental phobias in early childhood: A preliminary report. *Journal of Dentistry for Children,* 1974, *26,* 106.

Preparation of the Research Report

In the preceding section you saw a sample published article and the suggested content for each of the various sections of this article. However, you should realize that when you prepare a research report for submission to a journal for possible publication, the arrangement of the various components of the research report differ from that of the published research article. The primary difference is that various parts of the manuscript must appear on separate pages. The arrangement of the pages in the order in which they are to appear in the prepared manuscript and a brief explanation follows (see also Figures 14.1 and 14.2).

COVER PAGE.   The cover page appears first on a separate page. It consists of the title of the article, the author(s) name(s), and author(s) affiliation on the top portion of the page. A running head consisting of a shortened version of the title appears on the bottom half of the page and should consist of a maximum of 60 total spaces.

ABSTRACT.   The abstract is typed on the second page and is labeled as an abstract.

TEXT.   The text begins on the third page of the research report. The title of the report should be at the top of this page with the introduction following immediately thereafter and ending with the discussion section.

REFERENCE NOTES.   All reference notes follow the text and are to be typed on a separate page labeled *Reference Notes.* The first typed line of each note should be numbered and flush with the left margin and each succeeding line should be indented three spaces.

REFERENCES.   All references appear next on a separate page labeled *References.* References should be typed in the same manner as reference notes.

FOOTNOTES.   Footnotes appear on a separate page labeled *Foot-*
notes. The footnote number appears slightly above the line and is
followed by the footnote. The first line of each footnote is indented like
a paragraph. Footnotes appear in the same order in which they occur in
the text. The first footnote always represents any acknowledgement
and the author identification, and is not numbered.

TABLES.   Each table is to be typed on a separate page and ordered in
the manner in which it appears in the text.

FIGURE CAPTIONS.   Figure captions are *not* to be placed on the
figures but are to be typed on a separate page labeled *Figure Captions.*
Each figure caption should be indented and begin with the word *Figure*
followed by a period, the figure number, and the caption. Only the first
letter of the first word of the caption is capitalized.

FIGURES.   Each figure is to be presented on a separate page. On the
back of each page lightly write the title of the article, the number of
that figure, and indicate the top of the figure.

   The above represents the order of the pages of the final research
report. However, in preparing a report there are a number of other
regulations that need to be followed.

TYPING.   In typing the manuscript, double-space all material. The
rule is to set the typewriter on double-spacing and leave it there.

HEADINGS.   Headings should be rank ordered as follows: *Centered*
Main Heading, Flush Side Heading, Indented Paragraph Heading.
Main headings are underlined and centered, and the initial letters of
the key words are capitalized. Side headings are also underlined, and
the initial letters of the key words are capitalized, but the headings are
typed flush to the left margin. A paragraph heading is indented and
underlined but has only the initial letter of the first word capitalized.

ABBREVIATION.   Abbreviations are to be used sparingly. Generally speaking, use only those abbreviations that are conventional and
should be familiar to the reader, such as IQ, or abbreviate only when it
is necessary to save space and avoid cumbersome repetition. In all
cases, abbreviate metric units.

PHYSICAL MEASUREMENTS.   All physical measurements are to
be stated in metric units. If a measurement is expressed in nonmetric
units, it must be accompanied, in parentheses, by its metric equivalent.

Figure 14.1. Sample opening pages of a research report.

Figure 14.2. Sample final pages of a research report.

382   PRESENTATION OF STATISTICAL RESULTS.   When presenting the results of statistical tests in the text, give the name of the statistical test, followed by its degree of freedom, value, and probability level as follows:

$$t\ (36) = 4.52, p < .01$$
$$F\ (3, 52) = 17.36, p < .01$$

NUMBERS.   When expressing numbers in the text, the general rule is to use words to express any number that begins a sentence as well as any number below 10. Use figures to express all other numbers. There are several exceptions to this rule and the *APA Publication Manual* should be consulted for these exceptions. A second rule to follow in stating numbers is to use arabic and not roman numerals.

TABLES AND FIGURES.   Tables and figures are used only when they can convey and summarize the data more economically and clearly than can a lengthy discussion. The sample article presented above illustrates both a table and a figure, and these illustrations can be used as a model in preparing your research report. However, if you are attempting to prepare the report to submit it for possible publication, you should consult the *APA Publication Manual*, which explains in depth the numerous points to consider in preparing each of these. In preparing the text, you do not insert the table or figure where you want it. Instead, you indicate its approximate position by a clear break in the text with instructions clearly indicated as follows:

Insert Table 1 about here

---

or

Insert Figure 1 about here

REFERENCE CITATIONS.   In the text of the research report, particularly in the introduction section, you must reference other works you cite. The APA format is to use the author-date citation method, which involves inserting the author's surname and the publication date at the appropriate point as follows:

Doe (1975) investigated the. . . .
or
It has been demonstrated (Doe, 1975). . . .

With this information the reader could turn to the reference list and locate the complete information regarding the citation. Multiple citations involving the same author are arranged in chronological order:

Doe (1970, 1971, 1972, 1973)

and multiple citations involving different authors are arranged alphabetically as follows:

Several studies (Doe, 1970; Kelley, 1965; Mills, 1975) have revealed. . . .

Citations involving reference notes should include the surname of the author followed by the word "note" and the number of the note rather than the date:

Doe (Note 1)
or
(Doe, Note 1)
or
Doe (Note 1, Note 2)
or
(Doe, Note 1; Wilson, Note 4)

REFERENCE NOTES AND REFERENCE LISTS.   All citations in the text of the research report must be cited in the reference list or reference notes accurately and completely so that it is possible to identify the source of the citation. All references are to appear in alphabetical order. Rather than elaborate on the style of their presentation, I refer you to the reference list and reference note in the sample article. The reference list gives many examples that can be modeled with little difficulty. However, reference notes are more difficult due to the variation in the material. You should attempt to give enough information to be able to identify the source of the citation. This means that you should give the author, title, date, and any other identifying information.

FOOTNOTES.   There is one footnote that is a standard part of every article and consequently it is not numbered. Footnotes of acknowledgement and author identification are standard and should always appear as the *first* footnote. All other footnotes in the text be numbered consecutively with arabic superscript throughout the text. When typing footnotes, indent as if typing a paragraph and type them in the order

384   in which they appear in the text, with the superscript number corresponding to their superscript number in the text.

PAGE NUMBERING.   The pages of the total research report are to be numbered, using arabic numerals, in the upper right hand corner of the page beginning with the abstract page and continuing through the figure caption page (if figures exist in the report).

PAGE IDENTIFICATION.   In order to insure that the pages of the manuscript are not misplaced during the editorial process the first two or three words from the title are typed in the upper right hand corner of each page beginning with the abstract and continuing through the figure caption page.

At this point I have presented the basic format and many of the regulations to be followed in writing a research report that would conform to the APA format. In an attempt to integrate and illustrate some of these stylistic components, you are referred to Figures 14.1 and 14.2, which will illustrate the use of these basic components of a sample paper.

Writing Style

Up to this point I have given you the fundamental stylistic requirements for writing a research report that would correspond to the *APA Publication Manual.* However, you must still write the report, and many people have difficulty in communicating by means of the written word. Clear, concise writing is something that must be acquired by everyone. Unfortunately, many individuals conducting research have not yet mastered this skill; this becomes painfully apparent when they attempt to write the research report. Teaching the art of writing is beyond the scope of this text. However, for the student who has difficulty in writing, I recommend a short but excellent book by W. Strunk, Jr., and E. B. White, *The Elements of Style,* 2nd ed. (New York: Macmillan, 1972). This book is a classic and has the virtue of being a short book that offers clear, concise advice on achieving good writing style.

In conclusion, it is suggested that you read the very humorous remarks that H. F. Harlow made in the article, "Fundamental Principles for Preparing Psychology Journal Articles," *Journal of Comparative and Physiological Psychology,* 1976, 55, 893–896, regarding the content and style of writing the research report.

Bibliography

Abelson, R. P., and Miller, J. C. Negative persuasion via personal insult. *Journal of Experimental Social Psychology,* 1967, *3,* 321–333.

Adair, J. G. *The human subject.* Boston: Little, Brown, 1973.

Adair, J. G., and Schachter, B. S. To cooperate or to look good?: The subjects' and experimenters' perceptions of each others' intentions. *Journal of Experimental Social Psychology,* 1972, *8,* 74–85.

Agras, S., Leitenberg, H., Barlow, D. H., and Thompson, L. E. Instructions and reinforcement in the modification of neurotic behavior. *American Journal of Psychiatry,* 1969, *125,* 1435–1439.

Allen, K. E., Hart, B., Buell, J. S., Harris, F. R., and Wolf, M. M. Effects of social reinforcement on isolate behavior of a nursery school child. *Child Development,* 1964, *35,* 511–518.

Altemeyer, R. A. Subject pool pollution and the postexperimental interview. *Journal of Experimental Research in Personality,* 1971, *5,* 79–84.

Alumbaugh, R. V. Another "Malleus Maleficarum." *American Psychologist,* 1972, *27,* 897–899.

American Psychological Association, ad hoc Committee on Ethical Standards in Psychological Research. *Ethical principles in the conduct of research with human participants.* Washington, D.C.: American Psychological Association, Inc., 1973.

Anastasi, A. *Psychological testing* (3rd ed.). New York: Macmillan, 1968.

Anderson, B. F. *The psychology experiment: An introduction to the scientific method.* Belmont, Calif.: Brooks/Cole, 1966.

Argyris, C. Some unintended effects of rigorous research. *Psychological Bulletin,* 1968, *70,* 185–197.

Aronson, E. The effect of effort on the attractiveness of rewarded and unrewarded stimuli. *Journal of Abnormal and Social Psychology,* 1961, *63,* 375–380.

Aronson, E. Avoidance of inter-subject communication. *Psychological Reports,* 1966, *19,* 238.

Aronson, E., and Carlsmith, J. M. Performance expectancy as a determinant of actual performance. *Journal of Abnormal and Social Psychology,* 1963, *66,* 584–588.

Aronson, E., and Carlsmith, J. M. Experimentation in social psychology. In Lindzey, G., and Aronson, E. (Eds.) *The handbook of social psychology.* 2nd ed. Reading, Mass.: Addison-Wesley, 1968.

386   Aronson, E., and Cope, V. My enemy's enemy is my friend. *Journal of Personality and Social Psychology,* 1968, *8,* 8–12.

Aronson, E., and Linder, D. Gain and loss of esteem as determinants of interpersonal attractiveness. *Journal of Experimental Social Psychology,* 1965, *1,* 156–171.

Aronson, E., and Mills, J. The effect of severity of initiation on liking for a group. *Journal of Abnormal and Social Psychology,* 1959, *59,* 177–181.

Asch, S. E. Studies of independence and conformity: A minority of one against a unanimous majority. *Psychological Monographs,* 1956, *70,* No. 9 (Whole No. 416).

Ayllon, T. Intensive treatment of psychotic behavior by stimulus satiation and food reinforcement. *Behavioral Research Therapy.* 1963, *1,* 53–61.

Baer, D. M., Wolf, M. M., and Risley, T. R. Some current dimensions of applied behavior analysis. *Journal of Applied Behavior Analysis,* 1968, *1,* 91–97.

Bandura, A. *Principles of behavior modification.* New York: Holt, Rinehart and Winston, Inc., 1969.

Bandura, A., Ross, D., and Ross, S. A. Transmission of aggression through imitation of aggressive models. *The Journal of Abnormal and Social Psychology,* 1961, *63,* 575–582.

Bannister, D. Psychology as an exercise in paradox. *Bulletin of British Psychological Society,* 1966, *19,* 21–26.

Barber, T. X., *Pitfalls in human research: ten pivotal points.* New York: Pergamon Press, 1976.

Barber, T. X., Calverley, D. S., Forgione, A., McPeake, S. D., Chaves, J. F., and Brown, B. Five attempts to replicate the experimenter bias effect. *Journal of Consulting and Clinical Psychology,* 1969, *33,* 1–6.

Barber, T. X., and Silver, M. J. Fact, fiction, and the experimenter bias effect. *Psychological Bulletin Monograph,* 1968, *70,* 1–29. (a)

Barber, T. X., and Silver, M. J. Pitfalls in data analysis and interpretation: A reply to Rosenthal. *Psychological Bulletin Monograph,* 1968, *70,* 48–62. (b)

Barlow, D. H., and Hersen, M. Single-case experimental designs: Uses in applied clinical research. *Archives of General Psychiatry,* 1973, *29,* 319–325.

Baron, R. A. Threatened retaliation from the victim as an inhibitor of physical aggression. *Journal of Research in Personality,* 1973, *7,* 103–115.

Baron, R. A. Effects of victim's pain cues, victim's race, and level of prior instigation upon physical aggression. Unpublished manuscript, Purdue University, 1976.

Baumrind, D. Some thoughts on ethics of research: After reading Milgram's "Behavioral study of obedience." *American Psychologist,* 1964, *19,* 421–431.

Baumrind, D. Principles of ethical conduct in the treatment of subjects: Reaction to the draft report of the committee on ethical standards in psychological research. *American Psychologist,* 1971, *26,* 887–896.

Baumrind, D. Reactions to the May 1972 draft report of the ad hoc committee on ethical standards in Psychological Research. *American Psychologist,* 1972, *27,* 1083–1086.

Beach, F. A. The snark was a boojum. *American Psychologist,* 1950, *5,* 115–124.

Beach, F. A. Experimental investigations of species specific behavior. *American Psychologist,* 1960, *15,* 1–8.

Beckman, L., and Bishop, B. R. Deception in psychological research: A reply to Seeman. *American Psychologist,* 1970, *25,* 878–880.

Beecher, H. K. Pain: One mystery solved. *Science,* 1966, *151,* 840–841.

Bem, D. J. *Beliefs, attitudes, and human affairs.* Belmont, Calif.: Brooks/Cole, 1970.

Benjamin, L. S. A special latin square for the use of each subject "as his own control." *Psychometrika,* 1965, *30,* 499–513.

Bergin, A. E. Some implications of psychotherapy research for therapeutic practice. *Journal of Abnormal Psychology,* 1966, *71,* 235–246.

Bergin, A. E., and Strupp, H. H. New directions in psychotherapy research. *Journal of Abnormal Psychology,* 1970, *76,* 13–26.

Bergin, A. E., and Strupp, H. H. *Changing frontiers in the science of psychotherapy.* New York: Aldine-Atherton, 1972.

Berman, J. The volunteer in parole program: an evaluation. Lincoln: University of Nebraska, 1973. Cited in *Evaluation Studies: Annual Review,* edited by T. D. Cook, M. L. Del Rosario, K. M. Hennigan, M. M. Mark, and W. M. K. Trochim. Beverly Hills: Sage, 1978.

Bernstein, I., and Freeman, H. E. *Academic and entrepreneural research: Consequences of diversity in federal evaluation studies.* New York: Russell Sage, 1975.

Berscheid, E., Baron, R. S., Dermer, M., and Libman, M. Anticipating informed consent: An empirical approach. *American Psychologist,* 1973, *28,* 913–925.

Bijou, S. W., Peterson, R. F., Harris, F. R., Allen, K. E., and Johnston, M. S. Methodology for experimental studies of young children in natural settings. *Psychological Record,* 1969, *19,* 177–210.

Billewicz, W. Z. The efficiency of matched samples: an empirical investigation. *Biometrics,* 1965, *21,* 623–644.

Blanchard, E. B., and Young, L. D. Self-control of cardiac functioning: A promise as yet unfulfilled. *Psychological Bulletin,* 1973, *79,* 145–163.

Blumenthal, M., and Ross, H. L. Two experimental studies of traffic laws. Department of Transportation reports HS-800 825 (Vol. 1) and HS-800 826 (Vol. 2). Washington, D.C., 1973.

Boice, R. Domestication. *Psychological Bulletin,* 1973, *80,* 215–230.

Bolger, H. The case study method. In *Handbook of Clinical Psychology,* edited by B. B. Wolman, p. 28–39. New York: McGraw-Hill, 1965.

Boring, E. G. The nature and history of experimental control. *American Journal of Psychology,* 1954, *67,* 573–589.

388   Boruch, R. F. On common contentions about randomized field experiments. In *Evaluation studies review annual,* edited by G. Glass. Beverly Hills: Sage, 1976.

Box, G. E. P., and Jenkins, G. M. *Time-series analysis: Forecasting and Control.* San Francisco: Holden-Day, 1970.

Box, G. E. P., and Tiao, G. L. A change in level of a non-stationary time series. *Biometrics,* 1965, *52,* 181–192.

Bracht, G. H., and Glass, G. V. The external validity of experiments. *American Educational Research Journal,* 1968, *5,* 437–474.

Bradley, A. W. Self-serving bias in the attribution process: A reexamination of the fact or fiction question. *Journal of Personality and Social Psychology,* 1978, *36,* 56–71.

Brady, J. V. Ulcers in "executive monkeys." *Scientific American,* 1958, *199,* 95–100.

Brehm, J. W. Attitudinal consequences of commitment to unpleasant behavior. *Journal of Abnormal and Social Psychology,* 1960, *60,* 379–383.

Bridgman, P. W. *The logic of modern physics.* New York: Macmillan, 1927.

Brim, O. G., and Hoff, D. B. Individual and situational differences in desire for certainty. *Journal of Abnormal and Social Psychology,* 1957, *54,* 225–229.

Broden, M., Bruce, M., Mitchell, M., Carter, V., and Hall, R. V. Effects of teacher attention on attending behavior of two boys at adjacent desks. *Journal of Applied Behavior Analysis,* 1970, *3,* 199–203.

Brown, C. W., and Ghiselli, E. E. *Scientific method in psychology.* New York: McGraw-Hill, 1955.

Brown, R., Cayden, C. B., and Bellugi-Klima, U. The child grammar from I to III. In *Minnesota symposia on child psychology,* edited by J. P. Hill. Minneapolis: The University of Minnesota Press, 1969, *2,* 28–73.

Brown, W. F., Wehe, N. O., Zunker, V. G., and Haslam, W. L. Effectiveness of student-to-student counseling on the academic adjustment of potential dropouts. *Journal of Educational Psychology,* 1971, *62,* 285–289.

Brownell, W. A. The evaluation of learning under dissimilar systems of instruction. In *Introduction to research and evaluation,* edited by J. D. Finn. Buffalo: State University of New York at Buffalo, 1966.

Browning, R. M., and Stover, D. O. *Behavior modification in child treatment.* Chicago: Aldine-Atherton, 1971.

Bryk, A. S., and Weisberg, H. I. Use of the nonequivalent control group design when subjects are growing. *Psychological Bulletin,* 1977, *84,* 950–962.

Calder, R. *Science makes sense.* London: George Allen and Unwin Ltd., 1955.

Campbell, D. Factors relative to the validity of experiments in social settings. *Psychological Bulletin,* 1957, *54,* 297–312.

Campbell, D. T. Quasi-experimental design. In *International Encyclopedia of the Social Sciences,* 5, edited by D. L. Gills. New York: Macmillan and Free Press, 1968.

Campbell, D. T. Prospective: Artifact and control. In *Artifact in behavioral*

research, edited by R. Rosenthal and R. L. Rosnow. New York: Academic **389**
Press, 1969.

Campbell, D. T. Reforms as experiments. *The American Psychologist,* 1969, *24,* 409–429.

Campbell, D. T., and Boruch, R. F. Making the case for randomized assignments to treatments by considering the alternatives: Six ways in which quasi-experimental evaluations in compensatory education tend to underestimate effects. In *Evaluation and Experiment: Some critical issues in assessing social programs,* edited by C. A. Bennett and A. A. Lumsdaine. New York: Academic Press, 1975.

Campbell, D. T., and Erlebacher, A. How regression artifacts in quasi-experimental evaluations can mistakenly make compensatory education look harmful. In *Compensatory education: a national debate,* Vol. 3, *Disadvantaged Child,* edited by J. Hellmuth. New York: Brunner, Mazel, 1970.

Campbell, D. T., and Ross, H. L. The Connecticut crackdown on speeding: Time series data in quasi-experimental analysis. *Law and Society Review,* 1968, *3* (1), 33–53.

Campbell, D. T., and Stanley, J. C. *Experimental and quasi-experimental designs for research.* Chicago: Rand McNally, 1963.

Caporaso, J. A. Quasi-experimental approaches to social science. In *Quasi-experimental approaches,* edited by J. A. Caporaso and L. L. Ross, Jr. Evanston, Ill.: Northwestern University Press, 1973.

Caporaso, J. A. *The structure and function of European integration.* Pacific Palisades, Calif.: Goodyear Publishing Co., 1974.

Carlsmith, J. M., Collins, B. E., and Helmreich, R. L. Studies in forced compliance I: The effect of pressure for compliance on attitude change produced by face-to-face role playing and anonymous essay writing. *Journal of Personality and Social Psychology,* 1966, *4,* 1–3.

Carlson, R. Where is the person in personality research? *Psychological Bulletin,* 1971, *75,* 203–219.

Caro, F. G., ed. *Readings in evaluation research.* New York: Russell Sage, 1971.

Chapin, F. S. *Experimental designs in sociological research.* rev. ed. New York: Harper, 1955.

Chassan, J. B. *Research designs in clinical psychology and psychiatry.* New York: Appleton-Century-Crofts, 1967.

Christensen, L. Intrarater reliability. *The Southern Journal of Educational Research,* 1968, *2,* 175–182.

Christensen, L. Generality of personality assessment. *Journal of Consulting and Clinical Psychology,* 1973, *42,* 59–64.

Christensen, L. Strategies of perceiving others. Paper presented at Southwestern Psychological Association, El Paso, 1974.

Christensen, L. The negative subject: Myth, reality or a prior experimental experience effect. *Journal of Personality and Social Psychology,* 1977, *35,* 392–400.

390

Christensen, L. Evaluation apprehension; A viable concept. Submitted for publication, 1979.

Christensen, L. Positive self-presentation: A parsimonious explanation of subject bias. Submitted for publication, 1979.

Christensen, L., and Dickinson, R. What influences the subject's motive to look good? Paper read at the American Psychological Association, Chicago, September, 1975.

Christensen, L., and Wallace, L. Perceptual accuracy as a variable in marital adjustment. *Journal of Sex and Marital Therapy*, 1976, *2*, 130–136.

Christie, R. Some implications of research trends in social psychology. In *Perspectives in social psychology*, edited by O. Klineberg and R. Christie. New York: Holt, 1965.

Church, R. M. Systematic effect of random errors in the yoked control design. *Psychological Bulletin*, 1964, *62*, 122–131.

Cochran, W. G., and Cox, G. M. *Experimental designs.* New York: Wiley, 1957.

Conner, R. F. Selecting a control group: An analysis of the randomization process in twelve social reform programs. in *Evaluation Studies Annual Review*, edited by T. D. Cook, M. L. Del Rosario, K. M. Hennigan, M. M. Mark, and W. M. K. Trochim. Beverly Hills: Sage, 1978.

Conrad, H. S., and Jones, H. E. A second study of familial resemblances in intelligence. *39th Yearbook of the National Society for the Study of Education.* Chicago: University of Chicago Press, 1940 (II), 97–141.

Cook, T. D., Bean, J. R., Calder, B. J., Frey, R., Krovetz, M. L., and Reisman, S. R. Demand characteristics and three conceptions of the frequently deceived subject. *Journal of Personality and Social Psychology*, 1970, *14*, 185–194.

Cook, T. D., and Campbell, D. T. Experiments in field settings. In *Handbook of industrial and organizational research*, edited by M. D. Dunnette. Chicago: Rand McNally, 1975.

Cook, T. D., Gruder, C. L., Hennigan, K. M., and Flay, B. R. The history of the sleeper effect: Some logical pitfalls in accepting the null hypothesis. *Psychological Bulletin*, 1979, *86*, 662–679.

Cowles, M. F. N = 35: A rule of thumb for psychological researchers. *Perceptual and Motor Skills*, 1974, *38*, 1135-1138.

Cox, D. E., and Sipprelle, C. N. Coercion in participation as a research subject. *American Psychologist*, 1971, *26*, 726–728.

Cox, D. R. *Planning of experiments.* New York: Wiley, 1958.

Crano, W. D., Kenny, D. A., and Campbell, D. T. Does intelligence cause achievement?: A cross-lagged panel analysis. *Journal of Educational Psychology*, 1972, *53*, 258–275.

Cronbach, L. The two disciplines of scientific psychology. *American Psychologist*, 1957, *12*, 671–684.

Cronbach, L. Beyond two disciplines of scientific psychology. *American Psychologist*, 1975, *30*, 116–127.

Cronbach, L., and Furby, L. "How should we measure change"—or should we? *Psychological Bulletin*, 1970, 74, 68–80.

Dalkey, N. C. *The Delphi method: An experimental study of group opinion.* Santa Monica, Calif.: Rand Corporation, 1969.

D'Amato, M. R. *Experimental psychology methodology: Psychophysics and learning.* New York: McGraw-Hill, 1970.

Darley, J. M., and Latané, B. Bystander intervention in emergencies: diffusion of responsibility. *Journal of Personality and Social Psychology*, 1968, 8, 377–383.

Deese, J. *Psychology as science and art.* New York: Harcourt Brace Jovanovich, Inc., 1972.

Dinsmoor, J. A. Operant conditioning. In *Experimental methods and instrumentation in psychology*, edited by J. B. Sidowski. New York: McGraw-Hill, 1966, Ch. 10.

Dukes, W. F. N = 1. *Psychological Bulletin*, 1965, 64, 74–79.

Dunn, J. R., and Lupfer, M. Differentiation matching in school desegregation workshops. *Journal of Applied Psychology*, 1974, 4, 1, 24–35.

Ebbesen, E. B., and Haney, M. Flirting with death: Variables affecting risk taking at intersections. *Journal of Applied Social Psychology*, 1973, 3, 303–324.

Ebbinghaus, H. *Memory, a contribution to experimental psychology.* 1885. Translated by Ruger and Bussenius. New York: Teachers College, Columbia University, 1913.

Edgington, E. S. The design of one-subject experiments for testing hypotheses. *The Canadian Psychologist*, 1972, 3, 33–38. (a)

Edgington, E. S. N = 1 experiments: Hypothesis testing. *The Canadian Psychologist*, 1972, 13, 121–134. (b)

Edwards, A. L. *Statistical methods.* 2nd ed. New York: Holt, 1967.

Edwards, W., Guttentag, M. D., and Snapper, K. A decision-theoretic approach to evaluation research. In *Handbook of evaluation research*, Vol. 1, edited by E. L. Struening and M. D. Guttentag. Beverly Hills, Calif.: Sage, 1975.

Ehrlich, A. The age of the rat. *Human Behavior*, 1974, 3, 25–28.

Elashoff, J. D., and Thoresen, C. E. Choosing a statistical method for analysis of an intensive experiment. In *Single Subject research: Strategies for evaluating change*, edited by T. R. Kratochwill. New York: Academic Press, 1978.

Ellsworth, P. C. From abstract ideas to concrete instances: Some guidelines for choosing natural research settings. *American Psychologist*, 1977, 33, 604–615.

Ellsworth, P. C., Carlsmith, J. A., and Henson, A. The stare as a stimulus to flight in human subjects. *Journal of Personality and Social Psychology*, 1972, 21, 302–311.

Emery, F. W., and Trist, E. L. The causal texture of organizational environment. *Human Relations*, 1965, 18, 21–31.

392   Epstein, T. M., Suedfeld, P., and Silverstein, S. J. The experimental contact: Subject's expectations of and reactions to some behavior of experimenters. *American Psychologist*, 1973, *28*, 212–221.

Erlebacher, A., and Sekuler, R. Perceived length depends on exposure duration; Straight lines and Müller-Lyer Stimuli. *Journal of Experimental Psychology*, 1974, *103*, 724–728.

Eron, L. D., Huesmann, L. R., Lefkowitz, M. M., and Walder, L. D. Does television violence cause aggression? *American Psychologist*, 1972, *27*, 253–263.

Ethical aspects of experimentation with human subjects. *Daedalus*, 1969, *98*, No. 2.

Eysenck, H. I. The effects of psychotherapy: an evaluation. *Journal of Consulting Psychology*, 1952, *16*, 319–324.

Eysenck, H. J. *The biological basis of personality.* Springfield, Ill.: Charles C. Thomas, 1967.

Felton, G. S. The experimenter expectancy effect examined as a function of task ambiguity and internal-external control. *Journal of Experimental Research In Personality*, 1971, *5*, 286–294.

Ferguson, G. A. *Statistical analysis in psychology and education.* New York: McGraw-Hill, 1966.

Ferster, C. B., and Skinner, B. F. *Schedules of reinforcement.* New York: Appleton-Century-Crofts, Inc., 1957.

Festinger, G. L., and Carlsmith, J. M. Cognitive consequences of forced compliance. *Journal of Abnormal and Social Psychology*, 1959, *58*, 203–211.

Festinger, L. *A theory of cognitive dissonance.* Evanston, Ill.: Row, Peterson, 1957.

Fillenbaum, S. Prior deception and subsequent experimental performance: The faithful subject. *Journal of Personality and Social Psychology*, 1966, *4*, 532–537.

Fisher, R. A. *The design of experiments.* 1st ed. London: Oliver and Boyd, 1935.

Fode, K. L. The effects of experimenters' anxiety and subjects' anxiety, social desirability and sex, on experimenter outcome-bias. Unpublished doctoral dissertation, University of North Dakota, 1967.

Fouts, Roger S. Acquisition and testing of gestural signs in four young chimpanzees. *Science*, June 1, 1973.

Fox, J. G. A comparison of Gothic Elite and Standard Elite type faces. *Ergonomics*, 1963, *6*, 193–198.

Freedman, J. L., and Fraser, S. C. Compliance without pressure: The foot-in-the-door technique. *Journal of Personality and Social Psychology*, 1966, *4*, 195–202.

Freeman, H. E. The present status of evaluation research. In *Evaluation Studies Annual Review*, edited by M. Guttentag. Beverly Hills: Sage Publications, 1977.

Friedman, N. *The social nature of psychological research.* New York: Basic Books, 1967.

Friedson, E. The organization of medical practice. In *Handbook of medical sociology*, edited by H. E. Freeman, L. G. Reeder, and S. Levine. Englewood Cliffs, N. J.: Prentice Hall, 1972.

Gadlin, H., and Ingle, G. Through the one-way mirror: The limits of experimental self-reflection. *American Psychologist*, 1975, *30*, 1003–1009.

Gage, N. L., and Cronbach, L. J. Conceptual and methodological problems in interpersonal perception. *Psychological Review*, 1955, *62*, 411–422.

Gagné, R. M., and Baker, K. E. Stimulus pre-differentiation as a factor in transfer of training. *Journal of Experimental Psychology*, 1950, *40*, 439–451.

Gaito, J. Statistical dangers involved in counterbalancing. *Psychological Report*, 1958, *4*, 463–468.

Gaito, J. Repeated measurements designs and counterbalancing. *Psychological Bulletin*, 1961, *58*, 46–54.

Gardiner, P. C. and Edwards, W. Public values: Multi-attribute-utility measurement for social decision making. In *Human judgment and decision processes*, edited by M. F. Kaplan and S. Schwartz. New York: Academic Press, 1975.

Gelfand, D., and Hartmann, D. Behavior therapy with children: A review and evaluation of research methodology. *Psychological Bulletin*, 1968, *69*, 204–215.

Gentile, J. R., Roden, A. H., and Klein, R. D. An analysis-of-variance model for the intrasubject replication design. *Journal of Applied Behavior Analysis*, 1972, *5*, 193–198.

Gergen, K. J. The codification of research ethics: Views of a doubting Thomas. *American Psychologist*, 1973, *28*, 907–912.

Glass, G. V. Analysis of data on the Connecticut speeding crackdown as a time-series quasi-experiment. *Law and Society Review*, 1968, *3*(1), 55–76.

Glass, G. V., Tiao, G. C., and Maguire, T. O. The 1900 revision of German divorce laws. *Law and Society Review*, 1971, *5*, 539–62.

Glass, G. V., Willson, V. L., and Gottman, J. M. *Design and Analysis of Time Series.* Boulder, Colo.: Laboratory of Educational Research Press, 1975.

Goldberg, P. A. Expectancy, choice and the other person. *Journal of Personality and Social Psychology*, 1965, *2*, 895–897.

Gottman, J. M. N-of-one and N-of-two research in psychotherapy. *Psychological Bulletin*, 1973, *80*, 93–105.

Gottman, J. M., and Glass, G. V. *Analysis of interrupted time-series experiments.* In *Single Subject research. Strategies for evaluating change*, edited by T. R. Kratochwill. New York: Academic Press, 1978.

Gottman, J. M., and McFall, R. M. Self-monitoring effects in a program for potential high school dropouts: A time-series analysis. *Journal of Consulting and Clinical Psychology*, 1972, *39*, 273–281.

Gottman, J. M., McFall, R. M., and Barnett, J. T. Design and analysis of research using time series. *Psychological Bulletin*, 1969, *72*, 299–306.

Gottman, J. M., and Notarius, C. Sequential analysis of observational data

394   using Markov chains. *Single subject research: Strategies for evaluating change,* edited by T. R. Kratochwill. New York: Academic Press, 1978.

Greenwald, A. G. Consequences of prejudice against the null hypothesis. *Psychological Bulletin,* 1975, *82,* 1–20.

Greenwood, E. *Experimental sociology: A study in method.* New York: King's Crown Press, 1945.

Grice, G. R. Dependence of empirical laws upon the source of experimental variation. *Psychological Bulletin,* 1966, *66,* 488–498.

Guilford, J. P. *Fundamental statistics in psychology and education.* New York: McGraw-Hill Book Co., 1965.

Gustav, A. Students' attitudes toward compulsory participation in experiments. *Journal of Psychology,* 1962, *53,* 119–125.

Guttentag, M. Evaluation and Society. *Personality and Social Psychology Bulletin,* 1977, *3,* 31–410.

Hall, J. F., and Kobrick, J. L. The relationships among three measures of response strength. *Journal of Comparative and Physiological Psychology,* 1952, *45,* 280–282.

Hall, J. W., and Pierce, J. W. Recognition and recall by children and adults as a function of variations in memory encoding instructions. *Memory and Cognition,* 1974, *2,* 585–590.

Hall, R. V., ed. *Behavior management series: Part II, Basic principles.* Lawrence, Kans.: H. and H. Enterprises, 1971.

Hall, R. V., and Fox, R. W. Changing-criterion designs: An alternative applied behavior analysis procedure. In *New Developments in behavioral research: Theory, method, and application,* In honor of Sidney W. Bijou, edited by C. C. Etzel, G. M. LeBlanc, and D. M. Baer. Hillsdale, N. J.: Lawrence Erlbaum Associates, 1977.

Hartmann, D. P., and Hall, R. V. A discussion of the changing criterion design. *Journal of Applied Behavior Analysis,* 1976, *9,* 527–532.

Haslerud, G., and Meyers, S. The transfer value of given and individually derived principles. *Journal of Educational Psychology,* 1958, *49,* 293–298.

Haughton, E., and Ayllon, T. Production and elimination of symptomatic behavior. In *Case studies in behavior modification,* edited by L. P. Ullmann and L. Krasner. New York, Holt, 1965.

Hayes, K. J., and Hayes, C. Imitation in home-raised chimpanzee. *Journal of Comparative and Physiological Psychology,* 1952, *45,* 450–459.

Hayward, C. H. The ethics of doing research . . . and of not doing it. *American Journal of Mental Deficiency,* 1976, *81,* 311–317.

Heinemann, E. G. Photographic measurement of the retinal image. *American Journal of Psychology,* 1961, *74,* 440–445.

Heise, D. R. Problems in path analysis and causal inference. In *Sociological methodology,* edited by E. F. Borgatta and G. W. Bohrnstedt. San Francisco: Jossey-Bass, 1969.

Heise, D. R. Causal inference from panel data. In *Sociological methodology,* edited by E. F. Borgatta and G. W. Bohrnstedt. San Francisco: Jossey-Bass, 1969.

Helmstadter, G. C. *Research concepts in human behavior.* New York: Appleton-Century-Crofts, 1970.

Hersen, M., and Barlow, D. H. *Single case experimental designs: Strategies for studying behavioral change.* New York: Pergamon Press, 1976.

Hersen, M., Gullick, E. L., Matherne, P. M., and Harbert, T. L. Instructions and reinforcement in the modification of a conversion reaction. *Psychological Reports,* 1972, *31,* 719–722.

Hewett, F. M., Taylor, F. D., and Artuso, A. A. The Santa Monica project: Evaluation of an engineered classroom design with emotionally disturbed children. *Exceptional Children,* 1969, *35,* 523–529.

Higbee, K. L., and Wells, M. G. Some research trends in social psychology during the 1960's. *American Psychologist,* 1972, *27,* 963–966.

Holmes, D. S. Amount of experience in experiments as a determinant of performance in later experiments. *Journal of Personality and Social Psychology,* 1967, *7,* 403–407.

Holmes, D. S. Effectiveness of debriefing after a stress-producing deception. *Journal of Research in Personality,* 1973, *7,* 127–138.

Holmes, D. S. Debriefing after psychological experiments: I. Effectiveness of postdeception dehoaxing. *American Psychologist.* 1976, *31,* 858–867.

Holmes, D. S. Debriefing after psychological experiments: II. Effectiveness of postexperimental desensitizing. *American Psychologist,* 1976, *31,* 868–875.

Holmes, D. S., and Applebaum, A. S. Nature of prior experimental experience as a determinant of performance in a subsequent experiment. *Journal of Personality and Social Psychology,* 1970, *14,* 195–202.

Holmes, D. S., and Bennett, D. H. Experiments to answer questions raised by the use of deception in psychological research: I. Role playing as an alternative to deception; II. Effectiveness of debriefing after a deception; III. Effect of informed consent on deception. *Journal of Personality and Social Psychology,* 1974, *29,* 358–367.

Hovland, C. I., Lumsdaine, A. A., and Sheffield, F. D. *Experiments on mass communication.* Studies in Social Psychology in World War II, Vol. III, Princeton University, 1949.

Hurwitz, S., and Jenkins, V. The effects of experimenter expectancy on performance of sample learning tasks. Unpublished manuscript, Harvard University, 1966.

Hyman, R., and Berger, L. Discussion. In H. J. Eysenck (Ed.) *The effects of psychotherapy,* edited by H. J. Eysenck, pp. 81–86. New York: International Science Press, 1966.

Jackson, C. W., and Pollard, J. C. Some non-deprivation variables which influence the "effects" of experimental sensory deprivation. *Journal of Abnormal Psychology,* 1966, *71,* 383–388.

Johnson, J. M. Punishment of human behavior. *American Psychologist,* 1972, *27,* 1033–1054.

Johnson, R. F. Q. The experimenter attributes effect: A methodological analysis. *Psychological Record,* 1976, *26,* 67–78.

396   Johnson, R. W., and Adair, J. G. Experimenter expectancy vs. systematic recording errors under automated and nonautomated stimulus presentation. *Journal of Experimental Research in Personality,* 1972, 6, 88–94.

Johnson, R. W., and Ryan, B. J. Observer/recorder error as affected by different tasks and different expectancy inducements. *Journal of Experimental Research in Personality.* 1976, 10, 201–214.

Jones, R. A., and Cooper, J. Mediation of experimenter effects. *Journal of Personality and Social Psychology,* 1971, 20, 70–74.

Jones, R. R., Vaught, R. S., and Weinrott, M. Time-series analysis in operant research. *Journal of Applied Behavior Analysis,* 1977, 10, 151–166.

Jourard, S. *Disclosing man to himself.* New York: Van Nostrand, 1968.

Jung, J. *The experimenters dilemma.* New York: Harper, 1971.

Karhan, J. R. A behavioral and written measure of the effects of guilt and anticipated guilt on compliance for Machiavellians. Unpublished thesis, Texas A & M University, May 1973.

Kavanau, J. L. Behavior: Confinement, adaptation, and compulsory regimes in laboratory studies. *Science,* 1964, 143, 490.

Kavanau, J. L. Behavior of captive whitefooted mice. *Science,* 1967, 155, 1623–1639.

Kazdin, A. E. Methodological and assessment considerations in evaluating reinforcement programs in applied settings. *Journal of Applied Behavior Analysis,* 1973, 6, 517–531. (a)

Kazdin, A. E. The role of instructions and reinforcement in behavior changes in token reinforcement programs. *Journal of Educational Psychology,* 1973, 64, 63–71. (b)

Kazdin, A. E. Assessing the clinical or applied importance of behavior change through social validation. *Behavior Modification,* 1977, 1, 427–449.

Kazdin, A. E., and Kopel, S. A. On resolving ambiguities of the multiple-baseline design: problems and recommendations. *Behavior Therapy,* 1975, 6, 601–608.

Kelman, H. C. Human use of human subjects. *Psychological Bulletin,* 1967, 67, 1–11.

Kelman, H. C. *A time to speak.* San Francisco: Jossey Bass, 1968.

Kelman, H. C. The rights of the subject in social research: an analysis in terms of relative power and legitimacy. *American Psychologist,* 1972, 27, 989–1016.

Kempthorne, O. The design and analysis of experiments with some reference to educational research. In *Research design and analysis: second annual Phi Delta Kappa symposium on educational research,* edited by R. O. Collier, Jr., and S. M. Elam. Bloomington, Ind.: Phi Delta Kappa, 1961, 97–126.

Kendler, T. S., and Kendler, H. H. Reversal and nonreversal shifts in kindergarten children. *Journal of Experimental Psychology,* 1959, 58, 56–60.

Kendler, T. S., Kendler, H. H., and Learnard, B. Mediated responses to size and brightness as a function of age. *The American Journal of Psychology,* 1962, 75, 571–586.

Kennedy, J. L., and Uphoff, H. F. Experiments on the nature of extrasensory perception: III. The recording error criticism of extra-chance scores. *Journal of Parapsychology,* 1939, *3,* 226–245.

Kenny, D. A. A quasi-experimental approach to assessing treatment effects in the nonequivalent control group design. *Psychological Bulletin,* 1975, *82,* 345–362.

Kenny, D. A. Cross-Lagged Panel Correlation: A test for spuriousness. *Psychological Bulletin,* 1975, *82,* 887–903.

Kerlinger, F. N. *Foundations of behavioral research.* New York: Holt, 1964.

Kerlinger, F. Research in "education." In *Encyclopedia of educational research,* 4th ed., edited by R. Ebel, V. Nall, and R. Bauer. New York: Macmillan, 1969, pp. 1127–1144.

Kerlinger, F. Draft report of the APA committee on ethical standards in psychological research: A critical reaction. *American Psychologist,* 1972, *27,* 894–896.

Kerlinger, F. N. *Foundations of behavioral research.* New York: Holt, 1973.

Kerlinger, F. N., and Pedhazur, E. J. *Multiple regression in behavioral research.* New York: Holt Rinehart and Winston, 1973.

Kimmel, H. D., and Terrant, F. R. Bias due to individual differences in yoked control designs. *Behavior Research Methods and Instrumentation,* 1968, *1,* 11–14.

King, J. A. Relationships between early social experience and adult aggressive behavior in inbred mice. *Journal of Genetic Psychology,* 1957, *90,* 151–166.

Kingsbury, S. J., Stevens, D. P., and Murray, E. J. Evaluative apprehension in verbal conditioning: A test of four subject effects models. *Journal of Personality and Social Psychology,* 1975, *32,* 271–277.

Kirk, R. *Experimental design: Procedures for the behavioral sciences.* Belmont, Calif.: Brooks, Cole, 1968.

Kratochwill, T. R. Foundations of time-series research. In *Single Subject research: Strategies for evaluating change,* edited by T. R. Kratochwill. New York: Academic Press, 1978.

Kratochwill, T. R., and Brody, G. H. Single subject designs: A perspective on the controversy over employing statistical inference and implications for research and training in behavior modification. *Behavior Modification,* 1978, *2,* 291–308.

Krejcie, R. V., and Morgan, D. W. Determining sample size for research activities. *Educational and Psychological Measurement,* 1970, *30,* 607–610.

Kruglanski, A. W. The human subject in psychological experiment: Fact and artifact. In *Advances in Experimental Social Psychology,* edited by L. Berkowitz. New York: Academic Press, 1975.

Kruglanski, A. W. On the paradigmatic objections to experimental psychology: A reply to Gadlin and Ingle. *American Psychologist,* 1976, *31,* 655–663.

Lana, R. Pretest-treatment interaction effects in longitudinal studies. *Psychological Bulletin,* 1959, *56,* 293–300.

398   Lana, R. E. Pretest sensitization. In *Artifact in behavioral research,* edited by R. Rosenthal and R. L. Rosnow. New York: Academic Press, 1969.

Land, K. C. Principles of path analysis. In *Sociological methodology,* edited by E. P. Borgatta and G. W. Bohrnstedt. San Francisco: Jossey-Bass, 1969.

Langer, E. "Human experimentation: New York verdict affirms patient's rights." *Science,* 1966, *151,* 663–666.

Larrabee, L. G., and Kleinsasser, L. D. The effect of experimenter bias on WISC performance. Unpublished paper. *Psychological Associates,* St. Louis, 1967.

Lazarus, R. S., Yousem, H., and Arenberg, D. Hunger and perception. *Journal of Personality,* 1953, *21,* 312–328.

Lefkowitz, M., Blake, R. R., and Mouton, J. S. Status factors in pedestrian violation of traffic signals. *Journal of Abnormal and Social Psychology,* 1955, *51,* 704–705.

Leitenberg, H. The use of single-case methodology in psychotherapy research. *Journal of Abnormal Psychology,* 1973, *82,* 87–101.

Leitenberg, H., Agras, W. S., Allen, R., Butz, R., and Edwards, J. Feedback and therapist praise during treatment of phobia. *Journal of Consulting and Clinical Psychology,* 1975, *43,* 396–404.

Leitenberg, H., Agras, W. S., Thompson, L., and Wright, D. E. Feedback in behavior modification: An experimental analysis in two phobic cases. *Journal of Applied Behavior Analysis,* 1968, *1,* 131–137.

Leon, G. R. *Case histories of deviant behavior.* Boston: Holbrook Press, 1974.

LeUnes, A., Christensen, L., and Wilkerson, D. Institutional tour effects on attitudes related to mental retardation. *American Journal of Mental Deficiency,* 1975, *79,* 732–735.

Levenson, H., Gray, M., and Ingram, A. Current research methods in personality: Five years after Carlson's survey. *Personality and Social Psychology Bulletin,* 1976, *2,* 158–161.

Levin, H. M. Cost-effectiveness analysis in evaluation research. In *Handbook of evaluation research,* edited by M. Guttentag and E. L. Struening. Beverly Hills: Sage, 1975.

Levin, J. R., Marascuilo, L. A., and Hubert, L. J. N = Nonparametric Randomization tests. In *Single subject research: Strategies for evaluating change,* edited by T. R. Kratochwill. New York: Academic Press, 1978.

Levy, L. H. Reflections on replications and the experimenter bias effect. *Journal of Consulting and Clinical Psychology,* 1969, *33,* 15–17.

Liddle, G., and Long, D. Experimental room for slow learners. *The Elementary School Journal,* 1958, *59,* 143–149.

Liebert, R. M., and Baron, R. A. Some immediate effects of televised violence on children's behavior. *Developmental Psychology,* 1972, *6,* 469–475.

Liebert, R. M., Odem, R. D., Hill, J., and Huff, R. Effects of age and rule familiarity on the production of modeled language constructions. *Developmental Psychology,* 1969, *1,* 108–112.

Lindquist, E. F. *Design and analysis of experiments in psychology and education,* New York: Houghton Mifflin, 1953.

Lindzey, G., and Aronson, E. *The handbook of social psychology.* Reading, Mass.: Addison-Wesley, 1968.

Lockard, R. B. The albino rat: A defensible choice or a bad habit? *American Psychologist,* 1968, *23,* 734–742.

Lord, F. M. Statistical adjustments when comparing preexisting groups. *Psychological Bulletin,* 1969, *72,* 336–337.

Lowman, R. P. Animal research: Open season on scientists. *APA Monitor,* 1977, *8,* 6–7.

Lubin, A. The interpretation of significant interaction. *Educational and Psychological Measurement,* 1961, *21,* 807–817.

Lynne, L. E., Jr., and Salasin, S. Human services: Should we, can we make them available to everyone? *Evaluation,* 1974, Spring Special Issue, 4–5.

Lyons, J. On the psychology of the psychological experiment. In *Cognition-theory, research, promise,* edited by C. Schurer. New York: Harper, 1964.

Maguire, T. O., and Glass, G. V. A program for the analysis of certain time-series quasi-experiments. *Educational and Psychological Measurement,* 1967, *27,* 743–750.

Maier, N. R. F. *Frustration: The study of behavior without a goal.* New York: McGraw-Hill, 1949.

Maier, N. R. F. Experimentally produced neurotic behavior in the rat. (Paper presented at the meeting of the American Association for the Advancement of Science, Richmond, 1938.) In *Systems and theories in psychology,* edited by M. H. Marx and W. A. Hillix, p. 13. New York: McGraw-Hill, 1973.

Marks, I. M., and Gelder, M. G. Transvestism and fetishism: Clinical and psychological changes during Faradic aversion. *British Journal of Psychiatry,* 1967, *113,* 711–729.

Markus, H. Self-schemata and processing information about the self. *Journal of Personality and Social Psychology,* 1977, *35,* 63–78.

Martin, C. J., Boersma, F. J., and Cox, D. L. A classification of associative strategies in paired-associate learning. *Psychonomic Science,* 1965, *3,* 455–456.

Marwit, S. J. An investigation of the communication of tester-bias by means of modeling. Unpublished doctoral dissertation, State University of New York at Buffalo, 1968.

Marx, M. H. *Theories in contemporary psychology.* New York: Macmillan, 1963.

Marx, M. H., and Hillix, W. A. *Systems and theories in psychology.* New York: McGraw-Hill, 1973.

Masling, J. Role-related behavior of the subject and psychologist and its effects upon psychological data. *Nebraska Symposium on Motivation.* Lincoln: University of Nebraska Press, 1966, *14,* 67–103.

Matheson, D. W., Bruce, R. L., and Beauhamp, K. L. *Introduction to experimental psychology.* New York: Holt, 1970.

May, W. W. On Baumrind's four commandments. *American Psychologist,* 1972, *27,* 899–902.

400   McCullough, J. P., Cornell, J. E., McDaniel, and Mueller, R. K. Utilization of the simultaneous treatment design to improve student behavior in a first-grade classroom. *Journal of Consulting and Clinical Psychology*, 1974, *42*, 288–292.

McFall, R. M. Effects of self-monitoring on normal smoking behavior. *Journal of Consulting and Clinical Psychology*, 1970, *35*, 135–142.

McGinley, H., Kaplan, M., and Kinsey, T. Subject effects and demand characteristics. *Psychological Reports*, 1975, *36*, 267–278.

McGuigan, F. J. The experimenter: a neglected stimulus object. *Psychological Bulletin*, 1963, *60*, 421–428.

McNamara, J. R., and MacDonough, T. S. Some methodological considerations in the design and implementation of behavior therapy research. *Behavior Therapy*, 1972, *3*, 361–378.

McNemar, Q. Opinion-attitude methodology. *Psychological Bulletin*, 1946, *43*, 289–374.

Melamed, B. G., and Siegel, L. J. Reduction of anxiety in children facing hospitalization and surgery by use of filmed modeling. *Journal of Consulting and Clinical Psychology*, 1975, *43*, 511–521.

Mellgren, R. L., Nation, J. R., and Wrather, D. M. Magnitude of negative reinforcement and resistance to extinction. *Learning and Motivation*, 1975, *6*, 253–263.

Mellgren, R. L., Seybert, J. A., and Dyck, D. G. The order of continuous, partial and nonreward trials and resistance to extinction. *Learning and Motivation*, 1978, *9*, 359–371.

Menges, R. J. Openness and honesty versus coercion and deception in psychological research. *American Psychologist*, 1973, *28*, 1030–1034.

Michael, J. Statistical inference for individual organism research: Mixed blessing or curse? *Journal of Applied Behavior Analysis*, 1974, *7*, 697–653.

Milgram, S. Behavioral study of obedience. *Journal of Abnormal and Social Psychology*, 1963, *67*, 371–378.

Milgram, S. Group pressure and action against a person. *Journal of Personality and Social Psychology*, 1964, *69*, 137–143.

Milgram, S. Issues in the study of obedience: A reply to Baumrind. *American Psychologist*, 1964, *19*, 848–852.

Mill, J. S. *A system of logic.* New York: Harper, 1874.

Miller, A. G. Role playing: An alternative to deception? A review of the evidence. *American Psychologist*, 1972, *27*, 623–636.

Miller, N. E. Objective techniques for studying motivational effects of drugs on animals. In *Psychotropic drugs*, edited by S. Garettini and V. Ghetti. Amsterdam: Elsevier, 1957.

Mills, J. A procedure for explaining experiments involving deception. *Personality and Social Psychology Bulletin*, 1976, *2*, 3–13.

Mood, A. M. *Introduction to the theory of statistics.* New York: McGraw-Hill, 1950.

Morgan, C. T., and Morgan, J. D. Auditory induction of abnormal pattern of behavior in rats. *Journal of Comparative Psychology*, 1939, *27*, 505–508.

Morison, Robert S. "Gradualness, gradualness, gradualness" (I. P. Pavlov). **401**
American Psychologist, 1960, 15, 187–198.

Neale, J. M., and Liebert, R. M. Science and behavior: An introduction to methods of research. New Jersey: Prentice-Hall, 1973.

Nisbett, R. E., and Wilson, T. D. Telling more than we can know: Verbal reports on mental processes. Psychological Review, 1977, 84, 231–259.

Nisewander, W. A., and Price, J. M. Dependent variable reliability and the power of significance tests. Psychological Bulletin, 1978, 85, 405–409.

Oakes, W. External validity and the use of real people as subjects. American Psychologist, 1972, 27, 959–962.

Orne, M. T. On the social psychology of the psychological experiment: With particular reference to demand characteristics and their implications. American Psychologist, 1962, 17, 776–783.

Orne, M. T. Demand characteristics and the concept of quasi-controls. In Artifact in behavioral research, edited by R. Rosenthal and R. L. Rosnow. New York: Academic Press, 1969.

Packard, R. G. The control of "classroom attention": A group contingency for complex behaviors. Journal of Applied Behavior Analysis, 1970, 3, 13–28.

Page, M. M. Modification of figure-ground perception as a function of awareness of demand characteristics. Journal of Personality and Social Psychology, 1968, 9, 59–66.

Page, M. M. Social psychology of a classical conditioning of attitudes experiment. Journal of Personality and Social Psychology, 1969, 11, 177–186.

Page, M. M., and Kahle, L. R. Demand characteristics in the satiation-deprivation effect on attitude conditioning. Journal of Personality and Social Psychology, 1971, 20, 304–318.

Page, M. M., and Scheidt, R. J. The elusive weapons effect: demand awareness, evaluation apprehension, and slightly sophisticated subjects. Journal of Personality and Social Psychology, 1971, 20, 304–318.

Page, S., and Yates, E. Attitudes of psychologists toward experimenter controls in research. The Canadian Psychologist, 1973, 14, 202–207.

Pappworth, M. H. Human guinea pigs: Experimentation on man. Boston: Beacon Press, 1967.

Parsonson, B. S., and Baer, D. M. The analysis of and presentation of graphic data. In Single Subject research: strategies for evaluating change, edited by T. R. Kratochwill. New York: Academic Press, 1978.

Patton, M. Q. Utilization-focused evaluation. Beverly Hills: Sage Publications, 1978.

Paul, G. L. Behavior modification research: Design and tactics. In Behavior therapy appraisal and status, edited by C. M. Franks. New York: McGraw-Hill, 1969.

Pavlov, I. P. Lecturer on conditioned reflexes. Translated by W. H. Gantt. New York: International, 1928.

Payne, R. W., and Jones, H. G. Statistics for the investigation of individual cases. Journal of Clinical Psychology, 1957, 13, 115–121.

402   Pellegrini, R. J. Ethics and identity: A note on the call to conscience. *American Psychologist,* 1972, *27,* 896–897.

Pelz, D. C., and Andrews, F. M. Detecting causal priorities in panel study data. *American Sociological Review.* 1964, *29,* 836–848.

Pfungst, O. *Clever Hans* (the horse of Mr. Von Osten): *A contribution to experimental, animal, and human psychology.* Translated by C. L. Rahn. New York: Holt, Rinehart and Winston, 1911. (Republished, 1965).

Plutchik, Robert. *Foundations of experimental research.* New York: Harper, 1974.

Poulton, E. C., and Freeman, P. R. Unwanted asymmetrical transfer effects with balanced experimental designs. *Psychological Bulletin,* 1966, *66,* 1–8.

Pribram, K. H. *Languages of the brain: experimental paradoxes and principles in neuropsychology.* Englewood Cliffs, N. J.: Prentice-Hall, 1971.

Provus, M. *Discrepancy evaluation for educational program improvement and assessment.* Berkeley, Calif.: McCutchan, 1971.

Rankin, R. E., and Campbell, D. T. Galvanic skin response to Negro and white experimenters. *Journal of Abnormal and Social Psychology,* 1955, *51,* 30–33.

Raven, B. H., and Fishbein, M. Acceptance of punishment and change in belief. *Journal of Abnormal and Social Psychology,* 1961, *63,* 411–416.

Resnick, J. H., and Schwartz, T. Ethical standards as an independent variable in psychological research. *American Psychologist,* 1973, *28,* 134–139.

Revusky, S. H. Some statistical treatments compatable with individual organism methodology. *Journal of the Experimental Analysis of Behavior,* 1967, *10,* 319–330.

Richter, C. P. Rats, man, and the welfare state. *American Psychologist,* 1959, *14,* 18–28.

Riecken, H. W. A program for research on experiments in social psychology. In *Decisions, values and groups,* Vol. 2, edited by N. F. Washburne. New York: Pergamon Press, 1962.

Ring, K., Wallston, K., and Corey, M. Mode of debriefing as a factor affecting reaction to a Milgram-type obedience experiment: an ethical inquiry. *Representative Research in Social Psychology,* 1970, *1,* 67–88.

Risley, T. R. Behavior modification: An experimental-therapeutic endeavor. In *Behavior modification and ideal mental health services,* edited by L. A. Hammerlynd, P. O. Davison, and L. E. Ocker. Calgary, Alberta: University of Calgary, 1970.

Risley, T. R., and Wolf, M. M. Strategies for analyzing behavioral change over time. In *Life-Span developmental psychology: Methodological Issues,* edited by J. R. Nesselroade and H. W. Reese. New York: Academic Press, 1972.

Ritchie, E., and Phares, E. J. Attitude change as a function of internal-external control and communicator status. *Journal of Personality,* 1969, *37,* 429–443.

Robinson, J., and Cohen, L. Individual bias in psychological reports. *Journal of Clinical Psychology,* 1954, *10,* 333–336.

Rosenberg, M. J. The conditions and consequences of evaluation apprehension. In *Artifact in behavioral research,* edited by R. Rosenthal and R. L. Rosnow. New York: Academic Press, 1969.

403

Rosenthal, R. *Experimenter effects in behavioral research.* New York: Appleton-Century-Crofts, 1966.

Rosenthal, R. Interpersonal expectations: Effects of the experimenter's hypothesis. In *Artifact in Behavioral Research,* edited by R. Rosenthal and R. L. Rosnow. New York: Academic Press, 1969.

Rosenthal, R. Experimenter effects in behavioral research. 2nd ed. New York: Irvington, 1976.

Rosenthal, R. How often are our numbers wrong? *American Psychologist,* 1978, *33,* 1005–1007.

Rosenthal, R., and Fode, K. L. Three experiments in experimenter bias. *Psychological Reports,* 1963, *12,* 491–511. (a)

Rosenthal, R., and Fode, K. L. The effect of experimenter bias on the performance of the albino rat. *Behavioral Science,* 1963, *8,* 183–189. (b)

Rosenthal, R., Persinger, G. W., Vikan-Kline, L., and Mulry, R. C. The role of the research assistant in the mediation of experimenter bias. *Journal of Personality,* 1963, *31,* 313–335.

Rosenthal, R., and Rosnow, R. L. *The volunteer subject.* New York: John Wiley & Sons, 1975.

Rosnow, R. L., and Suls, J. M. Reactive effects of pretesting in attitude research. *Journal of Personality and Social Psychology,* 1970, *15,* 338–343.

Rossi, P. H., and Williams, W., eds. *Evaluating social programs: Theory practice and politics.* New York: Seminar Press, 1972.

Rozelle, R. M., and Campbell, D. T. More plausible rival hypotheses in the cross-lagged panel correlational technique. *Psychological Bulletin,* 1969, *71,* 74–80.

Rudner, R. S. *Philosophy of social science.* Englewood Cliffs, N. J.: Prentice-Hall, 1966.

Rugg, E. A. Ethical judgments of social research involving experimental deception. Unpublished doctoral dissertation, George Peabody College for Teachers, Nashville, Tenn. May 1975.

Rumenik, D. K., Capasso, D. R., and Hendrick, C. Experimenter sex effects in behavioral research. *Psychological Bulletin,* 1977, *84,* 852–877.

Sandell, R. G. Note on choosing between competing interpretations of cross-lagged panel correlations. *Psychological Bulletin,* 1971, *75,* 367–368.

Schachter, S., and Singer, J. E. Cognitive, social and physiological determinants of emotional state. *Psychological Review,* 1962, *69,* 379–399.

Schafer, R., and Murphy, G. The role of autism in visual figure-ground relationship. *Journal of Experimental Psychology,* 1943, *32,* 335–343.

Schaie, K. A general model for the study of developmental problems. *Psychological Bulletin,* 1965, *64,* 92–107.

Scholtz, J. A. Defense styles in suicide attempters. *Journal of Consulting and Clinical Psychology,* 1973, *41,* 70–73.

404   Schultz, D. P. The human subject in psychological research. *Psychological Bulletin*, 1969, *72*, 214–228.

Schutz, R. E., and Baker, R. L. The experimental analysis of behavior in educational research. *Psychology in the Schools*, July, 1968, 240–247.

Scriven, M. The methology of evaluation. In *Perspectives of curriculum evaluation*, edited by R. W. Tyler, R. M. Gagne, and M. Scriven, AERA monograph series on curriculum evaluation, No. 1. Chicago: Rand McNally, 1967.

Scriven, M. Pros and cons about goal-free evaluation, evaluation comment. *The Journal of Educational Evaluation*, 1972, *3*, 1–7.

Sears, R. R., Whiting, J. W. M., Nowlis, V., and Sears, P. S. Some child-rearing antecedents of aggression and dependency in young children. *Genetic Psychology Monographs*, 1953, *47*, 135–234.

Seaver, W. B., and Quarton, R. J. Social reinforcement of excellence: Dean's List and academic achievement. Paper presented at the 44th annual meeting of the Eastern Psychological Association, Washington, D.C., May, 1973.

Seeman, J. Deception in psychological research. *American Psychologist*, 1969, *24*, 1025–1028.

Selltiz, C., Jahoda, M., Deutsch, M., and Cook, S. W. *Research methods in social relations.* New York: Holt, 1959.

Shine, L. C. II, and Bower, S. M. A one-way analysis of variance for single-subject designs. *Educational and Psychological Measurements*, 1971, *31*, 105–113.

Shine, L. C. II. Five research steps designed to integrate the single-subject and multi-subject approaches to experimental research. *Canadian Psychological Review*, 1975, *16*, 179–183.

Shingles, R. D. Organizational membership and attitude change. In *Quasi-Experimental Approaches*, edited by J. A. Caporaso and L. L. Roos, Jr. Evanston, Ill.: Northwestern University Press, 1973.

Sidman, M. *Tactics of Scientific Research.* New York: Basic Books, 1960.

Sidowski, J. B., and Lockard, R. B. Some preliminary considerations in research. In *Experimental methods and instrumentation in psychology*, edited by J. B. Sidowski. New York: McGraw-Hill, 1966.

Sigall, H., Aronson, E., and Van Hoose, T. The cooperative subject: Myth or reality. *Journal of Experimental Social Psychology*, 1970, *6*, 1–10.

Silverman, I. The effects of experimenter outcome expectancy on latency of word association. *Journal of Clinical Psychology*, 1968, *24*, 60–63.

Silverman, I. The experimenter: A (still) neglected stimulus object. *The Canadian Psychologist*, 1974, *15*, 258–270.

Simon, J. L. *Basic research methods in social science.* New York: Random House, 1969.

Skinner, B. F. "Superstition" in the pigeon. *Journal of Experimental Psychology*, 1948, *38*, 168–172.

Skinner, B. F. *Walden two.* New York: Macmillan, 1948.   **405**

Skinner, B. F. *Science and human behavior.* New York: Macmillan, 1953.

Skinner, B. F. A case history in scientific method. *American Psychologist,* 1956, *11,* 221–223.

Skinner, B. F. *Beyond freedom and dignity.* New York: Knopf, 1971.

Skinner, B. F. A case history in scientific method. In *Cumulative Record,* New York: Appleton-Century-Crofts, 1972, p. 112.

Small-sample techniques. *The NEA Research Bulletin,* 1960, *36,* 99–104.

Smart, R. Subject selection bias in psychological research. *Canadian Psychologist,* 1966, *7a,* 115–121.

Smith, M. B. Some perspectives on ethical/political issues in social science research. *Personality and Social Psychology Bulletin,* 1976, *2,* 445–453.

Smith, R. E. The other side of the coin. *Contemporary Psychology,* 1969, *14,* 628–630.

Soloman, R. An extension of control group design. *Psychological Bulletin,* 1949, *44,* 137–150.

Solomon, R. L., and Lessac, M. S. A control group design for experimental studies of developmental process. *Psychological Bulletin,* 1968, *70,* 145–150.

Spence, K. W., Farber, I. E., and McFann, H. H. The relation of anxiety (drive) level to performance in competition and non-competition paired-associates learning. *Journal of Experimental Psychology,* 1956, *52,* 296–305.

Spinner, B., Adair, J. G., and Barnes, G. E. A reexamination of the faithful subject role. *Journal of Experimental Social Psychology,* 1977, *13,* 543–551.

Star, S. A., and Hughes, H. M. Report on an educational campaign: The Cincinnati plan for the United Nations. *American Journal of Sociology,* 1950, *55,* 389–400.

Stephen, A. S. Prospects and possibilities: The New Deal and the new social research. *Social Forces,* 1935, *13,* 515–521.

Stevens, S. S. Psychology and the science of science. *Psychological Bulletin,* 1939, *36,* 221–263.

Stratton, G. M. Vision without inversion of the retinal image. *Psychological Review,* 1897, *4,* 463–481.

Suchman, E. A. *Evaluation research: Principles and practice in public service and action programs.* New York: Russell Sage, 1967.

Sullivan, D. S., and Deiker, T. E. Subject-experimenter perception of ethical issues in human research. *American Psychologist,* 1973, *28,* 587–591.

Sutcliffe, J. P. On the role of "instructions to the subject" in psychological experiments. *American Psychologist,* 1972, *27,* 755–758.

Sween, J., and Campbell, D. T. *A study of the effect of proximally autocorrelated error on tests of significance for the interrupted time series quasi-experimental design.* Evanston, Ill.: Northwestern University, 1965.

406   Taffel, C. Anxiety and the conditioning of verbal behavior. *Journal of Abnormal and Social Psychology*, 1955, *51*, 496–501.

Tate, B. G., and Baroff, G. S. Aversive control of self-injurious behavior in a psychotic boy. *Behavior Research and Therapy*, 1966, *4*, 281–87.

Tedeschi, J. T., Schlenker, B. R., and Bonoma, T. V. Cognitive dissonance: Private ratiocination or public spectacle. *American Psychologist*, 1971, *26*, 685–695.

Tesch, F. E. Debriefing research participants: Though this be method there is madness to it. *Journal of Personality and Social Psychology*, 1977, *35*, 217–224.

Thigpen, C. H., and Cleckley, H. A case of multiple personality. *Journal of Abnormal and Social Psychology*, 1954, *49*, 135–151.

Thistlethwaite, D. L., and Campbell, D. T. Regression-discontinuity analysis: An alternative to the ex post facto experiment. *The Journal of Educational Psychology*, 1960, *51*, 309–317.

Timaeus, E., and Luck, H. E. Experimenter expectancy and social facilitation II: Stroop-test performance under the condition of audience. Unpublished manuscript, University of Cologne, 1968.

Tunnell, G. B. Three dimensions of naturalness: An expanded definition of field research. *Psychological Bulletin*, 1977, *84*, 426–437.

Underwood, B. J. Interference and forgetting. *Psychological Review*, 1957, *64*, 49–60.

Underwood, B. J. Verbal learning in the educative process. *Harvard Educational Review*, 1959, *29*, 107–117.

Underwood, B. J. *Experimental Psychology.* New York: Appleton-Century-Crofts, 1966.

Valenstein, E., Cox, V., and Kakolewski, J. Re-examination of the role of the hypothalamus in motivation. *Psychological Review*, 1970, *77*, 16–31.

Van Buskirk, W. L. An experimental study of vividness in learning and retention. *Journal of Experimental Psychology*, 1932, *15*, 563–573.

Vernon, H. M., Bedford, T., and Wyatt, S. *Two studies of rest pauses in industry.* Medical Research Council, Industrial Fatigue Research Board Report No. 25. London: His Majesty's Stationary Office, 1924.

Videbeck, R., and Bates, H. D. Verbal conditioning by a simulated experimenter. *Psychological Record*, 1966, *16*, 145–152.

Vinacke, E. Deceiving experimental subjects. *American Psychologist*, 1954, *9*, 155.

Wade, E. A., and Blier, M. J. Learning and retention of verbal lists: Serial anticipation and serial discrimination. *Journal of Experimental Psychology*, 1974, *103*, 732–739.

Walker, H. M., and Buckley, N. K. The use of positive reinforcement in conditioning attending behavior. *Journal of Applied Behavior Analysis*, 1968, *1*, 245–250.

Walker, H. M., and Lev, J. *Statistical inference.* New York: Holt, 1953.   **407**

Watson, J. B., and Rayner, R. Conditioned emotional reactions. *Journal of Experimental Psychology,* 1920, *3,* 1–14.

Watts, W. A. Relative persistence of opinion change induced by active compared to passive participation. *Journal of Personality and Social Psychology,* 1967, *5,* 4–15.

Webb, E. J., Campbell, D. T., Schwartz, R. D., and Sechrest, L. *Unobstructive measures: Nonreactive research in the social sciences.* Chicago: Rand McNally, 1966.

Weber, S. J., and Cook, T. D. Subject effects in laboratory research: An examination of subject roles, demand characteristics, and valid inference. *Psychological Bulletin,* 1972, *77,* 273–295.

Weiss, C. H. *Evaluation research.* Englewood Cliffs, N. J.: Prentice-Hall, Inc., 1972.

Weiss, C. H. The politicization of evaluation research. In *Evaluating action programs: Readings in social action and education,* edited by C. H. Weiss. Boston: Allyn and Bacon, Inc., 1972.

Weiss, J. M. Effects of coping behavior in different warning signal conditions on stress pathology. *Journal of Comparative and Physiological Psychology,* 1971, *77,* 1–13. (a)

Weiss, J. M. Effects of punishing and coping response (conflict) on stress pathology in rats. *Journal of Comparative and Physiological Psychology,* 1971, *77,* 14–21. (b)

Werts, C. E., and Lynn, R. L. A general linear model for studying growth. *Psychological Bulletin,* 1970, *73,* 17–22.

West, S. G., and Gunn, S. P. Some issues of ethics and social psychology. *American Psychologist,* 1978, *33,* 30–38.

Willems, E. P., and Raush, H. L., eds., *Naturalistic viewpoints in psychological research.* New York: Holt, 1969.

Wilson, D., and Donnerstein, E. Legal and ethical aspects of nonreactive social psychological research: An excursion into the public mind. *American Psychologist,* 1976, *31,* 765–773.

Windle, C. Test-retest effect on personality questionnaires. *Educational and Psychological Measurements,* 1954, *14,* 617–633.

Woodworth, R. S., and Sheehan, M. R. *Contemporary schools of psychology.* 3rd ed., New York: Ronald Press, 1964.

Wortman, C., and Brehm, J. Responses to uncontrollable outcomes: An integration of reactance theory and learned helplessness model. In *Advances in experimental social psychology,* Vol. 8, edited by L. Berkowitz. New York: Academic Press, 1975.

Wyer, R. S., Jr., Dion, K. L., and Ellsworth, P. C. An editorial. *Journal of Experimental Social Psychology,* 1978, *14,* 141–147.

Zadeh, L., Fu, K., Tanaka, K., and Shimwra, M., eds. *Fuzzy sets and their applications to cognitive and decision processes.* New York: Academic Press, 1975.

408   Zimbardo, P. G., Cohen, A. R., Weisenberg, M., Dworkin, L., and Firestone, I. Control of pain motivation by cognitive dissonance. *Science*, 1966, *151*, 217–219.

Zimney, G. H. *Method in experimental psychology.* New York: Ronald Press, 1961.

Zoble, E. J. Interaction of subject and experimenter expectancy effects in a tone length discrimination task. Unpublished AB thesis, Franklin and Marshall College, 1968.

Name Index

Abelson, R. P., 143–144
Adair, J. G., 103, 112, 152
Agras, S., 254–255
Allen, K. E., 242
Altemeyer, R. A., 305
Alumbaugh, R. V., 332
Andrews, F. M., 226
Applebaum, A. S., 324
Argyris, C., 101–102
Aronson, E., 41, 44, 67, 70, 73, 77, 78–79,
  80, 82, 84, 87, 103, 125, 142–143,
  145, 149, 151, 152, 157, 166, 179,
  304–305, 339, 347
Artuso, A. A., 241
Asch, S. E., 79
Ayllon, T., 16–17

Baer, D. M., 264
Baker, K. E., 142–143
Bandura, A., 5–6, 261–262
Bannister, D., 39
Barber, T. X., 109, 110, 114, 150
Barlow, D. H., 234, 235, 238, 243, 244,
  255, 259, 260, 262–263
Barnes, G. E., 103
Barnett, J. T., 217, 218, 224
Baroff, G. S., 239–240, 241
Baron, R. A., 55, 184–185, 341
Bates, H. D., 152
Baumrind, D., 332, 346
Beach, F. A., 298, 317
Beckman, L., 331
Bedford, T., 218–219
Beecher, H. K., 142
Bellugi-Klima, U., 32
Bennett, D. H., 344, 346
Berger, L., 234
Bergin, A. E., 234, 235
Berman, J., 287
Bernstein, I., 274, 285
Berscheid, E., 346

Bijou, S., 241, 258, 259, 260
Billewicz, W. Z., 130
Bishop, B. R., 331
Blake, R. R., 87
Blier, M. J., 92
Blumenthal, M., 286
Boersma, F. J., 303
Boice, R., 317
Bolger, H., 234
Bonoma, T. V., 104
Boring, E. G., 16, 37
Boruch, R. F., 203, 205, 209, 285–286
Box, G. E. P., 221
Bracht, G. H., 316, 317, 320, 324
Brady, J. V., 127–128
Brehm, J. W., 77
Bridgman, P. W., 8
Broden, M., 250–251
Brown, R., 32
Brown, W. F., 164
Brownell, W. A., 325
Bryk, A. S., 211
Buckley, N. K., 238

Calder, R., 13
Campbell, D., 175, 187
Campbell, D. T., 91–92, 98, 160–161,
  167, 170, 177, 198, 199, 202, 203,
  205, 209, 210, 216, 218, 222, 223,
  225, 226, 229, 316, 320, 344, 347
Capasso, D. R., 109
Caporaso, J. A., 217–218, 219–220, 222
Carlsmith, J. A., 43–44
Carlsmith, J. M., 53, 70, 77, 78–79, 80,
  82, 84, 87, 144, 149, 152, 304–305,
  339, 347
Carlson, R., 326
Caro, F. G., 285
Cayce, Edgar, 11
Cayden, C. B., 32
Christensen, L., 87, 103, 105, 145, 158, 169

410

Church, R. M., 128–129, 242
Cochran, W. G., 119
Cohen, L., 110
Collins, B. E., 87, 144
Conner, R. F., 286, 287
Conrad, H. S., 31
Cook, T. D., 103, 199, 202, 205, 216, 222, 229, 311, 324
Cooper, J., 112
Cope, V., 151
Corey, M., 346
Cowles, M. F., 302
Cox, D. E., 296
Cox, D. L., 303
Cox, D. R., 300–301
Cox, G. M., 119
Cox, V., 78
Crano, W. D., 225
Cronbach, L. J., 35, 174, 205, 209, 210, 266, 267, 320

Dalkey, N. C., 282
D'Amato, M. R., 133, 267
Darley, J. M., 54
Deese, J., 8–9, 26
Deiker, T. E., 347
Dickinson, R., 158
Dion, K. L., 146
Donnerstein, E., 348
Dukes, W. F., 234, 266
Dunn, J. R., 33–34
Dyck, D. G., 55

Ebbesen, E. B., 28–29
Ebbinghaus, H., 234
Edwards, A. L., 300
Edwards, W., 282
Ehrlich, A., 317
Elashoff, J. D., 264–265
Ellsworth, P. C., 43–44, 70–71, 146
Emery, F. W., 282
Epstein, T. M., 343
Erlebacher, A., 68, 203, 205, 209, 210
Eron, L. D., 227–228, 229
Eysenck, H. J., 234, 317

Felton, G. S., 112
Ferguson, G. A., 120
Ferster, C. B., 70
Festinger, L., 53
Fillenbaum, S., 102
Fishbein, M., 76–77
Fisher, R. A., 177
Fode, K. L., 111, 112, 113
Fouts, R. S., 73
Fox, J. G., 323
Fox, R. W., 255, 256, 257, 258
Fraser, S. C., 43
Freedman, J. L., 43

Freeman, H. E., 273, 274, 275–276, 279, 285, 289
Freeman, P. R., 265
Friedman, N., 105, 306
Friedson, E., 276
Furby, L., 174, 205, 209, 210

Gadlin, H., 40
Gage, N. L., 35
Gagné, R. M., 142–143
Gaito, J., 134
Gardiner, P. C., 282
Gelder, M. G., 249–250
Gelfand, D., 240, 242, 258
Gergen, K. J., 341–342
Glass, G. V., 221–222, 224, 262, 316, 317, 320, 324
Gottman, J. M., 217, 218, 221, 222, 224, 259, 262, 264
Gray, M., 326
Greenwald, A. G., 311
Grice, G. R., 267
Guilford, J. P., 300
Gunn, S. P., 341
Gustav, A., 101–102
Guttentag, M., 272–273, 282

Hall, J. F., 86
Hall, J. W., 72
Hall, R. V., 255, 256–257, 258
Haney, M., 28–29
Harlow, H. F., 384
Hartmann, D., 240, 242
Hartmann, D. P., 255, 256–257, 258
Haselrud, G., 187
Haughton, E., 16–17
Helmreich, R. L., 87, 144
Helmstadter, G. C., 10, 12, 27, 56, 58, 312
Hendrick, C., 109
Henson, A., 43–44
Hersen, M., 234, 235, 238, 243, 244, 255, 259, 260, 262–263, 265
Hewett, F. M., 241
Hillix, W., 7
Holmes, D. S., 324, 344, 346, 347*
Hubert, L. J., 264
Hughes, H. M., 211–212
Hurwitz, S., 111
Hyman, R., 234

Ingle, G., 40
Ingram, A., 326

Jackson, C. W., 101
Jenkins, G. M., 221
Jenkins, V., 111
Johnson, R. F. Q., 109, 149–150
Johnson, R. W., 112, 152

Jones, H. E., 31
Jones, R. A., 112
Jones, R. R., 263–264
Jourad, S., 102
Jung, J., 101, 108, 149

Kahle, L. R., 115
Kakolewski, J., 78
Kaplan, M., 103
Karhan, J. R., 87
Kavanau, J. L., 317
Kazdin, A. E., 250, 251–252, 262, 263, 266, 267–268
Kelman, H. C., 331, 335, 344
Kempthorne, O., 317
Kendler, H. H., 126–127, 320
Kendler, T. S., 126–127, 320
Kennedy, J. L., 107, 110
Kenny, D. A., 209, 210, 225, 228–229
Kerlinger, F. N., 2, 59–60, 89, 130, 165, 174, 186, 332
Kimmel, H. D., 129, 242
King, J. A., 5–6, 67
Kinsey, T., 103
Kirk, R., 178
Kleinsasser, L. D., 111
Kobrick, J. L., 86
Kopel, S. A., 251–252
Kratochwill, T. R., 235, 256, 257, 258, 265
Krejcie, R. V., 298
Kruglanski, A. W., 40, 103

Lana, R. E., 168, 170, 186–187, 326
Langer, E., 330
Larrabee, L. G., 111
Latané, B., 54
Learnard, B., 126–127
Lefkowitz, M., 87
Leitenberg, H., 237, 241–242, 244, 246, 248, 261, 265, 267
Leon, G. R., 161
Lessac, M. S., 175
LeUnes, A., 169
Levenson, H., 326
Levin, H. M., 289
Levin, J. R., 264
Levy, L. H., 114
Liddle, G., 96, 163
Liebert, R. M., 32, 55, 98
Linder, D., 73
Lindquist, E. F., 321
Lockard, R. B., 294, 295–296, 297–298, 302, 306, 318
Long, D., 96, 163
Lord, F. M., 205
Lubin, A., 321
Luck, H. E., 111
Lupfer, M., 33–34

Lynn, R. L., 210
Lynne, L. E., 283
Lyons, J., 106, 149

MacDonough, T. S., 261, 326
Maguire, T. O., 221
Maier, Norman, 7–8
Marascuilo, L. A., 264
Marks, I. M., 249–250
Martin, C. J., 303
Marwit, S. J., 111
Marx, M. H., 7, 36, 53
Masling, J., 102
May, W. W., 332
McCullough, J. P., 259
McFall, R. M., 217, 218, 224, 259
McGinley, H., 103
McGuigan, F. J., 107, 108, 148–149
McNamara, J. R., 261, 326
McNemar, Q., 318
Melamed, B. G., 353–374
Mellgren, R. L., 55, 81
Meyers, S., 187
Michael, J., 261
Milgram, S., 59–60, 346
Mill, J. S., 23–24
Miller, A. G., 344
Miller, J. C., 143–144
Miller, N. E., 71, 78
Mills, J., 41, 44, 67, 70, 73, 79, 82, 125, 142–143, 166, 305
Morgan, C. T., 7–8
Morgan, D. W., 298
Morgan, J. D., 7–8
Morison, Robert S., 24–27
Moulton, J. S., 87
Murphy, G., 115

Nation, J. R., 81
Neale, J. M., 98
Nisewander, W. A., 174–175
Notorious, C., 264

Oakes, W., 318
Orne, M. T., 102, 103, 146, 303

Packard, R. G., 265
Page, M. M., 115
Page, S., 146, 151
Pappworth, M. H., 331
Parsonson, B. S., 264
Patton, M. Q., 273, 281, 282, 283, 290
Paul, G. L., 265, 267, 268
Pavlov, I. P., 234
Pedhazur, E. J., 89
Pellegrini, R. J., 332
Pelz, D. C., 226
Pfungst, O., 106
Phares, E. J., 76–77, 82

412

Pierce, J. W., 72
Plutchik, Robert, 24, 71
Pollard, J. C., 101
Poulton, E. C., 265
Pribram, K. H., 37, 78
Price, J. M., 174–175
Provus, M., 276

Raven, B. H., 76–77
Resnick, J. H., 342–343
Ribicoff, A., 223
Richter, C. P., 317
Riecken, H. W., 102
Ring, K., 346
Risley, T. R., 236, 262
Ritchie, E., 75–76, 82
Robinson, J., 110
Roosevelt, F. D., 272
Rosenberg, M. J., 102
Rosenthal, R., 19, 35, 107–108, 110–111,
    112, 113–114, 146, 147, 148,
    150–151, 152, 320, 326
Rosenzweig, S., 100–101
Rosnow, R. L., 320, 326
Ross, D., 5–6
Ross, H. L., 223, 286
Ross, S., 5–6
Rossi, P. H., 285
Rozelle, R. M., 226
Rudner, R. S., 4
Rugg, E. A., 347
Rumenik, D. K., 109
Ryan, B. J., 112

Salasin, S., 283
Schachter, B. S., 103
Schachter, S., 77
Schafer, R., 115
Schaie, K., 32
Scheidt, R. J., 115
Schlenker, B. R., 104
Scholtz, J. A., 129–130
Schultz, D. P., 102
Schwartz, T., 342–343
Scriven, M., 274, 281, 282
Sears, R. R., 31
Seeman, J., 331
Sekuler, R., 68
Selltiz, C., 46, 77, 129, 168
Seybert, J. A., 55
Sheehan, M. R., 11
Shine, L. C., 267, 268
Shingles, R. D., 199–202, 203, 205
Sidman, M., 234, 255, 258, 266, 267
Sidowski, J. B., 294, 295–296, 297–298,
    302, 306, 318
Siegel, L. J., 353–374
Sigall, H., 103, 145, 157–158, 179
Silver, M. J., 110, 113, 150

Silverman, I., 111, 146–147
Silverstein, S. J., 343
Singer, J. E., 77
Sipprelle, C. N., 296
Skinner, B. F., 10, 15–16, 18, 19, 36,
    47–48, 70, 234, 267
Smith, R. E., 317
Snapper, K., 282
Solomon, R., 175, 177, 187
Solomon, R. L., 175
Spinner, B., 103
Stanley, J. C., 91–92, 98, 160–161, 167,
    170, 177, 218, 222, 316, 320
Star, S. A., 211, 212
Stephen, A. S., 273
Stevens, S. S., 8–9, 71
Strunk, W., Jr., 384
Strupp, H. H., 234–235
Suchman, E. A., 285
Suedfeld, P., 343
Sullivan, D. S., 347
Suls, J. M., 326
Sutcliffe, J. P., 302

Taffel, C., 342
Tate, B. G., 239–240, 241
Taylor, F. D., 241
Tedeschi, J. T., 104
Terrant, F. R., 129, 242
Tesch, 303, 305
Thoresen, C. E., 264–265
Tiao, G. C., 221
Timaeus, E., 111
Trist, E. L., 282
Tunnell, G. B., 43–44

Underwood, B. J., 39, 52, 324
Uphoff, H. F., 107, 110

Valenstein, E., 78
Van Buskirk, W. L., 325
Van Hoose, T., 103, 145, 157, 179
Vaught, R. S., 263–264
Vernon, H. M., 218–219
Videbeck, R., 152
Vinacke, E., 330

Wade, E. A., 92
Walker, H. M., 238
Wallston, K., 346
Watts, W. A., 95
Webb, E. J., 259
Weber, S. J., 103
Weinrott, M., 263–264
Weisberg, H. I., 211
Weiss, C. H., 273, 278, 279–280, 281,
    283, 285, 290
Werts, C. E., 210
West, S. G., 341

Name Index

White, E. B., 384
Wilkerson, D., 169
Williams, W., 285
Willson, V. L., 221, 222, 224
Wilson, D., 348
Wolf, M. M., 236
Woodworth, R. S., 11
Wrather, D. M., 81
Wundt, W., 234

Wyatt, S., 218–219
Wyer, R. S., Jr., 146

Yates, E., 146, 151

Zimbardo, P. G., 80
Zimney, G. H., 35
Zoble, E. J., 111

413

Subject Index

Abstract, research report, 353, 378, 380
After-only research design, 170–172, 178–179
Albino rat (*see also* Subjects, animal), 81, 295–296, 297–298, 317
American Psychological Association, 331–332
   code of ethics, 329, 331–340
   format for research report, 352–378
   guidelines for care of animals, 348–349
   journals, 352
   Publication Manual, 352–384
Analysis-of-variance design, 140, 157, 178–179
Animal research (*see also* Subjects, animal), ethics of, 348–350
Animals for Research (NAS), 295
Annual Review of Psychology, 57
Antecedent conditions (*see also* Independent variable), 15, 17, 66–67, 89, 197–198
Apparatus, 258–259
Artificiality, 28, 39–40, 44, 47
Authority, 11
Autocorrelation, 226, 228–229
Automation, 152

Baseline:
   condition, 237–238, 240, 242, 243
   defined, 258
   measure, 238–240
   multiple, 348–352
   stability, defined, 258–259
Before-after-four-group design, 175–177
Before-after research design, 172–175
Behavior control, 15–16, 17, 37
Behavior therapy, research, 234–235, 266
Between–subjects design (*see also* Randomized subjects design), 191, 194

Beyond Freedom and Dignity (Skinner), 15
Bias:
   controlling, 100–101
   experimenter, 35–36, 100–101, 105–114, 146–152, 325
   freedom from, 35–36, 90
   history effect, 94–96
   instrumentation, 97
   maturation, 96–97
   mortality, 99–100
   selection, 98–99
   subject, 101–105
Biased sample, 12–13
Blind technique, 150–151

Care and use of laboratory animals, 296
Carry-over effect, 133, 134, 136, 260
"Case History in Scientific Method" (Skinner), 47
Case study design, 161–162
Causal relationship, 6–7, 22–23, 31–32, 67, 118, 198, 225–228, 229–230, 265
Causation, 22–27, 31–32, 34, 91, 225–228
   chain of causality, 25
   canons (Mill), 23–24
      Joint Methods of Agreement and Difference, 24
      Method of Agreement, 23
      Method of Concomitant Variation, 24
      Method of Difference, 23
   causal agent, 23, 24–27
   defined, 23, 27
   descriptive analysis of cause of malaria, 24–27
   inferred, 31–32
   preponderant, 225–228
   probabilistic approach, 26

traditional view, 25–26
  necessary condition, 26
  sufficient condition, 26
Ceiling effect, 168
Cell (treatment combination), 180
  number of subjects in, 302
Change scores, 210–211
Cognitive dissonance theory, 53
College students (see also Subjects,
    human), 296, 318–320, 335–337
Commitment by subject, 85, 86, 87
Conceptual variable, 78
Conducting the experiment, 45–46
Confidentiality, 340
Constancy (see also Control), 37–38,
    92–100
  counterbalancing, 132–141
  matching, 123–132
  techniques for achieving, 118–155
Control (see also Constancy), 6–8, 13,
    15–16, 17, 37, 38, 43, 91–116
  of extraneous variables, 94–100,
    114–115, 119, 121–122, 165
  for rival hypotheses, 94–96, 98
  of sequencing effect, 114
  of subject-experimenter bias, 100–114,
    141–152
Control group, 165–166, 168, 171, 172,
    175, 199–216
  defined, 166
  nonequivalent, 199–216
Control techniques, 118–155, 165–166
Correlated-groups design, 187–189,
    189–190, 191–195
Correlation studies, 24, 31–32
Counterbalancing, 132–141
  intragroup, 137–140
  intrasubject, 135–137
  randomized, 140–141
  techniques for:
    building in extraneous variables,
      126–127
    holding variables constant, 125–126
    equating subjects, 129–132
    yoked control, 127–129
Cox formula, 300
Cross-lagged panel design, 224–230
Cross-over effect, 208–209
Cross-sectional studies, 32
Cyclic variations, 260–261

Daedalus (issue on ethics), 331
Data base, 35, 58
Data collection (see also Subjects),
    293–307
  internal analysis of data, 76–77
  procedure, 306–307
Debriefing, 303–305, 339–340, 346–347
  educational function, 303–304, 305
  ethical function, 303, 305
  methodological function, 304–305
Deception, 142–144, 334–335, 341–342,
    346–347
Dehoaxing, 346–347
Demand characteristics, 103–104, 107,
    111–112, 141, 146
Dependent variable, 66, 82–89
  commitment and, 85, 86, 87
  defined, 82
  disguised, 87
  measurement of, 87–89
  number of, 88–89
  reducing subject error, 86–88
  reliability of, 85–86
  selection of, 83–86
  sensitivity to independent variable, 83
  validity of, 86
Description, 14, 17
Descriptive experimentation:
  historical considerations, 233–234
  methodological considerations,
    258–265
  research designs, 235–258
  rival hypotheses, 265–266
Descriptive research approaches, 27–34
  characteristics, 27–28
  techniques:
    ex post facto studies, 33–34, 76
    field studies, 29–32, 33
    naturalistic observation, 28–29, 71
Design, 65–90, 156–195, 193–231
  after-only, 170–172, 178–179
  application of, 177–190
  appropriateness, 158–160, 170, 190
  before-after, 172–175
  before-after-four-group, 175–177
  choice of, 190–195
  correlated-groups, 187–189, 191–195
  criteria of, 165–168
  defined, 65, 156
  factorial, 177, 180–187, 189–190
  faulty, 160–165
  multisubject vs. single subject,
    266–268
  one-group before-after, 162–163
  one-shot case study, 161–162
  purpose illustrated, 157–160
  randomized subjects, 178–187,
    189–190, 191–195
  static group comparison, 164–165
Designing the experiment, 41, 45, 65–66
  decisions preceding, 65–90
Determinism, 15–16
Differential influence, 92–93, 147
Disguised experiment, 87, 143–144
Disruption effect, 325
Double blind placebo model, 141–142,
    150–151, 174

416

Ecological validity, 322–327
Elements of Style (Strunk and White), 384
Empiricism, 12–13
Environmental conditions, 322–323
Equiprobability of events, 121–122
ERIC (Educational Resources Information Center), 58
Error variance, 124–125, 188, 193–194
  defined, 193
Ethical principles in the conduct of research with human participants (APA), 332–340
Ethical Standards in Psychological Research committee, 331
Ethics, 71, 144, 198, 296, 303, 305, 329–350
  animal research (APA guidelines), 348–349
  code of ethics (APA), 329, 331–340
  consequences, 341
  ethical dilemma, 330
  responsibility of experimenter, 333–340
  restrictions, 71
Evaluation apprehension, 102
Evaluation research, 272–292
  comprehensive evaluation, 279–285
  cost analysis, 289
  cost benefit, 289
  cost-effectiveness, 289
  defined, 273
  dissemination, 290–291
  formative evaluation, 279, 281, 284
  formulating the research question, 280–283
  historical considerations, 272–273
  personal factor, 273–274
  purpose of evaluation, 281
  randomization, 285–287
  side effects, 289
  significance, 288
    practical, 288
    statistical, 288
  summative or impact evaluation, 281, 284–287
  target identification, 277–278
  types of activities, 274–284
    impact evaluation, 278–279
    process evaluation, 274–275, 283–284
    program implementation, 275–277
  utilization, 280, 290–291
Experiment, defined, 35
Experimental approach, 22–49
  advantages, 38–39
  defined, 22
  disadvantages, 39–40

  illustration, 40–42
  psychological, 35–38
    steps in, 44–46
  research setting, 42–44
  unformalized principles of scientific practice, 47
Experimental designs, 156–195
Experimental group, defined, 166
Experimenter attributes, 107–109
Experimenter bias, 35–36, 100–101, 105–114, 325
  control of, 146–152
    attribute errors, 147
    expectancy errors, 150–152
    recording errors, 147
  defined, 146
  randomization, 148–149
Experimenter expectancies, 109–114
  communication of effects, 112–113
  magnitude of effects, 113–114
Experimenter-participant agreement, 337–338
Experimenter responsibility (*see also* Ethics), 333–340
Explanation, 14–15, 17
Ex post facto studies, 33–34, 76, 77
External validity, 167, 316, 320
  ecological, 316, 322–327
  population, 316–322
Extraneous variables, 91–100, 114–115, 119, 121–122, 147, 165

Factorial designs, 177, 180–187, 189–190
  advantages, 186
  based on mixed model, 189–190
  difficulties, 185–186
Field experimentation, 43–44, 169
Field studies, 29–32, 33
  correlational, 31–32
  cross-sectional, 32
  ex post facto, 33–34, 76–77
  longitudinal, 32
  survey, 29–31
    defined, 29
Fisher factorial designs, 177
Freedom of choice, 333, 335
Frequency distribution control, 131–132
"Fundamental Principles for Preparing Psychology Journal Articles" (Harlow), 384

Gallop polls, 27, 30
Generalizability, 167
Generalization, 315–328
  defined, 316
  representative sample, 316, 317
GSR (galvanic skin response), 80

Hawthorne effect, 324–325
History effect, 94–96
Hypothesis, 12, 13, 24, 28, 45–46
  competing, 226
  formation, 45
  formulation, 61–63
  null, 310–311, 312
  orthogonal, 142
  personal involvement, 106–107
  rival, 94–96, 98, 116, 143, 163, 165,
    174, 265–266
  testability criterion, 62
  testing, 46, 69, 165, 308–311

Ideal constancy, 92–93
Identification of potential mistakes,
  35–36
Identification of problem, 45, 51–59
Independent variable, 65–82
  amount of, 68–69
  constructing, 69–71
  control of, 67, 72
  defined, 66–67
  defining operationally, 70–71
  establishing variation in, 72–77
    event manipulation, 73–74
    instructional manipulation, 72–73
    internal analysis, 76
    internal states measurement, 75–76
  main effect and, 181–184
  number of, 81–82
  presence vs. absence type, 67–68
  relation to concept, 77–81
  varying the type, 69
Information retrieval systems, 57–58
Informed consent, 144, 296, 341–342
Initial position, 169
Institute of Laboratory Animal Resources, 296
Instructions to subject, 302–303
Instrumentation, 97, 174, 258–259
Interaction, 181–187
  classic example of, 181
  disordinal, 321–322
  in factorial design, 181–187
  ordinal, 321
  selection by treatment, 320, 326
  testing, 186–187
Interactive feedback process, 225
Interdependent behaviors, 249–252
Internal invalidity, 98, 119
Internal validity, 92, 94, 95, 96, 123, 163,
  165, 168
  defined, 92, 94
Intuition, 10–11
Investigator (see Experimenter)

Knowledge, 3–4, 10–13
  methods of acquiring, 10–13

  nonscientific, 10–13
    authority, 11
    empiricism, 12–13
    intuition, 10–11
    rationalism, 11–12
    tenacity, 10
  scientific, 13

Laboratory experimentation, 44
Latin Square Design, 140
Literature review, 56–59
Locus of Control Scale, 75
Logic of inquiry, 4, 6
Longitudinal studies, 32

Main effect, 181–184
Manipulation of variables, 72–77, 91–
  100
Matching, 123–132
  building in the extraneous variable,
    126–127
  equating subjects, 129–132
  holding variable constant, 125–126
  of relevant variables, 188
  yoked control, 127–129
Maturation, 96–97
Mean difference, 147–148
Measurement of internal states, 75–77
Modeling technique, 5
Mortality bias, 99–100
Moving average model, 221–222, 224
Multiple-baseline design, 248–252
Multiple treatment interference, 323–
  324
Multivariate analysis of variance, 88–89

Natural setting, 193
Naturalistic observation, 28–29, 71
Naturalness, dimensions of, 44
NEA Research Division, sample size
  formula, 298
Necessary and sufficient conditions, 26
Nonreversible changes, 241–242, 248–
  249
Null hypothesis, 310–311, 312

Objectivity, 18–19, 35
Observation, 35–36
  naturalistic, 28–29
Observers, 97
One-group before-after design, 162–163
One-shot case study, 161–162
Ongoing process of science, 56, 63
Operational definition, 5, 6, 8–9, 13, 36,
  70–71, 80, 86, 275, 276
Operationism, 8–9
  defined, 8
Order effect, 132–134, 136, 140

Partial blind technique, 151–152
Participant (see Subject)
PASAR (Psychological Abstracts Search and Retrieval), 58
Personal factor, 273–274, 280, 283, 290
Personality variables, 75
Phenomenon, 36–38
  defined, 36
Pilot study, 306–307
Population (see also Subjects):
  experimentally accessible, 317–318
  target, 317–318
  validity, 316–322
Postexperimental inquiry, 146
Postexperimental interview, 303–305
Positive self-presentation, 103–105, 145–146
Precision control technique, 129–131
Prediction, 15, 17
Preponderant causality, 225–228
  prior cause, 226
  subsequent cause, 226
Pretesting, 80–81, 95–96, 97–98, 168–170, 306–307, 325–326
Pretesting effect, 325–326
Principles for the care and use of animals (APA), 349
Problem, 51–61
  defined, 59–60
  formulation, 59–61
  identification of, 45, 51–59
  review of literature, 56–59
  sources, 53–56
    everyday life, 54
    past research, 55–56
    practical issues, 54–55
    theories, 53–54
  specificity, 60–61
Professional meetings, 58–59
Psychological Abstracts, 57
Psychological experiment, 35–38, 44–46, 100–101
  social nature of, 100–101
  steps in, 44–46
Psychological journals, 46, 57, 352

Quasi-experimental designs, 197–231
  before-after, 199–216
    nonequivalent control group, 199–211
    simulated, 211–216
  cross-lagged panel design, 224–230
  defined, 198
  time series design, 217–224

Randomization, 119–123, 166, 174, 285–287
  assignment of subjects, 174, 178
  defined, 119

with single subject designs, 233–234
Randomized subjects design, 178–187, 191–195
  factorial, 180–187
  simple, 178–180
Random sample, defined, 120
Random selection, 316, 317
Rationalism, 11–12, 20
Reciprocal yoked control method, 242
References, in research report, 375, 378, 382–383
  citation, 382–383
  reference list, 383
  reference note, 375, 378, 383
Replication, 9–10, 13, 36, 85, 352
Representative sample, 316
Required standard error, 300
Research, 1–2, 12–13
  ability, 2
  approach to problem–solving, 2
  insight, 2
  knowledge about, 2
  ongoing process, 56, 63
  procedure, 1–2
  purpose, 51, 157
  settings, 42–44
Research question, 191
Research report, 351–384
  APA format, 352–378
  preparation of, 378–384
  writing, 46
  writing style, 384
Residual standard deviation, 300
Right to privacy, 330
Rival hypothesis, 94–96, 98, 116, 143, 163, 174, 265–266

Sample size, 298–302
  formula:
    Cox, 299
    NEA, 298
    precedent, 298
Sampling error, 30
Sampling techniques, 30
Schaie's model, 32
Science:
  basic assumptions, 19
  defined, 3–4, 10
  methodology, 4, 6–10, 13
  objectives, 13–17
    defined:
      control, 15–16
      description, 14
      explanation, 14–15
      prediction, 15
      understanding, 13–16
    illustrated, 16–17
  stereotypes, 2–3
  technique, 5–6

Scientific approach (*see also* Generalization), 13
  characteristics, 6–10
    control, 6–8, 13
    operational definition, 8–9, 13
    replication, 9–10, 13
  described, 13
  method *vs.* technique, 4–6
  uniqueness, 4
  unscientific methods, 10–13
Scientific knowledge:
  defined, 4
  purpose, 4, 13–17
Scientific process, 4, 44–48
  logical analysis, 44–46
  ongoing nature of, 56, 63
Scientist:
  approach to problem–solving, 2
  characteristics, 17–19, 47–48
    change, 19
    curiosity, 18, 53
    objectivity, 18–19
    patience, 18
  defined, 21
  role of, 17–18
  stereotypes, 2–3
Selection bias, 98–99
Selection by treatment interaction, 320, 326
Sensitivity, 168, 170
Sequencing effect, 114, 132, 136, 265–266
  carry–over effect, 133, 134, 136, 140, 260
  control of, 114
  linear, 136
  order effect, 132–134, 136, 140
Sequential technique, 301
Serendipity, 18, 43
Shingles study, 199–211
Significance level, 310, 311, 312
Significant difference, 309–310
Significant treatment effect, 171, 175
Single subject research design, 233–270
  historical considerations, 233–235
  methodological considerations, 258–265, 270
    baseline, 258–259
    changing only one variable, 259–260
    length of phase, 260–261
      carry-over effects, 260
      cyclic variations, 260–261
    rival hypotheses, 265–266
    statistical analysis, 261–265
    visual analysis, 261–265
  multisubject *vs.* single subject, 266–268
  stability, defined, 258
  techniques:

A-B-A design (withdrawal and reversal), 237–242
  changing-criterion design, 255–258
  interaction design, 243–248
  multiple-baseline design, 248–252
  multiple schedule design, 252–255
  time-series design, 235–237
Standard deviation, residual, 300
Standard techniques, 70
Standardized change score analysis, 210–211
Static group comparison design, 164–165
Stationarity, 228–229
  defined, 228
Statistical analysis, 209–211, 308
Statistical regression, 97–98, 203–204, 207
  defined, 98
Statistical testing, 157–158, 165, 191–195, 261–265, 308–312, 364–370
  potential errors, 311–312
  in research report, 364–370
  for significance, 157–158, 308–310
  in single-subject designs, 261–265
  variance, 191–195
Stereotypes:
  experimenter, 52
  scientist, 2–3
Subject bias, 101–105, 324–325
  control of, 141–146
    deception, 142–143
    disguised experiment, 143–144
    double blind placebo model, 141–142
    independent measurement of dependent variable, 144–145
    procedural control, 145–146
  errors of motivational attitude, 100
    observational attitude, 100
    personality influence, 100
  Hawthorne effect, 324–325
  novelty effect, 325
  positive self–presentation motive, 103–105
Subject error, 86–88
Subject pool, 296, 318, 335–337
Subjects, 294–307
  animal, 73, 74, 293–294, 294–298, 306, 317, 348–350
  college students as, 318–320
  commitment, 85, 86, 87
  confidentiality, 340
  debriefing, 303–305, 306, 339–340, 346–347
  dehoaxing, 346–347
  freedom of choice, 335
  human, 84–85, 293–294, 295, 306–307, 317, 318–320, 331, 332–340
  informed consent, 341–342